The World Book Student Information Finder

The World Book

STUDENT INFORMATION FINDER

Language Arts
and Social Studies

World Book, Inc.
a Scott Fetzer company
Chicago London Sydney Toronto

The World Book Student Information Finder

© 1988 World Book, Inc. All rights reserved. This volume may not be reproduced in whole or in part in any form without prior written permission from the publisher.

1990 Revised Printing

World Book, Inc.
525 West Monroe
Chicago, IL 60606

Portions of the text and certain illustrations previously published under the title
The World Book Student Handbook
Copyright © 1978, 1981 by
World Book-Childcraft International, Inc.

ISBN 0-7166-3231-4
Library of Congress Catalog Card No. 90-71009

Printed in the United States of America

b/ij

Staff

President
Peter Mollman

Publisher
William H. Nault

Editorial

Editor in Chief
Robert O. Zeleny

Executive Editor
Dominic J. Miccolis

Associate Editor
Maureen Mostyn Liebenson

Senior Editor
Karen Zack Ingebretsen

Permissions Editor
Janet T. Peterson

Freelance Editor
Kathy Klein

Indexer
Joyce Goldenstern

Writers
James I. Clark
William D. Leschensky
Mary Alice Molloy
Betty Van Wyk
Joseph A. Zullo

Cartographic Services
George Stoll, head

Research and Library Services
Mary Norton, director

Art

Art Director
Roberta Dimmer

Assistant Art Director
Joe Gound

Photography Director
John S. Marshall

Photographs Editor
Geralyn Swietek

Designer
Stuart Paterson

Production Artists
Kelly Shea
Ann Tomasic

Product Production

Manufacturing
Henry Koval, director
Sandra Van den Broucke,
  manager

Pre-Press Services
Jerry Stack, director

Production Control
Barbara Podczerwinski
Janice Rossing

During your years in school, you are asked to read and learn a tremendous amount of information. Sometimes it may seem to you—no matter how much you like school in general or any subject in particular—that you are almost overwhelmed by the many facts that you need to know.

The World Book Student Information Finder has been designed to help you review essential facts in nine key content areas: mathematics; physical sciences; earth sciences; life sciences; language, writing, and spelling; geography; world history and American history; biography; and United States Presidents and Canada's Prime Ministers. Reviewing the facts in a given area can help you maintain or regain your sense of perspective.

This key concept of *review* was foremost in the minds of the editors of THE WORLD BOOK ENCYCLOPEDIA when they planned and prepared this two-volume set. *The World Book Student Information Finder* is organized by units. Each unit presents the highlights of a content area in a clear, concise fashion. Naturally, two volumes cannot cover all the information you need to know, but a strong attempt was made to include the crucial highlights of your studies.

Helping you review your schoolwork is but one major purpose of the *Student Information Finder*. Another is to provide you with useful reference material. For example, you can look up the preferred method for using footnotes in a research paper.

You should familiarize yourself with the table of contents in the front of each volume before attempting to use the set. To make the best possible use of each volume, you should also consult the indexes frequently. Cross-references within the volumes will help you find related material.

The *Student Information Finder* is intended as a companion to your textbooks, your encyclopedia, other reference works, and books of other kinds. No book can take the place of all those others, but these volumes—properly used—can aid you in an important way.

This volume contains information on the language arts and social studies. You can use Unit 1, for example, to check on the rules of spelling—conveniently summarized in a running table. Or you can look up reference information on footnotes, bibliographies, punctuation, and capitalization. These are topics covered in the unit on writing, language, and spelling.

Unit 2 contains maps, population and area statistics, and important facts about the United States government. In addition, this unit presents a brief fact summary for each independent nation in the world—enabling you quickly and easily to look up such information as the population of Canada or the area of Tanzania.

For a chronology of important events in world history and American history, consult Unit 3. Key facts are arranged by chronological period, then by subject area—politics, social history, the arts, and so on. Thus, you can obtain an overview of major events.

Need reference material on famous people? Check Unit 4, which contains brief biographical entries for about 350 notable men and women from various fields and many countries.

Some famous people whom you have undoubtedly encountered often in your studies are the Presidents of the United States and the Prime Ministers of Canada. Unit 5 features a biography for each of the individuals who has served as President, with information about the individual's life and historical perspective about his place in American history. A reference table of important facts about Canada's Prime Ministers completes the unit.

Volume 1 of this set contains information on math and science.

The editors hope that this brief summary has given you ideas on how *The World Book Student Information Finder* can help you. Use of this book can give you not only a fund of important facts, but also many hours of interesting and pleasurable reading.

Contents

UNIT

1

Facts about Writing, Language, and Spelling

Have you ever thought about "words," not about any particular word, but what words are and what they do? Without words, it would be very difficult to communicate your feelings and ideas to other people. And other people would be unable to communicate their feelings and ideas to you. Words are just about the most important "thing" you have.

This unit will show you many interesting things about words. It will give you some rules by which words in English are spelled. It will present some facts about the English language. And it will describe some rules that will help you to become a better writer.

The Library of Congress is one of the largest
and most valuable research libraries in the world.

Rules for Spelling

The first rule of spelling is, "When in doubt, consult your dictionary." After you have looked up a word, make it yours by following these simple steps:

1. Copy the word carefully and neatly.
2. Visualize the word and remember how it looks.
3. Say each letter of the word in order.
4. Divide the word into syllables if it has more than one.
5. Study the difficult parts of the word.
6. Pronounce the word out loud.
7. Study the meaning of the word.
8. Make up a meaningful sentence of your own, using the word.
9. Use the word at the first opportunity in writing and conversation.

Once you know how to spell the basic word, most of your spelling difficulties arise when you modify that word in some way, either to form inflections or to change the part of speech.

The following table gives some helpful spelling rules. However, there are some exceptions to almost every rule. You should recognize the problem, learn the rule by learning to apply it, and then learn the exceptions.

Table of Spelling Rules

Problem	Rule	Some exceptions
Words with *i*'s and *e*'s: *believe, receive*	Use *i* before *e* except after *c* or when sounded like *a*, as in *neighbor* or *weigh*.	*ancient, financier, counterfeit, either, foreign, seize, weird*
Words ending in *cede: precede*	The root *cede* is always spelled this way except in four words and their various forms.	*supersede, exceed, proceed, succeed,* and their other forms *(superseded, exceeding, proceeds, succeeded)*
Words ending in *c: panic*	Insert *k* when adding an ending beginning with *e, i,* or *y: panicky*.	*arced, zincic*
Words ending in soft *ce* or *ge: trace, courage*	Retain the final *e* before adding *able* or *ous: traceable, courageous*.	
Words ending in silent *e: desire*	Drop the final *e* before suffixes beginning with a vowel: *desirable*.	*mileage*
Words ending in silent *e: love*	Retain the final *e* before a suffix beginning with a consonant: *lovely*.	*acknowledgment, argument, duly, judgment, ninth, wholly*
Words ending in *ie: die*	Change *ie* to *y* when adding *ing: dying*.	
Words ending in *oe: toe*	Retain the final *e* before a suffix beginning with any vowel except *e: toeing,* but *toed*.	

Spelling bees are held at local, state, and national levels for students of all ages. Winners may receive awards or prizes.

Problem	Rule	Some exceptions
Words ending in *y* preceded by a consonant: *occupy*	Change *y* to *i* before a suffix unless the suffix begins with *i*: *occupied*, but *occupying*.	
Adjectives of one syllable ending in *y*: *dry*	Retain *y* when adding a suffix: *drying*.	
Words of one syllable and words accented on the last syllable, ending in a single consonant preceded by a vowel: *sad, repel, occur*	Double the final consonant before a suffix beginning with a vowel: *sadden, repelled, occurred*.	*crocheting, ricocheted, filleted, transferable* (but *transferred*). Also, if the accent shifts to the first syllable when the suffix is added, the final consonant is not doubled: *deferred*, but *deference*.
Words ending in a consonant preceded by more than one vowel: *reveal, boil*	Do not double the consonant before a suffix beginning with a vowel: *revealed, boiling*.	
Words ending in more than one consonant: *help, confirm*	Do not double the final consonant: *helped, confirming*.	
Words not accented on the last syllable: *benefit, banquet*	Do not double the final consonant: *benefited, banqueted*.	
Words ending in *l*: *accidental*	Retain the *l* before a suffix beginning with *l*: *accidentally*.	Words ending in double *l* drop one *l* with the suffix *ly*: *hilly, fully*.
Prefixes and suffixes ending in *ll*: *all-, -full*	Omit one *l* in joining them to other words: *already, thankful*.	
Prefixes *dis-, il-, im-, in-, mis-, over-, re-,* and *un-*	Do not change the spelling of the root word: *dissatisfy, illiterate, immortal, innumerable, misspell, overrun, reenter, unnecessary*.	
Words ending in a double consonant: *possess, enroll*	Retain both consonants when adding suffixes: *possessor, enrolling*.	
Nouns ending in *f, fe, ff*: *handkerchief*	Form the plural by adding *s*: *handkerchiefs*.	Some nouns ending in *f* or *fe* form the plural by changing the *f* or *fe* to *ve* and adding *s*: *knives, elves, halves, calves, leaves, loaves, wives*.
Nouns ending in *y* preceded by a consonant: *army*	Form the plural by changing *y* to *i* and adding *es*: *armies*.	Proper nouns ending in *y* form the plural by adding *s*: "There are four *Marys* in this class."
Nouns ending in *ch, sh, j, s, x,* or *z*: *gas, church, bush, dress, box*	Form the plural by adding *es*: *gases, churches, bushes, dresses, boxes*.	
Nouns ending in *o* preceded by a vowel: *radio*	Form the plural by adding *s*: *radios*.	

Problem	Rule	Some exceptions
Some nouns ending in *o* preceded by a consonant: *tomato*	Form the plural by adding *es: tomatoes.*	*dittos, dynamos* For some nouns, either *s* or *es* is correct: *buffalos* or *buffaloes, volcanos* or *volcanoes.*
Compound nouns: *notary public, daughter-in-law, lieutenant general*	Make the modified word plural: *notaries public, daughters-in-law, lieutenant generals.*	
Letters, numbers, dates, signs, and words referred to as words	Form the plural by adding *'s:* two *x's,* four *7's,* the *1920's,* +*'s, and's.*	

Spelling Sounds   Certain letters or combinations of letters may sound like other letters. Knowing these letters should help you improve your spelling. Look at some letters and their sounds:

Table of Spelling Sounds

The letter *a* may sound like short *o* in some words.
The *o* sound in not = the *a* sound in watt.

The letters *o* and *ou* sometimes sound like short *u*.
The *u* sound in up = the *o* sound in done.
The *u* sound in up = the *ou* sound in touch.

Sometimes *y, u,* and *o* sound like short *i*.
The *i* sound in him = the *y* sound in hymn.
The *i* sound in him = the *u* sound in busy.
The *i* sound in him = the *o* sound in women.

At other times, *y* may sound like long *i*.
The *i* sound in ice = the *y* sound in rhyme.

Gh and *ph* sometimes sound like *f*.
The *f* sound in fur = the *gh* sound in enough.
The *f* sound in fur = the *ph* sound in phonics.

C, ck, ch, and *que* may sound like *k*.
The *k* sound in kill = the *c* sound in catastrophe.
The *k* sound in kill = the *ck* sound in buck.
The *k* sound in kill = the *ch* sound in chorus.
The *k* sound in kill = the *que* sound in antique.

In some words, *qu* sounds like *kw*.
The *kw* sound = the *qu* sound in queen.

The letters *ti* and *ci* may sound like *sh*.
The *sh* sound in shield = the *ti* sound in nation.
The *sh* sound in shield = the *ci* sound in social.

Sometimes *c* sounds like *s, ed* like *t, s* like *z,* and *n* like *ng*.
The *s* sound in space = the *c* sound in cent.
The *t* sound in sit = the *ed* sound in fixed.
The *z* sound in whiz = the *s* sound in desert.
The *ng* sound in going = the *n* sound in thank.

The letters *ei, ey, ai,* and *ay* sometimes sound like long *a*.
The *a* sound in snake = the *ei* sound in eight.
The *a* sound in snake = the *ey* sound in they.
The *a* sound in snake = the *ai* sound in gain.
The *a* sound in snake = the *ay* sound in pay.

The letter *i* may sound like long *e*.
The *e* sound in she = the *i* sound in machine.

Sometimes *g* and *dg* sound like *j*.
The *j* sound in jug = the *g* sound in register.
The *j* sound in jug = the *dg* sound in edge.

The letters *a, ai,* and *ay* may sound like short *e*.
The *e* sound in set = the *a* sound in many.
The *e* sound in set = the *ai* sound in said.
The *e* sound in set = the *ay* sound in says.

Review of Spelling Sounds

This exercise will give you the opportunity to review information on spelling sounds. Please do not write in this book, but place your answers on a separate sheet of paper.

An answer key follows the exercise.

1. Spell the short *o* sound in
   w__nd

2. Spell the short *u* sound in
   tr__ble, c__me, d__ble

3. Spell the short *i* sound in
   bic__cle, b__sy, w__men

4. Spell the long *i* sound in
   n__lon

5. Spell the *f* sound in
   ne__ew, lau__, em__asize, tou__, geogra__y, al__abet

6. Spell the *k* sound in
   pla____, an__or, ro__et, pi__ni__, or__estra, uni____, __ancel

7. Spell the *kw* sound in
   e__ator, __iet

8. Spell the *sh* sound in
   espe__ally, objec__on, pa__ent, an__ent, gra__ous

9. Spell the *s* sound in
   practi__e, pronoun__e, exer__ise

Answers

1. short *o* sound: wand
2. short *u* sound: trouble, come, double
3. short *i* sound: bicycle, busy, women
4. long *i* sound: nylon
5. *f* sound: nephew, laugh, emphasize, tough, geography, alphabet
6. *k* sound: plaque, anchor, rocket, picnic, orchestra, unique, cancel
7. *kw* sound: equator, quiet
8. *sh* sound: especially, objection, patient, ancient, gracious
9. *s* sound: practice, pronounce, exercise

2

Facts about Parts
of Speech

Grammar is a type of structure for words. When you study grammar, you study how words are put together to form sentences. Some patterns are correct, and others are not. The *parts of speech* are the basic building blocks for every sentence.

Traditional grammar books indicate eight parts of speech: (1) nouns; (2) verbs; (3) pronouns; (4) adjectives; (5) adverbs; (6) prepositions; (7) conjunctions; and (8) interjections.

Every word in this book belongs to one of those eight parts of speech. In fact, many words belong to more than one part of speech, depending on how they are used. *Cream*, for example, is a noun when you speak of cream for the coffee. *Cream* is an adjective when you use the term to describe something else, like cream pudding. And *cream* is a verb when you *cream* butter and sugar together to make a cake.

Very often, then, you need to know how a word is used in a sentence to label it properly. But that is not as hard as it sounds. Once you practice a little, you can sort words into their special categories with little trouble.

Nouns

Because they are probably the easiest to recognize, begin with nouns. You are a noun. So is every other person, every place, and every thing. You name it, and it is a noun: *baby, Susan, Mrs. Smith, England, ocean, river, avenue, Michigan, bridge.*

There are two kinds of nouns: common and proper. Proper nouns name particular persons, places, or things; they are capitalized (example: *Ohio*). Common nouns do not tell you which person, which place, or which thing; they are not capitalized (example: *state*).

Common nouns are divided into three groups: abstract, concrete, and collective. Abstract nouns name qualities, actions, and ideas: *courage, helpfulness, loyalty.* Most of the time, you can use *the* before abstract nouns, but not *a*. Ordinarily, you would not say *a helpfulness.*

Concrete nouns name material things that you can see or touch: *door, pencil, car.* Most of the time, you can use either *a* or *the* before a concrete noun, depending on the meaning you want to convey. Also, you can make concrete nouns plural—*doors, pencils, cars*—whereas ordinarily you would not say *courages* or *helpfulnesses.*

Collective nouns are singular in form, but they refer to a group of persons or things: *team, class, herd, set.* Collective nouns are usually followed by singular verbs: "Our *team was* defeated." But often they are followed by a plural verb, especially where they emphasize the individuals more than the groups. "The *people were* discontented."

Pronouns

Pronouns are substitutes. They take the place of nouns in speech and writing. Imagine how cumbersome language would be without them. We would have to say, "Mrs. Smith asked John to be careful with Mrs. Smith's car when John borrowed the car to take John's date home." However, it is easier to say, "Mrs. Smith asked John to be careful with her car when he borrowed it to take his date home."

Every pronoun must have an antecedent, or *that which goes before.* The antecedent is either stated or understood. In the example above, *Mrs. Smith, John,* and *car* are nouns, and the pronouns *her, he, his,* and *it* relieve you of the necessity of repeating the nouns.

There are five kinds of pronouns: (1) personal; (2) relative; (3) interrogative; (4) demonstrative (definite); and (5) indefinite.

Personal Pronouns. A pronoun that stands for the name of a person, a place, or a thing is called a personal pronoun. There are seven personal pronouns: *I, you, he, she, it, we,* and *they.* All seven are subject form. They "do" things. Any one of them will complete this key sentence: ". . . saw Mary." Each subject form has an object form: *me, you, him, her, it, us,* and *them.* They are receivers of some kind of action. Something happens "to" them. Any one of them will complete this key sentence: "Mary saw. . . ."

Most of the trouble with personal pronouns occurs in sentences using the linking verb *to be* and its many forms (including *is, are, am, was, were*). After linking verbs, the subject form of the personal pronoun should always be used: "It is *I*."

Choosing the right pronoun to follow a preposition—such as *to, for, at, between*—can be troublesome, too. Prepositions call for the object form of the pronoun. "She talked to Mary and *me*." (Note: *Mary and I* is wrong here.)

If you add *self* or *selves* to a personal pronoun, it becomes a compound form: *myself, yourself, herself, itself, ourselves, themselves*. This form may be intensive (giving emphasis) or reflexive (expressing action turned back on the subject). Do not use the compound form when you should use a simple personal pronoun. It is wrong to say, "My brother and *myself* are going." You may say, "I *myself* am going" (intensive) and you may also say "He shaves *himself*" (reflexive).

Relative Pronouns. A relative pronoun serves a double purpose: it connects two clauses, and it relates back to a noun or pronoun in a preceding clause. Words frequently used as relative pronouns are *that, which, what, who, whose, whom*. "She didn't buy the same book *that* he did." In this example, the word *that* refers back to the noun *book*. The compound relative pronouns in common use are *whoever, whichever*, and *whatever*.

Interrogative Pronouns. The interrogative pronouns, *who, which*, and *what*, are used to ask questions. They ask the identity, the nature, or the possessor of whatever is in question. "*Who* was there?" "*Which* of the books is yours?"

Demonstrative Pronouns. *This, these, that*, and *those* are pronouns that answer the question "Which?" by pointing out a particular person or thing. They are sometimes called definite pronouns. "*This* is the one I want." "*That* is all wrong." But *this, these, that*, and *those* may also be demonstrative adjectives. "*This* book is mine." "*That* day was a bad one."

Indefinite Pronouns. These are similar to the demonstrative pronouns in that they answer the question "Which?" But in so doing, they do not refer to definite persons or things. "*Somebody* took my pencil." "*Neither* will do the job." Other indefinite pronouns include *one, each, other, both, many*. Like demonstrative pronouns, many indefinite pronouns may also be used as adjectives. "*Both* boys were absent." "She had *many* dresses."

Adjectives

An *old* man; a *black* cat; a *long* bill. *Old, black,* and *long* have one thing in common that makes them all adjectives. Each is used to modify, or to give a more exact meaning to, a noun. It is not just any man, it is an *old* man; it is not just any cat, it is a *black* cat; it is not just any bill; it is a *long* bill.

Adjectives may be descriptive or limiting. Descriptive adjectives modify a noun by telling a quality or condition of the object named: a *short* stick, a *sad* girl, a *grassy* slope. Limiting adjectives point out the object talked about or indicate quantity: *this* book, *that* ring, *two* words. Notice that some limiting adjectives are regularly used as pronouns *(this, that, these, those)*. *A, an,* and *the,* called articles, are also limiting adjectives.

Word phrases and clauses may also act as adjectives. "The man *with the green hat* saw me." In addition to modifying nouns, adjectives modify a word or a phrase that is acting as a noun: "Going to school *is necessary*."

Verbs

The most important word in a sentence is the verb. A verb may express action, or it may express a state of being. In "John the ball." we have a subject, *John;* and we have an object, *ball.* But only after adding a verb, such as *threw,* do we have action, and a sentence. "John threw the ball." *Pull, strike, lift,* and *touch* are typical action verbs. Sometimes the action is mental rather than physical, as in "She *believed* the story."

As mentioned above, not all verbs express action. Those that do not may be either linking verbs or auxiliary verbs. Linking verbs merely link the subject of the sentence to another word, in order to make a statement. "Sara felt ill." The verb *felt* links the subject, *Sara,* with the word *ill,* to make a statement about Sara's health. Some linking verbs regularly used are *appear, be, become, grow, look, remain, seem, smell, sound, stay, taste.*

Auxiliary verbs are used in conjunction with other verbs to help form a verb tense, voice, or mood. "I studied" becomes "I *have* studied," with the addition of the helping, or auxiliary, verb *have.* Other common auxiliary verbs are *be, may, do, shall, will.*

Verbs may be either transitive or intransitive. A transitive verb takes an object. "He *lifted* the *hammer*." An intransitive verb does not take an object. "They *ran* fast." Many verbs are transitive in some sentences and intransitive in others.

"She *sang* the *song*" (transitive). "She simply is not able to *sing*" (intransitive).

Adverbs

Adverbs, like adjectives, give a more exact meaning to other words. But adjectives modify only nouns, and words or phrases acting as nouns. Adverbs modify verbs, adjectives, other adverbs, or entire sentences or clauses. "The boat was *absolutely* waterproof" (adverb modifying adjective). "The radio worked *unusually* well" (adverb modifying adverb). "I didn't go to school *yesterday*" (adverb modifying the rest of the sentence).

An adverb usually answers the question *how? when? where?* or *to what extent?* "He ran *quickly* down the road" (how). "She went to school *today*" (when). "She dropped the ball *there*" (where). "John sang *interminably*" (to what extent).

Interrogative adverbs ask questions themselves. "*Where* did she go?" "*Why* did she go?" Other common interrogative adverbs are *when* and *how*.

Conjunctive adverbs appear between clauses and serve the double function of connecting the two clauses and modifying one of those clauses. "You signed a contract; *therefore*, we demand payment." Other conjunctive adverbs are *however, moreover, still, otherwise, nevertheless.*

Words commonly used as adverbs are *almost, fast, very,* and most words ending in -ly: *badly, sorely, surely.*

Prepositions

Prepositions may be small words *(to, for, on, in)*, bigger words *(concerning, alongside)*, or even groups of words *(in spite of, as far as)*, but they all do the same thing—they show the relation of one word (usually a noun or a pronoun) to some other word in the sentence. Some of the relations shown may be:

In position—"The book is *on* the table."
In direction—"He walked *toward* the door."
In time—"She left *before* him."

Words frequently used as prepositions are *between, in, on, toward, at, with, of, up, for, down, over, by.*

Conjunctions

Conjunctions join together words or word groups. There are three kinds of conjunctions: coordinating, correlative, and subordinating.

Coordinating conjunctions are the simplest, linking two words or word groups that are grammatically equal. "She bought meat *and* potatoes." Other coordinating conjunctions are *but* and *yet*.

When two coordinating conjunctions are used together, they are called correlative conjunctions. "*Both* Henry *and* Bill are gone." Other correlative conjunctions are *either . . . or, though . . . yet*.

Subordinating conjunctions connect a subordinate clause to the main clause of a sentence. In this instance, the subordinating conjunction *because* introduces the subordinate clause. "May was happy *because* her mother was home." Other subordinating conjunctions are *when, as, since, if, unless, before*.

Interjections

Ouch! Oh! Ah! Alas! These are interjections. A unique thing about interjections is that they bear no grammatical relation to the other words in a sentence. They neither affect other words—as do adjectives—nor are they affected by other words—as are nouns. A second thing held in common by interjections is that they all express an emotion. *Ouch!* It hurts. *Alas!* It's a shame.

Other Kinds of Grammar

Recently, American linguists have presented new ways of looking at English that depart from traditional grammar. One approach, called "structural linguistics," analyzes English by concentrating on word endings, signal words, and the location of words in sentences.

Nouns, verbs, adjectives, and adverbs have endings that help identify them. Some of the more common endings for nouns include *-ance, -ence, -er, -ion, -ity, -ment, -ness,* and *-or*. Common verb endings are *-ate, -d, -ed, -en, -fy, -ing, -ize,* and *-t*. Common endings for adjectives are *-able, -al, -ant, -ary, -ed, -en, -ent, -ful, -ic, -ish, -less, -ous, -some,* and *-y*. A common adverb ending is *-ly*.

Certain words are called signal words because they announce that certain parts of speech are coming. *A, an, the, both, some,* and similar words signal nouns. Auxiliaries such as *may, have, will, can,* and *should* signal verbs. Prepositions such as *on, in,* and *of* signal nouns or pronouns. Of course, *both* and *some* are sometimes used as nouns, and *have* and other auxiliaries are sometimes verbs.

The position of a word in a sentence is also a good clue to part of speech because the English language contains certain sentence patterns. Consider the sentence "The _____ fumbled the ball.'' Without knowing the missing word, you can tell that it will be a noun. How? Because of its place in the sentence and its link with the signal word *the*.

Or consider the sentence ''The trugy deer gimfeled the grass.'' Even though you do not know the meaning of *gimfeled,* you can tell that it is a verb. How? Because of its place in the sentence and its *-ed* ending. You also know that *trugy* is an adjective because of its *-y* ending and its place in the sentence.

Another new approach to grammar, called ''generative transformational grammar,'' formulates logical procedures for ''generating'' new sentences. The basic unit of this grammar is the kernel sentence—an active, positive statement such as ''Jim is happy.'' By applying certain procedures, you can ''transform'' this kernel sentence into the following sentences:

> Jim is not happy. (negative transform)
> Is Jim happy? (question transform)

You can also transform two or more kernel sentences into a more complicated sentence. The sentence ''Mary smiled and walked away.'' is a transform of the kernel sentences ''Mary smiled'' and ''Mary walked away.'' The sentence ''The hungry person eats the pie'' is a transform of ''The person is hungry'' and ''The person eats the pie.'' The sentence ''I found somebody's ring'' is a transform of ''somebody had a ring'' and ''I found the ring.''

These two new approaches to grammar use terms not found in traditional grammar. For example, they discuss *morphemes,* which are single units of meaning expressed by a word or a part of a word.

> *girl* is one morpheme
> *girl's* is two morphemes (girl + possessive)
> *girls* is two morphemes (girl + plural)
> *girls'* is three morphemes (girl + plural + possessive)

The past tense morpheme is whatever is done to a verb to make it past tense. Usually, *-ed* is added to the end of the word. However, the past tense morpheme is not always shown this way.

> *help* is one morpheme
> *helped* is two morphemes (help + past)
> *teach* is one morpheme
> *taught* is two morphemes (teach + past)

The new grammars also classify words in a way slightly different from that of traditional grammar. All the parts of speech are classified under two main headings—content words and function words.

Content words contain many of the words that are called nouns, verbs, adjectives, and adverbs in traditional grammar. This category of words is constantly expanding because when new words are added to the language, they are almost always content words.

Even though they rarely change, function words are very important. Function words are the little words, like prepositions and conjunctions, that connect content words and hold sentences together. Some other important words are the following:

Auxiliaries. The auxiliaries are the familiar verb-helpers like *may, might, have, has, had, can, could, should*, and similar words.

Determiners. A determiner is used with a noun and limits the meaning of the noun. A determiner can be an article like *a, an,* or *the;* a demonstrative like *this, that, these,* or *those;* a number like *one, six,* or *thirteen;* a quantifier like *several of* or *many of;* or a possessive like *his* or *hers.* A determiner differs from an adjective in that a determiner usually does not make sense when it is used alone in the predicate. For example, green is an adjective when it is used with a noun. You can say "The green sweater shrank," or "The sweater is green." However, *the* when it is used with a noun is a determiner. You may say "The sweater is green," but you may not say, "Sweater is the."

Intensifiers. Intensifiers are words like *very, rather, quite,* and *somewhat.* They intensify or give more specific meaning to adjectives and adverbs.

Structural linguistics and transformational grammar are two new approaches to the study of the English language. No one knows how soon, if ever, either one will replace traditional grammar. However, many teachers of English are incorporating some of the ideas from these new grammars with the traditional approach. For example, consider the sentence "The lion devoured his trainer." In traditional grammar, the third word is called a verb because it expresses action. In structural linguistics, the third word is called a verb because of its position in the sentence and its *-ed* ending. When both the traditional and structural descriptions of a verb are combined into one definition, the advantages of both views are utilized, and the idea of what a verb is becomes clearer.

3

Facts about Style

Style, as it relates to writing, has two meanings. You use the word *style* to describe the creative or artistic manner in which an author writes prose or poetry. You can also use *style* to refer to such purely technical matters as capitalization and punctuation.

The creative side has to do with the way in which words are used by a writer to produce a specific effect or to bring out certain reactions from a reader. One writer may use long words and heavy, clumsy phrasing to give what might be considered a scholarly effect. Another writer may use simple, matter-of-fact words to say exactly the same thing.

Style, as explained on the following pages, deals specifically with technical matters. There are many possible variations of the basic styles given here. But the following rules and conventions represent preferred usage as it is taught in most schools in the United States.

Capitalization

One of the principal uses of capital letters is to distinguish proper nouns and proper adjectives from common nouns and adjectives. A proper noun is the name of a particular person, place, thing, or idea. A proper adjective is a proper noun used as an adjective or an adjective derived from a proper noun. A common noun is the name of any person, place, thing, or idea in a general class.

Proper Nouns	Common Nouns
Boston	city
Mary Smith	girl
Hatch Act	law

Here are some examples of proper adjectives: *Paris* fashions, *Reagan* administration, *Farmer-Labor* party, *New York* taxi drivers, *Steven Spielberg* film, *Persian* carpet.

Here are some general rules to follow when deciding whether to capitalize a word:

1. Capitalize the first word of a sentence or a word or phrase that has the force of a sentence.

   What are you doing? Nothing. Stop!

2. Capitalize the first word of a direct quotation that is a sentence or has the force of a sentence.

   Bob called, "Hurry up." Joe asked, "Why?"

3. Capitalize the first word of a complete statement following a colon.

   This is our conclusion: The trial was fair.

4. Capitalize the first word in the salutation and the first word of the complimentary close of a letter.

   Dear son: Gentlemen:
   With love,   Yours sincerely,

5. Capitalize the pronoun *I* whether used alone or in a contraction.

   She said I was right.   Now I've decided.

6. Capitalize the interjection *O*.

   Rejoice, O ye people.

7. Capitalize the names of the days of the week, months, and holidays.

   Saturday   February   Easter

8. Capitalize words showing family relationship when used instead of a name or as part of a name, but not when such words follow a possessive.

   I asked Father for a dime. He called Uncle Bob.
   I asked my father for a dime. He called my uncle.

9. Capitalize the first words and all other important words in the titles of books, newspapers, magazines, stories, poems, reports, songs, and other writings.

   A Tale of Two Cities   *Evening News*
   Business Week   "Born in the U.S.A."
   "To a Skylark"   *The Hobbit*

   Note: Capitalize prepositions, conjunctions, and articles only when they come at the beginning or end of a title or when they consist of five or more letters. This exception also applies to the other rules of capitalization.

10. Capitalize nicknames, other identifying names, and special titles and their abbreviations.

    Old Hickory   Richard the Lion-Hearted
    Senator Hunt   Mary Grow, Ph.D.

11. Capitalize the names of all political and geographical subdivisions, the names of all nationalities and tribes, words of direction designating a specific place, and the adjectives derived from such nouns.

    Chicago   Sioux Indians   Far East

12. Capitalize the names of streets, highways, plazas, parks, squares, buildings, and other specific locations, including common nouns and abbreviations.

    Alameda Boulevard   National Bank Building
    State Street

13. Capitalize the names of rivers, oceans, islands, mountains, and other geographical features, including the common nouns that are part of the proper names.

    Amazon River   Mount Olive
    Atlantic Ocean   Treasure Island

14. Capitalize the names of political parties and religious denominations and their members.

    Labor Party   The Baptist Church
    Republicans

15. Capitalize the names of organizations, business firms, and institutions.

    Boy Scouts of America   Harvard University
    Shell Oil Company   Franklin High School

16. Capitalize the word *Bible* and the names and designations of all sacred writings; also, capitalize all nouns and pronouns that refer to a specific Supreme Being.

    The Bible is sometimes called the Holy Writ.
    the Talmud
    The Lord is good.
    Great is His mercy.
    Buddha
    but: The Indians believed in many gods.

17. Capitalize the names of historical events, wars, treaties, laws, and documents.

    Gadsden Purchase   Battle of the Bulge
    Taft-Hartley Act   Civil War
    Bill of Rights   Treaty of Ghent

18. Capitalize the names of divisions, departments, and instrumentalities of government.

> Board of Education   Library of Congress

19. Capitalize the names of trains, planes, ships, satellites, and submarines.

> *Golden State Limited   Spirit of St. Louis*
> *Titanic   Nautilus*
> *Echo I*

20. Capitalize the names of stars, planets, constellations, and other astronomical designations.

> Venus   Big Dipper
> Sirius   Milky Way

21. Capitalize personified nouns.

> All Nature sang. Let not Evil triumph.

22. Capitalize the names of periods in the history of language, art, and literature.

> Old French   Age of Reason
> Renaissance   Dadaist period

23. Capitalize the names of war decorations.

> Purple Heart   Silver Star

24. Capitalize *Preface, Contents, Chapter, Index,* and other parts of a book when referring to a specific part.

Punctuation

Punctuation is used to make writing clear. The following punctuation rules present the main uses for each punctuation mark.

Apostrophe

,

1. Use the apostrophe to form the possessive of a noun.

> the tree's leaves   the boys' bicycles
> Mary's hat   the Johnsons' car
> Charles's book   Tom and Bob's mother

2. Use the apostrophe to show omission of one or more letters, words, or numbers.

> didn't (did not)   '79 (1979)
> o'clock (of the clock)

3. Use the apostrophe to show plurals of numbers, letters, and words discussed as words.

> two *4*'s   some *B*'s   too many *and*'s

Brackets

1. Use brackets within quotations to indicate explanations or your own comments.

    He replied, "She [Doris] is going."

2. Use brackets to indicate stage and acting directions in plays.

    CHARLES [waving arms]: Away with you!

3. Use brackets to correct a mistake in a quote.

    "The artist Le[o]nardo painted it."

4. Use brackets for parentheses within parentheses.

    (That was the color [red] he preferred.)

Colon

1. Use the colon after a complete statement followed by a list.

    Campers must take these items: bedding, linen, and cooking utensils.

2. Use the colon after the salutation of a business letter.

    Dear Sir: Gentlemen: Dear Mr. Harris:

3. Use the colon after a statement followed by a clause that extends, explains, or amplifies the preceding statement.

    Judges have a double duty: They must protect the innocent and punish the guilty.

4. Use the colon to separate parts of a citation.

    Elementary English XLIV: 114-123
    Exodus 4: 1

5. Use the colon to separate hours from minutes in indicating time.

    3:40 P.M.

Comma

1. Use the comma to separate the parts of an address.

    He lives at 23 First Avenue, Boise, Idaho.
    167 Park Boulevard, Rolling Acres, El Paso, Texas.

2. Use the comma to separate the day of the month and the month, or a special day, from the year.

    June 1, 1978   Independence Day, 1899

3. Use the comma after the greeting of an informal letter.

    Dear Alice,   My dear Uncle John,

4. Use the comma after the closing of a letter.

    Affectionately,   Sincerely yours,

5. Use the comma between words or phrases in a list or a series and before the *and* or the *or* that precedes the final item in a list.

   > Go up the road, across the river, and into the park.
   > The paper can be white, yellow, or blue.

6. Use the comma to set off the name of a person spoken to.

   > Bill, here is your cap.
   > Here is your cap, Bill.
   > Here, Bill, is your cap.

7. Use the comma to set off *yes, no, oh, first, second,* and similar words when these words introduce a sentence.

   > Yes, the letter came.   Oh, say can you see. . .
   > First, who is coming?   Second, why?

8. Use the comma to set off words that explain or define other words (appear in apposition).

   > Janet Jones, my cousin, won a speech award.
   > The bullet ricocheted, or bounced, off a brick wall.

9. Use the comma to set off long phrases and dependent clauses preceding the main clause of a sentence.

   > By the end of the week, most of the work was done.
   > To be a good jumper, a person needs strong legs.
   > Although the children were poorly dressed, they looked healthy.

10. Use the comma to separate long coordinate clauses of a compound sentence.

    > The building collapsed, but no one was hurt.
    > Snow fell during the night, and the ground was white by morning.

    However, two very brief independent clauses that are closely related to each other do not need a comma between them.

    > He sang and he danced.
    > The thunder rumbled and the lightning flashed.

11. Use the comma to indicate the omission of one or more words instead of repeating them.

    > The first game was exciting; the second, dull.
    > *shortened form of:*
    > The first game was exciting; the second was dull.

12. Use the comma before any title or its abbreviation that follows a person's name.

> H. W. McDowell, M.D.
> Sarah Caldwell, Secretary
> Byron Phelps, Dean of Students
> Patricia Brown, Ph.D.

13. Use the comma to set off words or phrases that suggest a break in thought, such as the connecting words *however, of course,* and *moreover.*

> You find, however, that small ones are rare.
> Of course, the winner received the medal.

14. Use the comma to set off participles, phrases, or clauses that add to the main thought of a sentence but are not essential to it.

> Climbing, Joe skinned his leg.
> The girls, busy as they were, found time to help.
> The final reports, which were completed today, give all totals.

15. Use the comma to separate identical or closely similar words in a sentence.

> Who he was, is a mystery.
> When you are eating, talking should stop.

16. Use the comma to separate adjacent words in a sentence that might be mistakenly joined in reading.

> To an Asian, Americans are foreigners.
> Just as we walked in, the window broke.
> Above, the girls made the beds; below, the boys swept the porch.
> I had to hurry, for the store was closing.

17. Use the comma to set off thousands, millions, billions, and other high numbers.

> 4,323   65,001   210,563,270

18. Use the comma to separate unrelated numbers in a sentence.

> By 1987, 30,000 people lived in the city.

19. Use the comma to set off coordinate phrases modifying the same noun.

> This lake is as deep as, but smaller than, Lake Erie.

20. Use the comma between sentence elements that suggest contrast or comparison.

> The more people he met, the lonelier he felt.
> The sooner we get started, the sooner we will finish.

Dash

1. Use the dash (— in handwriting or – – on a typewriter) before a summarizing statement introduced by *all, this,* or similar words.

   Bob, Bill, Harry—all found summer jobs.
   To defeat every opponent—this was his ambition.

2. Use the dash before a repeated word or expression in a sentence.

   He was a gentleman—a gentleman of the old school.

3. Use the dash to emphasize or define a part of a sentence.

   The Declaration of Independence—that glorious document—was written in 1776.

4. Use the dash to indicate an "aside" or point of view of the speaker.

   You may—though I doubt it—enjoy this book.

5. Use the dash to suggest halting or hesitant speech.

   "Well—I—ah—I didn't know," he stammered.

6. Use the dash to indicate a sudden break or interruption in a sentence.

   "I'm sorry, sir, but—." He was already through the gate.

Ellipses

1. Use ellipses (three spaced dots) within a quotation to indicate all places where a word or words have been omitted.

   "The house . . . was built in 1935."
   for:
   "The house on Elm Street was built in 1935."

2. Use ellipses at the end of a quotation to indicate words omitted before the period, but use four dots (the first dot is the period that indicates the end of the sentence).

   "He was a giant of a man. . . ."
   for:
   "He was a giant of a man and highly respected."

Exclamation Mark

!

1. Use the exclamation mark after a word, phrase, or sentence that expresses strong or sudden feelings.

   Ouch!   That hurts!   Good for you!

2. Use the exclamation mark to emphasize a command or strong point of view.

   Come here at once!
   We won't discuss this!

3. Use the exclamation mark to show sarcasm, irony, or amusement.

> You are a fine one to talk about lazy people!
> That should be an easy job for you!

Hyphen

—

The hyphen is most commonly used to mark the division of a word at the end of a line.

You may divide a word only between syllables, and only in such a way that each part of the hyphenated word contains at least two letters. If you are uncertain about where to break a word into syllables, always consult your dictionary.

In general, avoid dividing a word in a place where division would suggest an incorrect pronunciation—for example, *omni-potent*. Remember that pronunciation is not an accurate guide to syllabication. The word *babble,* for instance, is pronounced BAHB uhl and is syllabified *bab-ble*. Try to avoid dividing a word in a place where either part of the hyphenated word forms a word by itself; for example, *tar-tan*.

You should not divide a word that is a proper name; a number or a figure; a contraction; an abbreviation; a word of one syllable; or a word of five letters or less, regardless of the number of syllables.

The hyphen is also used to join word parts and to separate word parts.

Following are some specific rules about use of the hyphen.

1. You may divide between double consonants unless it is the root that ends in the double consonant.

    run-ning   remit-tance
    col-lection
    but:
    roll-ing   bless-edly
    miss-ing

2. You may divide between vowels when one vowel ends a syllable and another vowel begins a syllable.

    fluctu-ate   foli-age
    actu-ary

3. You may divide after a vowel that forms a one-letter syllable.

    presi-dent   deco-rate
    diminu-tive

4. You may divide before a suffix of three or more letters.

    port-able   transi-tion
    argu-ment

5. You may divide after a prefix of three or more letters.
   trans-mission   anti-climax
   pro-logue

6. You may divide a compound word *only* where a hyphen already occurs in the word.
   first-class   vice-president
   self-reliant

7. Use the hyphen in compound numbers between 21 and 99 when spelled out.
   twenty-one   thirty-sixth
   ninety-nine

8. Use the hyphen between the numerator and denominator of fractions that are spelled out and used as modifiers, unless one part of the fraction already contains a hyphen.
   two-thirds vote   one twenty-second piece
   one-fourth part   twenty-one thirtieths part
   but:
   Do not use the hyphen between the numerator and the denominator when the fraction is a noun.
   He bought one half.   He took four fifths.

9. Use the hyphen after the prefix *re* when the word being formed might be confused with a similar word.
   re-lay a carpet   re-cover a chair
   but:
   a relay race   recover from an illness

10. Use the hyphen after a prefix in these situations: when the prefix ends with the same letter with which the root word begins; when the root word begins with *w* or *y;* or when the root word begins with an initial capital letter. There are some exceptions to this rule; in these cases, your dictionary shows that the preferred spelling is without the hyphen, as in *cooperate.*
    de-emphasize   pre-Columbian   co-worker

11. Use a hyphen between the components of a compound adjective when it appears before the word or phrase it modifies.
    drive-in movie   would-be actor
    foreign-born person
    but
    The client was foreign born.

12. Do not hyphenate a compound adjective that includes an adverb ending in *ly* even when it is used before the word or phrase it modifies.

     It was a slowly moving train.
     but:
     It was a slow-moving train.

13. Use the hyphen in compounds containing a prepositional phrase, unless the dictionary shows that the preferred spelling is without the hyphen, as in *coat of arms*.

14. Use the hyphen after any prefix that precedes a proper noun or adjective.

     un-American   pre-Revolutionary   pro-Nazi

15. Use the hyphen after each item in a series when the last item requires a hyphen and the earlier items relate to that one.

     first-, second-, and third-grade pupils

16. Use the hyphen after *great* in describing generations or descent.

     great-great-grandfather   great-grandmother

17. Check your dictionary for words beginning with the prefixes *ante, after, pro, pre, super, ultra, non,* and *well.* Some of these words are hyphenated; some are not. Also check compound words beginning or ending with the words *boy, book, shop, store, mill, work, child, maker, payer, like, dealer, girl,* and *man.* Usage varies. Notice these examples:

     man-child   man in white   manslaughter

18. Use the hyphen to spell out a word or a name.

     s-e-p-a-r-a-t-e   D-i-s-r-a-e-l-i

Parentheses

1. Use parentheses around explanatory material in a sentence when this material has no essential connection with the rest of the sentence in which it occurs.

     To make holes, use an awl (a sharp, pointed tool).

2. Use parentheses to enclose sources of information within a sentence.

     One chapter in this book (Chapter IV) describes fish hatcheries.
     The population of Iowa is 2,913,808 (1980 census).

3. Use parentheses around numbers or letters that indicate subdivisions of a sentence.

> This committee has three duties: (a) to solicit members, (b) to collect dues, and (c) to send out receipts.

4. Use parentheses around figures that repeat a number written out.

> Enclosed is five dollars ($5.00).
> Please send forty-five (45) copies.

5. Other marks of punctuation are placed inside the parentheses when they belong with the parenthetical matter, rather than with the main body of the sentence.

> Carol's question ("Whom did you take to the dance?") produced a chill in the air.
> *but:*
> John walked to the store in all that snow (even though I asked him to stay home).

Period

1. Use the period after a statement.

> It is cold outside.

2. Use the period after a command.

> Please hurry.

3. Use the period after an initial.

> J. P. Jones

4. Use the period after an abbreviation or each part of most abbreviations.

> A.M.   lbs.   C.O.D.   yds.   Mr.   Mrs.

5. Use the period after each number or letter that begins a heading in an outline.

> Why I Like to Read
> I. Satisfies my curiosity
>   A. About people
>   1. In ages past
>   2. In the present
>   B. About things

Question Mark

1. Use the question mark after a direct question.

> How old is Bill?

2. Use the question mark after a statement followed by a short question.

> It's cold outside, isn't it?

3. Use the question mark after a word that indicates a question.
   What?   How?   Why?

Quotation Marks

" "

1. Use quotation marks to enclose the exact words of a speaker.
   Mary exclaimed, "I refuse to go!"

2. Use quotation marks around each part of a direct quotation when explanatory words come between the parts of the quotation.
   "This material," said the clerk, "washes easily."

3. Use quotation marks to enclose quoted words or quoted phrases that occur within a sentence.
   The leader told us we must "put our shoulders to the wheel."

4. Use quotation marks around the titles of songs or poems.
   We all sang "America."
   The child recited "Little Miss Muffet."

5. Use quotation marks around the titles of lectures, sermons, pamphlets, handbooks, chapters of a book, magazine articles, and any titled material that is less than a whole volume.
   "Rescued" was the most exciting chapter in the book.

6. Use quotation marks around a word or phrase explained or defined by the rest of the sentence.
   The "crib" in cribbage is made up of discards from players' hands.

7. In general writing, use quotation marks around a word to which attention is being called. In formal writing, underline the word to call attention to it.
   You have spelled "parallel" incorrectly.

8. Use quotation marks around a technical or trade name.
   Many people use "Jell-Right" in making jellies.

9. Use quotation marks around a word used in an unusual situation or with a slightly different meaning than usual.
   His "refuge" was a small room in the attic.
   She would not tell anyone her "secret."

10. Use quotation marks before the beginning of each stanza of a quoted poem and after the last stanza. Also use quotation marks before each paragraph of continuous quoted material and after the last paragraph.

11. Use single quotation marks for a quote within a quote.

    She said, "I won't until you say, 'Please.' "

12. Commas and periods are always placed inside the closing quotation marks (in ordinary usage in the United States).

    We all sang "America."

13. Semicolons and colons are always placed outside the closing quotation marks.

    John said, "I'll call you tomorrow"; but I have not heard from him yet.

    Here is what he did when he said, "I'll go": He closed the window, picked up his valise, and walked out the door.

14. Question marks and exclamation points are placed inside the closing quotation marks if they belong to the quotation.

    "Get out!" she shouted.

    but:

    What did you mean when you said, "I didn't know you were here"?

Semicolon

```
 •
 ,
```

1. Use the semicolon between the parts of a compound sentence if they are not joined by the conjunctions *and, but, or, for,* or *nor.*

   I must leave you now; you may join me later.

2. Use the semicolon before a conjuction connecting independent clauses when either or both clauses already contain commas.

   During the summer, he accomplished nothing; but finally, during the winter, he finished writing his book.

3. Use the semicolon after each clause in a series of three or more independent clauses.

   Bells rang; whistles shrieked; horns blared; and people screamed.

4. Use the semicolon before words like *therefore, however,* and *nevertheless* when they connect two independent clauses.

   Mr. Black is a busy man; nevertheless, he agreed to help on the committee.

5. Use the semicolon after listings when commas occur within the list.

   You will need to call Henrietta Hall, of the First Ward; Warren Holt, of the Second Ward; and Nancy Griffin, of the Third Ward.

6. Use the semicolon to set off lists, enumerations, and explanations introduced by expressions such as *for example, for instance, that is,* and *namely.*

> There are several reasons why this is a good factory site; namely, proximity to fuel, availability of raw materials, and abundance of skilled labor.

Underscoring

Words underscored in manuscript appear in italics when set in type.

1. Underscore the name of any book or complete volume.

> Tom Sawyer is a book about boyhood.

2. Underscore the name of a magazine or periodical.

> There are amusing cartoons in The New Yorker.

3. Underscore any foreign word that is not commonly used in English. Such words are labeled Latin, French, Italian, and so on in the dictionary, usually before the definition is given.

> The report dealt with de jure segregation.

4. Underscore the names of ships, pictures, and works of art.

> Titanic   The Last Supper   Rodin's The Thinker

5. Underscore any word or words considered not for their meaning but as words.

> But, for, and or are all conjunctions.

Virgule

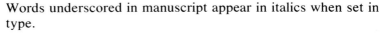

1. Use the virgule, or "slash mark," between two words to indicate that the meaning of either word pertains.

> The man and/or his wife may cash the check.

2. Use the virgule as a dividing line in special constructions like dates, fractions, and abbreviations.

> 10/7/77   3/4   1/2   c/o   B/W

3. Use the virgule when recording bibliographic matter to indicate where one line ends and another begins; for example, in recounting the position of words on the spine of a book.

> The/World Book/Encyclopedia/A/ Volume 1

4. Use the virgule with a run-in passage of poetry to indicate where one line ends and another begins.

> He recalled those famous lines by William Shakespeare: "This above all: to thine own self be true,/And it must follow, as the night the day,/Thou canst not then be false to any man."

4

Guide to
Preparing a Paper

When a teacher assigns a report or term paper, it is important to realize that there are many things that must be done before you pick up a pencil and begin writing. These preliminary steps include choosing a topic, doing background reading, doing research and taking notes, deciding on the approach your report will take, developing a thesis sentence, and preparing an outline. This section will tell you about these preliminary steps. It will also discuss the actual writing of the report. Rough and final drafts will be described, as will the process of revising your work. Practical information is given about how to create footnotes and a bibliography. Carefully following the steps in this section can help guarantee a better report in the end.

Choosing a Topic

In some cases, your teacher will assign a specific report topic or ask that you choose from a list of topics. In other cases, you will have the freedom to make your own choice. The following guidelines can be of help as you consider the possibilities.

Choose a Topic of Interest to You

You are going to be spending a lot of time preparing your report or term paper. Choosing an interesting topic will make the job less of a chore. That may seem obvious, but sometimes people need a little help seeing how their particular interests can fit into a term paper assignment. Let's suppose, for example, that you are asked to prepare a term paper about the Civil War. History may not be your favorite subject, but you just might be able to find a topic that fits right in with another interest. If you are an amateur photographer, for example, you might find it fascinating to write a report on Mathew Brady's photographs of the war. If you love music, a report on songs of the Civil War could turn out to be a lot of fun to prepare.

Narrow the Topic

Take into consideration the amount of time you have for the assignment and the required length. Then narrow your topic down to a manageable size. In general, it is better to cover a narrow topic in depth than to skim over a broad topic. For example, if you tried to prepare a report or term paper on such topics as the human body, William Shakespeare, or Maya Indians, you would quickly be buried under an avalanche of information. More appropriate topics would be how the human body fights disease, imagery in Shakespeare's *Macbeth,* and sculpture of the Maya Indians.

One way to begin narrowing your topic is to turn to an encyclopedia and look in the index under the heading that describes your general topic. Look at the index entries to see what articles are listed. Then check through some of the articles that seem particularly interesting and see how they are organized. A subheading within an article may give you an idea for a topic that you can cover adequately in your report.

Set up any materials you need in a comfortable, quiet place when you are ready to write.

**Check for
Availability of
Information**

Your report or term paper will never get off the ground if you cannot find enough information on your topic. A good way to check for availability of information is to look through your library catalog for the titles of books that relate to your topic. Check *The Readers' Guide to Periodical Literature* and the *New York Times Index* to see if there are magazine and newspaper articles available. If your search turns up promising titles, begin compiling a working bibliography, which is a list of books and articles to use as possible sources. If you cannot find any books or articles on your topic, it may be too narrow or too recent. You will have to choose something else.

**Background
Reading**

Once you have a topic in mind, do some background reading to get a good overview of the subject. An up-to-date encyclopedia can be an excellent starting point. Read through any articles that relate to your topic, and jot down ideas that occur to you about points you would like to cover in your report. It is likely that your background reading will turn up aspects of your topic that you didn't consider at first, and you may find yourself reshaping your original idea. Many encyclopedia articles include lists of sources to consult for further information on the topic. If you come across such lists, you can add to your working bibliography as you do your background reading.

**Formulating a
Thesis and an
Approach**

With your background reading completed, you are ready to begin putting your thoughts together in an organized fashion. This involves formulating a thesis—a statement that expresses the main idea or purpose of your report or term paper. Try to express this in a single sentence, known as a thesis sentence.

As you are thinking about your thesis sentence, you will need to consider what sort of approach you want your paper to take. A topic that inspires strong opinions may call for a pro-or-con approach. In this approach, you take a stand for or against a certain position, then back it up with supporting evidence. A similar approach is to prove or disprove a theory or idea. Some topics lend themselves to a chronological approach, in which events are described in the order in which they occurred. Other topics call for a descriptive approach or an explanatory approach. You may also choose to compare or contrast two or more things, or show a cause-and-effect relationship.

The approach you choose will affect your thesis. Here are some examples of thesis sentences. See if you can figure out which approach is used in each:

> Recent underwater research has revealed strange forms of aquatic life in the deepest parts of the ocean.

> Japanese schools use much different techniques to teach basic skills than schools in the United States do.

> The Electoral College should be abolished, and voters should elect the President of the United States directly.

The first thesis sentence sets the style for a descriptive approach. The second demonstrates a thesis that compares and contrasts. The third thesis sentence uses a pro-or-con approach.

Preparing a Preliminary Outline

Once you have decided on a thesis and an approach, you can continue to organize your thoughts by preparing a preliminary outline, which will guide your research. Your preliminary outline may be simply a list of points that you want to cover in your paper. It may take the form of a series of questions that you hope to answer. Remember that this is only a rough outline. Don't be too concerned about the order or completeness of the outline. It simply serves to give you some focus as you begin the task of doing research.

Doing Research

A good report or term paper depends on careful research. No matter how well you write, if your information is not complete and accurate, your paper will not be effective.

The first part of your research task is to find the best possible sources of information. The library is the first place that should come to mind when thinking about doing research. Without a doubt, it is a valuable storehouse of information. But be creative in your approach to research. You may find other resources that are equally helpful. Interviews or surveys may be appropriate for your particular topic. Some of your best information may come from a government agency or a professional association. The possibilities for good research information are by no means limited to books and magazines.

The second part of your research task is to record the information you find in an orderly manner. When the time comes to write your report, you will have to pull together bits and pieces of information that you have gathered from various sources. If you don't follow a carefully organized procedure for note taking, you can be faced with an overwhelming task.

Preparing a Final Outline

Good writing is well-organized writing. In a well-organized paper, related ideas are brought together to form main topics and subtopics, and topics follow one another in a logical fashion.

The key to good organization of a report or term paper is an outline. An outline serves as the skeleton of the paper. It lists the main topics and subtopics that are covered in the paper and shows how they are related to one another.

Preparing an outline is well worth the time. Making an outline forces you to organize your ideas before you begin writing, and it makes the actual writing task much easier. Your outline will show how you plan to get from your introduction to your conclusion.

Many teachers require that a formal outline be submitted as part of a term paper. For a shorter report, an outline may or may not be required. However, even if your teacher doesn't require an outline, you should take the time to prepare one.

How to Prepare an Outline

Begin by going back and reading over your notes. Then take another look at your thesis sentence. Does it still make sense? Did your research turn up information that leads you to think the thesis sentence should be changed somewhat? Remember, the thesis states the whole purpose of your paper. If you are not comfortable with it, you will be struggling when it comes time to write your report. Take the time now to refine your thesis so that it says exactly what you want it to.

Next, check your preliminary outline. Do the points in your preliminary outline still seem like appropriate topics to cover in your report? Are there new points you want to include? Do your notes indicate any information gaps that need to be filled in with additional research? Can some of your notes be set aside because they don't fit in with the purpose of your paper?

Once you have answered these questions, you are ready to separate your note cards into large divisions that correspond to the major points you plan to cover. These divisions will be the main headings in your outline, labeled with Roman numerals. For example, if you were writing a report on the Jamestown colony, your main headings might look like this:

I. Reasons the colony was founded

II. Difficulties faced by the settlers

III. Reasons for success

Look through your note cards for each main topic and see

how they can be divided into smaller groups. These smaller groups will be the subheadings in your outline, labeled with capital letters.

    I. Reasons the colony was founded
       A. Search for treasure
       B. Convert Indians to Christianity
       C. Grow agricultural products
   II. Difficulties faced by the settlers
       A. Poor climate
       B. Disease
       C. Indian attacks
       D. Crop failures
  III. Reasons for success
       A. Strong leadership
       B. Agricultural production
       C. Development of family life

It is not necessary to have a subtopic under every main topic, but if you have subtopics, there must be at least two. You can subdivide your subtopics even further, into outline headings labeled with Arabic numerals and small letters. Each topic of equal importance is indented equally.

  III. Reasons for success
       A. Strong leadership
          1. John Smith
          2. Lord De La Warr
       B. Agricultural production
          1. Food crops
          2. Tobacco for export
       C. Development of family life

Kinds of Outlines

There are two kinds of outlines: topic outlines and sentence outlines. They both use the same format, with headings labeled with Roman numerals, capital letters, Arabic numerals, and small letters. But they differ in how the headings are written.

The sample outline shown above is a topic outline. It uses simple phrases or clauses for each heading and subheading. The first word of each phrase or clause is capitalized, but periods are not used at the end of a phrase or clause.

A sentence outline uses the same format as a topic outline, but each heading and subheading must be expressed in a complete sentence. This kind of outline is more difficult to write, but it has an important advantage. Some of the sentences you write for your headings and subheadings can be used as topic sentences in your report. If the outline for the report on the Jamestown colony were written as a sentence outline, it might look like this:

I. The Jamestown colony was founded for three major reasons.
   A. The colonists hoped to find treasure.
   B. The colonists wanted to spread Christianity among the Indians.
   C. The colonists planned to grow crops that could not be grown in England.

II. The Jamestown settlers faced many difficulties.
   A. The colonists were unaccustomed to the sharp contrasts in seasonal climates.
   B. A poor diet and impure drinking water caused many colonists to die of various diseases.
   C. Hostile Indians attacked the colony repeatedly.
   D. Early attempts to grow grapes and silk were failures.

III. In spite of its problems, the Jamestown colony eventually succeeded.
   A. Strong leadership helped the colonists overcome their difficulties.
      1. John Smith made the colonists work and established trade with the Indians.
      2. Lord De La Warr arrived with new settlers and supplies in 1610.
   B. Agriculture formed the basis for the colony's economy.
      1. The colonists learned to grow Indian corn and raise hogs for their own food.
      2. The colonists grew a kind of tobacco that became an important export product.
   C. The arrival of women in the colony in 1619 led to the development of stable family life in Jamestown.

Writing the First Draft

With your notes organized and your outline before you, you are finally ready to begin writing your first draft. Believe it or not, most of the hard work is behind you. If you have done a careful job up to now, the writing task should proceed quite smoothly.

Let the Words Flow

Don't stare at the blank sheet of paper before you. Try to plunge right in. At this stage, you needn't worry about perfect grammar, punctuation, and spelling. It is more important to concentrate on getting your ideas down on paper in the orderly, logical fashion that you planned in your outline. Follow your notes carefully as you build paragraphs and move from one topic to another.

Write or type your first draft on one side of the paper only, with wide margins. If you write the draft out in longhand, skip every other line. If you type, set your typewriter or word processor for double- or triple-spacing. The extra space in the margins and between lines will give you plenty of room to make your corrections later.

Using Quotations

When you use a quotation, be careful to copy it exactly as it appears in your notes, and enclose it in quotation marks. There is one exception to the use of quotation marks. A quotation that takes up more than five typed lines of your paper should be single-spaced and indented from the body of the rest of the paper, with no quotation marks.

If you leave out part of a quotation, use an ellipsis (. . .) in place of the missing part. If you must add words of your own to make the meaning of a quotation clearer, enclose those words in brackets ([ ]).

It is important to observe these rules of punctuation whenever you use a direct quote from someone else. If you don't, you could be guilty of plagiarism—stealing someone else's words and passing them off as your own. Plagiarism applies not only to another person's words, but to their ideas, also. Here is where footnotes come in handy.

Footnotes

A footnote is an explanatory note placed at the bottom—or foot—of a page. Some footnotes give the reader more detailed information than can be presented easily in the text. Other footnotes tell the reader where a particular piece of information came from. The second kind are the ones that students most frequently use.

The main purpose of a footnote in a school report or term paper is to document sources—to give credit to the person whose words or ideas you are using in your paper. A teacher may or may not ask that you include footnotes in a short report. They almost always are required in a term paper.

When to Use a Footnote

In general, footnotes should be used for the following material: direct quotations, a restatement of someone else's words or ideas, and facts or statistics that a reader might have reason to question.

Sometimes it is difficult to know whether or not a footnote is necessary, especially when you are paraphrasing information. In general, information that is considered common knowledge does not require a footnote. For example, you would not use a footnote for such statements as, "Thomas Jefferson served as President of the United States from 1801 to 1809," or "The Sahara is the world's largest desert."

However, when you present an opinion or a theory that is not your own original thought, you need to cite the source with a footnote. And a footnote is a must if you make a statement that is contrary to what most authorities say about the topic. An example of this sort of statement would be "During the Civil War, most Northerners actually favored slavery."

Similarly, statistics that are not widely known require a footnote to clearly establish the authority and accuracy of the information. You would not need a footnote for the statement "The U.S. House of Representatives consists of 435 members." On the other hand, a footnote would be appropriate for a statement such as, "The highest point in Peru is 22,205 feet above sea level."

How to Write Footnotes

Keep track of footnotes as you write your first draft by putting a footnote number in the margin whenever you write something that needs documentation. On a separate sheet of paper, jot down the number and information about the source—title, author, and page number. You will need this information later on when you are preparing the actual footnotes. Number the footnotes consecutively throughout.

Within the text of your finished paper, a footnote is identified by its number, which appears slightly raised above the line at the end of the quotation or other material being footnoted. That same number appears before the footnote itself at the bottom of the page. The footnote number is raised slightly above the line. The first line of the footnote is indented.

Footnote form varies, and your teacher may have a particular preferred style that you should follow. Be consistent in the form you use for all your footnotes. If your teacher doesn't have a preference, the following examples show footnotes in a style that would be appropriate for school papers. Note that each part of the footnote is separated by a comma, and a period appears at the end.

A book with one author:
E. D. Hirsch, *Cultural Literacy,* p. 12.

A book with two authors:
Michael Griff and Ross Kenyon, *Computers in Schools,* p. 173.

An edited book:
Morton D. Zabel, ed., *The Portable Henry James,* p. 17.

A magazine article:
Michael E. Long, "What Is This Thing Called Sleep?," *National Geographic,* December 1987, p. 787.

A magazine article with no author:
"Yet Another Spy Arrest," *Time,* February 10, 1986, p. 53.

A newspaper article:
Marcienne S. Mattleman, "The Shame—and Costs—of Illiteracy," *The New York Times,* September 13, 1986, Sec. D, p. 29.

An encyclopedia article:
Dan M. Bass, "Petroleum," *The World Book Encyclopedia,* 1988, Vol. 15, p. 330.

A pamphlet or other work prepared by an institution:
National Dairy Council, "Your Food—Choice or Chance?," p. 2.

A personal interview:
David Halstead, Dodd County Councilman, personal interview, March 22, 1988.

For later references to a source that was cited earlier, you generally can use a shortened footnote form, such as the author's last name and the page number:

Reynolds, p. 456.

If you have more than one source by the same author, you should include a shortened form of the title, as well as the author, so the reader knows exactly which source you are citing:

Reynolds, *Dance,* p. 54.

Some teachers may prefer that you use traditional Latin abbreviations, such as *ibid.* and *op. cit.,* for later references. *Ibid.* is used when the footnoted source is the same as the one immediately preceding it. The abbreviation takes the

place of whatever information is identical in the two footnotes—author and title, for example. The page number may
differ. Here's an example:

> Ronald Eubanks, *The U.S. Supreme Court,* p. 35.
> *Ibid.,* p. 72.

Use *op. cit.* when the source you are citing has been cited before, but not in the footnote directly preceding it. Give the author's last name, *op. cit.,* and the page number, as in the following example:

> Paula J. Elkins, *Animal Behavior,* p. 231.
> Edmund Luboff, *The Zoo Environment,* p. 76.
> Elkins, *op. cit.,* p. 91.

End Notes

Some teachers prefer that you put all your footnotes on a separate sheet of paper at the end of your report, instead of putting them at the bottom of each page. These are called end
notes. They are prepared in the same way as footnotes, except that the number that appears before the note itself is not
raised, and it is followed by a period. Here's an example:

> 1. E. D. Hirsch, *Cultural Literacy,* p. 12.

The Bibliography

A bibliography is a list of the sources you used to prepare
your report or term paper—books, magazine articles, pamphlets, interviews, and so on. It should include only those
sources that you actually used in the final report, not those
that you consulted but eventually disregarded for one reason
or another. The purpose of the bibliography is to tell the
reader where you got your information and where the reader
could go to get additional information on the topic.

**How to Prepare a
Bibliography**

Bibliography entries are generally more complete than footnotes. The bibliography entries should provide information
about title, author, publisher, and publication date and place.
Entries for articles include the page numbers for the complete
article. The entries are listed in alphabetical order, according
to the authors' last names. Entries with no author are inserted
alphabetically according to the first word of the title (disre-
garding *a, an,* and *the*). In general, bibliography entries are
not numbered.

Your teacher may have a particular format for you to follow in your bibliography. If not, you can use the following
sample bibliography as a guide for preparing entries for var-

ious kinds of sources. Pay close attention to the punctuation marks (periods, commas, and colons) used to separate the various parts of each entry. Note also that the first line starts at the left margin, and additional lines within each entry are indented.

Bass, Dan M. "Petroleum." *The World Book Encyclopedia.* 1988, Vol. 15, pp. 330–350.

Griff, Michael, and Kenyon, Ross. *Computers in Schools.* Indianapolis: Park Avenue Press, 1983.

Halstead, David. Dodd County Councilman. Personal interview, March 22, 1988.

Hirsch, E. D. *Cultural Literacy.* Boston: Houghton-Mifflin Co., 1987.

Long, Michael E. "What Is This Thing Called Sleep?" *National Geographic,* December 1987, pp. 787–821.

Mattleman, Marcienne S. "The Shame—and Costs—of Illiteracy." *The New York Times,* September 13, 1986, sec. D, p. 29.

National Dairy Council. "Your Food—Choice or Chance?" Pamphlet no. 435, 1983.

"Yet Another Spy Arrest." *Time,* February 10, 1986, p. 53.

Zabel, Morton D., ed. *The Portable Henry James.* New York: Penguin Books, Inc., 1977.

If your bibliography includes more than one work by the same author, arrange the entries in alphabetical order according to title and begin the second entry with a line to replace the author's name:

Morison, Samuel Eliot. *The European Discovery of America.* New York: Oxford University Press, 1971.

————. *The Oxford History of the American People.* New York: Oxford University Press, 1965.

Preparing an Appendix

Some reports include tables, charts, graphs, diagrams, or other special material. If you do not wish to include such material in the body of the paper, it may be put together in a special section called an appendix. In your text, you can refer to the appendix material with a cross reference. For example, you might write, "For a table showing the number of immigrants arriving in the United States from 1850 to 1920, see Table I in the Appendix." Arrange your appendix items in the same order as they are referred to in the text.

Revising Your Work

With your first draft completed, the thought of going back to the beginning and revising your work may seem unbearable. But nobody writes a perfect paper the first time through. Good writing is usually achieved by rewriting—again and again, if necessary.

Actually, the best thing to do after you have finished your first draft is to ignore it for a while—an hour, a day, or even several days if time permits. You will be able to look at it with a fresh eye and do a much better job of revising if you give yourself a break from your work. When you are ready to take it up again, you will need to judge it critically for content, organization, and style, as well as such mechanical details as spelling, capitalization, and punctuation.

To begin your revision, read through your paper carefully. Reading it aloud can help you catch awkward phrasing, grammatical errors, and poor transitions. Reading it slowly and silently—word for word—can help you catch errors in spelling and punctuation. Keep a dictionary, thesaurus, and grammar guide handy. And use them.

Use a colored pencil to revise your work. If you want to add information, write the new material neatly above the line you are revising, or write it in the margin and use an arrow to show where it should be inserted in the text. If you want to take out material, don't erase it or black it out completely. Draw a circle around it or draw a light line through it. Then, if you later decide to restore it or move it somewhere else, it will be there when you need it.

Preparing the Final Copy

When you are satisfied that your work is the best it can be, you are ready to prepare the final copy. Take the time to do a neat, careful job. You have already invested a lot of time into your research and writing. Don't settle for anything less than a top-notch presentation of the final copy. The appearance of your finished work should make a good impression.

Style Guidelines

If your teacher has given you a style sheet or other guidelines, you should follow them precisely as you prepare your final copy. Some teachers are sticklers about such things as margins or paper quality. Don't ruin your chance to get an A+ because you neglected to observe the rules.

If you don't have a style sheet, use the following guidelines. Some of the guidelines—such as those dealing with outlines, bibliographies, and footnotes—will apply only to longer reports or term papers.

1. For a handwritten report, write on one side of the paper only, using standard-lined paper and black or dark blue ink. For a typewritten report, type on one side only, using high-quality white typing paper. Do not use onionskin paper. Make sure the type ball or metal keys are clean and the ribbon is dark.
2. Leave a margin of 1½ inches on the left edge and 1 inch on the top, bottom, and right edges of the paper.
3. Double-space the text of a typewritten report.
4. Type or print the title of the paper in all capital letters at the top of the first page of text.
5. Indent the first line of all paragraphs five spaces.
6. Single-space indented rather than run-in quotations.
7. Single-space the outline, but double-space between main headings.
8. Indent the first line of a footnote five spaces. Set the following lines flush with the left margin. Single-space lines within the footnote, and double-space between footnotes.
9. Begin each bibliography entry at the left margin. Indent additional lines within the entry five spaces. Single-space within each entry, and double-space between entries.
10. Prepare a title page, which contains the title, your name, and the date. You may also include the teacher's name and the course name. The title page should be flawless. If you make a typographical error on it, start over.
11. Number all pages except the title page. Use lower-case Roman numerals (i, ii, iii, etc.) for the outline pages and Arabic numerals for all other pages. Center the number at the bottom of the first page of the outline, the text, the "notes" page (if there is one), and the bibliography. Center the number at the top of all other pages.

Putting the Parts Together

A short report probably will consist of just a title page and the text of the paper. A longer report or term paper has more parts. The parts should be assembled in this order:

1. The title page
2. The final outline, including paper's title and thesis sentence
3. The text of the paper
4. A page titled "notes," which lists the footnotes if you did not put them at the bottom of each page
5. The bibliography
6. The appendix, if included

Fasten the paper in the upper left-hand corner, or put it in a folder or binder. If the teacher's guidelines allow for it, you may want to make a special cover for your report.

2

Places Around the World

Have you ever had to find the location of one of the nations of the world? Did you ever have to explain the structure and function of the federal government of the United States? Have you ever had to find the area or size of Canada or of Argentina? If so, then this unit contains useful information for you.

This unit is an overall review of geographic, political, and economic facts about the nations of the world. Use of this unit will help you to develop greater understanding of many of the places and events that fill today's news.

This map of the world, centered on Jerusalem, is
taken from an early 13th-century psalter.

A Political Atlas

This section presents information on the contemporary world that you might wish to consult and review for your social science or geography work. Included are ten political maps: the world, North America, the United States, Canada, South America, Europe, Asia, Africa, Australia, and the Middle East. Also included, to supplement the information on those maps, are tables of comparative population and comparative area (pages 46 and 47).

30 Largest Cities of the World by Population

Rank	City	Population*	Rank	City	Population*
1.	Mexico City, Mexico	10,061,000	16.	Tianjin, China	5,300,000
2.	Seoul, South Korea	9,645,932	17.	Karachi, Pakistan	5,208,170
3.	Tokyo, Japan	8,353,674	18.	Bangkok, Thailand	5,153,902
4.	Moscow, Soviet Union	8,275,000	19.	Rio de Janeiro, Brazil	5,093,232
5.	Bombay, India	8,227,332	20.	Delhi, India	4,884,234
6.	New York City, U.S.	7,071,639	21.	Leningrad, Soviet Union	4,295,000
7.	São Paulo, Brazil	7,033,529	22.	Santiago, Chile	4,225,299
8.	Shanghai, China	6,880,000	23.	Lima, Peru	4,164,597
9.	London, England	6,767,500	24.	Shenyang, China	4,130,000
10.	Jakarta, Indonesia	6,503,449	25.	Bogotá, Colombia	3,982,941
11.	Cairo, Egypt	6,052,836	26.	Pusan, South Korea	3,516,807
12.	Beijing, China	5,760,000	27.	Ho Chi Minh City, Vietnam	3,460,500
13.	Teheran, Iran	5,734,199	28.	Wuhan, China	3,340,000
14.	Hong Kong	5,705,000	29.	Calcutta, India	3,305,006
15.	Istanbul, Turkey	5,475,982	30.	Madras, India	3,276,622

*Latest census or government estimate.

30 Largest Countries of the World by Area

Rank	Country	In sq. mi.	In km^2
1.	Soviet Union	8,649,500	22,402,000
2.	Canada	3,849,674	9,970,610
3.	China	3,696,032	9,572,678
4.	United States	3,618,770	9,372,571
5.	Brazil	3,286,488	8,511,965
6.	Australia	2,966,150	7,682,300
7.	India	1,269,219	3,287,263
8.	Argentina	1,073,400	2,780,092
9.	Sudan	967,500	2,505,813
10.	Algeria	919,595	2,381,741
11.	Zaire	905,365	2,344,885
12.	Saudi Arabia	830,000	2,149,690
13.	Mexico	756,067	1,958,201
14.	Indonesia	741,101	1,919,443
15.	Libya	679,362	1,759,540
16.	Iran	636,300	1,648,000
17.	Mongolia	604,250	1,565,000
18.	Peru	496,225	1,285,216
19.	Chad	495,755	1,284,000
20.	Niger	489,200	1,267,000
21.	Angola	481,354	1,246,700
22.	Mali	478,841	1,240,192
23.	Ethiopia	471,778	1,221,900
24.	South Africa	471,445	1,221,037
25.	Colombia	440,831	1,141,748
26.	Bolivia	424,165	1,098,581
27.	Mauritania	397,956	1,030,700
28.	Egypt	386,662	1,001,449
29.	Tanzania	364,900	945,087
30.	Nigeria	356,669	923,768

*Latest census or government estimate.

30 Largest Countries of the World by Population

Rank	Country	Population*
1.	China	1,100,258,000
2.	India	853,532,000
3.	Soviet Union	288,239,000
4.	United States	250,372,000
5.	Indonesia	180,594,000
6.	Brazil	150,557,000
7.	Japan	123,749,000
8.	Bangladesh	116,000,000
9.	Pakistan	113,163,000
10.	Nigeria	112,765,000
11.	Mexico	88,560,000
12.	Vietnam	67,084,000
13.	Philippines	62,466,000
14.	West Germany	60,471,000
15.	Italy	57,380,000
16.	Great Britain	57,293,000
17.	Iran	56,800,000
18.	Turkey	56,549,000
19.	France	56,236,000
20.	Thailand	55,760,000
21.	Egypt	53,522,000
22.	Ethiopia	48,630,000
23.	South Korea	43,650,000
24.	Burma	41,279,000
25.	Spain	39,623,000
26.	Poland	38,441,000
27.	South Africa	37,922,000
28.	Zaire	35,330,000
29.	Argentina	32,361,000
30.	Colombia	31,863,000

Political Map of the World

This map shows each continent in a different color. The names of independent nations are printed in capital letters. Other political units are in upper- and lower-case letters.

Facts About the Continents

Asia has more land, people, and a higher population density than any other continent. People in Australia have a longer life expectancy than do people of any other continent.

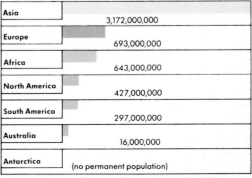

Area

Asia	17,006,000 sq. mi. (44,045,000 km²)
Africa	11,683,000 sq. mi. (30,259,000 km²)
North America	9,358,000 sq. mi. (24,237,000 km²)
South America	6,888,000 sq. mi. (17,840,000 km²)
Antarctica	5,400,000 sq. mi. (14,000,000 km²)
Europe	4,061,000 sq. mi. (10,517,000 km²)
Australia	2,966,000 sq. mi. (7,682,000 km²)

Population

Asia	3,172,000,000
Europe	693,000,000
Africa	643,000,000
North America	427,000,000
South America	297,000,000
Australia	16,000,000
Antarctica	(no permanent population)

Sources: Area and population figures are 1990 estimates based on the latest figures from official government and United Nations sources. Life expectancy figures are UN estimates for 1985-1990.

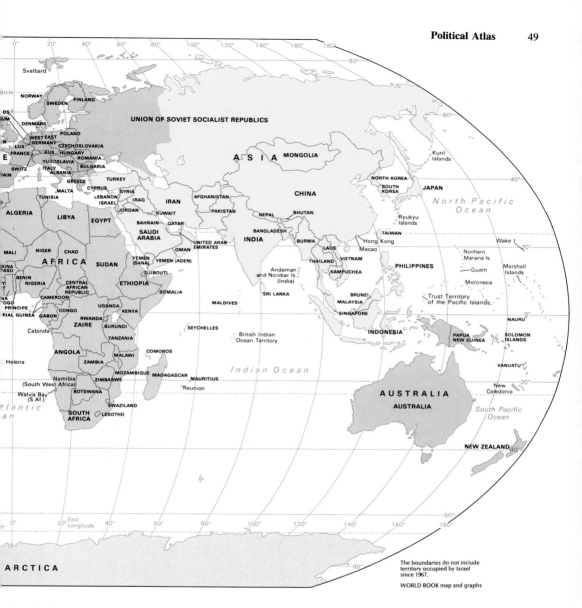

The boundaries do not include territory occupied by Israel since 1967.

WORLD BOOK map and graphs

Population Density

Asia	187 persons per sq. mi. (72 per km²)
Europe	171 persons per sq. mi. (66 per km²)
Africa	55 persons per sq. mi. (21 per km²)
North America	46 persons per sq. mi. (18 per km²)
South America	43 persons per sq. mi. (17 per km²)
Australia	6 persons per sq. mi. (2 per km²)
Antarctica	(no permanent population)

Life Expectancy

Australia	75.0 years
Europe	73.6 years
North America	71.9 years
South America	65.4 years
Asia	60.1 years
Africa	51.8 years
Antarctica	(no permanent population)

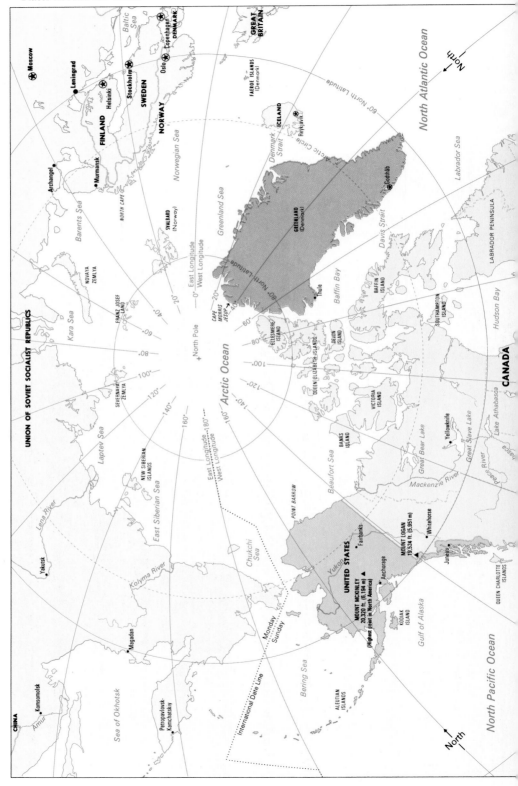

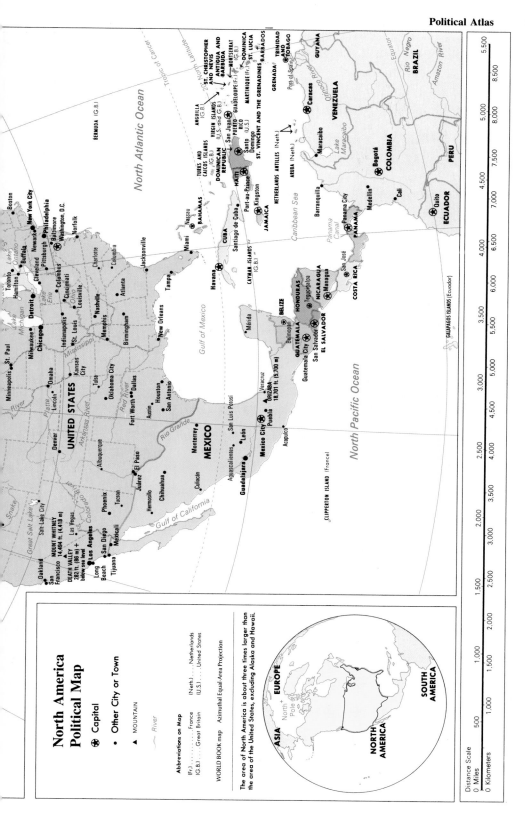

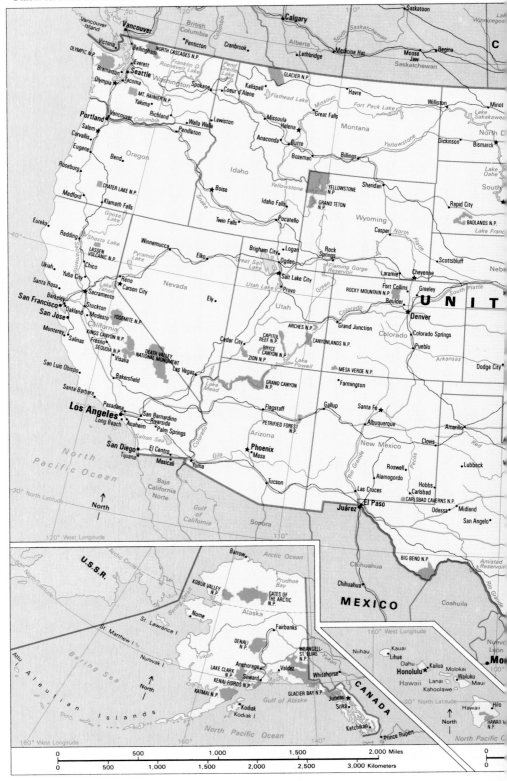

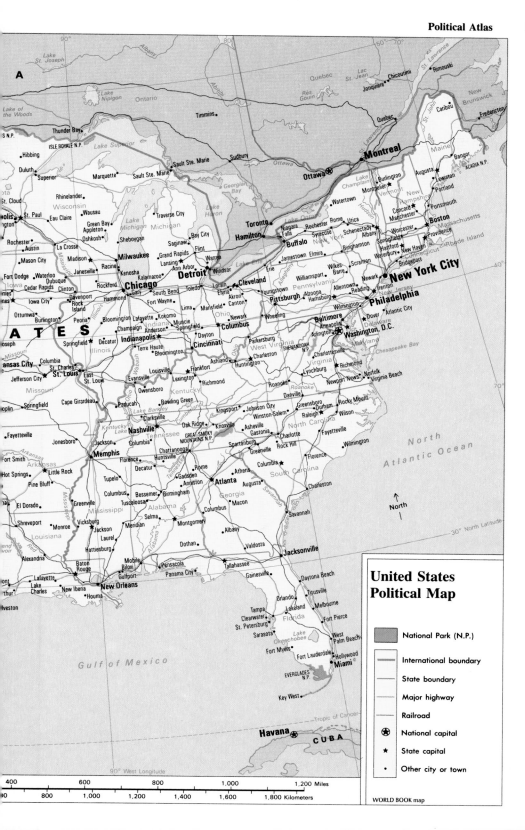

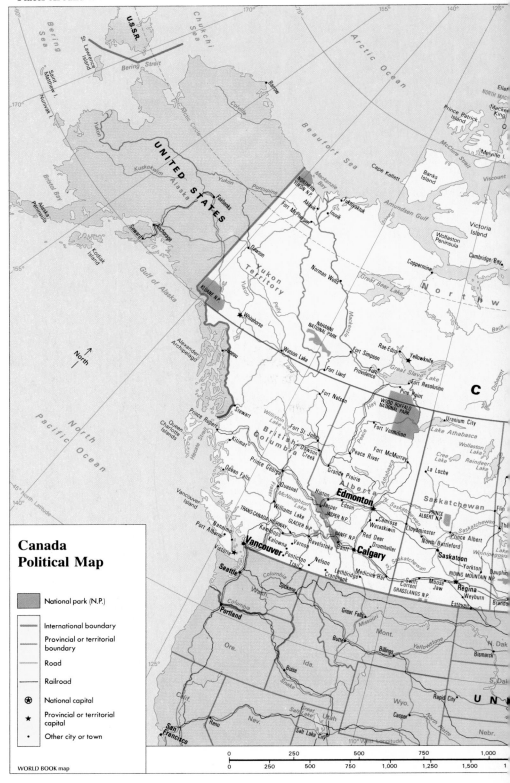

**Canada
Political Map**

National park (N.P.)

International boundary

Provincial or territorial
boundary

Road

Railroad

⊛ National capital

★ Provincial or territorial
capital

• Other city or town

WORLD BOOK map

ICELAND

Reykjavik ⊕

GREENLAND
(Denmark)

Arctic Circle

Thule

Baffin
Bay

re Island

and

er Sound

Bylot

Borden
Peninsula

Pond Inlet

Igloolik

Melville
Peninsula

Davis Strait

Disko
Island

Pangnirtung

Cumberland Sound

Baffin
Island

AUYUITTUQ
NATIONAL PARK

North
Atlantic Ocean

20°

35°

o r i e s

Foxe Basin

Southampton
Island

field Inlet

Coats I.

Mansel I.

D   A

Salluit

Ungava
Peninsula

Povungnituk

Cape Dorset

Hudson Strait

Akpatok I.

Iqaluit

Resolution I.

Cape Chidley

Gothab ⊕

Cape Farewell

35°

Labrador
Sea

North
↑
North
|

Ungava
Bay

ee Tatnam

Hudson Bay

Belcher
Islands

Kuujjuarapik

Feuilles

Kuujjuaq

Caniapiscau

Smallwood
Reservoir

Nain

Hopedale

Hamilton Inlet

Cartwright

ewfound

St. Anthony

45° North Latitude

50°

James
Bay

LG-2
Res.

LG-3
Res.

Chisasibi

LG-4
Res.

La Grande

Quebec

Labrador City

Schefferville

Happy Valley
Goose Bay
Churchill

Gagnon

Manicouagan Res.

Sept-Îles

Grand
Falls

Gander

GROS MORNE N.P.

Corner Brook

Stephenville

TRANS-CANADA
HIGHWAY

Channel-Port aux Basques

TERRA NOVA N.P.

St. John's

Mount Pearl

Cape Race

Akimiski I.

Fort Albany

Moosonee

Eastmain

Fort Rupert

Matagami

Lac
Mistassini

Chibougamau

Rés.
Gouin

Péribonca

Port-Cartier

Baie-Comeau

HAVRE-ST.-PIERRE
MINGAN ARCHIPELAGO N.P.

Anticosti I.

Gaspé

FORILLON N.P.

Gulf of
Saint Lawrence

Magdalen
Islands

ST.-PIERRE
AND MIQUELON
(France)

CAPE BRETON
HIGHLANDS N.P.

Glace Bay

Sydney

Albany

Ontario

Fort Albany

Hearst

Kapuskasing

Geraldton

Nipigon

Lake
Nipigon

kan

Bay

Lake Superior

PUKASKWA
N.P.

TRANS-CANADA HIGHWAY

Wawa

Sault
Ste. Marie

Sudbury

North Bay

Georgian
Bay

Lake
Huron

Timmins

Kirkland Lake

Noranda

Rouyn

Val-d'Or

Amos

La Tuque

LA MAURICIE N.P.

Shawinigan

Trois-Rivières

Pembroke

Mont-Laurier

Ottawa

Peterborough

Barrie

Oshawa

Lake Ontario

Kingston

Cornwall

Québec

St-Jean

Drummondville

Sherbrooke

St. John

Rivière-du-Loup

St. Lawrence

Edmundston

Fredericton

Campbellton

New
Brunswick

Moncton

Matane

Rimouski

Jonquière

Chicoutimi

Bathurst

Prince Edward
Island

Charlottetown

Summerside

Nova Scotia

Truro

Halifax ★

Dartmouth

KEJIMKUJIK N.P.

Yarmouth

Cape Sable

Bay of Fundy

Saint John

St. Stephen

Me.

N.H.

Vt.

N.Y.

Boston

Mass.

Providence

R.I.

Conn.

New York City

N.J.

Philadelphia

Pa.

Sable I.

North
Atlantic Ocean

Wis.

Milwaukee

Chicago

Mich.

Lake
Michigan

Grand
Rapids

Detroit

London

Windsor

Sarnia

Kitchener

Guelph

Hamilton

St. Catharines

Niagara Falls N.Y.

Toronto

Lake Erie

Cleveland

Toledo

Ohio

80° West Longitude

Albany

Syracuse

65°

Montreal

Ottawa ★

TES

65°

150°

35°

20°

25°

60°

	1,750		2,000		2,250		2,500		2,750		3,000 Miles

2,500	2,750	3,000	3,250	3,500	3,750	4,000	4,250	4,500	4,750 Kilometers

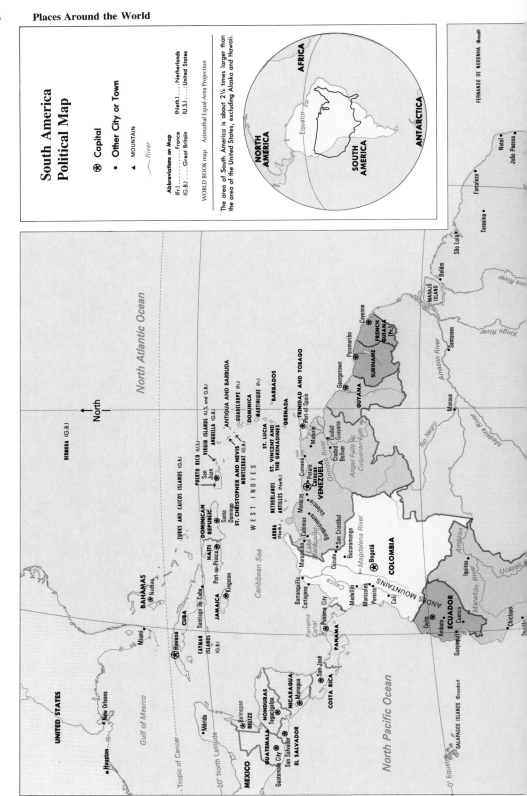

South America Political Map

Capital

Other City or Town

▲ MOUNTAIN

~ River

Abbreviations on Map
(Fr.).........France   (Neth.).....Netherlands
(G.B.).....Great Britain   (U.S.).....United States

WORLD BOOK map   Azimuthal Equal-Area Projection

The area of South America is about 2¼ times larger than the area of the United States, excluding Alaska and Hawaii.

NORTH AMERICA

AFRICA

Equator

SOUTH AMERICA

ANTARCTICA

North Atlantic Ocean

North

BERMUDA (G.B.)

Tropic of Cancer

20° North Latitude

UNITED STATES

Houston

New Orleans

Miami

Gulf of Mexico

Mérida

MEXICO

BELIZE
Belmopan

GUATEMALA
Guatemala City

EL SALVADOR
San Salvador

HONDURAS
Tegucigalpa

NICARAGUA
Managua

COSTA RICA
San José

PANAMA
Panama City

Panama Canal

BAHAMAS
Nassau

CUBA
Havana
Santiago de Cuba

CAYMAN ISLANDS (G.B.)

JAMAICA
Kingston

HAITI
Port-au-Prince

DOMINICAN REPUBLIC
Santo Domingo

TURKS AND CAICOS ISLANDS (G.B.)

PUERTO RICO (U.S.)
San Juan

VIRGIN ISLANDS (U.S. and G.B.)

ANGUILLA (G.B.)

ST. CHRISTOPHER AND NEVIS
MONTSERRAT (G.B.)

ANTIGUA AND BARBUDA

GUADELOUPE (Fr.)

DOMINICA

MARTINIQUE (Fr.)

ST. LUCIA

ST. VINCENT AND THE GRENADINES

BARBADOS

GRENADA

WEST INDIES

Caribbean Sea

ARUBA (Neth.)

NETHERLANDS ANTILLES (Neth.)

TRINIDAD AND TOBAGO
Port-of-Spain

Caracas

VENEZUELA

Maracaibo
Lake Maracaibo
Cabimas
Maracay
Valencia
Barquisimeto
Barinas
Petare
Cumaná
Maturín
Ciudad Guayana
Ciudad Bolívar

Orinoco River

Angel Falls

Coquenan Falls

GUYANA
Georgetown

SURINAME
Paramaribo

FRENCH GUIANA (Fr.)
Cayenne

Rio Negro

COLOMBIA
Bogotá

Barranquilla
Cartagena
Medellín
Manizales
Pereira
Cali
Cúcuta
Bucaramanga
San Cristóbal

Magdalena River

Cauca

ANDES MOUNTAINS

ECUADOR
Quito
Guayaquil
Ambato
Cuenca

GALAPAGOS ISLANDS (Ecuador)

Chiclayo

Marañón River

Amazon

Iquitos

Ucayali

Amazon River

Manaus

Madeira River

MARAJÓ ISLAND

Belém

São Luís

Teresina

Fortaleza

Natal

João Pessoa

Recife

FERNANDO DE NORONHA (Brazil)

Santarém

Xingu River

North Pacific Ocean

0° Equator

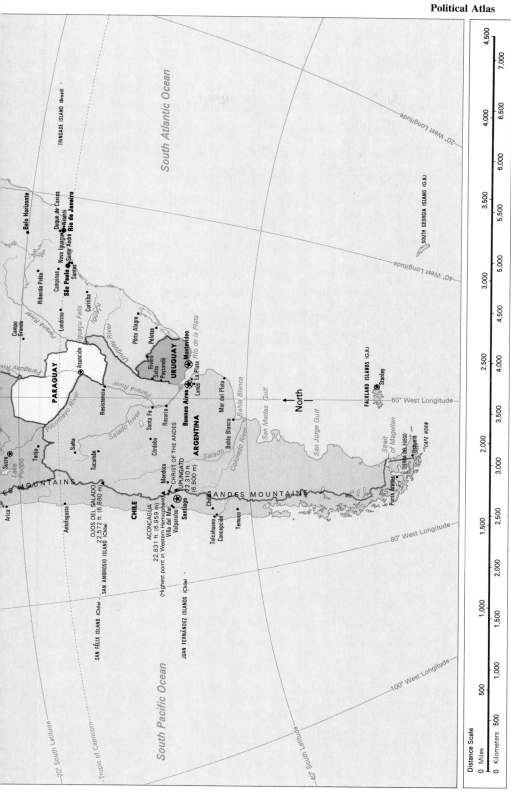

Distance Scale

Miles

Kilometers

Europe Political Map

⊛   Capital

●   Other City or Town

▲   MOUNTAIN

⌒   *River*

WORLD BOOK map

Azimuthal Equal-Area Projection

NORTH AMERICA

+ North Pole

ASIA

EUROPE

AFRICA

Arctic Circle

20° West Longitude

0° Prime Meridian

North

Norwegian Sea

●Akureyri

⊛Reykjavik

ICELAND

North Atlantic Ocean

60° North Latitude

FAEROE ISLANDS (Denmark)

SHETLAND ISLANDS

Trondheim

NORGE ... **NORWAY**   SW

Bergen●

HEBRIDES

ORKNEY ISLANDS

Oslo⊛

Lake Väner

SCOTLAND

NORTHERN IRELAND

Glasgow● ●Edinburgh

North Sea

Skagerrak

●Göteborg

Belfast●

Newcastle upon Tyne

DENMARK

Dublin⊛ ISLE OF MAN **ENGLAND**

Leeds● **GREAT BRITAIN**

Copenhagen⊛ ●Malmö

Liverpool●

IRELAND

Manchester●

Cork●

●Birmingham

Hamburg●

WALES

Cardiff●

Amsterdam●

The Hague⊛

West Berlin⊛ East Berlin●

●London⊛

NETHERLANDS

Essen●

●Düsseldorf

EAST GERMANY

English Channel

Antwerp●

Cologne●

Leipzig● ●Dresden

CHANNEL ISLANDS

Brussels⊛

Lille● **BELGIUM**

●Bonn

WEST GERMANY

Frankfurt●

Prague⊛

LUXEMBOURG

Paris⊛

CZECHOS

Nantes●

Stuttgart●

Loire River

Seine

Munich●

Vien

Bay of Biscay

FRANCE

Basel● Zurich●

Danube

AUSTRIA

Bern⊛ **LIECHTENSTEIN**

●Bordeaux

Lyon●

SWITZERLAND Geneva●

Graz●

Rhône

Turin● Milan●

Venice●

Zagreb

Bilbao●

Po River

Ebro River

●Toulouse

Genoa●

●Bologna

Duero River

Marseille●

MONACO

Florence●

SAN MARINO

●Porto

ANDORRA⊛

PORTUGAL

SPAIN

Saragossa●

ITALY

Lisbon⊛

Madrid⊛

Barcelona●

CORSICA

Adriatic Sea

Tagus River

VATICAN CITY⊛ ⊛Rome

Valencia●

SARDINIA

Tyrrhenian Sea

●Naples

Seville●

BALEARIC ISLANDS

●Málaga

40° North Latitude

Tangier● **GIBRALTAR** (Great Britain)

Mediterranean Sea

Palermo●

▲MO

SICILY ●Catan

⊛Rabat

Casablanca●

Algiers⊛

Tunis⊛

MALTA ●

MOROCCO

ALGERIA

TUNISIA

AFRICA

Distance scale

0 Miles		500		1,000		1,500

0 Kilometers	500	1,000	1,500	2,000	2,500

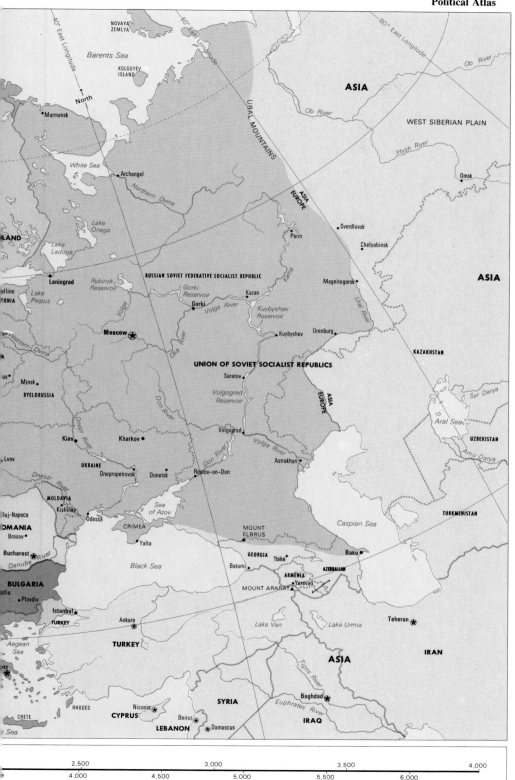

NOVAYA
ZEMLYA

Barents Sea

KOLGUYEV
ISLAND

40° East Longitude

80° East Longitude

80° East Longitude

Ob River

ASIA

North

• Murmansk

WEST SIBERIAN PLAIN

Ob River

URAL MOUNTAINS

Irtysh River

• Omsk

White Sea

• Archangel

Northern Dvina

ASIA
EUROPE

• Sverdlovsk

• Perm

• Chelyabinsk

Lake Onega

Lake Ladoga

LAND

• Leningrad

Rybinsk Reservoir

RUSSIAN SOVIET FEDERATIVE SOCIALIST REPUBLIC

Gorki Reservoir

• Gorki

Kazan •

Volga

Volga River

Kama

• Magnitogorsk

ASIA

Kuybyshev Reservoir

Ural River

allinn
ONIA

Lake Peipus

Moscow ✪

Oka River

• Kuybyshev

Orenburg •

KAZAKHSTAN

us •

UNION OF SOVIET SOCIALIST REPUBLICS

Saratov •

ASIA
EUROPE

Syr Darya

Minsk •

BYELORUSSIA

Volgograd Reservoir

Aral Sea

Western Dvina

Don River

Volgograd •

UZBEKISTAN

Kiev •

Kharkov •

Dnepr River

Volga River

Amu Darya

Lvov •

UKRAINE

• Dnepropetrovsk

Donetsk •

Don River

Rostov-on-Don •

Astrakhan •

Dnestr River

MOLDAVIA

Kishinev •

Odessa •

Sea of Azov

Caspian Sea

TURKMENISTAN

Cluj-Napoca •

OMANIA

Brasov •

CRIMEA

• Yalta

MOUNT
ELBRUS

Bucharest ✪

Danube River

Black Sea

Baku •

BULGARIA

ofia •

• Plovdiv

GEORGIA

Tbilisi •

Batumi •

AZERBAIJAN

ARMENIA • Yerevan

Teheran ✪

• Istanbul

TURKEY

• Ankara

MOUNT ARARAT •

Lake Van

Lake Urmia

Aegean Sea

TURKEY

IRAN

ASIA

RHODES

Nicosia •

CYPRUS

Beirut •

• Damascus

SYRIA

Tigris River

Baghdad ✪

IRAN

CRETE

LEBANON

Euphrates River

IRAQ

n Sea

2,500		3,000		3,500		4,000
4,000	4,500	5,000	5,500	6,000		

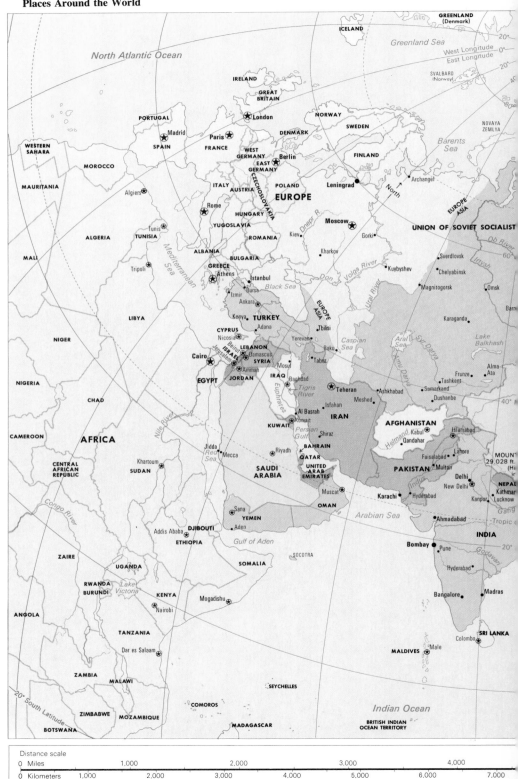

GREENLAND (Denmark)

ICELAND

North Atlantic Ocean

Greenland Sea

West Longitude 0°
East Longitude

20°

20°

40°

SVALBARD (Norway)

IRELAND

GREAT BRITAIN

London

NORWAY

SWEDEN

DENMARK

Bárents Sea

NOVAYA ZEMLYA

PORTUGAL

Madrid

SPAIN

Paris

FRANCE

WEST GERMANY

EAST GERMANY

Berlin

FINLAND

EUROPE ASIA

WESTERN SAHARA

MOROCCO

Algiers

ITALY

AUSTRIA

CZECHOSLOVAKIA

POLAND

EUROPE

Leningrad

North

Archangel

Rome

HUNGARY

Moscow

UNION OF SOVIET SOCIALIST

MAURITANIA

Tunis

YUGOSLAVIA

Kiev

Dnepr R.

Gorki

Ob River

MALI

ALGERIA

TUNISIA

Tripoli

ROMANIA

ALBANIA

BULGARIA

GREECE

Athens

Kharkov

Don

Volga River

Sverdlovsk

Kuybyshev

Chelyabinsk

Magnitogorsk

Omsk

60°

Irtysh

Ural River

LIBYA

Mediterranean Sea

Istanbul

Izmir

Bursa

Ankara

Black Sea

EUROPE ASIA

Tbilisi

Karaganda

Lake Balkhash

Barn

NIGER

CYPRUS

Nicosia

Konya

TURKEY

Adana

Yerevan

Caspian Sea

Aral Sea

Syr Darya

NIGERIA

LEBANON

Beirut

ISRAEL

Jerusalem

Cairo

Damascus

SYRIA

Amman

Mosul

Baku

Tabriz

Amu Darya

Alma-Ata

Frunze

Tashkent

Alma-Ata

CHAD

JORDAN

IRAQ

Baghdad

Tigris River

Teheran

Meshed

Ashkhabad

Samarkand

Dushanbe

40°

CAMEROON

AFRICA

EGYPT

Euphrates

Nile River

Isfahan

Al Basrah

Kuwait

IRAN

AFGHANISTAN

Kabul

Qandahar

Islamabad

MOUNT 29,028 ft.

KUWAIT

Persian Gulf

Shiraz

Faisalabad

Lahore

CENTRAL AFRICAN REPUBLIC

Khartoum

SUDAN

Jidda

Red Sea

Mecca

Riyadh

BAHRAIN

QATAR

UNITED ARAB EMIRATES

Muscat

PAKISTAN

Multan

Indus

Delhi

New Delhi

Karachi

Hyderabad

Kanpur

NEPAL

Kathmandu

Lucknow

Gang

SAUDI ARABIA

OMAN

Arabian Sea

Tropic

Sana

YEMEN

Aden

ZAIRE

Addis Ababa

DJIBOUTI

ETHIOPIA

Gulf of Aden

SOCOTRA

Ahmadabad

INDIA

20°

Bombay

Pune

Godavari

UGANDA

SOMALIA

Hyderabad

RWANDA BURUNDI

Lake Victoria

KENYA

Nairobi

Mogadishu

Bangalore

Madras

ANGOLA

TANZANIA

Dar es Salaam

SRI LANKA

Colombo

MALDIVES

Male

ZAMBIA

MALAWI

SEYCHELLES

ZIMBABWE

MOZAMBIQUE

20° South Latitude

COMOROS

MADAGASCAR

Indian Ocean

BRITISH INDIAN OCEAN TERRITORY

BOTSWANA

Congo River

Distance scale

0 Miles		1,000		2,000		3,000		4,000	
0 Kilometers	1,000	2,000	3,000	4,000	5,000	6,000	7,000		

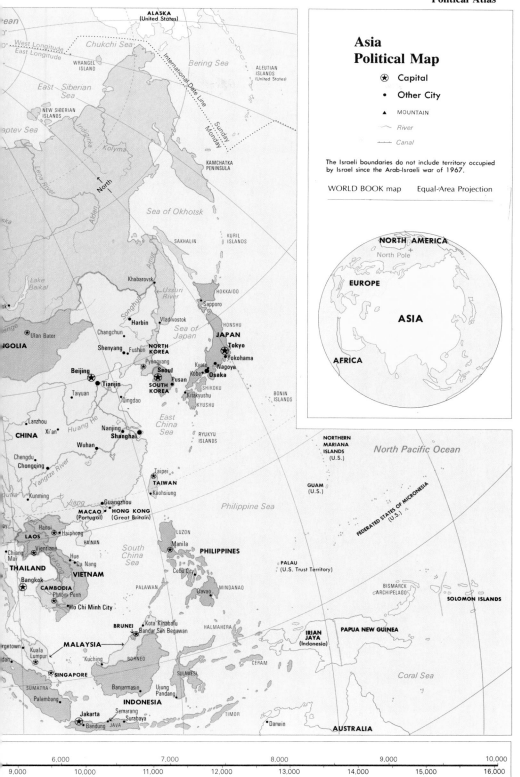

Asia
Political Map

⊛ Capital

• Other City

▲ MOUNTAIN

〜 River

⊣⊢ Canal

The Israeli boundaries do not include territory occupied by Israel since the Arab-Israeli war of 1967.

WORLD BOOK map   Equal-Area Projection

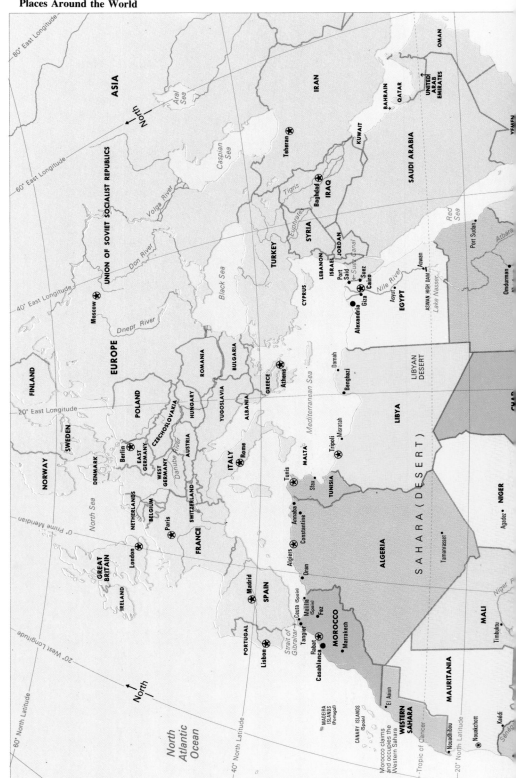

North Atlantic Ocean

60° North Latitude

40° North Latitude

20° West Longitude

0° Prime Meridian

North Sea

GREAT BRITAIN

IRELAND

London

NORWAY

SWEDEN

DENMARK

NETHERLANDS

BELGIUM

Paris

FRANCE

SWITZERLAND

WEST GERMANY

EAST GERMANY

Berlin

POLAND

CZECHOSLOVAKIA

AUSTRIA

HUNGARY

Danube River

FINLAND

EUROPE

20° East Longitude

UNION OF SOVIET SOCIALIST REPUBLICS

Moscow

40° East Longitude

Dnepr River

Don River

Volga River

60° East Longitude

80° East Longitude

ASIA

North

Aral Sea

Caspian Sea

Black Sea

ROMANIA

BULGARIA

YUGOSLAVIA

ALBANIA

GREECE

Athens

Mediterranean Sea

ITALY

Rome

PORTUGAL

Lisbon

SPAIN

Madrid

Strait of Gibraltar

Tangier

Ceuta (Spain)

Melilla (Spain)

Fez

Rabat

Casablanca

MOROCCO

Marrakech

Oran

Algiers

Annaba

Constantine

TUNISIA

Tunis

Sfax

MALTA

Tripoli

Misratah

LIBYA

SAHARA (DESERT)

ALGERIA

Tamanrasset

LIBYAN DESERT

Benghazi

Darnah

Port Said

Suez Canal

Suez

Cairo

Giza

Alexandria

ISRAEL

LEBANON

Nile River

Asyut

Aswan

ASWAN HIGH DAM

Lake Nasser

EGYPT

CYPRUS

TURKEY

SYRIA

JORDAN

Tigris

Euphrates

Baghdad

IRAQ

IRAN

Teheran

KUWAIT

SAUDI ARABIA

BAHRAIN

QATAR

UNITED ARAB EMIRATES

OMAN

YEMEN

Red Sea

Port Sudan

Omdurman

Atbara

CHAD

NIGER

Agadez

MALI

Timbuktu

Niger R.

MAURITANIA

Kaédi

Nouakchott

Nouadhibou

Senegal R.

WESTERN SAHARA

El Aaiun

Tropic of Cancer

20° North Latitude

CANARY ISLANDS (Spain)

MADEIRA ISLANDS (Portugal)

Morocco claims and occupies the Western Sahara

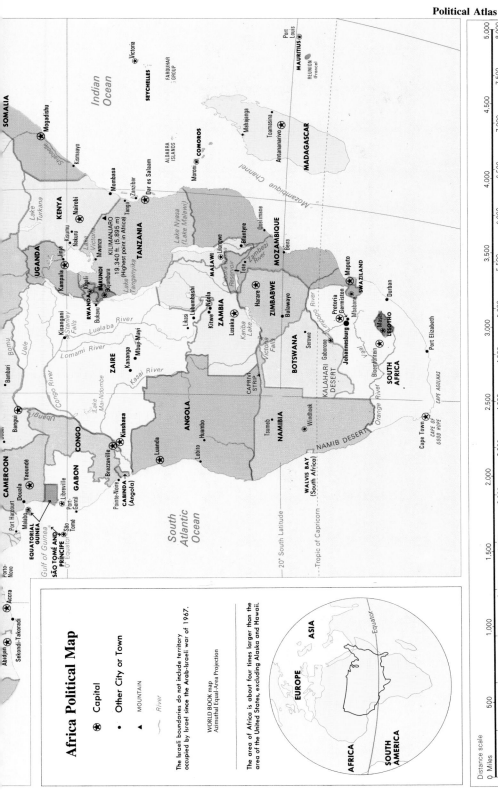

Africa Political Map

⊛ Capital

• Other City or Town

▲ MOUNTAIN

〜 River

The Israeli boundaries do not include territory occupied by Israel since the Arab-Israeli war of 1967.

WORLD BOOK map
Azimuthal Equal-Area Projection

The area of Africa is about four times larger than the area of the United States, excluding Alaska and Hawaii.

EUROPE   ASIA

AFRICA

SOUTH
AMERICA

Equator

Distance scale

| 0 Miles | 500 | 1,000 | 1,500 | 2,000 | 2,500 | 3,000 | 3,500 | 4,000 | 4,500 | 5,000 |
| 0 Kilometers 500 | 1,000 | 1,500 | 2,000 | 2,500 | 3,000 | 3,500 | 4,000 | 4,500 | 5,000 | 5,500 | 6,000 | 6,500 | 7,000 | 7,500 | 8,000 |

SOMALIA
Mogadishu

Indian
Ocean

Victoria
SEYCHELLES

FARQUHAR
GROUP

ALDABRA
ISLANDS   COMOROS
Moroni

Port
Louis
MAURITIUS
REUNION
(France)

Mahajanga

Toamasina
Antananarivo
MADAGASCAR

Mozambique Channel

Kismayo

Mombasa
KENYA
Nairobi
Nakuru

Lake
Turkana

UGANDA
Kampala
Jinja

Lake
Victoria
Mwanza

KILIMANJARO
19,340 ft. (5,895 m)
(Highest point in Africa)

Tanga
Zanzibar
Dar es Salaam

Lake Nyasa
(Lake Malawi)

RWANDA
Kigali
BURUNDI
Bujumbura
Bukavu

Lake
Tanganyika

TANZANIA

MALAWI
Lilongwe
Blantyre

Zambezi
River

Quelimane

Kisangani
Stanley
Falls

Lualaba
River

Lubumbashi
Ndola
Kitwe

Likasi

ZAMBIA
Lusaka

Tete
Beira

MOZAMBIQUE

Harare
ZIMBABWE
Bulawayo

Maputo
SWAZILAND
Mbabane
Durban

Lomami River

ZAIRE
Kananga
Mbuji-Mayi

Kasai River

Kariba
Lake

Victoria
Falls

Limpopo River

Pretoria
Germiston
Johannesburg
Bloemfontein

Maseru
LESOTHO

Port Elizabeth

Uele

Bambari

Lake
Mai-Ndombe

ANGOLA
Huambo

Serowe
BOTSWANA
Gaborone

KALAHARI
DESERT

SOUTH
AFRICA

Vaal
River

Bangui
Ubangi

Congo River

CONGO
Brazzaville
Kinshasa

Luanda
Lobito

Tsumeb

NAMIBIA
Windhoek

Orange River

CAPE OF
GOOD HOPE   CAPE AGULHAS

Cape Town

CAMEROON
Douala
Yaoundé

GABON
Libreville
Port-
Gentil

Pointe-Noire
CABINDA
(Angola)

CAPRIVI
STRIP

NAMIB DESERT

WALVIS BAY
(South Africa)

20° South Latitude

Tropic of Capricorn

South
Atlantic
Ocean

Port Harcourt
Malabo
EQUATORIAL
GUINEA
SÃO TOMÉ AND
PRÍNCIPE
São Tomé
Equator

Gulf of Guinea

Porto-
Novo

Accra

Abidjan
Sekondi-Takoradi

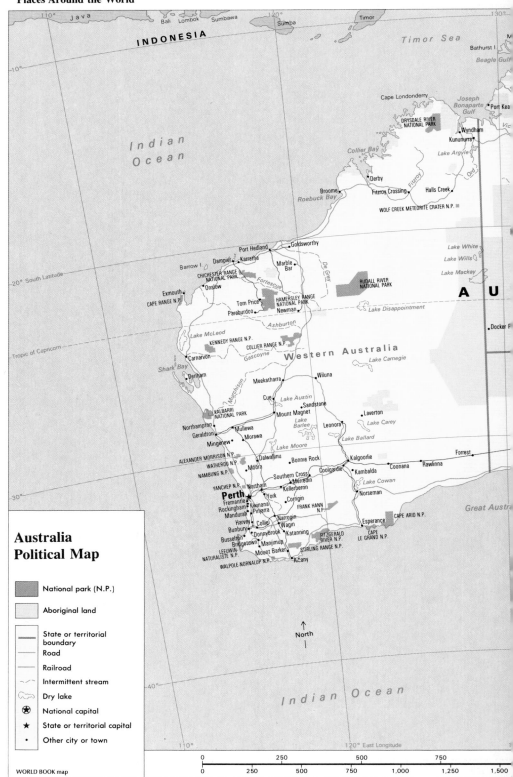

110°   Java   Bali Lombok Sumbawa   120°   Timor   130°

INDONESIA   Sumba   *Timor Sea*   Bathurst I.
                                                                                                        Beagle Gulf

-10°

                                                            Cape Londonderry   *Joseph*   Port Kea
                                                                                         Bonaparte
                                                                    DRYSDALE RIVER   *Gulf*   Vic
Indian   NATIONAL PARK   Wyndham
Ocean   Kununurra

                                                            Collier Bay   *Lake Argyle*
                                                                                          Ord

                                                                Derby
                                            Broome   Fitzroy Crossing   Halls Creek
                                            Roebuck Bay
                                                            WOLF CREEK METEORITE CRATER N.P.

                                    Port Hedland   Goldsworthy   *Lake White*
                                Dampier Karratha   *Lake Wills*
                Barrow I.   Marble   *De Grey*
                            CHICHESTER RANGE   Bar   *Lake Mackay*
                            NATIONAL PARK   *Fortescue*   RUDALL RIVER
-20° South Latitude   Onslow   NATIONAL PARK
        Exmouth   Tom Price HAMERSLEY RANGE   **A U**
        CAPE RANGE N.P.   Paraburdoo NATIONAL PARK
                                            Newman   *Lake Disappointment*
                                        Ashburton
                                                                                      Docker F
                    Lake McLeod   KENNEDY RANGE N.P.
Tropic of Capricorn   COLLIER RANGE N.P.
                Carnarvon   *Gascoyne*   *Western Australia*
        Shark Bay   *Lake Carnegie*
                Denham
                            Meekatharra   Wiluna
                            Cue   *Lake Austin*
                                            Sandstone
                    KALBARRI   Mount Magnet   *Lake*   Laverton
                    NATIONAL PARK   *Barlee*   *Lake Carey*
        Northampton   Mullewa   Leonora
        Geraldton   Morawa   *Lake Ballard*
            Mingenew   *Lake Moore*
ALEXANDER MORRISON N.P.   Dalwallinu   Kalgoorlie   Forrest
        WATHEROO N.P.   Moora   Bonnie Rock   Coolgardie   Coonana   Rawlinna
        NAMBUNG N.P.   Kambalda
                    Southern Cross   *Lake Cowan*
        YANCHEP N.P. Northam Merredin
                        Kellerbernn   Norseman
            Perth   York
        Fremantle   Corrigin
        Rockingham Kwinana   FRANK HANN
        Mandurah Pinjarra   N.P.
            Harvey Narrogin
        Bunbury Collie Wagin   Esperance   CAPE ARID N.P.
        Busselton Donnybrook Katanning
        Bridgetown Manjimup FITZGERALD   CAPE
        LEEUWIN- Mount Barker RIVER N.P. LE GRAND N.P.   *Great Austra*
        NATURALISTE N.P.   STIRLING RANGE N.P.
        WALPOLE-NORNALUP N.P.   Albany

-30°

↑
North
|

-40°   *Indian Ocean*

110°   120° East Longitude

Australia
Political Map

National park (N.P.)

Aboriginal land

State or territorial
boundary
Road
Railroad
Intermittent stream
Dry lake
National capital
State or territorial capital
Other city or town

0   250   500   750
0   250   500   750   1,000   1,250   1,500

Middle East Political Map

The map below shows the Middle East countries and surrounding countries. Asia, Africa, and Europe come together in this region. The smaller map, *right,* shows Arab territory that Israel has occupied since the Arab-Israeli war of 1967.

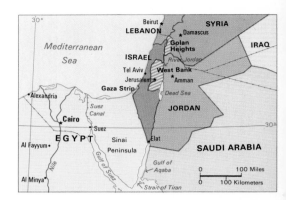

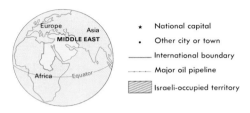

* ★ National capital
* • Other city or town
* —— International boundary
* ······· Major oil pipeline
* ▨ Israeli-occupied territory

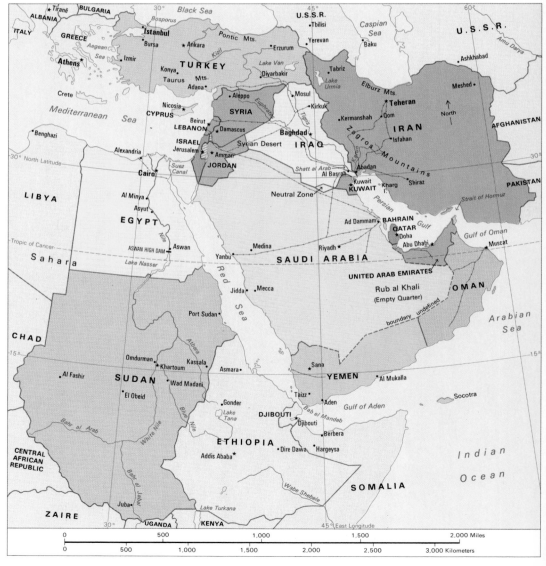

2

Facts about the United States

In this section, you will find a summary of useful information about the United States government and how it works. The section starts with a brief discussion of the United States Constitution, the document that serves as a basis for the government and its operations.

The Constitution

The federal government of the United States is based upon one of history's most remarkable documents, the Constitution of the United States. Drafted in 1787, and ratified by the required number of states in 1788, the Constitution is the oldest written national constitution in use today.

One of the major reasons for the success of the Constitution has been its flexibility—the ability to adjust to meet needs and changing times. Another reason for the long life of the Constitution has been the acceptance of its basic principles by the American people. These basic principles are (1) the idea of a limited government, (2) the concept of popular sovereignty, and (3) the idea of rule by law.

The principle of a limited government is achieved by granting certain powers to the federal government and by granting other powers to the various state governments. A few powers are shared. In this way, the Constitution ensures that the power of the federal government will remain limited because it can exercise only those powers granted by the Constitution. This system of dividing power between the federal government and the state government is called *federalism*. It is a system of government that was originated by the Founding Fathers when they wrote the Constitution.

The second basic principle of the Constitution is that of popular sovereignty. Simply stated, popular sovereignty is rule by the people. It is a basic principle found in all truly democratic societies—that is, societies in which the people have the power to determine and to control the policies of their government. The Constitution has provided for popular sovereignty by ensuring that the American people have the power to change the Constitution and to select officials.

Closely related to the idea of popular sovereignty is the idea of rule by law. Rule by law means that all citizens, regardless of their position, power, or prestige, are bound by the laws of the United States and are to be treated equally before the law. No one, from the President to the average citizen, is above the law. Instead, all citizens and all government officials must obey the laws and the Constitution of the United States.

In addition to establishing the basic principles of the government, the Constitution also establishes the structure of the federal government. In essence, this is done in the first three articles of the Constitution. These articles establish the powers and the structure of the executive, the legislative, and the judicial branches of our government.

Structure and Function of the Government

The Executive Branch. Every four years—on the first Tuesday after the first Monday in November in even-numbered years—the American voters cast their ballots and choose a President. The President is elected indirectly. The voters choose electors who are pledged to a particular presidential candidate. These electors then cast their ballots in December and the President is officially elected. The following month the President is inaugurated for a four-year term.

The oath that the President takes at the inauguration binds him to "preserve, protect, and defend the Constitution of the United States." The President also is bound by the Constitution to "take care that the laws be faithfully executed." The inaugural oath and the Constitution establish two basic functions of the presidency. These two functions are to follow the Constitution and to carry out and enforce the laws of the United States as the nation's chief executive.

As the nation's chief executive, the President is in charge of the executive branch of the federal government. This branch is made up of three parts. The first part is the President's Executive Office. This office has 10 branches that deal with a variety of concerns—from the federal budget to international trade negotiations. The second part of the executive branch consists of 13 executive departments: (1) State, (2) Treasury, (3) Defense, (4) Justice, (5) Interior, (6) Agriculture, (7) Commerce, (8) Labor, (9) Health and Human Services, (10) Housing and Urban Development, (11) Transportation,

(12) Energy, and (13) Education. The heads of these departments form the President's *Cabinet*—a group that advises the President. The third part of the executive branch consists of the various independent government agencies that are directed by the President.

In addition to his duties as chief executive, the President also functions in other roles. The Constitution, in Article II, Sections 2 and 3, specifies the additional responsibilities of the President. For example, the President is the commander in chief of the nation's armed forces and thus controls the military forces of the United States. The President also is given the power (with the advice and consent of the Senate) to make treaties and to appoint ambassadors. Therefore, the President is responsible for the nation's relations with other countries. Thus, he is also the nation's chief diplomat. The President functions as the nation's chief legislator when he exercises the legislative powers granted by the Constitution. These powers include recommending legislation to Congress, calling special sessions of Congress (when necessary), and signing or vetoing bills passed by Congress.

Over the years, some strong Presidents have used their power to influence the other two branches of government. But the principle of a *separation of power* and the system of *checks and balances* established by the Constitution (see page 71) have worked to maintain a balance of power among the three branches of the federal government.

The Legislative Branch. Congress and several administrative agencies make up the legislative branch of the federal government. Congress consists of two houses, the *Senate* and the *House of Representatives*. The two houses of Congress meet separately in the Capitol in Washington, D.C. The administrative agencies (for example, the Architect of the Capitol, the Congressional Budget Office, the General Accounting Office, the Library of Congress, the Government Printing Office, and the United States Botanic Garden) operate under the direction of Congress.

Article I, Section 8 of the Constitution establishes the powers and duties of Congress. Some of these powers are (1) to levy and collect taxes, (2) to coin and to regulate the value of money, (3) to borrow money, (4) to regulate commerce, and so on. To carry out these powers, Congress meets in annual sessions to pass needed legislation. This legislation, unless vetoed by the President or overruled by the federal courts, becomes part of the body of law that governs the nation.

Each house of Congress shares the powers granted by the

Constitution, with a few exceptions. For example, only the Senate has the power to confirm treaties and to approve certain presidential appointments. The House of Representatives, on the other hand, has the sole power to initiate tax legislation. And only the House of Representatives can bring charges of impeachment against a federal official. The Senate then has the sole power to try the individual.

Today, Congress has 535 members. There are 100 senators—two from each state as specified by the Constitution. This number changes only when a new state enters the Union and its senators enter Congress. The number of representatives is determined by Congress and it can be changed if Congress desires.

The 435 representatives in the House of Representatives are apportioned among the states based upon their population. Each state must have at least one representative. Thus, the largest state in population, California, has forty-five representatives plus two senators. In contrast, Alaska, Delaware, North Dakota, Vermont, and Wyoming—the smallest states in terms of population—each have only one representative and two senators. The number of representatives is reapportioned every ten years when a new census is taken.

The members of Congress are chosen by the voters. Congressional elections are held every two years in November of even-numbered years. Senators are elected for six-year terms, and representatives are elected for two-year terms. Thus, all representatives come up for election every two years. But since the terms for senators are staggered, only about one-third of the Senate is chosen in each election.

Normally, Congress begins its annual session in January of each year. During a typical session, it is not unusual to have nearly 10,000 bills introduced for consideration. But for a bill to become a law it must pass both houses of Congress and be signed, or at least not vetoed, by the President. To handle this enormous workload, Congress has developed a process that enables members of Congress to consider only those bills that reflect the needs of at least a part of the American society (see page 72).

The Judicial Branch. The federal courts—the judicial branch of the federal government—derive their jurisdiction and powers from Article III of the Constitution. Today, this branch consists of the Supreme Court, about 90 district courts, 11 courts of appeal, and a number of special courts. These special courts deal with such matters as taxes, patents, and customs duties.

All federal judges are appointed by the President and approved by the Senate. These judges serve for life (or during good behavior) and can only be removed from office through impeachment and conviction.

The highest court of the land is the Supreme Court of the United States. It is the only federal court that is specifically mentioned in the Constitution. It has a chief justice and eight associate justices. The Supreme Court's jurisdiction and its powers are covered in Article III, Section 2 of the Constitution. However, the Constitution also gives Congress the power to decide what type of cases the Supreme Court can hear on appeal from lower federal courts and, in some cases, from state courts.

The Constitution also provides that the other federal courts are to be established by Congress. Of these courts, the district courts handle most of the cases involving federal laws or the Constitution. Decisions from the district courts can be appealed to the courts of appeal and, from there, to the Supreme Court if the Supreme Court decides to accept them. Cases involving the Constitution may also be appealed from state courts to the federal courts.

An important power of the federal courts—the power of *judicial review*—is not mentioned in the Constitution. Judicial review is the power of a federal court to overrule an act of a government official or a law that is in violation of the Constitution. This power applies to acts of government officials at all levels, and to laws passed by local, state, and federal legislatures.

The federal courts' power of judicial review grew out of actions by the federal courts early in the nation's history. It was firmly established in 1803 in the case of *Marbury v. Madison* when the Supreme Court declared part of a law passed by Congress as unconstitutional. From that time on, judicial review has become an accepted power of the judicial branch of the federal government.

Features of the Federal Government

The Separation of Power and the System of Checks and Balances. The Constitution divides the powers of the federal government among the three branches. Congress has the power to pass laws, the President has the power to enforce the laws, and the courts have the power to interpret and apply the laws as cases arise. By and large, each of the three branches is independent and does not share its power with the other branches. For example, Congress does not enforce the laws it passes. And the President does not pass laws he enforces.

Similarly, the federal courts cannot interpret or apply a law until a case involving a law or the Constitution comes before a federal court.

This separation of power among the three branches of government is maintained by a built-in system of *checks and balances*. In this system of checks and balances, each branch of government has some means of checking or limiting the actions of the other branches. Congress, for example, can check the actions of the President through its exclusive power to appropriate—make available—money. Thus, while the President may order a program to begin, it cannot be started until Congress makes the needed money available. Congress also has the power to maintain a check upon the courts through its power to remove judges through impeachment and conviction. However, Congress also can be checked by the other branches as well. The President has the power to veto bills passed by Congress. And the federal courts have the power to declare laws passed by Congress unconstitutional. In the final analysis, the Constitution has established a federal government composed of three branches, each with powers that check and balance the powers of the other branches.

How a Bill Becomes a Law. The process through which a bill becomes a law differs slightly in the Senate and in the House of Representatives. But the basic steps are the same. By following a bill as it progresses through the House of Representatives and then through the Senate, you can understand the logic and the sequence of the legislative process.

Normally, a bill originates in one of three ways. First it may be proposed by individual citizens or by an interest group that represents a specific group within American society. Second, a bill may originate with a member of Congress. Third, a bill may be proposed by the executive branch or by an agency of the federal government. Today, most major bills begin in the executive branch.

Once a bill is proposed, the next step is to get it introduced. Every bill must be introduced by a member of Congress. It must be "sponsored" by a senator or a representative. In this example, it will be sponsored by a member of the House of Representatives.

When the proposed bill is written in its proper legal form it is placed in a basket (called a "hopper") on the floor of the House of Representatives. The Clerk of the House reads the bill (by title only). This is called the first reading. The bill is then assigned a number and sent to the Government Printing Office to be printed.

After the bill is printed, it is sent to the Speaker of the House (the presiding officer) and assigned to an appropriate committee. After the committee or a subcommittee studies the bill, the committee can take several actions. It can release, or *report out,* the bill with a recommendation to pass it; revise the bill and release it; or lay it aside so that the House cannot vote on it. Laying the bill aside is called *tabling.* If the committee approves the bill, it is sent to the House floor for consideration. At this point, the bill is put on a House Calendar. The bill then must wait its turn for consideration. However, if the bill is an important one, it can be pushed ahead of other bills by the House Rules Committee.

When the bill comes up for consideration, it receives a second reading, in full, and copies are distributed to the members of the House. The bill is then debated. At this point, it may be amended and/or approved, or it may be sent back to the committee for further consideration and adjustment. If a majority of the House approves the bill, it then receives its third reading (by title only) and is voted on again. If the bill passes—receives a majority vote—it is signed by the Speaker of the House and sent to the Senate for its consideration.

Upon reaching the Senate, the bill begins to go through the same steps again. The bill receives a first reading and is assigned to a Senate committee for study. Once again, the bill may die in committee, or it may be amended, rewritten, and/or approved. If the bill survives the committee, it is sent to the floor of the Senate. The bill is then placed on the Senate Calendar, and it must wait its turn unless pushed ahead by unanimous consent—without objection.

When its turn arrives, the bill receives a second reading, in full, and it is debated. The bill may be returned to the committee, or it may be amended, rejected, or approved. If approved, the bill receives its third reading (by title only) and is voted on again. If the bill receives a majority vote, it is passed. It is then signed and sent to the White House for the President's signature. However, before a bill can be sent to the President, any differences in the version passed by the House and the version passed by the Senate must be resolved. Therefore, if changes have been made in the Senate, the bill must be returned to the House for its approval. If the House of Representatives does not agree to the changes, a conference committee—made up of members from both houses—is appointed to resolve the differences. When an agreement is finally reached, the bill is sent back to both houses for their approval. If the bill is approved by both houses, it is then sent to the President.

The President, when he receives the bill, can do one of four things. First, he can sign the bill and it becomes a law. Second, he can refuse to sign the bill, and in ten days (excluding Sunday) it becomes a law without his signature. Third, he can veto the bill and send it back to Congress with the reasons for the veto. Congress then can override the President's veto, but it takes a two-thirds vote of both houses to do so. If Congress fails to override the veto, the bill is dead. Fourth, the President can "pocket veto" the bill. This can be done if after the bill arrives at the White House, Congress adjourns within ten days. The President then can decline to take action and the bill dies.

Obviously, the process that a bill must go through to become a law is complicated and time-consuming. Of the more than 20,000 bills usually introduced during a term of Congress (two annual sessions), only a few survive beyond the committee stage. And of those that do survive, only a very few actually become laws. The process effectively screens out most of the less important bills that are introduced each year. It also ensures that the bills passed are widely supported.

Amending the Constitution. Not all changes in the nation's laws must take the form of a bill. The basic law of the United States is the Constitution, and it can be changed to meet new needs or the wishes of the people. The Constitution is changed with an amendment.

Over the years, more than 7,000 amendments to the Constitution have been considered. But to date, only 33 of these have been approved by Congress. And of these, only 26 have been ratified by the states.

Ten of the 26 amendments were ratified in 1791, and they form what is known as the *Bill of Rights*. Freedom of speech, freedom of religion, the right to assemble or meet publicly, and freedom from unreasonable searches by the government—these are some of the basic rights guaranteed to all American citizens in the Bill of Rights.

Amendments can originate in two ways. They can begin in Congress, receive the approval of two-thirds of both houses, and be sent to the states for ratification. They also can originate in a national convention called by Congress on the request of two-thirds of the state legislatures. However, as yet, none of the amendments has begun in a national convention.

Ratification of a proposed amendment can be done in one of two ways. The first method is by the approval of the amendment by the legislatures of three-fourths of the states. The second method is through approval by state ratification conventions in three-fourths of the states. This second method has been used only once.

Unlike most state constitutions, the Constitution of the United States has had relatively few amendments. One reason for this is that over the years the Constitution has proved flexible enough to meet most new conditions. Another reason is the acceptance by the American people of the basic principles of government contained in the Constitution.

Suggested Reading on American Government

This reading list will help you further explore topics from American history and government reviewed in this section. The suggested books are frequently recommended in high school classrooms.

The books probably can be found in your school or public library. If not, your librarian may arrange to get them for you from other sources.

If you ask, your librarian can also suggest additional resources on American history and government that will help expand your knowledge and enjoyment of the subject.

Bailey, Thomas A., and Kennedy, David M. *The American Pageant: A History of the Republic*. 2 vols. 7th ed. Boston: D.C. Heath & Co., 1983.

Beard, Charles A., and Beard, Mary R. *The Beards' New Basic History of the United States*. New York: Doubleday & Co., 1968.

Bedford, Henry F., and Colbourn, Trevor. *The Americans: A Brief History*. 2 vols. 4th ed. New York: Harcourt Brace Jovanovich, 1985.

Chambers, William N., and Burnham, Walter D., eds. *The American Party System: Stages of Political Development*. 2nd ed. New York: Oxford University Press, 1975.

Commager, Henry Steele, ed. *Documents of American History*. 9th ed. New York: Appleton-Century-Crofts, 1974.

Curti, Merle. *The Growth of American Thought*. 3rd ed. New Brunswick, N.J.: Transaction Books, 1981.

Dictionary of American History. 8 vols. rev. ed. New York: Charles Scribner's Sons, 1976.

Ferguson, John H. *The American Federal Government*. 14th ed. New York: McGraw-Hill, 1981.

Hofstadter, Richard. *The American Political Tradition and the Men Who Made It*. 2nd ed. New York: Alfred A. Knopf, 1973.

Magruder, Frank. *Magruder's American Government*. rev. ed. Edited by William A. McClenaghan. Boston: Allyn & Bacon, 1980.

Morison, Samuel E., and others. *The Growth of the American Republic*. 2 vols. 7th ed. New York: Oxford University Press, 1980.

Nevins, Allan, and Commager, Henry Steele. *A Short History of the United States*. 6th ed. New York: Alfred A. Knopf, 1976.

Todd, Lewis Paul, and Curti, Merle E. *Rise of the American Nation*. New York: Harcourt Brace Jovanovich, 1977.

Table of the States

State	Date of entry into Union	Capital city	Largest city**	Area in square miles	Area in square kilometers	Population*	Rank by popu- lation*	Popular name
Alabama	1819	Montgomery	Birmingham	51,705	133,915	3,893,978	22	Yellowhammer State
Alaska	1959	Juneau	Anchorage	591,004	1,530,700	401,851	50	Last Frontier
Arizona	1912	Phoenix	Phoenix	114,000	295,260	2,718,425	29	Grand Canyon State
Arkansas	1836	Little Rock	Little Rock	53,187	137,754	2,286,419	33	Land of Opportunity
California	1850	Sacramento	Los Angeles	158,706	411,049	23,668,562	1	Golden State
Colorado	1876	Denver	Denver	104,091	269,595	2,889,964	28	Centennial State
Connecticut	1788	Hartford	Bridgeport	5,018	12,977	3,107,576	25	Constitution State
Delaware	1787	Dover	Wilmington	2,044	5,295	594,338	47	First State
Florida	1845	Tallahassee	Jacksonville	58,664	151,939	9,746,421	7	Sunshine State
Georgia	1788	Atlanta	Atlanta	58,910	152,576	5,463,087	13	Empire State of the South
Hawaii	1959	Honolulu	Honolulu	6,471	16,759	964,691	39	Aloha State
Idaho	1890	Boise	Boise	83,564	216,432	944,038	41	Gem State
Illinois	1818	Springfield	Chicago	56,345	145,934	11,427,414	5	Land of Lincoln
Indiana	1816	Indianapolis	Indianapolis	36,185	93,720	5,490,260	12	Hoosier State
Iowa	1846	Des Moines	Des Moines	56,275	145,753	2,913,808	27	Hawkeye State
Kansas	1861	Topeka	Wichita	82,277	213,098	2,364,236	32	Sunflower State
Kentucky	1792	Frankfort	Louisville	40,409	104,660	3,660,257	23	Bluegrass State
Louisiana	1812	Baton Rouge	New Orleans	47,752	123,677	4,206,098	19	Pelican State
Maine	1820	Augusta	Portland	33,265	86,156	1,125,030	38	Pine Tree State
Maryland	1788	Annapolis	Baltimore	10,460	27,092	4,216,941	18	Old Line State
Massachusetts	1788	Boston	Boston	8,284	21,456	5,737,081	11	Bay State
Michigan	1837	Lansing	Detroit	58,527	151,586	9,262,070	8	Wolverine State
Minnesota	1858	St. Paul	Minneapolis	84,402	218,601	4,075,970	21	Gopher State
Mississippi	1817	Jackson	Jackson	47,689	123,515	2,520,631	31	Magnolia State
Missouri	1821	Jefferson City	St. Louis	69,697	180,516	4,916,759	15	Show Me State
Montana	1889	Helena	Billings	147,046	380,848	786,690	44	Treasure State
Nebraska	1867	Lincoln	Omaha	77,355	200,350	1,569,825	35	Cornhusker State
Nevada	1864	Carson City	Las Vegas	110,561	286,532	799,184	43	Silver State
New Hampshire	1788	Concord	Manchester	9,297	24,032	920,610	42	Granite State
New Jersey	1787	Trenton	Newark	7,787	20,169	7,365,011	9	Garden State
New Mexico	1912	Santa Fe	Albuquerque	121,593	314,925	1,303,445	37	Land of Enchantment
New York	1788	Albany	New York City	49,108	127,189	17,558,072	2	Empire State
North Carolina	1789	Raleigh	Charlotte	52,669	136,413	5,881,813	10	Tar Heel State
North Dakota	1889	Bismarck	Fargo	70,702	183,119	652,717	46	Flickertail State

State	Date of entry into Union	Capital city	Largest city**	Area in square miles	Area in square kilometers	Population*	Rank by population*	Popular name
Ohio	1803	Columbus	Cleveland	41,330	107,044	10,797,624	6	Buckeye State
Oklahoma	1907	Oklahoma City	Oklahoma City	69,956	181,186	3,025,495	26	Sooner State
Oregon	1859	Salem	Portland	97,073	251,419	2,633,149	30	Beaver State
Pennsylvania	1787	Harrisburg	Philadelphia	45,308	117,348	11,864,751	4	Keystone State
Rhode Island	1790	Providence	Providence	1,212	3,140	947,154	40	Ocean State
South Carolina	1788	Columbia	Columbia	31,113	80,582	3,122,814	24	Palmetto State
South Dakota	1889	Pierre	Sioux Falls	77,116	199,730	690,768	45	Sunshine State
Tennessee	1796	Nashville	Memphis	42,114	109,152	4,591,120	17	Volunteer State
Texas	1845	Austin	Houston	266,807	691,030	14,227,574	3	Lone Star State
Utah	1896	Salt Lake City	Salt Lake City	84,899	219,889	1,461,037	36	Beehive State
Vermont	1791	Montpelier	Burlington	9,614	24,900	511,456	48	Green Mountain State
Virginia	1788	Richmond	Norfolk	40,767	105,586	5,346,797	14	Old Dominion
Washington	1889	Olympia	Seattle	68,139	176,479	4,132,204	20	Evergreen State
West Virginia	1863	Charleston	Huntington	24,231	62,759	1,950,258	34	Mountain State
Wisconsin	1848	Madison	Milwaukee	56,153	145,436	4,705,642	16	Badger State
Wyoming	1890	Cheyenne	Cheyenne	97,809	253,326	469,557	49	Equality State

*1980 census.
**Latest available data.

Table of Principal Territories and Dependencies of the United States

Territory	Location	Date acquired	Capital	Area in sq. mi.	Area in km²	Population**
American Samoa	In the South Pacific	1900-25	Pago Pago	76	197	37,000
District of Columbia	East coast of the U.S.	1791	*	69	179	638,432
Guam	In the Mariana Island group in the Pacific Ocean	1898	Agana	212	549	120,000
Puerto Rico	Southeast of Florida in the Caribbean Sea	1898	San Juan	3,515	9,103	3,282,000
Trust Territory of the Pacific Islands	In the Pacific Ocean near the equator	1947	Koror	192	497	13,000
Virgin Islands	Between the Caribbean Sea and the Atlantic Ocean, east of Puerto Rico	1917	Charlotte Amalie	132	342	111,000

*The district is the capital of the United States.
**Latest available estimate.

Continents of the World

Continent	Area in sq. mi.	in km²	Rank by area	Population	Rank by pop.	Density Persons per sq. mi.	Persons per km²	Rank by density
Africa	11,683,000	30,259,000	2	643,000,000	3	55	21	3
Antarctica	5,400,000	14,000,000	5	0	7	0	0	7
Asia	17,006,000	44,045,000	1	3,172,000,000	1	187	72	1
Australia	2,966,000	7,682,000	7	16,000,000	6	6	2	6
Europe	4,061,000	10,517,000	6	693,000,000	2	171	66	2
North America	9,358,000	24,237,000	3	427,000,000	4	46	18	4
South America	6,888,000	17,840,000	4	297,000,000	5	43	17	5

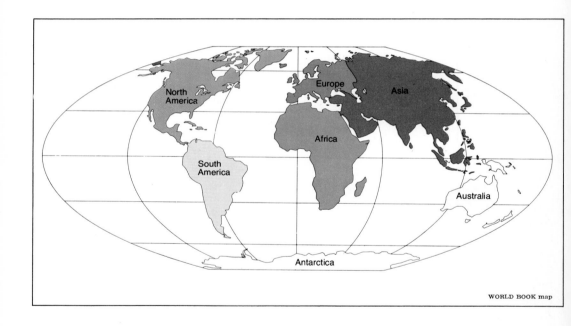

WORLD BOOK map

Nations of the World

This section contains "facts in brief" for all the independent nations of the world. Countries appear according to their commonly known names. In parentheses, you will also find a formal or official name for each country. Other useful facts then follow, including the name of the capital, the area of the country, its type of government, its largest cities, population figures, and brief information about its economy.

For more detailed information about the U.S. government, see Section 2 of this Unit. A world map and regional maps can be found in Section 1 of the Unit, along with tables of comparative information about the world's countries.

Afghanistan

(Democratic Republic of Afghanistan) Afghanistan is located in southwestern Asia. It is bordered by the Soviet Union, China, Pakistan, and Iran. About 85 per cent of the labor force works in agriculture.
Capital: Kabul.
Area: 251,773 sq. mi. (652,090 km^2).
Government: Republic.
Largest cities: Kabul (1,036,407) and Qandahar (191,345).
Population: 1990 estimate—15,885,000; density—63 persons per sq. mi (24 per km^2).
Economy: Mainly agricultural, with some mining and limited manufacturing.

Albania

(People's Socialist Republic of Albania) Albania is located on the eastern coast of the Adriatic Sea. It is bordered by Yugoslavia and Greece. Most of its workers are farmers.
Capital: Tiranë.
Area: 11,100 sq. mi. (28,748 km^2).
Government: Communist dictatorship.
Largest cities: Tiranë (260,000), Shkodër (62,500), and Durrës (61,000).
Population: 1990 estimate—3,248,000; density—293 persons per sq. mi. (113 per km^2).
Economy: Mainly agricultural, with some mining and forestry, but very limited manufacturing and fishing.

Algeria

(Democratic and Popular Republic of Algeria)
Algeria is located in northern Africa. It is bordered by Morocco, Western Sahara, Mauritania, Mali, Niger, Tunisia, and Libya. Most of its workers are farmers or herders.
Capital: Algiers.
Area: 919,595 sq. mi. (2,381,741 km^2).
Government: Republic.
Largest cities: Algiers (1,721,607) and Oran (663,504).
Population: 1990 estimate—25,174,000; density—27 persons per sq. mi. (10 per km^2).
Economy: Mainly agricultural, with some mining and limited manufacturing.

Andorra

(Valleys of Andorra)
Andorra is located in the Pyrenees mountains in western Europe. It is bordered by Spain and France. Most of its workers are involved in the tourist trade.
Capital: Andorra.
Area: 180 sq. mi. (465 km^2).
Government: Principality.
Largest cities: Andorra (16,000) and Escaldes (7,372).
Population: 1990 estimate—49,000; density—273 persons per sq. mi. (105 per km^2).
Economy: Based mainly on tourism, with some farming and limited mining.

Angola

(People's Republic of Angola)
Angola is located on the southwestern coast of Africa. It is bordered by Zaire, Zambia, Congo, and Namibia. Most of Angola's workers are engaged in agriculture.
Capital: Luanda.
Area: 481,354 sq. mi. (1,246,700 km^2).
Government: Socialist dictatorship.
Largest cities: Luanda (600,000) and Huambo (61,885)
Population: 1990 estimate—10,000,000; density—21 persons per sq. mi. (8 per km^2).
Economy: Mainly agricultural, with limited mining and developing industries.

Antigua and Barbuda

(Antigua and Barbuda)
Antigua and Barbuda is a country composed of three islands, Antigua, Barbuda, and Redonda. It is located in the Caribbean Sea about 430 miles (692 kilometers) north of Venezuela. Most workers are engaged in the tourist industry.
Capital: St. John's.
Area: 171 sq. mi. (442 km^2).
Government: Constitutional monarchy.
Largest city: St. John's (24,000).
Population: 1979 census—83,000; density—485 persons per sq. mi. (187 per km^2).
Economy: Mainly tourism, with some farming and manufacturing.

Argentina

(Argentine Republic)
Argentina is located in southeastern South America. It is bordered by Chile, Bolivia, Paraguay, Brazil, and Uruguay. Most of Argentina's workers are engaged in manufacturing, farming, ranching, meat packing, and the processing of farm products.
Capital: Buenos Aires.
Area: 1,073,400 sq. mi. (2,780,092 km^2).

Government: Republic (military rule).
Largest cities: Buenos Aires (2,908,001), Córdoba (968,664), and Rosario (875,623).
Population: 1990 estimate—32,361,000; density—30 persons per sq. mi. (12 per km²).
Economy: Mainly industrial production, service industries, agriculture, and trade, with some mining.

Australia

(Commonwealth of Australia)
Australia is both a continent and a country. It lies between the Indian Ocean and the South Pacific Ocean. Most of the workers in Australia are engaged in manufacturing, service industries, and trade.
Capital: Canberra.
Area: 2,966,150 sq. mi. (7,682,300 km²).
Government: Constitutional monarchy.
Largest cities: Sydney (2,989,070), Melbourne (2,645,484), and Brisbane (1,037,815).
Population: 1990 estimate—16,365,000; density—6 persons per sq. mi. (2 per km²).
Economy: Based mainly on agriculture and mining, with increasing manufacturing.

Austria

(Republic of Austria)
Austria is located in central Europe. It is bordered by Switzerland, Liechtenstein, West Germany, Czechoslovakia, Hungary, Italy, and Yugoslavia. Most of Austria's workers are employed in manufacturing, services, and trade.
Capital: Vienna.
Area: 32,377 sq. mi. (83,855 km²).
Government: Federal republic.

Largest cities: Vienna (1,515,666), Graz (243,405), Linz (197,962), Salzburg (138,213), and Innsbruck (116,110).
Population: 1990 estimate—7,493,000; density—231 persons per sq. mi. (89 per km²).
Economy: Mainly manufacturing and trade, with some agriculture and forestry, but limited mining.

Bahamas

(The Commonwealth of the Bahamas)
Bahamas is a country composed of about 3,000 islands in the northern part of the West Indies. Most workers are engaged in the tourist industry.
Capital: Nassau.
Area: 5,385 sq. mi. (13,878 km²).
Government: Constitutional monarchy.
Largest cities: Nassau (132,000) and Freeport (15,277).
Population: 1990 estimate—251,000; density—47 persons per sq. mi. (18 per km²).
Economy: Based mainly on tourism and related activities.

Bahrain

(The State of Bahrain)
Bahrain is an island country in the Persian Gulf in southwest Asia. Most of the land is desert, and most of the workers in Bahrain are employed in the oil industry or by the government.
Capital: Manama.
Area: 264 sq. mi. (685 km²).
Government: Emirate.
Largest cities: Manama (121,986) and Al Muharraq (44,567).
Population: 1990 estimate—516,000; density—1,947 persons per sq. mi. (750 per km²).

Economy: Based mainly on the production and refining of oil, with limited construction, fishing, and manufacturing.

Bangladesh

(People's Republic of Bangladesh)
Bangladesh is a nation in South Asia. It is bordered by India and Burma. About 80 per cent of the workers are engaged in agriculture.
Capital: Dhaka.
Area: 55,598 sq. mi. (143,998 km^2).
Government: Republic.
Largest cities: Dhaka (2,365,695) and Chittagong (1,391,877).
Population: 1990 estimate—116,000,000; density—2,086 persons per sq. mi. (806 per km^2).
Economy: Mainly agricultural, with some limited industry.

Barbados

(Barbados)
Barbados is an island country in the West Indies. It lies about 250 miles (402 km) northeast of Venezuela. About 50 per cent of its workers are engaged in agriculture, the tourist trade, and other service industries.
Capital: Bridgetown.
Area: 166 sq. mi. (431 km^2).
Government: Constitutional monarchy.
Largest city: Bridgetown (7,519).
Population: 1990 estimate—260,000; density—1,566 persons per sq. mi. (605 per km^2).
Economy: based mainly on tourism, trade, and agriculture.

Belgium

(Kingdom of Belgium)
Belgium is located in northwestern Europe. It is bordered by the Netherlands, West Germany, Luxembourg, and France. Most workers in Belgium are found in manufacturing or service industries.
Capital: Brussels.
Area: 11,783 sq. mi. (30,519 km^2).
Government: Constitutional monarchy.
Largest cities: Antwerp (185,021), Brussels (137,738), and Ghent (236,540).
Population: 1990 estimate—9,895,000; density—840 persons per sq. mi. (324 per km^2).
Economy: Mainly industrial and commercial, with limited agriculture.

Belize

(Belize)
Belize is located in Central America. It is bordered by Mexico and Guatemala. Most of its workers are in agriculture, forestry, and fishing.
Capital: Belmopan.
Area: 8,867 sq. mi. (22,965 km^2).
Government: Constitutional monarchy.
Largest city: Belize City (49,750).
Population: 1990 estimate—182,000; density—21 persons per sq. mi. (8 per km^2).
Economy: Based mainly on agriculture, with limited fishing and industry.

Benin

(People's Republic of Benin)
Benin is located in West Africa. It is bordered by Burkina Faso, Niger, Nigeria, and Togo. More than 50 per cent

of the nation's workers are engaged in agriculture.
Capital: Porto-Novo.
Area: 43,484 sq. mi. (112,622 km²).
Government: Republic (military rule).
Largest cities: Contonou (178,000) and Porto-Novo (144,000).
Population: 1990 estimate—4,737,000; density—109 persons per sq. mi. (42 per km²).
Economy: Based mainly on agriculture.

Bhutan

(Kingdom of Bhutan)
Bhutan is located in south-central Asia. It is bordered by China, India, and Tibet. Almost all the people in Bhutan are engaged in farming or the raising of livestock.
Capital: Thimphu.
Area: 17,950 sq. mi. (46,500 km²).
Government: Monarchy.
Largest city: Thimphu (8,922)
Population: 1990 estimate—1,513,000; density—86 persons per sq. mi. (33 per km²).
Economy: Almost entirely agricultural and pastoral, but with very limited mining.

Bolivia

(Republic of Bolivia)
Bolivia is located in South America. It is bordered by Brazil, Paraguay, Argentina, Chili, and Peru. About 46 per cent of the labor force is engaged in agriculture.
Capital: Sucre (official); La Paz (actual).
Area: 424,165 sq. mi. (1,098,581 km²).
Government: Republic.
Largest cities: La Paz (881,404), Santa Cruz (376,912), Cochabamba

(281,962), and Oruro (132,213).
Population: 1990 estimate—7,311,000; density—17 persons per sq. mi. (7 per km²).
Economy: Mainly agricultural, with manufacturing and mining growing in importance.

Botswana

(Republic of Botswana)
Botswana is located in southern Africa. It is bordered by Namibia, Zimbabwe, and South Africa. Most of the workers are engaged in agriculture and mining.
Capital: Gaborone.
Area: 224,607 sq. mi. (581,730 km²).
Government: Republic.
Largest cities: Gaborone (96,000), Francistown (25,000).
Population: 1990 estimate—1,283,000; density—6 persons per sq. mi. (2 per km²).
Economy: Based mainly on agriculture and herding, but with a growing mining industry.

Brazil

(Federative Republic of Brazil)
Brazil is located in South America. It is bordered by every country in South America except Chile and Ecuador. About 30 per cent of the workers are engaged in agriculture, and most of the rest are employed in the nation's growing industries or in service occupations.
Capital: Brasília.
Area: 3,286,488 sq. mi. (8,511,965 km²).
Government: Federal republic.
Largest cities: São Paulo (7,033,529), Rio de Janeiro (5,093,232), and Belo Horizonte (1,442,483).

Population: 1990 estimate—150,557,000; density—46 persons per sq. mi. (18 per km²).
Economy: Based mainly on industry and services.

Brunei

(Brunei, Abode of Peace)
Brunei lies on the north coast of the island of Borneo. Petroleum and natural gas found beneath the coastal waters of Brunei have brought wealth to the country. The petroleum and gas industry employs about 10 per cent of the labor force.
Capital: Bandar Seri Begawan
Area: 2,226 sq. mi. (5,765 km²).
Government: Monarchy
Largest City: Bandar Seri Begawan (36,987).
Population: 1990 estimate—277,000; density—124 persons per sq. mi. (48 persons per km²).
Economy: Based mainly on the petroleum and gas industry.

Bugaria

(People's Republic of Bulgaria)
Bulgaria is located in southeastern Europe on the Balkan Peninsula. It is bordered by Romania, Turkey, Greece, and Yugoslavia. Many of the nation's workers are employed in industry and services, while others are farmers.
Capital: Sofia.
Area: 42,823 sq. mi. (110,912 km²).
Government: Communist dictatorship.
Largest cities: Sofia (1,056,945) and Plovdiv (350,438).
Population: 1990 estimate—8,985,000; density—210 persones per sq. mi. (81 per km²).

Economy: Primarily industrial, with some agriculture.

Burkina Faso

(Burkina Faso)
Burkina Faso (formerly Upper Volta) is a nation located in western Africa. It is bordered by Mali, Niger, Benin, Togo, Ghana, and the Ivory Coast. Most of Burkina Faso's workers are engaged in farming or raising livestock.
Capital: Ouagadougou.
Area: 105,869 sq. mi. (274,200 km²).
Government: Republic (military rule).
Largest city: Ouagadougou (442,223).
Population: 1990 estimate—8,996,000; density—85 persons per sq. mi. (33 per km²).
Economy: Based mainly upon farming and the raising of livestock.

Burma

Union of Myanmar
Burma is located in Southeast Asia. It is bordered by China, Laos, Thailand, Bangladesh, and India. About 70 per cent of the workers are engaged in agriculture and forestry, and most of the rest are factory workers, craftspeople, or merchants.
Capital: Rangoon.
Area: 261,218 sq. mi. (676,552 km²).
Government: Military rule.
Largest cities: Rangoon (1,315,964) and Mandalay (472,512).
Population: 1990 estimate—41,279,000; density—158 persons per sq. mi. (61 per km²).
Economy: Mainly agriculture and forestry, with some limited mining.

Burundi

(Republic of Burundi)
Burundi is located in central Africa. It is bordered by Rwanda, Tanzania, and Zaire. Almost all of its people are engaged in agriculture.
Capital: Bujumbura.
Area: 10,747 sq. mi. (27,834 km^2).
Government: Republic.
Largest city: Bujumbura (151,000).
Population: 1990 estimate—5,450,000; density—507 persons per sq. mi. (196 per km^2).
Economy: Mainly agricultural, with very limited industry.

Cambodia

(State of Cambodia)
Cambodia is located in Southeast Asia. It is bordered by Thailand, Laos, and Vietnam. Almost all of its people are engaged in agriculture.
Capital: Phnom Penh.
Area: 69,898 sq. mi. (181,035 km^2).
Government: Communist dictatorship.
Largest city: Phnom Penh (700,000).
Population: 1990 estimate—6,993,000; density—100 persons per sq. mi. (39 per km^2).
Economy: Based mainly on agriculture.

Cameroon

(United Republic of Cameroon)
Cameroon is located in west-central Africa. It is bordered by Chad, the Central African Republic, Congo, Gabon, Equatorial Guinea, and Nigeria. Most of the workers are engaged in agriculture.
Capital: Yaoundé.
Area: 183,569 sq. mi. (475,442 km^2).
Government: Republic.

Largest cities: Douala (1,000,000) and Yaoundé (313,706).
Population: 1990 estimate—11,236,000; density—61 persons per sq. mi. (24 per km^2).
Economy: Based mainly on agriculture.

Canada

(Canada)
Canada is the second largest nation in area in the world. It is located in North America, and it is bordered by the United States. A large majority of workers in Canada are employed in manufacturing, service occupations, or in wholesale and retail trade.
Capital: Ottawa.
Area: 3,849,674 sq. mi. (9,970,610 km^2).
Government: Constitutional monarchy.
Largest cities: Montreal (1,015,420), Calgary (636,104), Toronto (612,289), Winnipeg (594,551), Edmonton (573,982), and Vancouver (431,147).
Population: 1990 estimate—26,279,000; density—7 persons per sq. mi. (3 per km^2).
Economy: Mainly manufacturing, with trade and services contributing significantly.

Cape Verde

(Republic of Cape Verde)
Cape Verde is an island country composed of 10 islands and 5 islets in the Atlantic Ocean. It lies north of the equator, off the west coast of Africa. Many of the people are engaged in agriculture and fishing.
Capital: Praia.
Area: 1,557 sq. mi. (4,033 km^2).
Government: Republic.
Largest cities: Praia (49,000) and Mindelo (28,797).

Population: 1990 estimate—378,000;
  density—243 persons per sq. mi. (94
  per km^2).
Economy: Based largely upon agriculture
  and fishing, with limited mining.

Central African Republic

(Central African Republic)
The Central African Republic is located
in the center of Africa. It is bordered by
Chad, Sudan, Zaire, Congo, and Cameroon. About half of its workers live in
country areas.
Capital: Bangui.
Area: 240,535 sq. mi. (622,984 km^2).
Government: Republic (military rule).
Largest cities: Bangui (473,817) and Ber-
  bérati (93,000).
Population: 1990 estimate—2,911,000;
  density—12 persons per sq. mi. (5 per
  km^2).
Economy: Based mainly on farming,
  with some mining and very limited
  manufacturing.

Chad

(Republic of Chad)
Chad is located in north-central Africa.
It is bordered by Libya, Sudan, the Cen-
tral African Republic, Niger, Nigeria,
and Cameroon. Most of the workers are
engaged in agriculture, hunting, fishing,
and food gathering.
Capital: N'Djamena.
Area: 495,755 sq. mi. (1,284,000 km^2).
Government: Republic.
Largest cities: N'Djamena (511,700) and
  Sarh (50,000).

Population: 1990 estimate—5,674,000;
  density—11 persons per sq. mi. (4 per
  km^2).
Economy: Based almost entirely on agriculture.

Chile

(Republic of Chile)
Chile is located on the southwest coast
of South America. It is bordered by
Peru, Argentina, and Bolivia. Only about
15 percent of its work force is engaged
in agriculture. Most of the other workers
are employed in manufacturing, mining,
and service occupations.
Capital: Santiago.
Area: 292,258 sq. mi. (756,945 km^2).
Government: Military rule.
Largest cities: Santiago (4,225,299), Viña
  del Mar (307,308), and Valparaíso
  (266,876).
Population: 1990 estimate—13,185,000
  density—45 persons per sq. mi. (17
  per km^2).
Economy: Based mainly on mining and
  manufacturing.

China

(People's Republic of China)
China is located in eastern and central
Asia. It is bordered by Russia, Afghani-
stan, India, Nepal, Pakistan, Bhutan,
and a number of other Asian nations.
More than three-fourths of China's
workers are engaged in agriculture and
fishing.
Capital: Beijing.
Area: 3,696,032 sq. mi. (9,572,678 km^2).
Government: Communist dictatorship.
Largest cities: Shanghai (6,880,000),
  Beijing (5,760,000), Tianjin (5,300,000),
  and Shenyang (4,130,000).

Population: 1990 estimate—
1,100,258,000; density—298 persons
per sq. mi. (115 per km^2).
Economy: Based primarily on agriculture, though industries are developing.

Colombia

(Republic of Colombia)
Colombia is located in northwestern
South America. It is bordered by Vene-
zuela, Brazil, Peru, Ecuador, and Pan-
ama. A large portion of the labor force is
engaged in agriculture.
Capital: Bogotá.
Area: 440,831 sq. mi. (1,141,748 km^2).
Government: Republic.
Largest cities: Bogotá (3,982,941) and
Medellín (1,468,089).
Population: 1990 estimate—31,863,000;
density—72 persons per sq. mi. (28
per km^2).
Economy: Mainly agricultural and some
mining, with growing industries.

Comoros

(Federal and Islamic Republic of the
Comoros)
Comoros is an island nation of Africa. It
is composed of several islands located in
the Indian Ocean. Most workers are en-
gaged in agriculture.
Capital: Moroni.
Area: 863 sq. mi. (2,235 km^2).
Government: Republic.
Largest city: Moroni (17,267).
Population: 1990 estimate—518,000;
density—600 persons per sq. mi. (232
per km^2).
Economy: Almost entirely agricultural.

Congo

(People's Republic of the Congo)
Congo is located in west-central Africa.
It is bordered by Cameroon, the Central
African Republic, Zaire, Angola, and
Gabon. Most of the workers are engaged
in agriculture.
Capital: Brazzaville.
Area: 132,047 sq. mi. (342,000 km^2).
Government: Republic (military rule).
Largest cities: Brazzaville (596,200),
Pointe-Noire (135,000), and Dolisie
(25,000).
Population: 1990 estimate—2,183,000;
density—17 persons per sq. mi. (6 per
km^2).
Economy: Based mainly on agriculture
and forestry, with some mining.

Costa Rica

(Republic of Costa Rica)
Costa Rica is located in Central America. It is bordered by Nicaragua and
Panama. About 25 per cent of its workers are engaged in agriculture, and about
20 per cent are in manufacturing. Most
of the others work in service occupations.
Capital: San José.
Area: 19,730 sq. mi. (51,100 km^2).
Government: Democratic republic.
Largest cities: San José (241,464), Li-
món (42,082), and Alajuela (33,865).
Population: 1990 estimate—3,017,000;
density—153 persons per sq. mi. (59
per km^2).
Economy: Mainly agricultural, but there
is growing industry.

Cuba

(Republic of Cuba)
Cuba is an island nation in the Caribbean Sea. It lies in the West Indies, about 90 miles (140 kilometers) south of Florida. About 22 per cent of the Cuban workers are engaged in forestry, fishing, and agriculture; 30 per cent in services; and 21 per cent in manufacturing.
Capital: Havana.
Area: 42,804 sq. mi. (110,861 km^2).
Government: Socialist republic (Communist dictatorship).
Largest cities: Havana (1,924,886), Santiago de Cuba (345,772), and Camagüey (245,235).
Population: 1990 estimate—10,297,000; density—241 persons per sq. mi. (93 per km^2).
Economy: Based on services, agriculture, and manufacturing.

Cyprus

(Republic of Cyprus)
Cyprus is an island nation located in Southwest Asia in the northeast corner of the Mediterranean Sea. About 40 per cent of the workers are engaged in manufacturing.
Capital: Nicosia.
Area: 3,572 sq. mi. (9,251 km^2).
Government: Republic.
Largest cities: Nicosia (163,700) and Limassol (80,600).
Population: 1990 estimate—701,000; density—196 persons per sq. mi. (76 per km^2).
Economy: Based on agriculture, manufacturing, mining, and tourism.

Czechoslovakia

(The Czech and Slovak Federal Republic)
Czechoslovakia is located in central Europe. It is bordered by Poland, the Soviet Union, Hungary, Austria, and East and West Germeny. About 34 per cent of its workers are engaged in industry and almost 19 per cent in government and other services.
Capital: Prague.
Area: 49,373 sq. mi. (127,876 km^2).
Government: Republic (government determined by free elections).
Largest cities: Prague (1,189,828), Brno (383,443), Bratislava (409,100), and Ostrava (325,431).
Population: 1990 estimate—15,659,000; density—317 persons per sq. mi. (122 per km^2).
Economy: Mainly manufacturing, with some agriculture.

Denmark

(Kingdom of Denmark)
Denmark is located in northern Europe. It is bordered by West Germany. Most of the workers in Denmark are employed in manufacturing or service occupations. Only about 7 per cent of the workers are engaged in agriculture, forestry, and fishing.
Capital: Copenhagen.
Area: 16,632 sq. mi. (43,077 km^2).
Government: Constitutional monarchy.
Largest cities: Copenhagen (472,729), Århus (253,761), Odense (172,851), and Ålborg (154,878).
Population: 1990 estimate—5,119,000; density—308 persons per sq. mi. (119 per km^2).
Economy: Mainly manufacturing.

Djibouti

(Republic of Djibouti)
Djibouti is a small nation located in eastern Africa. It lies on the western shore of the Gulf of Aden, and it is bordered by Ethiopia and Somalia. Djibouti is an extremely poor and underdeveloped country with a high unemployment rate. Most of the workers are involved in livestock herding.
Capital: Djibouti.
Area: 8,958 sq. mi. (23,200 km^2).
Government: Republic.
Largest city: Djibouti (200,000).
Population: 1990 estimate—337,000; density—38 persons per sq. mi. (15 per km^2).
Economy: Based almost entirely on shipping and railway transportation.

Dominica

(Commonwealth of Dominica)
Dominica is a small island country in the Caribbean Sea. It lies north of the Venezuelan coast. More than 60 per cent of the nation's workers are engaged in agriculture.
Capital: Roseau.
Area: 290 sq. mi. (751 km^2).
Government: Republic.
Largest city: Roseau (11,000).
Population: 1990 estimate—98,000; density—338 persons per sq. mi. (130 per km^2).
Economy: Based on the export of agricultural goods, with some food processing, tourism, and mining.

Dominican Republic

(Dominican Republic)
The Dominican Republic is located on the island of Hispaniola between the North Atlantic Ocean and the Caribbean Sea. About 50 per cent of the nation's workers are engaged in agriculture.
Capital: Santo Domingo
Area: 18,816 sq. mi. (48,734 km^2).
Government: Republic.
Largest cities: Santo Domingo (1,313,000) and Santiago (278,638).
Population: 1990 estimate—7,172,000; density—381 persons per sq. mi (147 per km^2).
Economy: Based mainly on agriculture, with some manufacturing.

Ecuador

(Republic of Ecuador)
Ecuador is located in South America. It is bordered by Colombia and Peru. About 48 per cent of Ecuador's workers are engaged in agriculture, forestry, and fishing. About 27 per cent are employed in manufacturing and services.
Capital: Quito.
Area: 109,484 sq. mi. (283,561 km^2).
Government: Republic.
Largest cities: Guayaquil (1,199,344), and Quito (866,472).
Population: 1990 estimate—10,782,000; density; 98 persons per sq. mi. (38 per km^2).
Economy: The mainstay of the economy is service industries and manufacturing, with agriculture and some mining.

Egypt

(Arab Republic of Egypt)
Egypt is a nation that lies in the northeastern corner of Africa. It is bordered by Israel, Sudan, and Libya. About 38 per cent of the workers in Egypt are engaged in agriculture, and about 44 per cent are engaged in service occupations.
Capital: Cairo.

Area: 386,662 sq. mi. (1,001,449 km²).
Government: Republic.
Largest cities: Cairo (6,052,836), Alexandria (2,917,327), and Giza (1,870,508).
Population: 1990 estimate—53,522,000; density—138 persons per sq. mi. (53 per km²).
Economy: Largely based on services and industry, with agriculture and mining.

El Salvador

(Republic of El Salvador)
El Salvador is a nation in Central America. It is bordered by Honduras and Guatemala. Almost 60 per cent of its workers are engaged in agriculture, and about 20 per cent are employed in various industries.
Capital: San Salvador.
Area: 8,124 sq. mi. (21,041 km²).
Government: Republic.
Largest cities: San Salvador (452,614), Santa Ana (135,186), and San Miguel (86,722).
Population: 1990 estimate—5,655,000; density—696 persons per sq. mi. (269 per km²).
Economy: Based mainly on farming and the export of agricultural products.

Equatorial Guinea

(Republic of Equatorial Guinea)
Equatorial Guinea is a nation in western Africa. It is bordered by Cameroon and Gabon. Many workers are engaged in agriculture.
Capital: Malabo on Bioko.
Area: 10,831 sq. mi. (28,051 km²).
Government: Military rule.
Largest city: Malabo (15,253).

Population: 1990 estimate—411,000; density—38 persons per sq. mi. (15 per km²).
Economy; Based on agriculture, forestry, and fishing.

Ethiopia

(Ethiopia)
Ethiopia is a nation located in northeastern Africa. It is bordered by Sudan, Djibouti, Somalia, and Kenya. Most of the workers in Ethiopia are engaged in agriculture.
Capital: Addis Ababa.
Area: 471,778 sq. mi. (1,221,900 km²).
Government: Military rule.
Largest cities: Addis Ababa (1,413,000) and Asmara (275,385).
Population: 1990 estimate—48,630,000; density—103 persons per sq. mi. (40 per km²).
Economy: Largely dependent upon agriculture, with some mining but very limited industry.

Fiji

(Fiji)
Fiji is an island nation in the South Pacific Ocean. It is composed of more than 800 islands. Most of the workers are engaged in agriculture.
Capital: Suva.
Area: 7,056 sq. mi. (18,274 km²).
Government: Republic.
Largest cities: Suva (64,000) and Lautoka (22,672).
Population: 1990 estimate—772,000; density—109 persons per sq. mi. (42 per km²).
Economy: Based upon agriculture and the export of agricultural products, with some tourism and manufacturing.

Finland

(Republic of Finland)
Finland is a nation located in northern
Europe. It is bordered by Norway, the
Soviet Union, and Sweden. Almost 55
per cent of Finland's workers are em-
ployed in manufacturing or in service industries. Only 12 per cent of the nation's
workers are engaged in agriculture, forestry, and fishing.
Capital: Helsinki.
Area: 130,559 sq. mi. (338,145 km^2).
Government: Republic.
Largest cities: Helsinki (481,927) and
  Tampere (167,951).
Population: 1990 estimate—4,981,000;
  density—38 persons per sq. mi. (15
  per km^2).
Economy: Mainly based upon services
  and industry, with agriculture, commerce, forestry, and trade also important.

France

(French Republic)
France is a nation located in Western
Europe. It is bordered by Belgium, Luxembourg, West Germany, Switzerland,
Italy, Monaco, Andorra, and Spain. Almost 68 per cent of France's workers
are engaged in manufacturing, trade, or
service occupations. Only about 8 per
cent of the French workers are engaged
in agriculture, forestry, and fishing.
Capital: Paris.
Area: 210,026 sq. mi. (543,965 km^2).
Government: Parliamentary democracy.
Largest cities: Paris (2,176,243), Mar-
  seille (874,436), Lyon (413,095), Toulouse (347,995), and Nice (337,085).

Population: 1990 estimate—56,236,000;
  density—268 persons per sq. mi. (103
  per km^2).
Economy: Mainly industrial, with some
  agriculture.

Gabon

(Gabonese Republic)
Gabon is a nation located on the west
coast of Africa. It is bordered by Equa-
torial Guinea, Cameroon, and the
Congo. About 65 per cent of Gabon's
workers are engaged in agriculture.
Capital: Libreville.
Area: 103,347 sq. mi. (267,667 km^2).
Government: Republic.
Largest cities: Libreville (350,000) and
  Port-Gentil (85,000).
Population: 1990 estimate—1,172,000;
  density—11 persons per sq. mi. (4 per
  km^2).
Economy: Based largely upon agriculture
  and forestry.

Gambia

(Republic of The Gambia)
Gambia is a nation located in western
Africa. It is bordered by Senegal. Most
of the workers in Gambia are engaged in
agriculture.
Capital: Banjul.
Area: 4,361 sq. mi. (11,295 km^2).
Government: Republic.
Largest city: Banjul (44,000).
Population: 1990 estimate—820,000;
  density—188 persons per sq. mi. (73
  per km^2).
Economy: Mainly agricultural.

Germany, East

(German Democratic Republic)
East Germany is a nation located in
north-central Europe. It is bordered by
Poland, Czechoslovakia, and West Germany. More than half of East Germany's
workers are employed in manufacturing
and trade. Only about 11 per cent of its
workers are engaged in agriculture and
forestry.
Capital: East Berlin.
Area: 41,768 sq. mi. (108,178 km^2).
Government: East Germany is undergo-
  ing reunification with West Germany.
Largest cities: East Berlin (1,202,895),
  Leipzig (554,595), and Dresden
  (519,860).
Population: 1990 estimate—16,645,000,
  including East Berlin; density—400
  persons per sq. mi. (154 per km^2).
Economy: Based largely on industry and
  services.

Germany, West

(Federal Republic of Germany)
West Germany is a nation located in
north-central Europe. It is bordered by
Denmark, the Netherlands, East Germany, Czechoslovakia, Austria, Switzerland, France, Belgium, and Luxembourg. About 72 per cent of the workers
are engaged in manufacturing, trade, or
service occupations.
Capital: Bonn.
Area: 96,005 sq. mi. (248,651 km^2).
Government: Parliamentary democracy.
Largest cities: West Berlin (1,860,084),
  Hamburg (1,579,884), and Munich
  (1,266,549).
Population: 1990 estimate—60,471,000,
  including West Berlin; density—629
  persons per sq. mi. (243 per km^2).

Economy: Mainly industrial, with trade,
  finance, and agriculture as important
  segments.

Ghana

(Republic of Ghana)
Ghana is a nation located in western Africa. It is bordered by Burkina Faso,
Togo, and Ivory Coast. Over two-thirds
of the workers in Ghana are engaged in
agriculture, and most of the other workers are employed in mining or service
occupations.
Capital: Accra.
Area: 92,100 sq. mi. (238,537 km^2).
Government: Military rule.
Largest cities: Accra (964,879) and Ku-
  masi (260,286).
Population: 1990 estimate—15,020,000;
  density—163 persons per sq. mi. (63
  per km^2).
Economy: Mainly agriculture, with some
  mining.

Great Britain

(United Kingdom of Great Britain and
Northern Ireland)
Great Britain is a nation composed of
two large islands (Great Britain and part
of Ireland) and many small islands that
lie off the northwest coast of Europe. It
is bordered by the Republic of Ireland.
Most of the nation's workers are employed in industry and service occupations.
Capital: London.
Area: 94,248 sq. mi. (244,100 km^2).
Government: Constitutional monarchy.
Largest cities: Greater London
  (6,767,500), Birmingham (1,007,500),
  and Glasgow (733,794).

Population: 1990 estimate—57,293,000; density—608 persons per sq. mi. (235 per km^2).
Economy: Based mainly upon manufacturing and services.

Greece

(Hellenic Republic)
Greece is a nation located in southeastern Europe. It is bordered by Bulgaria. Yugoslavia, Albania, and Turkey. About 34 per cent of the workers in Greece are employed in manufacturing or service occupations; about 29 per cent, in farming, fishing, and forestry.
Capital: Athens.
Area: 50,962 sq. mi. (131,990 km^2).
Government: Republic.
Largest cities: Athens (885,737), Salonika (406,413), and Piraeus (196,389).
Population: 1990 estimate—10,053,000; density—197 persons per sq. mi. (76 per km^2).
Economy: Based mainly on industry and services, with agriculture also contributing.

Grenada

(State of Grenada)
Grenada is an island nation that is located in the Windward Islands of the West Indies. Most of Grenada's workers are engaged in agriculture, forestry, or fishing.
Capital: St. George's.
Area: 133 sq. mi. (344 km^2).
Government: Constitutional monarchy.
Largest city: St. George's (7,500).
Population: 1990 estimate—96,000; density—722 persons per sq. mi. (279 per km^2).
Economy: Mainly agriculture, fishing, and tourism.

Guatemala

(Republic of Guatemala)
Guatemala is a nation located in Central America. It is bordered by Mexico, Honduras, Belize, and El Salvador. About 66 per cent of its workers are engaged in agriculture, fishing, and forestry.
Capital: Guatemala City.
Area: 42,042 sq. mi. (108,889 km^2).
Government: Republic.
Largest cities: Guatemala City (754,243) and Quezaltenango (62,719).
Population: 1990 estimate—9,117,000; density—217 persons per sq. mi. (84 per km^2).
Economy: Mainly agricultural, with trade and industry also significant.

Guinea

(Republic of Guinea)
Guinea is a nation in western Africa. It is bordered by Guinea-Bissau, Senegal, Mali, Ivory Coast, Liberia, and Sierra Leone. Most of its workers are engaged in agriculture.
Capital: Conakry.
Area: 94,926 sq. mi. (245,857 km^2).
Government: Military rule.
Largest cities: Conakry (763,000) and Kankan (50,000).
Population: 1990 estimate—6,871,000; density—72 persons per sq. mi. (28 per km^2).
Economy: Based mainly upon agriculture and mining, with some commerce.

Guinea-Bissau

(Republic of Guinea-Bissau)
Guinea-Bissau is a nation located on the west coast of Africa. It is bordered by

Senegal and Guinea. More than half its workers are engaged in agriculture.
Capital: Bissau.
Area: 13,948 sq. mi. (36,125 km²).
Government: Military rule.
Largest city: Bissau (109,214).
Population: 1990 estimate—985,000; density—71 persons per sq. mi. (27 per km²).
Economy: Based largely upon agriculture.

Guyana

(Cooperative Republic of Guyana)
Guyana is a nation located on the northeast coast of South America. It is bordered by Suriname, Brazil, and Venezuela. Most of its workers are engaged in agriculture or mining.
Capital: Georgetown.
Area: 83,000 sq. mi. (214,969 km²).
Government: Republic.
Largest cities: Georgetown (72,049) and New Amsterdam (17,782).
Population: 1990 estimate—868,000; density—10 persons per sq. mi. (4 per km²).
Economy: Based on agriculture and mining.

Haiti

(Republic of Haiti)
Haiti is a nation located on the western third of the island of Hispaniola in the Caribbean Sea. Most of its workers are engaged in agriculture.
Capital: Port-au-Prince.
Area: 10,714 sq. mi. (27,750 km²).
Government: Military rule.
Largest city: Port-au-Prince (719,000).

Population: 1990 estimate—5,777,000; density—539 persons per sq. mi. (208 per km²).
Economy: Based on agriculture and tourism.

Honduras

(Republic of Honduras)
Honduras is a nation located in Central America. It is bordered by Nicaragua, El Salvador, and Guatemala. About 53 per cent of the workers in Honduras are engaged in agriculture, fishing, and forestry.
Capital: Tegucigalpa.
Area: 43,277 sq. mi. (112,088 km²).
Government: Republic (military rule).
Largest cities: Tegucigalpa (571,400) and San Pedro Sula (372,800).
Population: 1990 estimate—5,144,000; density—119 persons per sq. mi. (46 per km²).
Economy: Mainly agriculture, with some mining and limited manufacturing.

Hungary

(Hungarian People's Republic)
Hungary is a nation located in central Europe. It is bordered by Czechoslovakia, the Soviet Union, Romania, Yugoslavia, and Austria. More than 52 per cent of Hungary's workers are employed in manufacturing and service occupations. About 23 per cent of its workers are engaged in agriculture and forestry.
Capital: Budapest.
Area: 35,920 sq. mi. (93,032 km²).
Government: Republic (government determined by free elections).
Largest cities: Budapest (2,075,990), Debrecen (211,823), Miskolc (211,660), and Szeged (182,137).

Population: 1990 estimate—10,545,000; density—249 persons per sq. mi. (113 per km²).
Economy: Mainly industrial, with some contribution from agriculture.

Iceland

(Republic of Iceland)
Iceland is an island nation located in the North Atlantic Ocean. About 20 per cent of the workers are engaged in fishing or in the fish-processing industry. Only about 15 per cent of the workers are farmers.
Capital: Reykjavík.
Area: 39,800 sq. mi. (103,000 km²).
Government: Republic.
Largest cities: Reykjavík (87,106) and Kopavogur (13,533).
Population: 1990 estimate—250,000; density—6 persons per sq. mi. (2 per km²).
Economy: Mainly fishing and fish processing, with some agriculture and manufacturing.

India

(Union of India)
India is a large nation located in southern Asia. It is bordered by China, Nepal, Bhutan, Bangladesh, Burma, and Pakistan. About 72 per cent of India's workers are engaged in agriculture, forestry, and fishing.
Capital: New Delhi.
Area: 1,269,219 sq. mi. (3,287,263 km²).
Government: Federal republic.
Largest cities: Bombay (8,227,332), Delhi (4,884,234), Calcutta (3,305,006), Madras (3,276,622), and Hyderabad (2,187,262).

Population: 1990 estimate—853,532,000; density—672 persons per sq. mi. (260 per km²).
Economy: Based mainly on agriculture, with some mining and manufacturing.

Indonesia

(Republic of Indonesia)
Indonesia is an island nation in Southeast Asia. It is bordered by Malaysia and Papua New Guinea. About 55 per cent of Indonesia's workers are engaged in agriculture, fishing, and forestry; about 25 per cent are in manufacturing and trade.
Capital: Jakarta.
Area: 741,101 sq. mi. (1,919,443 km²).
Government: Republic.
Largest cities: Jakarta (6,503,449), Surabaya (2,027,913), Bandung (1,462,637), and Medan (1,378,955).
Population: 1990 estimate—180,594,000; density—244 persons per sq. mi. (94 per km²).
Economy: Mainly agriculture, with some manufacturing.

Iran

(Islamic Republic of Iran)
Iran is a nation located in southwestern Asia. It is bordered by the Soviet Union, Afghanistan, Pakistan, Iraq, and Turkey. About 36 per cent of Iran's workers are engaged in agriculture. Most of the other workers are employed in the petroleum industry or other industries.
Capital: Teheran.
Area: 636,300 sq. mi. (1,648,000 km²).
Government: Islamic republic.
Largest cities: Teheran (5,734,199), Meshed (1,119,748), Isfahan (926,601), and Tabriz (852,296).

Population: 1990 estimate—56,800,000; density—89 persons per sq. mi. (34 per km²).

Economy: Based mainly on oil production and agriculture.

Iraq

(Republic of Iraq)
Iraq is a nation located in southwestern Asia. It is bordered by Turkey, Iran, Kuwait, Saudi Arabia, Jordan, and Syria. About 30 per cent of Iraq's workers are engaged in agriculture, and about 32 per cent are employed in the petroleum industry or service occupations.

Capital: Baghdad.

Area: 169,235 sq. mi. (438,317 km²).

Government: Republic.

Largest city: Baghdad (2,969,000).

Population: 1990 estimate—18,048,000; density—107 persons per sq. mi. (41 per km²).

Economy: Based mainly on the oil industry and agriculture.

Ireland

(Republic of Ireland)
Ireland is a nation located in northwestern Europe. It is bordered by Great Britain and Northern Ireland. About 61 per cent of Ireland's workers are employed in manufacturing, trade, or service occupations.

Capital: Dublin.

Area: 27,136 sq. mi. (70,283 km²).

Government: Republic.

Largest cities: Dublin (502,749) and Cork (133,271).

Population: 1990 estimate—3,637,000; density—134 persons per sq. mi. (52 per km²).

Economy: Mainly industrial, with some agriculture.

Israel

(State of Israel)
Israel is a nation located in southwestern Asia. It is bordered by Lebanon, Syria, Jordan, and Egypt. About 60 per cent of the workers in Israel are employed in manufacturing and mining, in government service, and in other service occupations.

Capital: Jerusalem.

Area: 8,019 sq. mi. (20,770 km²)*.

Government: Republic.

Largest cities: Jerusalem (424,400), Tel Aviv-Yafo (325,700), and Haifa (226,100).

Population: 1990 estimate—4,585,000; density—572 persons per sq. mi. (221 per km²)**.

Economy: Based largely upon manufacturing and commerce, with some agriculture.

*Does not include 3,900 sq. mi. (10,100 km²) of Arab territory occupied since 1967.

**Including Israeli citizens living in occupied territory.

Italy

(Italian Republic)
Italy is a nation located in southern Europe. It is bordered by Switzerland, Austria, Yugoslavia, and France. More than 69 per cent of Italy's workers are engaged in manufacturing, trade, or service occupations. Only about 12 per cent of Italy's workers are engaged in agriculture, forestry, and fishing.

Capital: Rome.

Area: 116,320 sq. mi. (301,268 km²).

Government: Parliamentary democracy.

Largest cities: Rome (2,830,569), Milan (1,634,638), Naples (1,210,503), Turin (1,103,520), and Genoa (760,300).

Population: 1990 estimate—57,380,000; density—493 persons per sq. mi. (190 per km²).

Economy: Based mainly on manufacturing, with commerce and agriculture also contributing.

Ivory Coast

(Republic of the Ivory Coast)
Ivory Coast is a nation located in western Africa. It is bordered by Mali, Burkina Faso, Ghana, Liberia, and Guinea. Most of the workers are engaged in agriculture.

Capital: Abidjan.

Area: 124,504 sq. mi. (322,463 km²).

Government: Republic.

Largest cities: Abidjan (1,850,000) and Bouaké (230,000).

Population: 1990 estimate—12,053,000; density—97 persons per sq. mi. (37 per km²).

Economy: Mainly based upon agriculture, forestry, and fishing.

Jamaica

(Jamaica)
Jamaica is an island nation in the West Indies, about 90 miles (140 kilometers) south of Cuba in the Caribbean Sea. About a fourth of Jamaica's workers are engaged in agriculture. Others are employed in manufacturing and service occupations.

Capital: Kingston.

Area: 4,244 sq. mi. (10,991 km²).

Government: Constitutional monarchy.

Largest cities: Kingston (104,041), Montego Bay (43,754), and Spanish Town (40,731).

Population: 1990 estimate—2,520,000; density—594 persons per sq. mi. (229 per km²).

Economy: Manufacturing, mining, agriculture, and tourism.

Japan

(Japan)
Japan is an island nation located in the North Pacific Ocean, off the northeast coast of Asia. Over 60 per cent of the Japanese workers are employed in industry or service occupations; only about 10 per cent are engaged in agriculture and fishing.

Capital: Tokyo.

Area: 145,870 sq. mi. (377,801 km²).

Government: Constitutional monarchy.

Largest cities: Tokyo (8,353,674), Yokohama (2,992,644), Osaka (2,636,260), and Nagoya (2,116,350).

Population: 1990 estimate—123,749,000; density—848 persons per sq. mi. (328 per km²).

Economy: Mainly based upon manufacturing and trade.

Jordan

(Hashemite Kingdom of Jordan)
Jordan is a nation located in the Middle East. It is bordered by Syria, Iraq, Saudi Arabia, Israel and the West Bank. Most of its workers are engaged in service industries.

Capital: Amman.

Area: 35,475 sq. mi. (91,880 km²).

Government: Constitutional monarchy.

Largest cities: Amman (900,000) and Az Zarqa (306,500).

Population: 1990 estimate—3,065,000; density—86 persons per sq. mi. (33 per km²).

Economy: Mainly based upon services and industry, with some agriculture.

Kenya

(Republic of Kenya)
Kenya is a nation located in eastern Africa. It is bordered by Sudan, Ethiopia, Somalia, Tanzania, and Uganda. More workers in Kenya are engaged in agriculture than in any other activity.
Capital: Nairobi.
Area: 224,081 sq. mi. (580,367 km^2).
Government: Republic.
Largest cities: Nairobi (827,775) and Mombasa (341,148).
Population: 1990 estimate—25,081,000; density—112 persons per sq. mi. (43 per km^2).
Economy: Mainly agricultural, with growing manufacturing.

Kiribati

(Republic of Kiribati)
Kiribati is a small island country in the southwest Pacific Ocean. It consists of 33 islands scattered over about 2 million square miles (5 million square kilometers) of ocean. Most of its people are engaged in agriculture and fishing.
Capital: Tarawa.
Area: 277 sq. mi. (717 km^2).
Government: Republic.
Largest city: Tarawa (22,148).
Population: 1990 estimate—69,000; density—249 persons per sq. mi. (96 per km^2).
Economy: Based mainly on agriculture, with some trade and limited mining.

Korea, North

(Democratic People's Republic of Korea)
North Korea is a nation located in the northern portion of a peninsula in northeastern Asia that projects southeastward from China. It is bordered by China, the Soviet Union, and South Korea. About 50 per cent of its workers are engaged in agriculture.
Capital: Pyongyang.
Area: 46,540 sq. mi. (120,538 km^2).
Government: Communist dictatorship.
Largest cities: Pyongyang (2,639,448), Hamhung (525,000), Sinuiju (500,000), Chongjin (754,128), and Kaesong (345,642).
Population: 1990 estimate—22,965,000; density—493 persons per sq. mi. (191 per km^2).
Economy: Mainly based upon manufacturing and mining, with limited agriculture.

Korea, South

(Republic of Korea)
South Korea is a nation located in the southern portion of a peninsula in northeastern Asia that projects southeastward from China. It is bordered by North Korea. About 50 per cent of South Korea's workers are engaged in service activities, and about 25 per cent are in industry.
Capital: Seoul.
Area: 38,625 sq. mi. (99,106 km^2).
Government: Republic.
Largest cities: Seoul (9,645,932), Pusan (3,516,807), Taegu (2,030,672), and Inchon (1,387,491).
Population: 1990 estimate—43,650,000; density—1,130 persons per sq. mi. (440 per km^2).
Economy: Based mainly on service industries, manufacturing, and agriculture.

Kuwait

(State of Kuwait)
Kuwait is a nation located at the north

end of the Persian Gulf in southwestern
Asia. It is bordered by Iraq and Saudi
Arabia. Most workers in Kuwait are em-
ployed by the government or work in
business or the oil industry.
Capital: Kuwait.
Area: 6,880 sq. mi. (17,818 km²)*.
Government: Emirate.
Largest cities: Hawalli (130,565), As Sal-
imiyah (113,943), and Kuwait (78,116).
Population: 1990 estimate—2,096,000;
density—305 persons per sq. mi. (117
per km²).
Economy: Based almost entirely upon
oil.
*Includes offshore islands.

Laos

(Lao People's Democratic Republic)
Laos is a nation located in Southeast
Asia. It is bordered by China, Vietnam,
Kampuchea, Thailand, and Burma. Al-
most all of the workers in Laos are en-
gaged in agriculture.
Capital: Vientiane.
Area: 91,430 sq. mi. (236,800 km²).
Government: Socialist republic (Commu-
nist dictatorship).
Largest cities: Vientiane (264,277), Sa-
vannakhet (50,691), and Pakxé
(44,860).
Population: 1990 estimate—4,070,000;
density—45 persons per sq. mi. (17
per km²).
Economy: Based almost entirely on agriculture.

Lebanon

(Republic of Lebanon)
Lebanon is a nation located in south-
western Asia at the eastern end of the
Mediterranean Sea. It is bordered by

Syria and Israel. Most of Lebanon's
workers are engaged in agriculture, service occupations, or industry.
Capital: Beirut.
Area: 4,015 sq. mi. (10,400 km²).
Government: Republic.
Largest cities: Beirut (702,000) and Tripoli (175,000).
Population: 1990 estimate—2,947,000;
density—734 persons per sq. mi. (283
per km²).
Economy: Based mainly on trade and
commerce, with agriculture and industry also important.

Lesotho

(Kingdom of Lesotho)
Lesotho is a nation surrounded by the
Republic of South Africa. Most of its
workers are engaged in raising livestock
and food crops.
Capital: Maseru.
Area: 11,720 sq. mi. (30,355 km²).
Government: Military rule.
Largest city: Maseru (109,382).
Population: 1990 estimate—1,757,000;
density—150 persons per sq. mi. (58
per km²).
Economy: Based mainly on agriculture.

Liberia

(Republic of Liberia)
Liberia is a nation located on the west
coast of Africa. It is bordered by
Guinea, Ivory Coast, and Sierra Leone.
Most of the workers are engaged in agri-
culture.
Capital: Monrovia.
Area: 43,000 sq. mi. (111,370 km²).
Government: Republic.
Largest city: Monrovia (421,058).
Population: 1990 estimate—2,552,000;

density—59 persons per sq. mi. (23 per km^2).

Economy: Based mainly on service industries and mining, with agriculture and trade also important.

Libya

(Great Socialist People's Libyan Arab Jamahiriya)
Libya is a nation located on the northern coast of Africa. It is bordered by Egypt, Sudan, Chad, Niger, Algeria, and Tunisia. Most of Libya's workers are engaged in service industries and agriculture.

Capital: Tripoli.
Area: 679,362 sq. mi. (1,759,540 km^2).
Government: Jamahiriya*.
Largest cities: Tripoli (990,697) and Benghazi (368,000).
Population: 1990 estimate—4,356,000; density—6 persons per sq. mi. (2 per km^2).
Economy: Based mainly on production of oil.

*The Libyan government's name for a kind of republic.

Liechtenstein

(Principality of Liechtenstein)
Liechtenstein is a small nation located in south-central Europe. It is bordered by Austria and Switzerland. More than half of Liechtenstein's workers are employed in manufacturing or trade.

Capital: Vaduz.
Area: 62 sq. mi. (160 km^2).
Government: Constitutional monarchy.
Largest city: Vaduz (4,920).
Population: 1990 estimate—28,000; density—452 persons per sq. mi. (175 per km^2).

Economy: Based mainly on industry and trade, with some agriculture.

Luxembourg

(Grand Duchy of Luxembourg)
Luxembourg is a small nation located in northwestern Europe. It is bordered by Belgium, West Germany, and France. About 33 per cent of the workers in Luxembourg are employed in the nation's steel mills, and only about 6 per cent of its workers are engaged in agriculture.

Capital: Luxembourg.
Area: 998 sq. mi. (2,586 km^2).
Government: Constitutional monarchy.
Largest city: Luxembourg (76,640).
Population: 1990 estimate—367,000; density—368 persons per sq. mi. (142 per km^2).
Economy: Largely based upon mining, industry, and tourism.

Madagascar

(Democratic Republic of Madagascar)
Madagascar is an island nation located in the Indian Ocean about 240 miles (386 kilometers) southeast of Africa. About 80 per cent of its workers are engaged in agriculture.

Capital: Antananarivo.
Area: 226,658 sq. mi. (587,041 km^2).
Government: Republic (military rule).
Largest cities: Antananarivo (662,585) and Fianarantsoa (73,000).
Population: 1990 estimate—11,969,000; density—53 persons per sq. mi. (20 per km^2).
Economy: Mainly agricultural, with some mining and very limited industry.

Malawi

(Republic of Malawi)
Malawi is a small nation located in southeastern Africa. It is bordered by Tanzania, Mozambique, and Zambia. Most of Malawi's workers are engaged in agriculture.
Capital: Lilongwe.
Area: 45,747 sq. mi. (118,484 km²).
Government: Republic.
Largest cities: Blantyre (229,000), Lilongwe (186,000), and Zomba (16,000).
Population: 1990 estimate—8,198,000; density—179 persons per sq. mi. (69 per km²).
Economy: Almost entirely agricultural.

Malaysia

(Malaysia)
Malaysia is a nation located in Southeast Asia. It covers the southern portion of the Malay Peninsula and most of the northern portion of the island of Borneo. It is bordered by Thailand and Indonesia. About half of the workers in Malaysia are engaged in agriculture.
Capital: Kuala Lumpur.
Area: 127,317 sq. mi. (329,749 km²).
Government: Constitutional monarchy.
Largest cities: Kuala Lumpur (937,875) and George Town (250,578).
Population: 1990 estimate—17,344,000; density—136 persons per sq. mi. (53 per km²).
Economy: Depends heavily on the production of petroleum and tin, with some manufacturing and agriculture.

Maldives

(Republic of Maldives)
Maldives is a small nation composed of about 1,200 islands located in the Indian Ocean. Most of the nation's workers are engaged in the fishing industry.
Capital: Male.
Area: 115 sq. mi. (298 km²).
Government: Republic.
Largest city: Male (46,334).
Population: 1990 estimate—215,000; density—1,869 persons per sq. mi. (721 per km²).
Economy: Based on the fishing industry, which is government controlled, and tourism.

Mali

(Republic of Mali)
Mali is a nation located in western Africa. It is bordered by Algeria, Niger, Burkina Faso, Ivory Coast, Guinea, Senegal, and Mauritania. Most of its workers are engaged in agriculture and raising livestock.
Capital: Bamako.
Area: 478,841 sq. mi. (1,240,192 km²).
Government: Republic (military rule).
Largest cities: Bamako (404,022) and Mopti (35,000).
Population: 1990 estimate—8,278,000; density—17 persons per sq. mi. (7 per km²).
Economy: Based mainly upon farming and livestock raising.

Malta

(Republic of Malta)
Malta is an island nation in the Mediterranean Sea. It is composed of two main islands and several smaller islands. The large majority of Malta's workers are employed in industry, primarily shipbuilding and repairing.
Capital: Valletta.

Area: 122 sq. mi. (316 km²).
Government: Republic.
Largest cities: Sliema (20,095), Birkir-
kara (16,832), Qormi (15,784), and
Valletta (14,249).
Population: 1990 estimate—350,000;
density—2,868 persons per sq. mi.
(1,108 per km²).
Economy: Based mainly on shipbuilding
and ship repairing, with very limited
agriculture and tourism.

Mauritania

(Islamic Republic of Mauritania)
Mauritania is a nation located in western
Africa. It is bordered by Western Sa-
hara, Algeria, Mali, and Senegal. About
90 per cent of the workers are engaged
in farming and livestock herding.
Capital: Nouakchott.
Area: 397,956 sq. mi. (1,030,700 km²).
Government: Military rule.
Largest cities: Nouakchott (350,000) and
Nouadhibou (21,961).
Population: 1990 estimate—2,021,000;
density—5 persons per sq. mi. (2 per
km²).
Economy: Based mainly on agriculture,
with some small industry and mining.

Mauritius

(Mauritius)
Mauritius is an island nation located in
the Indian Ocean, about 500 miles (800
kilometers) east of Madagascar. About
one-third of the nation's workers raise or
process sugar.
Capital: Port Louis.
Area: 788 sq. mi. (2,040 km²).
Government: Constitutional monarchy.
Largest cities: Port Louis (138,482),
Beau Bassin (83,714), and Curepipe
(54,356).

Population: 1990 estimate—1,105,000;
density—1,402 persons per sq. mi.
(542 per km²).
Economy: Based mainly upon the raising
and processing of sugar and sugar by-
products.

Mexico

(United Mexican States)
Mexico is a nation located in North
America. It is bordered by the United
States, Belize, and Guatemala. About 50
per cent of Mexico's workers are en-
gaged in services; many others are em-
ployed in manufacturing and agriculture.
Capital: Mexico City.
Area: 756,067 sq. mi. (1,958,201 km²).
Government: Republic.
Largest cities: Mexico City (10,061,000)
and Guadalajara (1,725,000).
Population: 1990 estimate—88,560,000;
density—117 persons per sq. mi. (45
per km²).
Economy: Based mainly on services,
with increasing manufacturing, trade,
and petroleum.

Monaco

(Principality of Monaco)
Monaco is one of the smallest nations in
the world. It lies along the Mediterranean Sea and is bordered on three sides
by France. Most workers are employed
in tourist and service occupations, controlled by the government.
Capital: Monaco.
Area: 0.73 sq. mi. (1.9 km²).
Government: Principality.
Largest cities: Monte Carlo (11,599) and
La Condamine (11,438).
Population: 1990 estimate—29,000; density—39,726 persons per sq. mi.
(15,263 per km²).

Economy: Based mainly on tourism, with some small, local industries.

Mongolia

(Mongolian People's Republic)
Mongolia is a nation located in east-central Asia. It is bordered by the Soviet Union and China. Most of the nation's workers are engaged in livestock herding, and they live and work on cooperatively owned livestock farms.
Capital: Ulan Bator.
Area: 604,250 sq. mi. (1,565,000 km²).
Government: Communist dictatorship.
Largest city: Ulan Bator (515,000).
Population: 1990 estimate—2,185,000; density—4 persons per sq. mi. (1 per km²).
Economy: Based mainly on livestock raising and related industries, with some developing industry.

Morocco

(Kingdom of Morocco)
Morocco is a nation located in northwest Africa. It is bordered by Algeria and Western Sahara. About 40 per cent of its workers are engaged in farming and fishing.
Capital: Rabat.
Area: 177,117 sq. mi. (458,730 km²).
Government: Constitutional monarchy.
Largest cities: Casablanca (2,139,204), Rabat (518,616), Fez (448,823), and Marrakech (439,728).
Population: 1990 estimate—25,169,000; density—142 persons per sq. mi. (55 per km²).
Economy: Based mainly on agriculture and mining.

Mozambique

(People's Republic of Mozambique)
Mozambique is a nation located on the southeastern coast of Africa. It is bordered by Swaziland, South Africa, Zimbabwe, Zambia, Malawi, and Tanzania. Almost all of its workers are engaged in agriculture.
Capital: Maputo.
Area: 308,642 sq. mi. (799,380 km²).
Government: Communist dictatorship.
Largest cities: Maputo (510,000), Nampula (120,188), and Beira (110,752).
Population: 1990 estimate—15,627,000; density—51 persons per sq. mi. (20 per km²).
Economy: Based on agriculture and trade, with some limited industry.

Nauru

(Republic of Nauru)
Nauru is an island nation located in the central Pacific Ocean, just south of the equator. Most workers in Nauru are employed in the phosphate industry.
Capital: None.
Area: 8 sq. mi. (21 km²).
Government: Republic.
Largest city: None; population concentrated in coastal settlements and villages.
Population: 1990 estimate—9,000; density—1,110 persons per sq. mi. (428 per km²).
Economy: Based almost entirely on the production of phosphate for export, with a government-owned shipping industry.

Nepal

(Kingdom of Nepal)
Nepal is a nation located in south-central Asia. It is bordered by China and India. About 90 per cent of the workers in Nepal are engaged in agriculture.
Capital: Kathmandu.
Area: 56,827 sq. mi. (147,181 km^2).
Government: Constitutional monarchy.
Largest city: Kathmandu (150,402).
Population: 1990 estimate—19,157,000; density—337 persons per sq. mi. (130 per km^2).
Economy: Based mainly on agriculture, with some limited local industry.

The Netherlands

(Kingdom of the Netherlands)
The Netherlands is a nation located in northwestern Europe. It is bordered by West Germany and Belgium. Most of the workers are in manufacturing, mining, commerce, and service occupations.
Capital: Amsterdam.
Area: 14,405 sq. mi. (37,310 km^2).
Government: Constitutional monarchy.
Largest cities: Amsterdam (687,397), Rotterdam (558,832), and The Hague (449,338).
Population: 1990 estimate—14,765,000; density—1,024 persons per sq. mi. (396 per km^2).
Economy: Based mainly on service industries, manufacturing, and commerce.

New Zealand

(New Zealand)
New Zealand is an island nation located in the Southwest Pacific Ocean. It is composed of two principal islands and many smaller islands. More than half of New Zealand's workers are engaged in industry or in service occupations, and about 11 per cent are in agriculture, forestry, and fishing.
Capital: Wellington.
Area: 103,883 sq. mi. (269,057 km^2).
Government: Constitutional monarchy.
Largest cities: Auckland (820,754), Wellington (325,697), and Christchurch (299,373).
Population: 1990 estimate—3,402,000; density—33 persons per sq. mi. (13 per km^2).
Economy: Based mainly on manufacturing, farming, and trade.

Nicaragua

(Republic of Nicaragua)
Nicaragua is a nation located in Central America. It is bordered by Honduras and Costa Rica. Almost half of Nicaragua's workers are engaged in agriculture, fishing, and forestry; and most of the rest are employed in industry and in service occupations.
Capital: Managua.
Area: 50,200 sq. mi. (130,000 km^2).
Government: Republic (Junta).
Largest cities: Managua (677,680) and León (83,693).
Population: 1990 estimate—3,606,000; density—72 persons per sq. mi. (28 per km^2).
Economy: Based mainly on agriculture, with industry and commerce growing in importance.

Niger

(Republic of Niger)
Niger is a nation located in West Africa. It is bordered by Algeria, Libya, Chad,

Nigeria, Benin, Burkina Faso, and Mali. Most of the workers farm or herd livestock.
Capital: Niamey.
Area: 489,200 sq. mi. (1,267,000 km²).
Government: Republic (military rule).
Largest cities: Niamey (360,000) and Zinder (58,400).
Population: 1990 estimate—7,095,000; density—14 persons per sq. mi. (5 per km²).
Economy: Based almost entirely on agriculture.

Nigeria

(Federal Republic of Nigeria)
Nigeria is a nation located on the west coast of Africa. It is bordered by Niger, Chad, Cameroon, and Benin. About 67 per cent of the workers in Nigeria are engaged in agriculture.
Capital: Lagos.
Area: 356,669 sq. mi. (923,768 km²).
Government: Military rule.
Largest cities: Lagos (1,149,200) and Ibadan (885,300).
Population: 1990 estimate—112,765,000; density—316 persons per sq. mi. (122 per km²).
Economy: Based mainly upon agriculture and the production of oil.

Norway

(Kingdom of Norway)
Norway is a nation located in northern Europe. It is bordered by Sweden, Finland, and the Soviet Union. Most of Norway's workers are employed in the nation's industries or in service occupations.
Capital: Oslo.
Area: 149,405 sq. mi. (386,958 km²).

Government: Constitutional monarchy.
Largest cities: Oslo (449,220) and Bergen (208,915).
Population: 1990 estimate—4,213,000; density—28 persons per sq. mi. (11 per km²).
Economy: Based largely upon manufacturing and trade.

Oman

(Sultanate of Oman)
Oman is a small nation located on the southeast tip of the Arabian Peninsula. It is bordered by the United Arab Emirates, Yemen, and Saudi Arabia. Most of Oman's workers are engaged in agriculture or work in the oil industry.
Capital: Muscat.
Area: 82,030 sq. mi. (212,457 km²).
Government: Sultanate.
Largest cities: Matrah (20,000), Salalah (10,000), and Nazwa (10,000).
Population: 1990 estimate—1,469,000; density—18 persons per sq. mi. (7 per km²).
Economy: Based mainly on the oil industry and agriculture.

Pakistan

(The Islamic Republic of Pakistan)
Pakistan is a nation located in south Asia. It is bordered by Iran, Afghanistan, China, and India. About half of Pakistan's workers are engaged in agriculture.
Capital: Islamabad.
Area: 307,374 sq. mi. (796,095 km²).
Government: Republic.
Largest cities: Karachi (5,208,170), Lahore (2,952,689), Lyallpur (1,104,209), Rawalpindi (794,843), and Hyderabad (751,529).

Population: 1990 estimate—113,163,000; density—368 persons per sq. mi. (142 per km²).
Economy: Based mainly on agriculture, with some service industries and manufacturing.

Panama

(Republic of Panama)
Panama is a nation located in Central America. It is bordered by Colombia and Costa Rica. About a fourth of the workers in Panama are engaged in agriculture; many others are employed in commerce, trade, manufacturing, and transportation.
Capital: Panama City.
Area: 30,193 sq. mi. (78,200 km²).
Government: Republic.
Largest cities: Panama City (389,172) and San Miguelito (156,611).
Population: 1990 estimate—2,421,000; density—80 persons per sq. mi. (31 per km²).
Economy: Based mainly on agriculture and transportation.

Papua New Guinea

(Papua New Guinea)
Papua New Guinea is a nation that occupies the eastern half of the island of New Guinea and a chain of smaller islands. It is bordered by Indonesia. Most of the people in Papua New Guinea are engaged in subsistence agriculture.
Capital: Port Moresby.
Area: 178,704 sq. mi. (462,840 km²).
Government: Constitutional monarchy.
Largest cities: Port Moresby (122,761) and Lae (45,100).
Population: 1990 estimate—3,824,000; density—21 persons per sq. mi. (8 per km²).

Economy: Based almost entirely upon agriculture, with some limited manufacturing and mining.

Paraguay

(Republic of Paraguay)
Paraguay is a nation located in South America. It is bordered by Brazil, Argentina, and Bolivia. About 45 per cent of the workers in Paraguay are engaged in agriculture.
Capital: Asunción.
Area: 157,048 sq. mi. (406,752 km²).
Government: Republic.
Largest cities: Asunción (457,210) and Fernando de la Mora (66,450).
Population: 1990 estimate—4,278,000; density—27 persons per sq. mi. (11 per km²).
Economy: Based mainly on agriculture, with some manufacturing.

Peru

(Republic of Peru)
Peru is a nation located on the west coast of South America. It is bordered by Ecuador, Colombia, Brazil, Bolivia, and Chile. Most of the workers in Peru are engaged in agriculture; but fishing, mining, and manufacturing also employ many workers.
Capital: Lima.
Area: 496,225 sq. mi. (1,285,216 km²).
Government: Republic.
Largest cities: Lima (4,164,597), Callao (313,316), and Arequipa (302,316).
Population: 1990 estimate—22,330,000; density—45 persons per sq. mi. (17 per km²).
Economy: Based largely on manufacturing, mining, agriculture, and fishing.

Philippines

(Republic of the Philippines)
The Philippines is an island nation composed of more than 7,000 islands. It is located off the coast of Southeast Asia. About 48 per cent of the workers are engaged in agriculture, forestry, or fishing.
Capital: Manila.
Area: 116,000 sq. mi. (300,000 km²).
Government: Parliamentary republic.
Largest cities: Manila (1,630,485), Quezon City (1,165,865), Davao (610,375), and Cebu (490,281).
Population: 1990 estimate—62,466,000; density—539 persons per sq. mi. (208 per km²).
Economy: Mainly manufacturing, services, mining, and agriculture.

Poland

(Polish People's Republic)
Poland is a nation located in central Europe. It is bordered by the Soviet Union, Czechoslovakia, and East Germany. About 29 per cent of the Polish workers are occupied in agriculture and forestry, 34 per cent in manufacturing, and 15 per cent in service industries.
Capital: Warsaw.
Area: 120,728 sq. mi. (312,683 km²).
Government: Republic (government determined by free elections).
Largest cities: Warsaw (1,659,400), Łódź (847,900), and Kraków (740,100).
Population: 1990 estimate—38,441,000; density—318 persons per sq. mi. (123 per km²).
Economy: Based mainly upon manufacturing and heavy industries.

Portugal

(Portuguese Republic)
Portugal is a nation located in western Europe. It is bordered by Spain. Most of the Portuguese workers are engaged in agriculture, forestry, or fishing.
Capital: Lisbon.
Area: 34,340 sq. mi. (88,941 km²).
Government: Republic.
Largest cities: Lisbon (817,627) and Porto (330,199).
Population: 1990 estimate—9,903,000; density—288 persons per sq. mi. (111 per km²).
Economy: Based mainly upon manufacturing, with service industries, agriculture, and fishing also important.

Qatar

(The State of Qatar)
Qatar is a nation located in southwestern Asia, on a peninsula that reaches into the Persian Gulf. It is bordered by Saudi Arabia and the United Arab Emirates. The greatest number of Qatar's workers are engaged in the oil industry.
Capital: Doha.
Area: 4,416 sq. mi. (11,437 km²).
Government: Emirate.
Largest city: Doha (217,294).
Population: 1990 estimate—418,000; density—95 persons per sq. mi. (37 per km²).
Economy: Based mainly upon the oil industry, with very limited agriculture.

Romania

(Socialist Republic of Romania)
Romania is a nation located in southeastern Europe. It is bordered by the Soviet Union, Bulgaria, Yugoslavia, and Hun-

gary. About 36 per cent of Romania's workers are engaged in agriculture and forestry.
Capital: Bucharest.
Area: 91,700 sq. mi. (237,500 km²).
Government: Republic (government determined by free elections).
Largest cities: Bucharest (1,961,189), Iaşi (310,158), Timişoara (309,258), and Cluj-Napoca (299,786).
Population: 1990 estimate—23,279,000; density—254 persons per sq. mi. (98 per km²).
Economy: Based mainly upon manufacturing, mining, and agriculture.

Rwanda

(Republic of Rwanda)
Rwanda is a nation located in east-central Africa. It is bordered by Uganda, Tanzania, Burundi, and Zaire. Almost all the workers in Rwanda are engaged in agriculture.
Capital: Kigali.
Area: 10,169 sq. mi. (26,338 km²).
Government: Republic.
Largest cities: Kigali (117,749) and Butare (21,700).
Population: 1990 estimate—7,222,000; density—710 persons per sq. mi. (274 per km²).
Economy: Based mainly upon agriculture, with some limited mining.

Saint Christopher and Nevis

(St. Christopher and Nevis)
St. Christopher and Nevis is an island nation in the Caribbean Sea. It is composed of two islands, St. Christopher (commonly called St. Kitts) and Nevis. Most workers are engaged in agriculture.
Capital: Basseterre.

Area: 101 sq. mi. (262 km²).
Government: Constitutional monarchy.
Largest city: Basseterre (14,725).
Population: 1990 estimate—44,400; density—440 persons per sq. mi. (171 per km²).
Economy: Agriculture and some tourism.

Saint Lucia

(St. Lucia)
St. Lucia is a small island country composed of a single island in the Caribbean Sea. It lies about 240 miles (386 kilometers) north of Venezuela. Most of its workers are engaged in agriculture.
Capital: Castries.
Area: 238 sq. mi. (616 km²).
Government: Constitutional monarchy.
Largest city: Castries (52,868).
Population: 1990 estimate—143,000; density—601 persons per sq. mi. (232 per km²).
Economy: Based mainly on agriculture.

Saint Vincent and the Grenadines

(St. Vincent and the Grenadines)
St. Vincent and the Grenadines is an island country composed of about 100 islands in the Caribbean Sea. It lies about 200 miles (320 kilometers) north of Venezuela. Most of its people work on farms.
Capital: Kingstown.
Area: 150 sq. mi. (388 km²).
Government: Constitutional monarchy.
Largest city: Kingstown (18,830).
Population: 1990 estimate—117,000; density—780 persons per sq. mi. (302 per km²).
Economy: Based mainly on agriculture, with some fishing, manufacturing, and tourism.

San Marino

(The Most Serene Republic of San Marino)
San Marino is the smallest republic in
Europe. It is located in the Apennine
Mountains, and it is entirely surrounded
by Italy. Most of the workers in San
Marino are engaged in agriculture, man-
ufacturing, or in service occupations re-
lated to tourism.
Capital: San Marino.
Area: 24 sq. mi. (61 km²).
Government: Republic.
Largest city: San Marino (4,179).
Population: 1990 estimate—23,000; den-
   sity—958 persons per sq. mi. (377 per
   km²).
Economy: Based upon tourism, agricul-
   ture, and limited local manufacturing.

São Tomé and Príncipe

(Democratic Republic of São Tomé and
Príncipe)
São Tomé and Príncipe is an island nation composed of two large islands and
several smaller ones that lie about 180
miles (290 kilometers) off the west coast
of Africa. Most of its workers are engaged in agriculture.
Capital: São Tomé.
Area: 372 sq. mi. (964 km²).
Government: Republic.
Largest city: São Tomé (34,997).
Population: 1990 estimate—123,000;
   density—331 persons per sq. mi. (128
   per km²).
Economy: Based almost entirely on agriculture and fishing.

Saudi Arabia

(Kingdom of Saudi Arabia)
Saudi Arabia is a nation located on the
Arabian Peninsula in the Middle East. It
is bordered by Jordan, Iraq, Kuwait,
Qatar, the United Arab Emirates, Oman,
and Yemen. About 33 per cent of the nation's workers are engaged in agriculture, forestry, and fishing, and about
30 per cent work in construction and
trade jobs. Only about 2 per cent of all
Saudi workers are employed by the
oil industry.
Capital: Riyadh.
Area: 830,000 sq. mi. (2,149,690 km²).
Government: Monarchy.
Largest cities: Riyadh (1,380,000), Jidda
   (1,210,000), and Mecca (463,000).
Population: 1990 estimate—12,939,000;
   density—16 persons per sq. mi. (6 per
   km²).
Economy: Based mainly upon the oil industry and agriculture.

Senegal

(Republic of Senegal)
Senegal is a nation located in northwest
Africa. It is bordered by Mauritania,
Mali, Gambia, Guinea, and Guinea-Bis-
sau. Most of Senegal's workers are en-
gaged in agriculture, fishing, mining, and
service occupations.
Capital: Dakar.
Area: 75,750 sq. mi. (196,192 km²).
Government: Republic.
Largest cities: Dakar (978,523), Thiès
   (117,333), and Kaolack (106,899).
Population: 1990 estimate—7,360,000;
   density—97 persons per sq. mi. (38
   per km²).
Economy: Based mainly upon agriculture, with commerce and mining also
   important.

Seychelles

(Republic of Seychelles)
Seychelles is an island nation composed of approximately 90 islands in the Indian Ocean. About a third of the nation's workers are employed by the government. Only about 15 per cent are farmers.
Capital: Victoria.
Area: 175 sq. mi. (453 km^2).
Government: Republic.
Largest city: Victoria (23,000).
Population: 1990 estimate—71,000; density—406 persons per sq. mi. (157 per km^2).
Economy: Based mainly on tourism with a growing fishing industry.

Sierra Leone

(Republic of Sierra Leone)
Sierra Leone is a nation located in western Africa. It is bordered by Guinea and Liberia. Most of the nation's workers are engaged in agriculture.
Capital: Freetown.
Area: 27,699 sq. mi. (71,740 km^2).
Government: Republic.
Largest city: Freetown (469,776).
Population: 1990 estimate—4,146,000; density—150 persons per sq. mi. (58 per km^2).
Economy: Based mainly on agriculture and mining.

Singapore

(Republic of Singapore)
Singapore is an island nation that lies south of the Malay Peninsula in Southeast Asia. Most of the workers in Singapore are employed in industry or service occupations.
Capital: Singapore.
Area: 239 sq. mi. (618 km^2).
Government: Republic.
Largest city: Singapore (2,308,200).
Population: 1990 estimate—2,704,000; density—11,313 persons per sq. mi. (4,375 per km^2).
Economy: Based primarily upon trade and commerce, with manufacturing also important.

Solomon Islands

(Solomon Islands)
Solomon Islands is an island country in the South Pacific Ocean. It lies about 1,000 miles (1,610 kilometers) northeast of Australia. Most of the workers are engaged either in agriculture, including fishing, or in administration and social services.
Capital: Honiara.
Area: 10,639 sq. mi. (27,556 km^2).
Government: Constitutional monarchy.
Largest city: Honiara (30,499).
Population: 1990 estimate—329,000; density—31 persons per sq. mi. (12 per km^2).
Economy: Based upon fishing and forestry.

Somalia

(Somali Democratic Republic)
Somalia is a nation located in eastern Africa. It is bordered by Djibouti, Kenya, and Ethiopia. About 60 per cent of its workers are nomads.
Capital: Mogadishu.
Area: 246,201 sq. mi. (637,657 km^2).
Government: Republic (military rule).
Largest city: Mogadishu (444,882).

Population: 1990 estimate—7,597,000;
density—31 persons per sq. mi. (12
per km^2).
Economy: Based mainly upon agriculture, including the raising of livestock.

South Africa

(Republic of South Africa)
South Africa is a nation located on the
southern tip of Africa. It is bordered by
Namibia, Botswana, Zimbabwe, Lesotho, Swaziland, and Mozambique.
Most of South Africa's workers are employed in agriculture, mining, manufacturing, or in service occupations.
Capitals: Cape Town (legislative); Pretoria (administrative); Bloemfontein (judicial).
Government: Republic.
Area: 471,445 sq. mi. (1,221,037 km^2).
Largest cities: Cape Town (789,580), Johannesburg (703,980), and Pretoria
(435,100).
Population: 1990 estimate—37,922,000;
density—80 persons per sq. mi. (31
per km^2).
Economy: Based mainly upon mining
and manufacturing, with some agriculture.

Spain

(Spanish State)
Spain is a nation located in Western Eu-
rope. It occupies most of the Iberian
Peninsula. It is bordered by France, An-
dorra, and Portugal. About 52 per cent
of its workers are employed in the na-
tion's service industries.
Capital: Madrid.
Area: 194,885 sq. mi. (504,750 km^2).
Government: Parliamentary monarchy.

Largest cities: Madrid (3,123,713), Bar-
celona (1,694,064), Valencia (738,575),
and Seville (668,356).
Population: 1990 estimate—39,623,000;
density—202 persons per sq. mi. (78
per km^2).
Economy: Based mainly upon services,
manufacturing, and agriculture.

Sri Lanka

(Democratic Socialist Republic of
Sri Lanka)
Sri Lanka is an island nation located in
the Indian Ocean off the southeastern tip
of India. Most of its workers are en-
gaged in agriculture.
Capital: Colombo.
Area: 25,333 sq. mi. (65,610 km^2).
Government: Republic.
Largest cities: Colombo (616,000) and
Dehiwala-Mount Lavinia (169,000).
Population: 1990 estimate—17,218,000;
density—680 persons per sq. mi. (262
per km^2).
Economy: Based mainly upon agriculture
and mining.

Sudan

(Democratic Republic of the Sudan)
Sudan is the largest nation in Africa. It
is located in northeastern Africa. It is
bordered by Egypt, Ethiopia, Kenya,
Uganda, Zaire, the Central African Re-
public, Chad, and Libya. Most of its
workers are engaged in agriculture.
Capital: Khartoum.
Area: 967,500 sq. mi. (2,505,813 km^2).
Government: Republic.
Largest cities: Omdurman (526,827) and
Khartoum (476,218).

Population: 1990 estimate—25,004,000;
density—26 persons per sq. mi. (10
per km^2).
Economy: Based mainly upon agriculture.

Suriname

(Republic of Suriname)
Suriname is a nation located on the
northeastern coast of South America. It
is bordered by French Guiana, Brazil,
and Guyana. Most of its workers are
employed in the mining industry or in
agriculture.
Capital: Paramaribo.
Area: 63,037 sq. mi. (163,265 km^2).
Government: Republic.
Largest city: Paramaribo (150,000).
Population: 1990 estimate—404,000;
density—6 persons per sq. mi. (2 per
km^2).
Economy: Based mainly upon mining
and metal processing, with some
agriculture.

Swaziland

(Kingdom of Swaziland)
Swaziland is a nation located in southern
Africa. It is almost entirely surrounded
by South Africa, except for a small area
that borders Mozambique. Most of its
workers are engaged in agriculture and
livestock herding.
Capitals: Mbabane (administrative) and
Lobamba (traditional).
Area: 6,704 sq. mi. (17,363 km^2).
Government: Monarchy.
Largest city: Mbabane (38,636).
Population: 1990 estimate—779,000;
density—116 persons per sq. mi. (45
per km^2).
Economy: Based mainly upon agriculture
and mining, with some manufacturing.

Sweden

(Kingdom of Sweden)
Sweden is a nation located in northern
Europe on the Scandinavian Peninsula.
It is bordered by Finland and Norway.
Most workers are employed in manufac-
turing, government, and business.
Capital: Stockholm.
Area: 170,250 sq. mi. (440,945 km^2).
Government: Constitutional monarchy.
Largest cities: Stockholm (653,455) and
Göteborg (424,085).
Population: 1990 estimate—8,363,000;
density—49 persons per sq. mi. (19
per km^2).
Economy: Based mainly upon natural re-
sources, manufacturing, and various
service industries.

Switzerland

(Switzerland)
Switzerland is a nation located in central
Europe. It is bordered by West Germany, Austria, Liechtenstein, Italy, and
France. About 30 per cent of its workers
are employed in manufacturing; about 40
per cent, in commerce or service occupations.
Capital: Bern.
Area: 15,943 sq. mi. (41,293 km^2).
Government: Federal republic.
Largest cities: Zurich (351,545), Basel
(174,606), and Geneva (159,895).
Population: 1990 estimate—6,535,000;
density—410 persons per sq. mi. (158
per km^2).
Economy: Based mainly upon manufacturing and agriculture, with tourism
and other services also important.

Syria

(The Syrian Arab Republic)
Syria is a nation located in southwestern Asia. It is bordered by Turkey, Iraq, Jordan, Israel, and Lebanon. About 40 per cent of the Syrian workers are engaged in service activities, and about 15 per cent work in the nation's industries.
Capital: Damascus.
Area: 71,498 sq. mi. (185,180 km²).
Government: Socialist popular democracy.
Largest cities: Damascus (1,200,000) and Aleppo (961,000).
Population: 1990 estimate—12,491,000; density—175 persons per sq. mi. (67 per km²).
Economy: Based mainly upon services, agriculture, commerce, and industry.

Taiwan

(Republic of China)
Taiwan is an island nation composed of one major island and several small islands located off the coast of mainland China. About 50 per cent of its workers are employed in the nation's industries or in service occupations.
Capital: Taipei.
Area: 13,900 sq. mi. (36,000 km²)*.
Government: Republic.
Largest cities: Taipei (2,220,427) and Kaohsiung (1,172,977).
Population: 1990 estimate—20,454,000; density—1,472 persons per sq. mi. (568 per km²).
Economy: Based mainly upon manufacturing and foreign trade.

*Area does not include the islands of Quemoy and Matsu.

Tanzania

(United Republic of Tanzania)
Tanzania is a nation located in eastern Africa. It is bordered by Kenya, Uganda, Mozambique, Malawi, Zambia, Rwanda, Burundi, and Zaire. Most of its workers are engaged in agriculture.
Capital: Dar es Salaam.
Area: 364,900 sq. mi. (945,087 km²).
Government: Republic.
Largest cities: Dar es Salaam (870,020), Mwanza (110,611), and Tanga (103,409).
Population: 1990 estimate—25,955,000; density—71 persons per sq. mi. (27 per km²).
Economy: Based mainly on agriculture, services, and manufacturing, with some mining.

Thailand

(Land of the Free)
Thailand is a nation located in Southeast Asia. It is bordered by Laos, Kampuchea, Malaysia, and Burma. More than 75 per cent of the workers in Thailand are engaged in agriculture.
Capital: Bangkok.
Area: 198,115 sq. mi. (513,115 km²).
Government: Constitutional monarchy.
Largest cities: Bangkok (5,153,902), Chiang Mai (100,146), and Hat Yai (98,091).
Population: 1990 estimate—55,760,000; density—281 persons per sq. mi. (109 per km²).
Economy: Based mainly upon agriculture and manufacturing, with some mining.

Togo

(Republic of Togo)
Togo is a nation located in western Africa. It is bordered by Burkina Faso, Benin, and Ghana. About 80 per cent of its workers are engaged in agriculture, and a small percentage work in the nation's mining industry.
Capital: Lomé.
Area: 21,925 sq. mi. (56,785 km^2).
Government: Presidential regime.
Largest city: Lomé (366,476).
Population: 1990 estimate—3,451,000; density—157 persons per sq. mi. (61 per km^2).
Economy: Based largely upon agriculture, with mining also important.

Tonga

(Kingdom of Tonga)
Tonga is an island nation located in the South Pacific Ocean. It is composed of about 150 islands located 400 miles (640 kilometers) west of Fiji. Almost all of Tonga's workers are engaged in agriculture or in fishing.
Capital: Nukualofa.
Area: 289 sq. mi. (748 km^2).
Government: Constitutional monarchy.
Largest city: Nukualofa (18,000).
Population: 1990 estimate—101,000; density—349 persons per sq. mi. (135 per km^2).
Economy: Based almost entirely upon agriculture.

Trinidad and Tobago

(Republic of Trinidad and Tobago)
Trinidad and Tobago is an island nation composed of two islands located in the West Indies. Most of the nation's work-ers are employed in the oil industry, manufacturing, or construction.
Capital: Port-of-Spain.
Area: 1,980 sq. mi. (5,128 km^2).
Government: Republic.
Largest cities: Port-of-Spain (59,649) and San Fernando (36,650).
Population: 1990 estimate—1,283,000; density—648 persons per sq. mi. (250 per km^2).
Economy: Based mainly upon the production and the refining of oil.

Tunisia

(Republic of Tunisia)
Tunisia is a nation located in northern Africa. It is bordered by Libya and Algeria. About 40 per cent of Tunisia's workers are engaged in farming or the raising of livestock.
Capital: Tunis.
Area: 63,170 sq. mi. (163,610 km^2).
Government: Republic.
Largest cities: Tunis (596,654) and Sfax (171,297).
Population: 1990 estimate—8,095,000; density—128 persons per sq. mi. (49 per km^2).
Economy: Based mainly upon the production of phosphates and petroleum, agriculture, and some industries.

Turkey

(Republic of Turkey)
Turkey is a nation in southwestern Asia and southeastern Europe. It is bordered by the Soviet Union, Iran, Iraq, Syria, Greece, and Bulgaria. About 58 per cent of Turkey's workers are engaged in agriculture, forestry, and fishing; and about 11 per cent are employed in the nation's manufacturing.

Capital: Ankara.
Area: 301,382 sq. mi. (780,576 km²).
Government: Republic (military rule).
Largest cities: Istanbul (5,475,982) and
  Ankara (2,235,035).
Population: 1990 estimate—56,549,000;
  density—184 persons per sq. mi. (71
  per km²).
Economy: Based mainly upon agricul-
  ture, but the nation's industries are
  expanding rapidly.

Tuvalu

(Tuvalu)
Tuvalu is a small country consisting of
nine islands in the South Pacific Ocean.
It lies about 2,000 miles (3,200 kilometers) northeast of Australia. Tuvalu has
poor soil, few natural resources, and almost no manufacturing or mining. The
people produce copra (dried coconut
meat) and weave baskets and mats for
export. Many young islanders also work
on ocean ships.
Capital: Funafuti.
Area: 10 sq. mi. (26 km²).
Government: Constitutional monarchy.
Largest city: Funafuti (900).
Population: 1990 estimate—7,000; density—697 persons per sq. mi. (269 per
  km²).
Economy: Based mainly on the export of
  copra and handicrafts.

Uganda

(Republic of Uganda)
Uganda is a nation located in east-central
Africa. It is bordered by Zaire, Sudan,
Kenya, Tanzania, and Rwanda. Most of
the workers in Uganda are engaged in
farming or in herding.
Capital: Kampala.

Area: 91,074 sq. mi. (235,880 km²).
Government: Republic.
Largest cities: Kampala (458,423) and
  Jinja (189,540).
Population: 1990 estimate—17,593,000;
  density—193 persons per sq. mi. (75
  per km²).
Economy: Mainly based on agriculture,
  with very limited mining.

Union of Soviet Socialist Republics

(Union of Soviet Socialist Republics)
The Union of Soviet Socialist Republics,
also commonly known as the Soviet
Union, is a large nation located in northern Eurasia. The U.S.S.R. stretches
from the Baltic Sea to the North Pacific
Ocean. It is the largest nation in area in
the world. It is bordered by Norway,
Finland, Poland, Czechoslovakia, Hungary, Romania, Turkey, Iran, Afghanistan, China, Mongolia, and North Korea. Twenty-nine per cent of the workers
in the U.S.S.R. are employed in manufacturing, mining, and utilities.
Capital: Moscow.
Area: 8,649,500 sq. mi. (22,402,000 km²).
Government: Communist dictatorship.
Largest cities: Moscow (8,275,000), Leningrad (4,295,000), Kiev (2,409,000),
  Tashkent (1,986,000), and Kharkov
  (1,536,000).
Population: 1990 estimate—288,239,000;
  density—33 persons per sq. mi. (13
  per km²).
Economy: Based mainly upon industry,
  services, and agriculture.

United Arab Emirates

(United Arab Emirates)
The United Arab Emirates is a federation of seven independent Arab states lo-

cated in southwestern Asia. It is bordered by Qatar, Oman, and Saudi Arabia. Most of its workers are employed in the nation's oil industry.
Capital: Abu Dhabi.
Area: 32,278 sq. mi. (83,600 km^2).
Government: Emirate.
Largest cities: Abu Dhabi (242,975) and Dubayy (76,000).
Population: 1990 estimate—1,602,000; density—50 persons per sq. mi. (19 per km^2).
Economy: Based mainly upon the production and refining of oil.

United States

(United States of America)
The United States is a large nation located in North America. It is bordered by Canada and Mexico. A large majority of its workers are employed in nonagricultural industries or services.
Capital: Washington, D.C.
Area: 3,618,770 sq. mi. (9,372,571 km^2).
Government: Republic.
Largest cities: New York City (7,071,639), Chicago (3,005,072), Los Angeles (2,968,597), Philadelphia (1,688,210), Houston (1,595,138), and Detroit (1,203,399).
Population: 1990 estimate—250,372,000; density—69 persons per sq. mi. (27 per km^2).
Economy: Based mainly upon manufacturing, commerce, and trade.

Uruguay

(Eastern Republic of Uruguay)
Uruguay is a small country in South America. It is located on the southeastern coast of South America, and it is bordered by Brazil and Argentina. About 16 per cent of its workers are engaged in farming or the raising of livestock.
Capital: Montevideo.
Area: 68,500 sq. mi. (177,414 km^2).
Government: Republic.
Largest cities: Montevideo (1,247,920), Salto (80,787), and Paysandú (75,081).
Population: 1990 estimate—3,130,000; density—46 persons per sq. mi. (18 per km^2).
Economy: Based mainly upon agriculture.

Vanuatu

(Republic of Vanuatu)
Vanuatu is an island country in the South Pacific Ocean. It consists of a group of 12 principal islands and many smaller ones which lie about 1,000 miles (1,600 kilometers) northeast of the Queensland coast of Australia. Most of its people are engaged in agriculture and raising livestock.
Capital: Port-Vila.
Area: 4,700 sq. mi. (12,200 km^2).
Government: Republic.
Largest city: Port-Vila (25,000).
Population: 1990 estimate—164,000; density—35 persons per sq. mi. (13 per km^2).
Economy: Based mainly on agriculture, with tourism also important.

Vatican City

(The State of Vatican City)
Vatican City is the smallest independent state in the world. It lies entirely within the city of Rome, Italy. Vatican City is the spiritual and governmental center of the Roman Catholic Church. Vatican City is under the direction of the pope.
Area: 0.17 sq. mi. (0.44 km^2).

Population: 1990 estimate—1,000; density—5,884 persons per sq. mi. (2,272 per km^2).
Economy: All residents are connected with the activities of the Roman Catholic Church.

Venezuela

(Republic of Venezuela)
Venezuela is a nation located on the northern coast of South America. It is bordered by Colombia, Brazil, and Guyana. About 15 per cent of its workers are engaged in agriculture, and about 20 per cent are employed in the oil industry.
Capital: Caracas.
Area: 352,145 sq. mi. (912,050 km^2).
Government: Federal republic.
Largest cities: Caracas (1,261,116), Maracaibo (1,151,933), Valencia (889,228), and Barquisimeto (681,961).
Population: 1990 estimate—19,744,000; density—56 persons per sq. mi. (22 per km^2).
Economy: Based mainly upon the production of oil and on manufacturing and agriculture.

Vietnam

(Socialist Republic of Vietnam)
Vietnam is a nation located in the eastern part of the Indochinese Peninsula in Southeast Asia. It is bordered by China, Laos, and Kampuchea. About 70 per cent of the workers in Vietnam are engaged in agriculture.
Capital: Hanoi.
Area: 127,242 sq. mi. (329,556 km^2).
Government: Communist dictatorship.
Largest cities: Ho Chi Minh City (3,460,500), Hanoi (1,443,500), Hai-

phong (1,190,900), and Da Nang (492,194).
Population: 1990 estimate—67,084,000; density—527 persons per sq. mi. (204 per km^2).
Economy: Based mainly upon agriculture.

Western Samoa

(Independent State of Western Samoa)
Western Samoa is an island nation in the South Pacific Ocean. It lies about 1,700 miles (2,740 kilometers) northeast of New Zealand. It is composed of two main islands and several smaller islands. About 70 per cent of its workers are engaged in agriculture and fishing.
Capital: Apia.
Area: 1,093 sq. mi. (2,831 km^2).
Government: Parliamentary.
Largest city: Apia (36,000).
Population: 1990 estimate—170,000; density—156 persons per sq. mi. (60 per km^2).
Economy: Mainly based on agriculture.

Yemen

(Republic of Yemen)
Yemen is a nation located in the southern part of the Arabian Peninsula in southwestern Asia. It is bordered by Saudi Arabia and Oman. About 75 per cent of its workers are engaged in farming and the raising of livestock.
Capital: Sana.
Area: 203,887 sq. mi. (528,038 km^2).
Government: Republic.
Largest cities: Sana (427,185) and Aden (271,590).
Population: 1990 estimate—10,848,000; density—53 persons per sq. mi. (21 per km^2).

Economy: Based mainly upon agriculture, light industry, oil refining, and port facilities.

Yugoslavia

(Socialist Federal Republic of Yugoslavia)
Yugoslavia is a nation in the Balkan Peninsula in southeastern Europe. It is bordered by Italy, Austria, Hungary, Romania, Bulgaria, Greece, and Albania. About 52 per cent of the nation's workers are engaged in industry and manufacturing.
Capital: Belgrade.
Area: 98,766 sq. mi. (255,804 km²).
Government: Socialist republic.
Largest cities: Belgrade (1,455,046), Zagreb (763,293), and Skopje (503,449).
Population: 1990 estimate—23,853,000; density—242 persons per sq. mi. (93 per km²).
Economy: Based mainly upon manufacturing and the mining industry, with some agriculture.

Zaire

(Republic of Zaire)
Zaire is a nation located in south-central Africa. It is bordered by the Congo, the Central African Republic, Sudan, Uganda, Rwanda, Burundi, Tanzania, Angola, and Zambia. Most of its workers are engaged in agriculture.
Capital: Kinshasa.
Area: 905,365 sq. mi. (2,344,885 km²).
Government: Presidential regime.
Largest cities: Kinshasa (2,222,981) and Kananga (460,091).
Population: 1990 estimate—35,330,000; density—39 persons per sq. mi. (15 per km²).

Economy: Based mainly upon the mining industry, with very limited manufacturing.

Zambia

(Republic of Zambia)
Zambia is a nation located in south-central Africa. It is bordered by Zaire, Tanzania, Malawi, Mozambique, Zimbabwe, Botswana, Namibia, and Angola. Many of its workers are employed in construction and mining.
Capital: Lusaka.
Area: 290,586 sq. mi. (752,614 km²).
Government: Republic.
Largest cities: Lusaka (818,994), Kitwe (341,000), and Ndola (323,000).
Population: 1990 estimate—8,459,000; density—29 persons per sq. mi. (11 per km²).
Economy: Based mainly upon the mining industry, with construction and agriculture also important.

Zimbabwe

(Zimbabwe)
Zimbabwe is a nation located in southern Africa. It is bordered by Zambia, Mozambique, South Africa, and Botswana. Most of the workers are engaged in agriculture.
Capital: Harare.
Area: 150,804 sq. mi. (390,580 km²).
Government: Republic.
Largest cities: Harare (656,100) and Bulawayo (363,000).
Population: 1990 estimate—9,700,000; density—64 persons per sq. mi. (25 per km²).
Economy: Based on mining and agriculture.

3

Important Dates in History

Did you know that Julius Caesar was killed in 44 B.C.? Do you know what events were taking place in literature and art at the time of Napoleon's conquest of Europe? Do you know in approximately what year the colonial period ended in the history of the United States?

This unit is a review of important dates and events in history. For convenience, the unit has been divided into sections, one on world history and one on the history of the United States. Those sections are further divided by subject area—arts, sciences, philosophy, and so on—and by time periods.

In 1682, an expedition led by Sieur de La Salle
lands on the coast of the Gulf of Mexico.

121

1

World History

The following section outlines some important dates in world history. The section is divided into seven categories: (1) political events, (2) social events, (3) religion, (4) philosophy, (5) literature, (6) the arts, including music, and (7) science and technology. Chronologically, the history is divided into these broad headings: Prehistory and Ancient Times (?-476 A.D.); The Middle Period (477-1492); The Early Modern Period (1493-1699); European Ascendancy (1700-1899); Since 1900 (1900-Present). Each heading encompasses an important historical epoch.

You can use this unit to gain overall perspective on the events that make up world history. And you can use this unit to review key points in history or find areas of interest to explore further.

Gutenberg, in his workshop, shows a proof sheet made by using the type mold he invented in about 1440.

Prehistory and Ancient Times

Political Events

8000 B.C.   People are nomads
During this period, people are organized into small tribes and clans. These tribes and clans follow a nomadic existence, traveling constantly to find sources of food.

8000 B.C.- 3500 B.C.   Settlements begin
Agriculture and the domestication of animals begin. A steady food supply permits people to form settlements.

3500 B.C.   Cities in India
The cities of Mohenjodaro and Harappa are formed in the Indus Valley.

3200 B.C.   Sumerian city-states
A system of sophisticated city-states emerges in the southern part of Mesopotamia, called Sumer.

3100 B.C.   Egypt united
The city-states of Lower and Upper Egypt are united by Menes, also called Na'rmer. Menes' reign marks the beginning of the First Dynasty.

2330 B.C.   Sumer united
The state of ancient Sumer is created by Sargon of Akkad.

1830 B.C.   Rise of Babylon
The First Dynasty of Babylon is founded by King Sumuabum.

1728 B.C.- 1686 B.C.   Hammurabi the Great
Hammurabi of Babylon completes the conquest of Mesopotamia.

1600 B.C.   First Hittite state
The Kingdom of the Hittites, a warlike people who later are to control much of the Middle East, is founded by Labarnas.

1600 B.C.   Rise of Crete
The Minoan culture is solidified on the island of Crete in the Mediterranean Sea. Under a powerful monarchy based in the city of Knossos on Crete, the Minoans expand their influence throughout the Mediterranean area.

1570 B.C.- 1370 B.C.   The Egyptian Empire
The power of the Egyptian state is increased and expanded under the rule of a succession of vigorous soldier kings.

1500 B.C.   Shang Dynasty begins
Kings of the Shang Dynasty establish control over the Yellow River plain in China.

1450 B.C.- 1200 B.C.   The Hittite Empire
The Hittite Kingdom expands into Syria, Palestine, and portions of Mesopotamia.

1290 B.C.- 1224 B.C.   Reign of Ramses II
Ramses II helps restore Egyptian power with a series of military campaigns against the Hittites.

1200 B.C.   India invaded
Aryan tribes from the Iranian Plateau invade and begin the conquest of India.

1115 B.C.- 1078 B.C.   Middle Assyrian Empire
King Tiglath-pileser I develops the Assyrian state into a tightly centralized military machine. He helps create an empire that stretches from

Prehistory and Ancient Times
Political Events (*Continued*)

the Mediterranean Sea to the Persian Gulf.

1100 B.C.   **Greece invaded**
The Dorians invade Greece, destroying the Mycenaean civilization, a civilization that was closely related to the Minoan. The Dorian invaders plunge the Greek Peninsula into a ''Dark Age'' that lasts until about 800 B.C.

1100 B.C.-   **Phoenician expan-**
888 B.C.   **sion**
Based in the Mediterranean cities of Sidon and Tyre, the Phoenicians begin a policy of political and economic expansion.

1027 B.C.   **China centralized**
The Western Chou Dynasty is established in China. The Chou state features a strong king supported by a military aristocracy based on land tenure.

1020 B.C.   **Kingdom of Israel**
Saul is anointed the first king of the Israelites.

1000 B.C.   **King David of**
Israel
Under King David, the city of Jerusalem is captured and made the capital of the Kingdom of Israel.

900 B.C.   **Etruscans settle**
Italy
The Etruscans, a group of people from Asia Minor, settle the Italian Peninsula.

800 B.C.-   **Revival in Greece**
600 B.C.   The city-states that later will dominate the Greek Peninsula begin to rebuild. These include Athens, Sparta, Corinth, and Thebes.

760 B.C.   **Greeks in Italy**
Colonists from the Greek Peninsula establish settlements in southern Italy.

753 B.C.   **Rome founded**
The traditional date for the founding of the city of Rome by Romulus.

605 B.C.-   **Nebuchadnezzar II**
562 B.C.   The Neo-Babylonian Empire, led by King Nebuchadnezzar II, the Great, establishes control over much of the Middle East.

550 B.C.   **Persian Empire**
founded
Cyrus the Great establishes an empire that extends from the Indus River to the Mediterranean Sea.

517 B.C.   **Persians invade**
India
Under Darius I, a Persian army occupies the city of Gandhara in India.

509 B.C.   **The Roman Republic**
Traditional date for the end of the monarchy and the founding of the Roman Republic.

500 B.C.   **Kingdom of Kush**
The central African Kingdom of Kush is founded.

490 B.C.-   **The Persian Wars**
479 B.C.   Greek city-states led by Athens and Sparta beat back Persian attempts to conquer the Greek Peninsula.

477 B.C.   **Delian League**
founded
Several Greek city-states under the leadership of Athens form an alliance to offset the growing power of Sparta.

460 B.C.-   **First Peloponne-**
446 B.C.   **sian War**
The Delian League wages

war against
Sparta.

**431 B.C.-
404 B.C.   Great Peloponnesian War**
With aid from
Persia, Sparta de-
feats Athens.

**359 B.C.-
336 B.C.   Rise of Macedonia**
The Peloponne-
sian Wars leave
the Greek city-
states weak and
divided. The un-
rest is ended by
the intervention
of King Philip of
Macedonia who
defeats an allied
Greek army at
the Battle of
Chaeronea in 338
B.C.

336 B.C.   Philip assassinated
After enforcing
the formation of a
Hellenic League
and declaring war
on Persia, Philip
II is assassinated.
He is succeeded
by his son, Alex-
ander III, the
Great.

333 B.C.   Battle of Issus
Alexander the
Great defeats the
Persians under
Darius III, thus
laying the founda-
tion for the crea-
tion of a great
world empire.

**321 B.C.-
184 B.C.   Maurya Empire
grows**
The Emperor
Chandragupta
founds the
Maurya Dynasty
in India.

300 B.C.   Aksum founded
The kingdom of
Aksum is
founded in what
is today Ethiopia.

272 B.C.   Asoka's empire
The Emperor
Asoka of India
increases the po-
litical, economic,
and cultural influ-
ence of the In-
dian Empire.

**264 B.C.-
241 B.C.   First Punic War**
Carthage and
Rome wage war
to settle which
city-state will
control the Medi-
terranean Sea.
The war ends
with Carthage
and Rome sharing
control of Sicily.

221 B.C.   Unity in China
The Ch'in Dy-
nasty restores a
strong govern-
ment in China.

**218 B.C.-
201 B.C.   Second Punic War**
Led by Hannibal,
Carthage renews
its war against
Rome. After nu-
merous early vic-
tories, Hannibal's
army is defeated
by a Roman army
at the Battle of
Zama (202 B.C.).

**202 B.C.   Han Dynasty be-
gins**
The Han family,
a warrior clan,
seizes control of
the government
of China.

**149 B.C.-
146 B.C.   Third Punic War**
The Roman Gov-
ernment becomes
alarmed over a
revival of Cartha-
ginian power.
When Carthage
becomes involved
in a conflict with
a Roman ally,
Rome uses the
occasion to de-
clare war. The
city-state of Car-
thage is obliter-
ated.

**149 B.C.-
148 B.C.   Romans in Greece**
Rome intervenes
in the Fourth Ma-
cedonian War.
Macedonia be-
comes a Roman
province.

146 B.C.   Greece occupied
The city-state of
Corinth is de-
stroyed by a Ro-
man army. The
remaining Greek
city-states pay
tribute to Rome.

60 B.C.   First Triumvirate
Julius Caesar,
Crassus, and
Pompey join in
alliance to divide
control of Rome.

**58 B.C.-
51 B.C.   Caesar in Gaul**
Julius Caesar
conquers Gaul,
gaining for him-
self the reputa-
tion of a vigorous
hero and skillful
general.

51 B.C.   Triumvirate ends
The death of
Crassus (53 B.C.)
and Pompey's

Prehistory and Ancient Times
Political Events (*Continued*)

fear of Caesar's growing popularity cause an end to the alliance.

48 B.C.   **Pompey assassinated**
After Caesar's victory at the Battle of Pharsalus, Pompey flees to Egypt, where he is executed by the king, Ptolemy XII.

48 B.C.–
45 B.C.   **Caesar triumphant**
Campaigns in Egypt, Syria, and Spain leave Caesar the master of the Roman state.

44 B.C.   **Caesar dies**
A conspiracy of nobles assassinates Caesar.

27 B.C.   **Caesar Octavianus**
After a long period of civil war, Gaius Julius Caesar Octavianus, the great-nephew of Julius Caesar, gains control of the Roman state. He takes the titles Imperator and Augustus. Augustus Caesar's rule marks the beginning of the Roman Empire.

Note: All dates given from this point are dates A.D.

64   **Rome burns**
A crisis in government is caused by a great fire that destroys much of the city of Rome. The Emperor Nero deflects criticism by blaming the Christians.

66–70   **Revolt in Judea**
The Jewish people revolt against Roman occupation. The revolt is crushed when the city of Jerusalem is captured and destroyed by Titus.

84   **Romans take Britain**
The Roman General Agricola completes the conquest of Britain.

135   **Jewish Diaspora**
A second Jewish revolt is crushed, and the Jewish people are forced to leave their homeland.

284   **A new order begins**
The Emperor Diocletian divides the Roman Empire into two parts, each part ruled by a separate emperor.

300   **The Mayas in America**
The Maya Indians develop the first of the important civilizations to flourish in America.

306   **Age of Constantine**
Constantine I the Great becomes co-emperor with Galerius of the Roman Empire. In 324, Constantine reunites the empire under his sole rule.

320   **India's Golden Age**
The Gupta Dynasty seizes power in India ending five centuries of disorder and disunity.

330   **A new Roman capital**
Constantine I moves the capital of the empire from Rome to the city of Byzantium on the Bosporus. The city is renamed Constantinople.

360   **Japan enters the scene**
The Korean Peninsula is conquered by a Japanese army.

410   **Sack of Rome**
The Visigoths, led by Alaric, loot and burn the city of Rome.

451   **Attila the Hun**
Led by Attila, a
large force of bar-
barian tribesmen
invades the Ro-
man Empire.

476   **Fall of Rome**
Traditional date
for the end of the
Roman Empire in
the West.
Odoacer, a Goth
serving as a gen-
eral in the Roman
army, deposes
Romulus Augus-
tulus.

Social Events

3200 B.C.   **Sumerians
organize**
Sumerian society
is divided into
formal classes
made up of
priests, soldiers,
and free citizens.

2500 B.C.   **Egypt's society
frozen**
Egypt's rigid so-
cial structure,
which lasts with
little modification
for 2000 years,
takes shape.

1700 B.C.   **Code of laws
written**
*The Code of
Hammurabi* is
the earliest exam-
ple of a written
law code.

1200 B.C.   **Caste system in
India**
The caste system
is introduced in
India by Aryan
invaders.

**1027 B.C.-
256 B.C.**   **China's Mandate
of Heaven**
The Chinese de-
velop a belief in a
"Mandate of
Heaven," one of
the first declara-
tions of a peo-
ple's right to re-
volt against an
unpopular gov-
ernment.

750 B.C.   **Ancient Greek society**
The poet Homer
presents a vivid
picture of the so-
cial structure of
ancient Greece in
the epics the *Iliad*
and the *Odyssey*.

594 B.C.   **Solon's reforms**
Solon institutes a
reform and codifi-
cation of the laws
and constitution
of the city-state
of Athens.

133 B.C.   **Reform in Rome**
Tiberius Grac-
chus, a noble-
man, is elected to
public office on a
platform of social
reform. His aim
is to break up
large estates and
redistribute land
to the poor.

123 B.C.   **Reformers fail**
Gaius Gracchus
fails in his at-
tempts to carry
through the land
reform program
proposed by his
brother Tiberius.

Note: All dates
given from this
point are dates
A.D.

212   **Edict of Caracalla**
Extends Roman
citizenship to all
free inhabitants
of the empire.

Religion

5000 B.C.   **Neolithic religion**
Neolithic peoples
decorate sacred
caves and build
stone temples to
worship various
animal-gods and
fertility god-
desses.

3500 B.C.   **New gods emerge**
People of the
Near East de-
velop highly for-
malized religions
revolving about
deities in human
form representing
cosmic forces and
fertility.

1370 B.C.   **Akhenaton reigns**
The Egyptian
King Akhenaton
attempts to intro-
duce monothe-
ism, the worship
of one god, into
Egypt's religious
system.

1200 B.C.   **Jews claim one
God**
The Hebrews,
also called Jews,
develop and
spread their idea
of one God.

Prehistory and Ancient Times
Religion (*Continued*)

600 B.C.   **Zoroaster's religion**
The Persian prophet Zoroaster formulates a religion that interprets the universe as a struggle between good and evil.

587 B.C.   **Temple destroyed**
The Temple in Jerusalem is destroyed by Babylonians who occupy the kingdom of Judah.

563 B.C.   **Buddha is born**
Buddha is born in Nepal. He founds Buddhism, which becomes one of the major religions of the world.

516 B.C.   **Second temple built**
The Hebrews complete the Second Temple in Jerusalem.

270 B.C.   **Hinduism formalized**
The collection of cults and beliefs that become the Hindu religion begins to be organized by the Brahmins.

8 B.C.   **Jesus is born**
Jesus of Nazareth is born in Judea, a Roman province. He is the founder of Christianity, which becomes the dominant religion of the Western Hemisphere.

Note: All dates given from this point on are dates A.D.

29   **Christ crucified**
Traditional date for the execution of Christ by the Romans in Jerusalem.

70   **Second temple razed**
Roman forces capture Jerusalem and destroy the Jews' Second Temple.

200   **Jewish laws compiled**
Rabbi Judah Hanasi completes the *Mishnah,* the first compilation of Jewish law and tradition.

249   **Christians persecuted**
The Roman Emperor Decius orders the first general persecution of Christians.

300   **Aksum converted**
The Kingdom of Aksum in Africa is converted to Christianity.

305   **Monasticism begins**
Saint Anthony forms the first Christian monastic community in the Egyptian desert.

313   **Edict of Milan**
Constantine, by the Edict of Milan, grants Christians in the Roman Empire freedom of religion.

325   **Christians consult**
The first ecumenical council of the Christian church meets in the city of Nicaea.

360   **Buddhism spreads**
Buddhist missionaries from China begin the conversion of the people of Japan.

392   **Christianity recognized**
Under Theodosius I, Christianity becomes the official state religion of the Roman Empire.

405   **Vulgate completed**
Saint Jerome completes the *Vulgate,* a revision of the Latin Bible which for centuries is the only version authorized by the Roman Catholic Church.

Philosophy

2700 B.C. **Imhotep the Sage**
The Egyptian Imhotep considers the rules of correct conduct for a proper life.

1100 B.C. **Egypt's pessimism**
The *Tales of Wenamun* consider the meaning of life.

600 B.C. **Milesian philosophers**
Traditional date for the formal beginning of Greek philosophy by Thales, Anaximander, and Anaximenes of the city of Miletus.

551 B.C. **Confucius born**
Confucius, the most respected and influential philosopher in Chinese history, is born. His ideas stress the need to develop moral character.

530 B.C. **Pythagoras teaches**
Pythagoras, a Greek philosopher, teaches that number is the essence of all things.

469 B.C. **Birth of Socrates**
The philosopher Socrates is born in Athens. He becomes a martyr to freedom of thought.

427 B.C. **Plato born**
Plato is born in Athens. He writes *The Republic,* a work that tries to define justice in a perfect state.

384 B.C. **Birth of Aristotle**
Aristotle, Plato's greatest pupil, is born. He is the foremost scholar of the ancient world.

124 B.C. **Confucius accepted**
The Chinese government establishes the Imperial University to educate government officials in Confucian ideals.

106 B.C. **Birth of Cicero**
Cicero becomes the leading Roman philosopher, specializing in ethics and jurisprudence.

Note: All dates given from this point are dates A.D.

161-180 **Roman Stoicism**
The Roman Emperor Marcus Aurelius becomes the leading exponent of the Stoic philosophy.

354-430 **St. Augustine**
The *City of God* and other writings by St. Augustine form the basis of philosophical thought during the Middle Ages.

Literature

2500 B.C. **Epic poems written**
The *Epic of Gilgamesh* and the *Epic of Creation,* the oldest epic poems in world literature, are written in Mesopotamia.

1800 B.C. **Egyptian literature**
The high point of ancient Egyptian literature with such classics as *King Khufu and the Magicians* and *The Shipwrecked Sailor* written.

750 B.C. **Greek epics written**
The Greek Homer composes the *Iliad* and the *Odyssey,* two famous classical epics.

500 B.C. **Hindu literature**
The classic Hindu religious epic, the *Mahabharata,* begins to take form.

500 B.C. **Lyric poetry begins**
Greek poets develop and use the lyric meter in poetry.

480 B.C.- **Greek drama**
404 B.C. **flourishes**
Greek dramatists
Sophocles, Euri-
pides, and Aes-
chylus develop
the tragedy. Aris-
tophanes writes
his most popular
comedies.

450 B.C. **Historical writing**
Herodotus, called
the "Father of
History," writes
a history of the
Persian Wars.

400 B.C. **History flourishes**
In the tradition of
Herodotus, the
Greek historians
Thucydides and
Xenephon con-
tinue the story of
Greece's conflict
with Persia.

70 B.C.- **Writings of Cicero**
43 B.C. The writings of
Cicero, a master
of Latin prose,
dominate Roman
literature during
his lifetime.

28 B.C. **Roman history**
The Roman histo-
rian Livy pub-
lishes his first
work.

19 B.C. **Virgil writes epic**
The Roman poet
Virgil writes the
Aeneid, an epic
poem considered
the greatest work
of Latin litera-
ture.

Note: All dates
from this point
are dates A.D.

50 **Chinese literature**
The Chinese his-
torian Pan Ku be-
gins compiling a
history of past
Chinese emper-
ors.

75 **Biography begins**
The Greek Plu-
tarch writes a se-
ries of biogra-
phies of the lives
of famous Greeks
and Romans.

80 **Tacitus writes**
The most famous
Roman historian
Tacitus begins
writing his fa-
mous study of
German tribes in
Gaul.

161- **The emperor-**
180 **writer**
The Emperor
Marcus Aurelius
writes and pub-
lishes his *Medita-
tions.*

The Arts

13,000 **Neolithic Spain**
B.C. Neolithic hunters
paint pictures of
animals on rock
walls and ceilings
of caves near Al-
tamira, Spain.

7500 B.C. **Neolithic Africa**
Neolithic hunters
in what is today
the Sahara paint
pictures on ex-
posed walls of
rock of people
hunting animals.

5000 B.C. **Prehistoric Italy**
Crudely engraved
pottery in Italy is
gradually re-
placed with re-
fined, attractively
painted vases.

4500 B.C. **Where Joshua**
fought
The walled city
of Jericho of
Biblical fame is
built. Potters
fashion glazed
ware and vessels
decorated with
geometric de-
signs.

4000 B.C. **Grecian idols**
Neolithic Greeks
form small sculp-
tures in both clay
and stone. Fe-
male idols are the
favorite subject.

3000 B.C. **Bronze age cul-**
ture
Using bronze,
craftsmen are
able to produce
more intricate
and sophisticated
jewelry and art-
works than neo-
lithic craftsmen
had been able to
make from stone.

2850 B.C.- **Egyptian architec-**
2052 B.C. **ture**
The monumental
Sphinx of Giza
and Pyramid of
Khufu rise in des-
ert sands.

2000 B.C.- **Isle of Crete**
1700 B.C. Minoan architects
design and build
huge, rambling

palaces on the Island of Crete.

1750 B.C.   **Egyptian jewelry**
Men and women wear collars of stringed beads, silver ear loops, and bracelets. Advances are made in the design of copper jewelry.

1347 B.C.-   **Egypt's legacy**
1335 B.C.   Egyptian craftsmen and artists produce a treasure of jewelry, ornaments, art objects, and decorated weapons and household items for King Tutankhamon.

1100 B.C.   **Iron is used**
The use of iron for the production of decorated weapons and jewelry begins.

438 B.C.   **The Greeks build**
The Parthenon, a temple to honor the goddess Athena, is built in Athens. The Parthenon marks the development of the classic Greek style.

300 B.C.   **Praxiteles sculpts**
Praxiteles creates a timeless masterpiece in a statue of Hermes, messenger of the gods.

200 B.C.-   **Classic Greek**
100 B.C.   **sculpture**
Aphrodite, a Greek goddess, is forever immortalized in marble. As Venus de Milo, she stands in the Louvre, Paris.

Note: All dates given from this point are dates A.D.

200-   **Early frescoes**
300   **done**
Early Christians decorate their underground graves, or catacombs, with frescoes. The paintings are spiritual and symbolic of life to come.

Science and Technology

8000 B.C.   **Agriculture begins**
The planting of crops and the domestication of wild animals begin in the Middle East.

7000 B.C.-   **Tools improved**
3600 B.C.   Neolithic and early Bronze Age people develop important tools such as the wheel, plow, and water wheel.

3000 B.C.-   **Writing begins**
2500 B.C.   The earliest known examples of cuneiform writing begin to be used in Sumer.

2800 B.C.-   **Pyramids built**
2100 B.C.   Leaders of the ancient world in engineering and architecture, the Egyptians build huge pyramids along the Nile River.

2000 B.C.   **First major canal**
The Egyptians construct a canal connecting the Nile River and the Red Sea.

1750 B.C.   **Trade grows**
Egyptian, Babylonian, and Minoan trade and industry flourish. Mathematics and astronomy are studied extensively.

1500 B.C.   **Iron used**
The Hittites introduce the use of iron to western Asia and Egypt.

1500 B.C.-   **Chinese bronze**
1027 B.C.   **work**
During the Shang dynasty, the Chinese become skilled at casting bronze.

1400 B.C.   **The Phoenician alphabet**
The Phoenicians develop an alphabet of 22 characters. This alphabet is so successful that it is adopted by both the Greeks and Romans.

1000 B.C. **Phoenicians explore**
Great seagoing traders, the Phoenicians are probably the first Mediterranean people to sail the Atlantic Ocean, perhaps reaching the British Isles.

600 B.C. **Mayas develop calendar**
The Mayas develop an accurate calendar.

500 B.C. **Medical school founded**
Darius I founds a medical school in Egypt. It is the first scientific institution supported by a government.

460 B.C.- **Athens is trade**
430 B.C. **center**
Athens becomes the center of manufacturing and trade in the Mediterranean region.

400 B.C. **Medical advances**
The Greek physician Hippocrates teaches that diseases have natural, not supernatural, causes.

330 B.C. **Aristotle and science**
Aristotle's studies in logic and the classification of plants and animals contribute to the foundations of science.

312 B.C. **Appian Way begun**
The Appian Way is begun. It is the first important link in an extensive system of Roman roads.

300 B.C. **Euclidean geometry**
The Greek mathematician Euclid formulates the basic concepts of geometry.

300 B.C. **Numerals developed**
The Hindus develop the symbols that we still use today for numerals.

287 B.C. **Archimedes born**
Archimedes, a great Greek scientist, is born. He discovers the principle of specific gravity, the law of floating bodies, and the theory of the lever.

221 B.C.- **Great Wall of**
206 B.C. **China**
The Great Wall of China is completed by the Ch'in kings. The wall protects the country from invaders.

50 B.C. **Romans build**
Roman engineers continue construction of sophisticated aqueducts and bridges. Experiments in the use of concrete are begun.

Note: All dates given from this point are dates A.D.

105 **Paper invented**
The Chinese invent paper, using the bark of mulberry trees.

150 **Anatomy studied**
The Greek physician Galen lays the foundation for the study of anatomy and physiology.

150 **Ptolemy's theory**
The Greek astronomer Ptolemy develops a theory that the earth is the center of the universe.

The Middle Period

Political Events

486 **Frankish state founded**
Traditional date for
the founding of the
Merovingian Dynasty
and the Frankish
Kingdom.

497 **Gothic Italy**
Theodoric, King of
the Ostrogoths, is rec-
ognized ruler of Italy
by the emperor of the
Roman Empire in the
East.

500 **Huns in India**
Hun raiders weaken
the power of Aryan
kingdoms in India.

527- **Eastern Empire solidi-**
565 **fied**
The Eastern Empire is
solidified during the
reign of Emperor Jus-
tinian I at Constanti-
nople.

589 **China revival**
The Sui Dynasty is
victorious over an alli-
ance of petty kings
and warlords.

622 **A new power**
Traditional date for
the beginning of the
Commonwealth of Is-
lam by Muhammad in
the city of Medina in
Arabia.

635- **Islamic expansion**
738 Under a succession of
vigorous generals,
Muslim political and
military power ex-
pands from Arabia.

645 **Japan reorganizes**
The Fujiwara clan
seizes power in Japan,
initiating a period of
sweeping political re-
form.

661 **Muslim Empire**
The Omayyad Cali-
phate is founded. Cap-
ital of the first Muslim
Empire is established
at Damascus in Syria.

690 **West African Empire**
The Songhai Empire
on the middle Niger
dominates West Af-
rica.

711 **Muslims in Spain**
The Muslims begin
their conquest of
Spain.

732 **Battle of Tours**
Led by Charles Mar-
tel, the Franks beat
back a Muslim inva-
sion of Europe.

751 **New Frankish Dynasty**
The Merovingian Dy-
nasty falls and the
Carolingian Dynasty is
founded by Pepin the
Short, a descendant of
Charles Martel.

768- **Charles the Great**
814 The son of Pepin the
Short, Charles shares
rule with his brother
until 771. Charles is
known in history as
Charlemagne.

800 **New western empire**
Pope Leo III crowns
Charlemagne emperor
of the Roman Empire
in the West.

843 **Treaty of Verdun**
Charlemagne's empire
is divided into east-
ern, central, and west-
ern kingdoms.

862 **First Russian Dynasty**
Rurik, a Viking war-
lord, captures the
Russian city-state of
Novgorod.

871- **Alfred of England**
899 Alfred the Great,
Saxon King of Eng-
land, battles Viking
raiders and begins the
rebuilding of England.

878 **Vikings defeated**
Alfred the Great de-
feats the Vikings at
the Battle of Eding-
ton.

880 **Expansion in Russia**
The Viking Prince
Oleg establishes con-
trol over the city-state
of Novgorod and the
city-state of Kiev.
This marks the found-
ing of the Kievan
Principality.

935- **Unrest in Japan**
941 Local warlords and
military clans break
the power of the cen-
tral government. Ja-
pan is divided by doz-
ens of warring
factions.

960   **Sung Dynasty**
A period of weakness
and civil war in China
is ended by the acces-
sion of the Sung Dy-
nasty.

962   **Holy Roman Empire
founded**
Otto I, the Great, a
descendant of Charle-
magne, is crowned
Emperor. He changes
his title from Roman
Emperor in the West
to Holy Roman Em-
peror.

969   **Fatimids conquer
Egypt**
The Fatimid Dynasty
gains control of Egypt
and founds the city of
Cairo.

987   **Capetian Dynasty
founded**
Hugh Capet is elected
King of the West
Franks. His state be-
comes the basis for
the modern state of
France.

995   **Fujiwara revival**
Michinaga, head of
the Fujiwara clan,
helps to restore the
authority of the cen-
tral government of Ja-
pan.

998-   **Muslim India expands**
1030   Mahmud of Ghazni
leads raids into Hindu
India.

1000   **Kingdom of Ghana**
The Kingdom of
Ghana in West Africa,
with its capital at the
city of Kumbi,
reaches its high point.

1037   **Iran conquered**
The Muslim Seljuk
Turks conquer most
of the Muslim Arab
kingdoms in Iran.

1066   **Normans invade Eng-
land**
William the Duke of
Normandy invades
England and defeats
the Anglo-Saxon King
Harold at the Battle of
Hastings.

1071   **Battle of Manzikert**
The Seljuk Turks de-
stroy Byzantine power
in Asia Minor.

1100   **New African states**
The Kingdom of Diara
and the Kingdom of
Sosso succeed Ghana
as the leading powers
in West Africa.

1154- **England consolidated**
1399   The House of Plantag-
enet begins the organi-
zation of the state of
England.

1180- **France consolidated**
1223   Philip II Augustus,
King of France, con-
solidates the French
monarchy and formal-
izes the organization
of the French state.

1187   **Jerusalem recaptured**
A Muslim army led by
Saladin recaptures the
city of Jerusalem from
Christian Europeans.

1190   **Mongols rise**
The war chief Temujin
begins the creation of
a Mongol Empire in
central Asia.

1192   **Shogun rules Japan**
Yoritomo, leader of
the Minamoto clan,
becomes the first Sho-
gun, or "Great Gen-
eral," to rule Japan.
The office of emperor
becomes purely cere-
monial.

1200   **Growth of Mali**
The Kingdom of Mali
politically and militar-
ily dominates West
Africa.

1206   **Mongol Empire
founded**
Temujin is elected
Genghis Khan, or
"Emperor within the
Seas" of the Mongols.

1215   **Magna Carta**
The English nobility
forces King John to
accept a charter rec-
ognizing the rights un-
der the law of English
nobles.

1237- **Mongols in Europe**
1240   Mongol armies occupy
Russia and attack Po-
land and Hungary.

1271   **Mongols in China**
Kublai Khan leads the
Mongols to the final
conquest of China. He
founds the Yüan Dy-
nasty, which rules
China until 1368.

1273   **Rise of the Hapsburgs**
Rudolf of Hapsburg is
elected King of Ger-
many. The Hapsburg

family plays an impor-
tant role in European
politics until the 20th
century.

1274- **Mongols in Japan**
1281 The Japanese govern-
ment turns back two
attempts by Mongols
from China to invade
Japan.

1290 **Ottoman State begins**
The Seljuk prince
Othman founds a prin-
cipality called Oth-
manli. From this base,
the Turkish Muslim
state that becomes the
Ottoman Empire
grows.

1300 **Italian revival**
Italian city-states such
as Florence, Venice,
and Genoa begin
achieving political
power through domi-
nation of Europe's
trade and banking.

1312- **Mandingo Empire**
1337 The Emperor Mansa
Musa, a vigorous po-
litical and military
leader, consolidates a
brilliant and powerful
state centered in the
city of Timbuktu in
West Africa.

1336- **Civil war in Japan**
1392 A long period of un-
rest occurs, during
which various clans
battle for control of
Japan.

1337 **Hundred Years' War
begins**
The war is fought be-
tween France and

England, over English
claims to the throne
of France. The war
ends in 1453 with Eng-
land's claims
thwarted.

1346 **Battle of Crécy**
During the Hundred
Years' War, this bat-
tle marks the defeat
of French knights by
English bowmen.

1356 **Battle of Poitiers**
During the Hundred
Years' War, the
French forces are dec-
imated by an English
army led by the Black
Prince.

1368 **Ming Dynasty founded**
The Ming Dynasty be-
gins its 300-year rule
of China.

1369- **Mongol unrest**
1405 Tamerlane, a Mongol
Khan, ravages central
Asia, Mesopotamia,
India, and Turkey.

1380 **Battle of Kulikovo**
A Russian force de-
feats a Mongol army,
marking the beginning
of the Mongol with-
drawal from Russia.

1421 **New capital for China**
The capital of China is
moved to the city of
Peking.

1428 **Battle of Orléans**
Joan of Arc leads a
French army to vic-
tory over the English.
The battle is the turn-
ing point toward a

final French victory in
the Hundred Years'
War.

1453 **Constantinople falls**
The Ottoman Turks
capture the city of
Constantinople. This
marks the end of the
Roman Empire in the
East.

1455 **Wars of the Roses
begin**
The House of York
and the House of Lan-
caster battle for the
throne of England.

1462- **Ivan III, the Great**
1505 A brilliant political
leader, he begins the
consolidation of the
modern Russian state.

1485 **Wars of the Roses end**
Henry Tudor, mem-
ber of a branch of the
House of Lancaster,
defeats Richard III of
the House of York at
the Battle of Bos-
worth Field.

1492 **Spain consolidated**
King Ferdinand and
Queen Isabella com-
plete the reconquest
of Spain. The last
Muslims are expelled
from Spanish soil.

Social Events

527- **Justinian's Code com-
565 piled**
The Code of Justinian
organizes Roman law.
The code becomes the
basis for law as it de-
velops in many Euro-
pean and Latin-Amer-
ican countries.

The Middle Period
Social Events (*Continued*)

700-   European feudalism
1000   Europe's social structure is frozen by feu-
dalism, which organ-
izes society into
rigidly defined classes.

970   University started
The University of Al-
Azhar is founded in
Cairo. The Arab Mus-
lims are among the
first to establish uni-
versities.

1000-   The guild system
1200   Merchants and craftsmen form guilds to
protect profits and as
mutual aid societies.

1085   Domesday survey
William the Con-
queror orders a cen-
sus of people and
goods in England.

1100-   Universities in Europe
1300   Universities develop
out of schools at ca-
thedrals and monas-
teries. The universi-
ties organize and
formalize the teaching
of law, medicine, and
theology.

1100-   Rise of towns
1400   New social structures
begin to emerge as
towns, which had de-
cayed since Roman
times, begin to reor-
ganize.

1185-   Kamakura period
1333   A feudal structure is
gradually formalized
and consolidated in
Japan.

1300   League formed
Merchants from cities
in northern Germany
form the Hanseatic
League to protect
their commercial in-
terests, and advance
their social goals.

1347-   The Black Death
1350   The Black Death, a
form of bubonic
plague, destroys a
fourth of the popula-
tion of Europe. Eu-
rope's social structure
is completely over-
turned as a result of
the plague.

1450-   Slave trade flourishes
1865   Europeans take as
many as 10 million
people from Africa to
work as slaves.

Religion

**480   Church's influence
grows**
After the fall of
Rome, the Roman
Catholic Church be-
comes the most pow-
erful political and so-
cial influence in
Western Europe.

500   *Talmud* completed
Jewish scholars in
Mesopotamia com-
plete the *Talmud*.

500   Nubians converted
The Nubian kingdoms
in Africa are con-
verted to Christianity.

529   Monte Cassino opens
St. Benedict founds
the monastery of
Monte Cassino and
organizes what be-
comes the Benedictine
order of monks.

**610   Muhammad begins
preaching**
Muhammad, founder
of Islam, begins
preaching in Mecca.

622   Islamic era begins
Muhammad travels se-
cretly to Medina. His
journey, called the
"Hegira," marks the
traditional beginning
of the religion of Is-
lam.

652   *Koran* written
The teachings of Mu-
hammad are collected
into a book, called the
Koran. The *Koran* re-
mains to this day the
basic foundation of
the religion of Islam.

756   Donation of Pepin
Pepin the Short, King
of the West Franks,
grants the papacy au-
thority over lands in
central Italy, thus es-
tablishing the Papal
States.

1000-   Judaic Golden Age
1300   The Jewish community in Spain and
North Africa, under
tolerant Muslim gov-
ernments, enjoys a
spiritual and cultural
golden age.

1054   Christianity divided
Rivalries between the
church at Rome and
the church at Con-
stantinople result in a
separation between
Eastern Orthodox
churches and the Ro-
man Catholic Church.

1099 **First Crusade**
Led by Godfrey of
Bouillon, Christian
crusaders capture the
city of Jerusalem from
the Muslims.

1231 **Inquisition begins**
Pope Gregory IX be-
gins the Inquisi-
tion, a special court to
investigate people sus-
pected of heresy.

1302 **Papal power grows**
Pope Boniface VIII is-
sues a papal docu-
ment, *Unam Sanc-
tam.* It declares that
the kings of nations
are subject to the
Holy Roman emperor,
and the emperor's
power is derived from
the pope.

1378- **Papacy divided**
1417 The *Great Schism* results in several Roman
Catholic churchmen
claiming to be the
pope at the same
time. The dispute is
settled at the Council
of Constance.

1380 **English Bible**
The first complete
English translation of
the Bible is made by
John Wycliffe, an
English priest.

1492 **Spanish Jews expelled**
Ferdinand and Isa-
bella expel all Jews
from Spain

Philosophy
524 **Death of Boethius**
Boethius, the last
classical philosopher,
is executed.

600 **Chinese influence
spreads**
The ethical system of
Confucius spreads to
Japan where it influ-
ences Japanese
thought.

800 **Carolingian revival**
Philosophy and learn-
ing are revived at the
court of Charlemagne
by such men as Al-
cuin and Einhard.

1100- **European philosophy**
1200 The height of scholas-
ticism in Europe, fea-
turing such figures as
Bernard of Clairvaux,
Anselm, and Peter
Abélard.

1150 **Classical revival**
The Muslim philoso-
pher Averroës revives
interest in Plato and
Aristotle.

1225- **St. Thomas Aquinas**
1274 A great theologian
and philosopher of the
Christian church, St.
Thomas Aquinas ar-
gues that faith rests
on a rational founda-
tion and that philoso-
phy does not conflict
with Christianity.

1300- **Rise of humanism**
1500 European philosophy
begins to turn from
study of the spiritual
to study of the mate-
rial as "people" be-
come the center of the
universe.

Literature
700 **A new epic**
The Anglo-Saxon epic
poem, *Beowulf,* is
written.

712 **Literature in Japan**
The first known exam-
ple of Japanese litera-
ture, the *Record of
Ancient Things,* is
published.

780 **Early encyclopedia**
The Chinese historian
Tu Yu compiles an
encyclopedia, a chro-
nology of world his-
tory.

810 **European revival**
After a long period of
decay, a revival of lit-
erature in Europe be-
gins with publication
of Einhard's *Life of
Charlemagne.*

935 **Japanese poetry**
The height of Japa-
nese classical poetry
is marked by the pub-
lication of the *Kokin-
shū,* an anthology of
over a thousand well-
known poems.

1000 **Japanese classic**
The noblewoman
Lady Murasaki writes
The Tale of Genji, still
considered to be the
greatest Japanese
novel.

1100 **Frankish epic poetry**
The French epic
poem, *Song of Ro-
land,* is written.

1100 **Muslim poetry popular**
A Persian Muslim
poet, Omar Khayyam,
writes *The Rubaiyat,*
a collection of qua-
trains that gains popu-
larity throughout the
Muslim world.

Literature (*Continued*)

1200   Age of German epics
The German epic,
*Song of the Nibe-
lungs,* is collected and
written down.

1321   Dante popular
The Italian author
Dante Alighieri writes
the *Divine Comedy,*
the first serious liter-
ary work written in a
modern European lan-
guage.

1348-   *The Decameron*
1353   *The Decameron,* a
collection of short sto-
ries, is written by Gio-
vanni Boccaccio. His
style is copied by
writers all over Eu-
rope.

1350-   Petrarch writes poems
1374   A founder of the humanist movement, Pe-
trarch writes more
than 400 poems.

1350   Revival in Japan
After a period of liter-
ary decline, there oc-
curs a revival of liter-
ature symbolized in
the style of lyric
drama called *No.*

1377   Robin Hood
The first stories fea-
turing Robin Hood ap-
pear in England.

1400   Chaucer publishes
The English writer
Geoffrey Chaucer
publishes his major
work, *The Canterbury
Tales.*

The Arts

532-   Hagia Sophia built
537   Byzantine Emperor
Justinian builds the
Church of the Holy
Wisdom in Constanti-
nople. It is better
known as the Hagia
Sophia.

540-   Early music
604   The Gregorian chant,
a form of singing with-
out musical accom-
paniment, is devel-
oped by churchmen
under St. Gregory I,
the Great.

700-   Manuscripts illumi-
800   **nated**
The Books of Kells,
an illuminated manu-
script, is completed.

**800   Charlemagne
and the arts**
Charlemagne builds
the cathedral at Aix-
la-Chapelle. He
encourages a revival
of art.

900   Celtic stonework
Celtic stonemasons in
Ireland carve com-
plex, highly decorated
crosses to mark
graves.

1000   Jewelers flourish
Rulers wear crowns of
gold and silver stud-
ded with precious
stones.

1100   New art style
A style of architec-
ture, sculpture, and
painting called the ro-
manesque reaches its
highest development.

The style is derived
from classical Roman
forms.

1163   Early gothic style
One hundred and fifty
years of work begins
on Notre Dame Ca-
thedral in Paris,
France. The gothic
style replaces roman-
esque as the prevail-
ing art form in Eu-
rope.

1200   Classic Chinese artist
Hsia Kuei paints
idealized Chinese
landscapes on silk
scrolls. He paints in
ink.

1200   The Byzantine style
Byzantine artists de-
velop a distinctive
style, concentrating
on the outward
expression of inner
spirituality.

1305   Painting revival
The Italian master
Giotto paints *The De-
scent from the Cross.*
He introduces realism
into paintings.

1320-   Realism reinforced
1330   Simone Martini paints
the St. Martino chapel
below the church of
St. Francis of Assisi
in Siena, Italy. The
pictures are scenes
from the life of St.
Martin and the style
continues the trend to-
ward realism begun by
Giotto.

1359   Viennese gothic
Work begins on the
nave of St. Stephen's

Cathedral in the city of Vienna.

1415 **Donatello masterpiece**
The Italian sculptor Donatello creates *St. George* in marble. A relief below the statue pictures *St. George Killing the Dragon.*

1434 **Flemish symbolism**
Jan van Eyck paints *The Arnolfini Wedding.* Christ is represented by a single lighted candle.

1450 **Monk and artist**
Fra Angelico, a Dominican monk and artist, paints one of his most famous creations. It is titled *The Annunciation.*

1450- **Persian art**
1537 Persian painter Kamal ad-Din Bihzad excels in painting miniatures. He draws both battle and nature scenes.

1478 **Classical revival**
Sandro Botticelli is inspired by the myth of

Venus. His painting, *Birth of Venus,* marks a revival of classicism in art.

1485 **Italian genius**
Leonardo da Vinci paints the *Madonna of the Rocks.* He is one of the greatest of the Italian Renaissance painters.

Science and Technology

500 **Theories of the earth**
Hindu astronomers and mathematicians develop theories about the rotation of the earth.

600 **Zero developed**
Hindu mathematicians develop the concept of zero and the use of decimal places in mathematics.

770 **Wood-block printing**
The Chinese invent wood-block printing.

800 **Number system adopted**
The Arabs adopt from India the number sys-

tem that we use today.

960- **Inventions in China**
1279 During the Sung Dynasty, the Chinese invent the magnetic compass, gunpowder, and movable type for printing.

1267 **Roger Bacon**
Roger Bacon, an English scientist, writes *Opus maius,* a summary of his system of knowledge.

1346 **Gunpowder in Europe**
Gunpowder is used during the Battle of Crécy, probably for the first time in Europe.

1440 **Movable type used**
Johannes Gutenberg, a German printer, is the first European to use movable type.

1454 **First book printed**
Johannes Gutenberg prints the Latin Bible, the first large book printed in Europe using movable type.

The Early Modern Period

Political Events

1492 **America reached**
Christopher Columbus reaches land in the Western Hemisphere.

1493 **Songhai revival**
Led by Askia Muhammad, the Songhai Empire enjoys a final

burst of military expansion.

1497 **Cabot in Canada**
John Cabot explores islands off the coast of what is today Canada.

1498 **Da Gama in India**
Vasco da Gama, a Portuguese navigator,

reaches India by sailing around Africa.

1509 **Henry VIII of England**
Henry VIII ascends the throne of England.

1516 **Hapsburg dynasty grows**
Charles Hapsburg becomes Charles I, King

Political Events (*Continued*)

of Spain, and Charles
V, Holy Roman Em-
peror.

1517 **Songhai defeated**
The Haussa Confeder-
ation wins a war
against Songhai.

1517 **Luther**
Martin Luther's break
with the Church of
Rome causes political
unrest in Europe.

1519- **Cortés in Mexico**
1521 The Aztec Empire in
what is today Mexico
is destroyed by Her-
nando Cortés.

1520 **Ottomans expand**
Suleiman I, the Mag-
nificent, greatest of
the Turkish sultans,
ascends the throne.

1526 **The Mogul Empire**
Babar, a descendant
of Tamerlane, estab-
lishes Muslim control
over most of northern
India.

1529 **Turks at Vienna**
The forces of Sulei-
man I penetrate Eu-
rope to the city of Vi-
enna where they
mount an unsuccess-
ful siege.

1532 **Peru invaded**
A Spanish force led
by Francisco Pizarro
lands in what is today
Peru.

1533 **First czar**
Ivan IV, the Terrible,
is the first Russian
ruler to use the title
czar.

1537 **Italian decline**
The Italian city-states
begin to fall under the
control of France,
Spain, and the Holy
Roman Empire.

1543 **Portuguese in Japan**
First Europeans visit
Japan, establishing
trade relations be-
tween Europe and Ja-
pan.

1552 **Russian expansion**
Russian forces move
eastward, capturing
control of the Volga
River.

1555 **Peace of Augsburg**
Temporarily halts civil
war in the Holy Ro-
man Empire.

1556 **New king in Spain**
The Holy Roman Em-
peror Charles abdi-
cates. He leaves the
Kingdom of Spain to
his son, Philip II.

1558 **Elizabeth I, Tudor**
Elizabeth I becomes
Queen of England.
She reigns until 1603,
during a period of ex-
pansion.

1562- **Civil war in France**
1598 Catholics and Protestants (the Huguenots)
fight eight wars for
control of the French
throne.

1568- **Japan active**
1600 One of the most vigorous periods in Japa-
nese history, marked
by the expansion of
Japanese influence
abroad.

1571 **Empire of Kanem**
The Empire of Kanem
in Africa gains control
of most of the terri-
tory around Lake
Chad.

1571 **Battle of Lepanto**
An allied European
fleet defeats the Turk-
ish fleet, marking the
beginning of the end
of Muslim control of
the Mediterranean
Sea.

1588 **Armada defeated**
The key battle in a
major war between
Spain and England,
the Spanish Armada,
or fleet, is completely
defeated.

1589 **New French dynasty**
The House of Bour-
bon, which rules
France until 1792,
gains the throne.

1592 **Japanese expansion**
A Japanese army of
over 200,000 men in-
vades Korea but is de-
feated.

1598 **Edict of Nantes**
The civil wars in
France are ended by
the Edict of Nantes.

1600- **Tokugawa Shogunate**
1867 The capital of Japan is
established at the city
of Edo (Tokyo). The

Tokugawa family gains and retains the title of Shogun. The title of Emperor remains purely honorary as shoguns rule Japan.

1603   House of Stuart
King James VI of Scotland becomes James I of England as the Tudor family dies out.

1608   Quebec founded
The French explorer Champlain founds the city of Quebec.

1613   Romanov rule in Russia
Michael Romanov becomes Czar of all the Russians, founding the dynasty that rules Russia until 1917.

1618-   The Thirty Years' War
1648 What is today Germany is devastated by 4 major wars that are together called the Thirty Years' War.

1624   Richelieu in France
Cardinal Richelieu becomes chief minister of France.

1627   Shah Jahan rules India
The Mogul emperor Shah Jahan gains the throne of India.

1642-   Civil War in England
1648 The Roundheads (Puritan supporters of Parliament) battle the Cavaliers (Anglican supporters of the king) for control of England's government.

1643-   Louis XIV in France
1715 The reign of Louis XIV, the most famous of the French monarchs. France pursues a vigorous policy designed to control Europe.

1644   Manchus conquer China
The Manchus, a group of people from what is today Manchuria, gain control of China and rule until 1912.

1648   Treaty of Westphalia
The treaty ends the Thirty Years' War.

1649   English monarchy falls
The parliamentary party, victorious in the Civil War, executes King Charles I.

1652   Cape Town founded
Dutch settlers led by Jan van Riebeeck found the city and Cape Colony at the southern tip of Africa.

1653   Cromwell gains power
Control of England, which is now a commonwealth (republic), is seized by Oliver Cromwell.

1656   Ottoman revival begins
The decline of the Ottoman Empire is temporarily reversed by grand vizier (prime minister) Muhammad Kiuprili.

1660   English monarchy restored
Parliament restores the monarchy. Charles II becomes king.

1660   Mandingo Empire falls
The Kingdom of Segu and the Kingdom of Kaarta replace the Mandingo Empire as the chief states along the upper Niger in Africa.

1682-   Liberation of Hungary
1699 After having occupied Hungary for many years, the Ottoman Turks are driven out by the armies of the Holy Roman Empire.

1688-   The Glorious Revolu-
1689 **tion**
King James II, in conflict with Parliament, flees from England. Parliament offers the throne to James's daughter Mary, and her husband William of Orange.

1689-   Peter I of Russia
1725 Known as Peter the Great, this czar begins to modernize Russia.

1697-   Charles XII of Sweden
1718 For a short period of time, Sweden becomes a first-class power. Charles follows a vigorous political and military policy in East Europe.

Social Events

1500-   Europe's middle class
1700 The feudal structure decays as the traditional nobility is gradually replaced by a rising middle class made up of bankers, merchants, and successful craftsmen.

1689   **English Bill of Rights**
William and Mary, joint rulers of England, accept the Bill of Rights. This document assures the basic civil rights of English citizens.

Religion

1517   **Reformation begins**
The Protestant Reformation begins when Martin Luther, a Roman Catholic priest, protests certain practices of the Roman Catholic Church.

1520-   **Reformation spreads**
1536   Swedish and Danish kings make Lutheranism the state religion of Sweden, Finland, Norway, and Denmark.

1534   **English reformation**
An act of Parliament declares that the king, not the pope, is the head of the church in England.

1536   **Calvin prominent**
The Institutes of the Christian Religion by John Calvin offers a systematic presentation of Protestant beliefs.

1545-   **The Counter Reforma-**
1563   **tion**
At the Council of Trent, the Roman Catholic Church responds to the Protestant Reformation with internal reforms. Many of the abuses that had caused the Protestant Reformation are corrected.

1555   **Peace of Augsburg**
A compromise, known as the peace of Augsburg, allows the ruler of each German state to determine whether Catholicism or Lutheranism will be its official religion.

1560   **Scottish Reformation**
Protestantism, introduced by John Knox, becomes the state religion of Scotland.

1563   ***Thirty-nine Articles***
The *Thirty-nine Articles* organize the teachings of Anglicanism, a moderate form of Protestantism, which becomes the state religion of England.

1598   **Edict of Nantes**
The Edict of Nantes gives French Protestants religious freedom and civil rights.

1611   **The King James Bible**
Scholars complete a new version of the Bible in the English language as authorized by King James.

1647   **Quakers founded**
The Society of Friends, also called Quakers, is founded in England.

Philosophy

1530-   **The social contract**
1596   The French philosopher Jean Bodin introduces the idea that the state is the result of a social contract.

1532   ***The Prince* published**
In *The Prince,* Niccolò Machiavelli, an Italian statesman, urges rulers to use any means to achieve their goals.

1533-   **Essays by Montaigne**
1592   In a series of essays, the French writer Montaigne expresses his doubt about the ability of reason to find truth.

1605   **The scientific method**
Francis Bacon, an English philosopher, writes *The Advancement of Learning.* He calls for the development of a logical methodology for the study of natural phenomena.

1632   **Galileo's masterpiece**
Galileo, considered the founder of modern experimental science, writes *A Dialogue on the Two Principal Systems of the World.*

1637-   **Age of Descartes**
1650   The French philosopher René Descartes says that truth can be found through the use of reason alone. He is considered the founder of modern philosophy.

1651 **The *Leviathan***
English political philosopher Thomas Hobbes publishes his major work, *Leviathan,* a work studying man's relationship to the state.

1663 **Spinoza writes**
In his writings, the Dutch philosopher Baruch Spinoza writes that the highest good man can attain is the intellectual love of God.

1685- **Berkeley's "idealism"**
1753 George Berkeley, an Irish philosopher, argues that nothing exists unless it is perceived by the mind. His philosophy is called "idealism."

1690 **John Locke**
An English philosopher, John Locke, publishes his major work, *An Essay Concerning Human Understanding.* His writing has great influence on political science.

Literature
1500 **Erasmus shakes Europe**
Christian humanist Desiderius Erasmus writes *Praise of Folly,* ridiculing the manners of the day.

1516 ***Utopia* written**
An English scholar, Thomas More, writes *Utopia,* an account of an ideal society.

1532- **Works by Rabelais**
1534 A Frenchman, François Rabelais, writes *Gargantua and Pantagruel,* a comic satire of French society.

1599- **Height of Shakespeare**
1608 At the height of his career, William Shakespeare writes several comedies and almost all of the tragedies which have made him the world's most famous playwright.

1600 **Japanese drama**
The classical Japanese dramatic form, the Kabuki, is developed.

1605 **Cervantes publishes**
The Spanish writer Miguel de Cervantes publishes his great work, *Don Quixote.*

1616 **Jonson famous**
Ben Jonson is the first playwright to publish an edition of his own works.

1635 **De Vega dies**
The most noted of the early Spanish writers, Lope de Vega, dies.

1636 **New French drama**
Pierre Corneille, called the founder of French heroic comedy, stages *The Cid,* a play which sets new standards for drama.

1662 **A Molière masterpiece**
Jean Baptiste Poquelin (Molière), the greatest French writer of comedy, produces *The School for Wives,* his first stage triumph.

1664 **Racine begins**
Jean Racine stages his first tragedy, *La Thébaïde.*

1667 **Milton's masterpiece**
English poet John Milton writes the great epic, *Paradise Lost.*

1681 **Poem by Dryden**
English poet laureate John Dryden writes the poem *Absalom and Achitophel.*

The Arts
1498- **The *Pietà* completed**
1499 At age 23, Michelangelo creates the *Pietà.* In this sculpture Mary cradles the lifeless body of Christ.

1503 ***Mona Lisa* completed**
Da Vinci completes what has become the world's most famous painting, the *Mona Lisa.*

1504 **Raphael emerges**
Raphael, Italian Renaissance painter, paints the *Marriage of the Virgin.* It is one of his early masterpieces.

1506 **Da Vinci's influence**
Influenced by Da Vinci's *Madonna of the Rocks,* Raphael paints the *Madonna of the Goldfinch.*

The Early Modern Period
The Arts (*Continued*)

1511   Michelangelo as painter
Michelangelo, known primarily as a sculptor, is immortalized as a painter by his work in the Sistine Chapel in the Vatican.

1550   Book of Kings
Early kings of Persia are illustrated in the *Book of Kings*. It is one of the greatest works of Persian miniaturists.

1565   Flemish master
Pieter Bruegel the Elder, a great Flemish master, paints *Return of the Hunters*, a classic of the early Flemish style.

1575   English church music
Thomas Tallis, called the "Father of English Church Music," joins William Byrd to publish a set of motets, a kind of church music. The title is *Sacred Songs for Chorus*.

1581   First ballet
A royal wedding in Paris plays host to Italian dancers performing the *Ballet Comique de la Reine*.

1586   A new style
El Greco of Spain joins the great masters of all times with his painting *The Burial of Count Orgaz*. El Greco's use of slightly distorted forms sets new styles for art.

1598   Bernini born
Gian Lorenzo Bernini, baroque artist who designs the plaza of St. Peter's Church in Rome, is born in Italy.

1611   Peter Paul Rubens
Rubens, the Flemish master, helps to define the baroque style in his oil, *Elevation of the Cross*.

1642   Rembrandt prominent
The Night Watch, the most famous of Rembrandt's paintings, is completed. He paints many religious and mythological scenes.

1653   Taj Mahal built
The Indian ruler Shah Jahan builds an exquisite tomb, the Taj Mahal.

1660   Painted sunlight
Young Woman with a Water Jug is painted in oils by Jan Vermeer.

1685-   Age of Bach
1750   Johann Sebastian Bach, as composer, musician, and choirmaster, sets the format for what is called the baroque style in music.

Science and Technology

1500   Da Vinci's experiments
Leonardo da Vinci uses observation and experiments to make many discoveries in anatomy, aerodynamics, and architectural engineering.

1543   Modern astronomy
The Polish astronomer Nicolaus Copernicus rediscovers the theory that the earth moves around the sun. He lays the foundation for modern astronomy.

1600   Modern science founded
The Italian physicist Galileo founds modern experimental science.

1609   Astronomy expands
Johannes Kepler establishes astronomy as an exact science.

1628   Harvey publishes
William Harvey publishes his theory on the circulation of blood.

1650   Microscope made
Anton van Leeuwenhoek produces the first practical microscope.

1687   The new physics
Sir Isaac Newton publishes the *Principia*, which summarizes basic laws of mechanics.

European Ascendancy

Political Events

1700-1721 Great Northern War
Sweden is thoroughly defeated and replaced by Russia as the leading power in the Baltic.

1701-1714 War of Spanish Succession
An alliance of England, Holland, and the Holy Roman Empire goes to war against Louis XIV of France, who has established his grandson as King of Spain. The allies fear union of France and Spain.

1713 Treaty of Utrecht
The treaty marks the official end of the War of Spanish Succession though some fighting continues until 1714.

1713-1740 Rise of Prussia
Under the leadership of King Frederick William I, Prussia begins its rise to leadership in Germany.

1714 New English dynasty
The Stuart dynasty dies out without direct heirs, and the House of Hanover is given the throne.

1717 The English in India
The British East India Company begins its penetration of India.

1740-1786 Frederick II, the Great
Under the vigorous political and military leadership of Frederick II, Prussia becomes a leading power.

1740-1748 Austrian War
Also known as the War of Austrian Succession, the war begins when Maria Theresa inherits the throne of Austria. European monarchs, led by Frederick II of Prussia, refuse to recognize the right of a woman to inherit this throne.

1751 Chinese in Tibet
A Chinese force invades and occupies Tibet.

1756-1763 Seven Years' War
The war begins over boundary disputes between British and French colonies in North America.

1762-1796 Catherine II, the Great
Catherine, the most famous Russian czarina (queen), continues the reforms begun by Peter the Great.

1763 Treaty of Paris
The treaty ends the Seven Years' War, leaving England the world's leading power.

1772 Poland divided
The first of three partitions of Poland. The territory of Poland is divided between Austria (the Holy Roman Empire), Prussia, and Russia.

1775-1783 American Revolution
Thirteen of Britain's North American colonies revolt.

1780-1790 Austrian reform
Joseph II becomes Emperor of Austria, and begins a period of reform designed to modernize the empire.

1783 Treaty of Paris
The United States is recognized as a sovereign nation.

1789 French Revolution
The Estates General meets in France, marking the beginning of the French Revolution.

1793 Louis XVI executed
The French revolutionary government orders the execution of King Louis XVI.

1793 Ottoman reform
The Sultan Selim III issues the *New Regulations* which call for comprehensive reform of the Ottoman Empire.

Political Events (*Continued*)

1795   **Unrest in Japan**
Beginning of the de-
cline of the authority
of the shogunate in
Japanese government.

1796   **Napoleon in Italy**
Napoleon Bonaparte
comes into promi-
nence by leading
French forces to
smashing victories in
Italy.

1796   **Unrest in China**
A period of govern-
ment weakness and
rebellion against the
government begins.

1799   **French dictatorship**
Napoleon is elected
First Consul and be-
comes military dicta-
tor of France.

1804   **Napoleon emperor**
Napoleon Bonaparte
is crowned Emperor
of the French.

1812   **Napoleon in Russia**
The beginning of the
end for the First
French Empire as Na-
poleon suffers defeat
in Russia.

1814   **Napoleon abdicates**
The Bourbons are re-
stored to the throne of
France.

1815   **Battle of Waterloo**
Napoleon attempts to
regain power. He is
crushed at Waterloo
by a joint British and
Prussian army.

1815   **Congress of Vienna**
The nations of Europe
gather in Vienna to re-
store order after the
upheavals caused by
Napoleon.

1824   **Spain loses colonies**
Spain's colonies in
what is now South
America declare and
gain independence.

1830-   **British reform**
1846   A series of laws reform the political sys-
tem of England.

1841-   **First Opium War**
1842   The weakness of the
Chinese government
is demonstrated when
the Chinese fail to
stop British sale of
opium in China.

1847   **Liberian Republic**
Supported by the
United States, freed
slaves found the first
Black African Repub-
lic.

1848   **European unrest**
Democratic revolu-
tions against monar-
chies break out all
over Europe.

1848   **A new France**
The French monarchy
is overthrown again,
and the Second
French Republic is de-
clared.

1852   **Second Empire**
Napoleon III, a de-
scendant of Napoleon
Bonaparte, over-
throws the French Re-
public, and founds the
Second Empire.

1853   **Perry in Japan**
The United States
Commodore Matthew
C. Perry heads a dele-
gation to Japan, the
first outsiders to land
in force for many
years.

1853-   **Crimean War**
1856   Russian attempts to
annex Turkish terri-
tory are blocked by
Great Britain and
France.

1857-   **Sepoy Mutiny**
1858   British control of India is shaken as In-
dian troops revolt
against English offi-
cers.

1861   **Italy unified**
Led by Count Cavour,
the Kingdom of Pied-
mont expels the Aus-
trians and founds the
modern Italian state.

1862   **Bismarck prominent**
Otto von Bismarck
becomes prominent in
the Prussian govern-
ment and begins his
drive to make Prussia
pre-eminent in Ger-
many.

1867   **Dominion of Canada**
The British parliament
grants Canada domin-
ion status.

1868   **Disraeli ministry**
Benjamin Disraeli,
leader of the English
Conservative Party,
forms his first, but
short-lived, ministry.

1868	**Gladstone ministry** William Gladstone, leader of the English Liberal Party and Disraeli's great adversary, forms his first ministry.		Austria-Hungary, and Italy is engineered by Bismarck.			attempt to block British expansion.

1868 **Gladstone ministry**
William Gladstone, leader of the English Liberal Party and Disraeli's great adversary, forms his first ministry.

1868 **Meiji Restoration**
The Emperor Mutsuhito eliminates the shogunate and embarks Japan on a program of modernization.

1870 **Franco-Prussian War**
Bismarck tricks Napoleon III into a war that proves disastrous for France.

1870 **Republican France**
The defeat of Napoleon III by Bismarck causes the founding of the Third French Republic.

1871 **Germany unified**
Bismarck uses the prestige gained by Prussia in the war with France to gain support for declaration of the German Empire.

1875 **The British in Suez**
Disraeli secretly purchases control of the Suez Canal from Egypt.

1877 **The British in Africa**
The British government annexes the South African Republic.

1882 **The Triple Alliance**
An anti-French alliance of Germany,

Austria-Hungary, and Italy is engineered by Bismarck.

1885 **Indians unite**
The Indian National Congress is founded to work for independence for India.

1888 **Kaiser Wilhelm II**
Wilhelm II, the last German Kaiser (emperor), comes to the throne.

1890 **American unity**
The Pan American Union is founded.

1894 **Czar Nicholas II**
Nicholas II, the last Russian czar, comes to the throne.

1894- **Dreyfus Affair**
1906 Captain Dreyfus, a Jewish officer in the French Army, is wrongfully convicted of treason. The struggle to acquit Dreyfus, because of the anti-Semitic overtones of the case, rocks France.

1896- **Young Turks**
1908 A movement led by young Turkish military officers struggles to reform the decaying Ottoman Empire.

1898 **Spanish-American War**
Defeat by the United States marks Spain's end as a great power.

1899- **Boer War**
1902 Dutch settlers in southern Africa (Boers) unsuccessfully

attempt to block British expansion.

1899 **Peace conference**
The first International Peace Conference is held at The Hague.

Social Events

1764 **Penal reform started**
Beccaria of Italy publishes *On Crimes and Punishments*. The book provides impetus for penal reform.

1776 **Colonies rebel**
Basing their ideas on many social thinkers, American thinkers produce the *Declaration of Independence*. This document supports the natural right of citizens to rebel against a government that has become unresponsive to the needs of the governed.

1777 **English prison reform**
A study by John Howard leads to prison reform in England.

1789 **French declare rights**
The Declaration of the Rights of Man and of the Citizen, written by representatives of all classes of French society, becomes a landmark in the story of human liberty.

1791 **Americans declare rights**
The first 10 amendments to the new United States Constitution explain and protect the fundamental rights and free-

doms of every citizen. These first 10 amendments become known as the *Bill of Rights.*

1802   **Child labor limited**
The First Factory Act in Great Britain limits the working hours of children.

1804   **Code Napoleon issued**
Napoleon combines many local French civil laws into one code. The Code Napoleon recognizes many human liberties and civil rights and influences law codes around the world.

1807   **Slave trade abolished**
The British Parliament forbids the slave trade throughout the Empire.

1832   **Britain liberalizes**
The First Reform Act in Britain gives the middle class greater voice in government.

1841   **Mentally-ill cared for**
Dorothea Dix of the United States leads a drive for better treatment of mentally-ill patients.

1844   **Consumer cooperatives**
A group of English weavers opens a co-operative store. This marks the beginning of the modern consumer-cooperative movement.

1858-   **Serfdom abolished**
1861   Alexander II abolishes serfdom in Russia with a series of laws culminating in the Emancipation Edict of 1861.

1863   **U.S. slavery abolished**
The Emancipation Proclamation outlaws slavery in the United States.

1864   **Red Cross founded**
The International Red Cross is founded, originally to care for sick and wounded soldiers.

1870   **British education**
Great Britain establishes a national system of education, thereby recognizing the right of every child in Britain to a minimum level of education.

1878   **Salvation Army founded**
William Booth founds the Salvation Army in England. The intent of the organization is to help improve living conditions for poor workers in English cities.

1881-   **French education**
1886   Free public education is established in France.

1891   ***Rerum Novarum***
Pope Leo XIII issues an encyclical giving the Roman Catholic Church's position on

social affairs and the conditions of the working classes.

Religion

1744   **Methodism founded**
John Wesley organizes a series of meetings that mark the formal beginning of Methodism.

1844   **YMCA founded**
The Young Men's Christian Association is founded in England.

1869-   **Papal authority set**
1870   Vatican Council I declares the pope infallible, that is, incapable of error, when dealing with matters concerning faith and morals.

1870   **Papal states lost**
The government of Italy claims sovereignty over the Papal States. The papacy's political authority is limited to Vatican City.

1897   **Zionism begins**
Theodor Herzl founds the Zionist movement, a movement to reestablish in Palestine the nation of Israel.

Philosophy

1700-   **The Enlightenment**
1800   Building on foundations laid by such men as Descartes, Hobbes, and Locke, European thinkers publicize the ideas of respect for human reason and human rights.

1739-1740   Hume's epistemology
In his major work, *A Treatise of Human Nature,* David Hume argues that knowledge is limited to experience and that complete understanding of any event or natural phenomenon is not possible.

1762   Rousseau's romanticism
In his book *The Social Contract,* Jean Jacques Rousseau gives his views on government as the expression of the general will of all the people. His ideas influenced the French Revolution.

1776   Adam Smith's economics
A Scottish philosopher, Adam Smith, writes *The Wealth of Nations.* He establishes the importance of world trade and control of sources of raw materials to the economic growth of nations.

1781   Kant critiques reason
German philosopher Immanuel Kant writes the *Critique of Pure Reason.* The book explores the nature and limits of the human mind.

1820   Hegel on history
In his writings, the German philosopher Georg Hegel estab-

lishes the philosophy of history as an important field of study.

1824   Comte and sociology
Auguste Comte, founder of the philosophy known as "positivism," originates a concept of social science which he calls sociology.

1843-1845   Existentialism begins
The Danish philosopher Søren Kierkegaard is considered one of the founders of "existentialism." He writes about the nature of religious faith.

1843   The utilitarian movement
John Stuart Mill, leader of the utilitarian movement, writes *System of Logic,* his chief work.

1859   Evolution explodes
Charles Darwin, an English biologist, writes *Origin of Species.* He believes that living things evolved from simpler forms with the fittest species surviving and weaklings sacrificed by nature.

1860   Spencer's evolutionism
In his writing, British philosopher Herbert Spencer tries to work out a philosophy, based on the scientific discoveries of his day, which can be applied to the interpretation of all reality.

1863   Idealism attacked
Ernest Renan, a French philosopher, attacks democracy as an idealist system, calling instead for government by an intellectual elite.

1867   *Das Kapital* published
In his major work, *Das Kapital,* the German philosopher Karl Marx describes the flaws of the free enterprise system and develops an evolutionary explanation for the flow of history.

1870-1900   Darwin extended
Darwin's notion of biological evolution and survival of the fittest is applied to society in a movement termed "Social Darwinism." It is used to justify the exploitation of the economically weak by the economically strong.

1872-1888   Nietzsche emerges
German philosopher Friedrich Nietzsche teaches that the driving force of change through history is the "will to power."

1888   Romantic revival
Led by the French philosopher Henri Bergson, European thinkers begin a reaction against materialism, claiming that intuition and not intellect is the best vehicle for interpreting reality.

European Ascendancy

Literature

1714   Pope prominent
Alexander Pope publishes his most famous poem, *Rape of the Lock*.

1726   A famous satire
Jonathan Swift writes *Gulliver's Travels*, a satire of life in 18th century England.

1754   Fielding dies
The English novelist Henry Fielding dies. His *The History of Tom Jones, a Foundling* is a landmark in the development of the novel.

1755   Johnson's dictionary
Samuel Johnson, the greatest English writer of his day, completes his often humorous *Dictionary of the English Language*.

1759   *Candide* written
The French author Voltaire writes the philosophical tale *Candide*.

1759   Scottish poet is born
Robert Burns, the national poet of Scotland, is born.

1780   Motoori writes
A revival of Japanese interest in Japan's early history is begun by Motoori, who writes the *Exposition of the Record of Ancient Things*.

1791   Boswell's biography
James Boswell sets new standards for the art of biography with his *The Life of Samuel Johnson*.

1796   Birth of Haliburton
Thomas Chandler Haliburton, called the "father of American humor," is born in Nova Scotia.

1799   Schiller's masterpiece
Friedrich Schiller, second only to Goethe as a German author, publishes his greatest drama, *Wallenstein*.

1799   Balzac born
The French writer Honoré de Balzac is born. He becomes a leading 19th century novelist.

1801   Romanticism begins
François-René de Chateaubriand writes the romantic novel *Atala*.

1804   Popular Schiller
Schiller's play *William Tell* achieves popularity all over Europe.

1806   Wordsworth prominent
William Wordsworth writes the poem, "Ode: Intimations of Immortality."

1810   Medieval revival
Sir Walter Scott, a Scottish romantic writer, produces *The Lady of the Lake*, a long verse poem that marks a romantic revival of interest in the Middle Ages.

1812-1815   Grimm brothers publish
Two brothers, Jakob and Wilhelm Grimm, publish a book of traditional German fairy tales. This book is considered part of the Medieval revival.

1816   Latin-American novel
José Joaquin Fernandez de Lizardi writes *The Itching Parrot*, a novel about the Mexican Revolution and the first novel published in Latin America.

1817   Keats begins
John Keats, the English poet, publishes his first volume, titled *Poems*.

1818   Mary Shelley writes
Mary Wollstonecraft Shelley publishes her classic novel *Frankenstein, or The Modern Prometheus*.

1818   Shelley in Italy
Percy Bysshe Shelley, leading English romantic poet, moves to Italy where he enjoys his most productive period.

1823   Major work by Byron
Lord Byron begins his major work, the epic poem *Don Juan*.

1829   Balzac emerges
Balzac begins publication of his monumental, many-volumed work, *The Human Comedy*.

1831   **Stendhal publishes**
Marie Henri Beyle (Stendhal), one of the first writers of psychological novels, publishes *The Red and The Black*.

1831   **Romanticism continues**
Victor Hugo, leader of the romantic movement in France, publishes *The Hunchback of Notre Dame*.

1832   **Age of Goethe**
The writer Goethe, called by many Germany's greatest writer, completes his most famous work *Faust*, a verse play.

1835   **Classic fairy tales**
Danish writer Hans Christian Andersen publishes the first of the 168 fairy tales that will make his name a household word.

1846   **Sand prominent**
Amantine Lucile Aurore Dupin (George Sand) publishes her finest novel *The Haunted Pool*.

1847   **Charlotte Brontë writes**
Charlotte Brontë writes *Jane Eyre*, her most famous work.

1847   **Emily Brontë writes**
Emily Brontë, the sister of Charlotte, writes the classic *Wuthering Heights*.

1847   **Anne Brontë prominent**
The third of the Brontë sisters, Anne, publishes *Agnes Grey*, her most famous work.

1848   **Thackeray gains fame**
English novelist William Makepeace Thackeray publishes *Vanity Fair*, his famous satire of British society.

1850   **Novel by Dickens**
Charles Dickens writes *David Copperfield*, one of his many novels describing social conditions in 19th-century England.

1854   **Canadian prominent**
French-Canadian poet Octave Crémazie begins writing religious and patriotic poems.

1857   **Flaubert publishes**
French novelist Gustave Flaubert writes *Madame Bovary*, a study of 19th century middle-class morality.

1860   **Birth of Chekhov**
Anton Chekhov, Russia's most famous playwright, is born.

1860   **Quebec poets write**
The School of Quebec poets use French-Canadian patriotism as their dominant theme.

1861   **Nature poet born**
Archibald Lampman, called Canada's finest nature poet, is born.

1862   **Novel by Turgenev**
Russian novelist Ivan Sergeevich Turgenev writes *Fathers and Sons*, the first in a distinguished line of psychological novels by Russian authors.

1865-   **Tolstoy's major work**
1869   Russian novelist Leo Tolstoy writes *War and Peace*.

1866   **Classic Russian novel**
Russian novelist Fyodor Dostoevsky writes *Crime and Punishment*.

1867   **Spanish poet born**
Rubén Darío, one of the most important Spanish-language poets, is born in Nicaragua.

1867   **Novel by Isaacs**
Jorge Isaacs of Colombia writes the classic Latin-American novel *Maria*.

1870   **Strindberg writes**
Swedish writer August Strindberg begins writing. His plays influence the development of naturalism and expressionism in drama.

1872-   **Spanish folk tales**
1902   Ricardo Palma edits a 10-volume collection of folk tales of Latin America.

1874   **Canadian writer born**
Lucy Maud Montgomery, author of *Anne of Green Gables*, is born.

European Ascendancy
Literature (*Continued*)

1879   Social drama
Norwegian dramatist
Henrik Ibsen writes *A
Doll's House.* Ibsen is
known as the father of
modern drama, con-
centrating on works
that explore the social
problems of the day.

1880   *Orion* published
With the publication
of *Orion,* Sir Charles
G. D. Roberts lays the
foundation for a dis-
tinctive Canadian lit-
erary form.

1885   Zola prominent
French naturalist au-
thor Émile Zola writes
Germinal.

1892   German revival
Gerhart Hauptmann
publishes *The Weav-
ers.* The play de-
scribes the revolt of
exploited workers.

1897   Dracula born
The British author
Bram Stoker publishes
the classic horror story
Dracula.

1898   Gordon publishes
Canadian author
Charles Gordon, writ-
ing under the name
Ralph Connor, pub-
lishes the classic Ca-
nadian novel *Black
Rock.*

The Arts

1710   After the Fire
Architect Christopher
Wren redesigns St.
Paul's Cathedral after
the Great Fire of Lon-
don.

1717   Orchestral suite
Water Music, an or-
chestral suite, by
George Frideric Han-
del debuts in England.

1717   The rococo style
The rococo style, fea-
turing intricate orna-
mentation, is typified
by the French painter
Antoine Watteau. He
portrays members, of
the French nobility off
for a holiday on the
island of Cythera in
*The Embarkation for
Cythera.*

1729   Bach's greatest work
Johann Sebastian
Bach completes what
many believe to be his
greatest work, *The
Passion According to
St. Matthew.*

1732   Haydn born
Known as the father
of the symphony,
composer Joseph
Haydn is born in Aus-
tria.

1762-   Mozart prominent
1791   Wolfgang Amadeus
Mozart completes
over 600 works in a
brief 36-year life span.
His work marks the
transition from ba-
roque to classical mu-
sic forms.

1770-   Age of Beethoven
1827   Ludwig van Beethoven refines the
classical symphonic
style in his nine sym-
phonies. Beethoven's
style affects compos-
ers throughout the
19th century.

1770   Danish sculptor
The Danish sculptor
Bertel Thorvaldsen is
born. His most fa-
mous work is the *Lion
of Lucerne.*

1784   The classical revival
Ancient Roman my-
thology inspires
Jacques Louis David
of France. He paints
*The Oath of the Hora-
tii.*

**1787   Mozart's greatest
opera**
Wolfgang Amadeus
Mozart's opera, *Don
Giovanni,* is per-
formed for the first
time in Prague.

1797   Schubert born
Franz Schubert, com-
poser of music in
many forms, is born
in Austria. He begins
writing music when he
is 13 years old.

1810-   Art in Canada
1871   Pioneer Canadian
painter Paul Kane re-
cords North American
Indian life in his vivid
paintings.

1810   Polish genius born
Frédéric Chopin, a
master of piano com-
position, is born near
Warsaw, Poland.

1833   Brahms born
Johannes Brahms, a
great German com-
poser, is born. His
many works will in-
clude symphonies and
collections of mood-
setting songs.

**1836   Schumann's major
work**
Robert Schumann of
Germany composes
Fantasia in C major.

1838   New artistic realism
Camille Corot paints
A View near Volterra,
in which nature is
realistically inter-
preted.

1839   Cézanne born
Paul Cézanne, a
founder of cubism and
abstract art, is born in
France.

1840   Rodin born
Auguste Rodin, prom-
inent 19th-century
sculptor, is born in
France.

**1846   Mendelssohn promi-
nent**
Felix Mendelssohn's
oratorio, *Elijah,* is
first performed in
England.

1855   Realism expands
Gustave Courbet
paints a masterpiece
of realism. He calls it
The Artist's Studio.

1859   Wagner prominent
The German com-
poser Richard Wagner
completes his major
opera *Tristan and
Isolde.*

1863   New style in art
French artist Edouard
Manet concentrates
on presenting beauty
as an ideal in his
painting *Luncheon on
the Grass.*

1874   The Viennese waltz
Johann Strauss, Jr.,
composes *Die Fleder-
maus.* He is known as
the "Waltz King."

**1881   Impressionist land-
mark**
*The Luncheon of the
Boating Party,* an
impressionist painting
by Pierre Renoir, is
completed.

1888   Van Gogh works
Vincent Van Gogh
captures *The Night
Café* on canvas. An-
other of his best-
known paintings is
Sunflowers, a robust
still life.

**1892   Tchaikovsky
prominent**
The Nutcracker Suite,
a major work by Rus-
sian composer Peter
Tchaikovsky, is com-
pleted. Besides operas
and ballet music, he
composes many con-
certos for piano and
violin.

1897   Gauguin's romanticism
Paul Gauguin idealizes
the people of the
South Sea Islands.
Representative of his
work is *Where Do We
Come From? What
Are We? Where Are
We Going?*

**Science and
Technology**

1700   Seed drill invented
Jethro Tull invents the
seed drill. It helps to
revolutionize agricul-
ture.

1730   Biology classifications
Carolus Linnaeus de-
velops the method of
classifying plants and
animals.

1738   Industry grows
The roller-spinning
machine is patented
by John Wyatt. It is
the forerunner of
sweeping advances in
the textile industry.

1766   Hydrogen discovered
Sir Henry Cavendish
discovers hydrogen,
which he calls "in-
flammable air."

1769   Steam engine improved
James Watt of Scot-
land patents an im-
proved steam engine.
It becomes the chief
source of power for
industry.

1774   Oxygen discovered
Joseph Priestley dis-
covers oxygen.

**1777   Modern chemistry
begins**
Antoine Lavoisier lays
the foundation for
modern chemistry
when he explains that
an object unites with
oxygen when it burns.

European Ascendancy
Science and Technology (*Continued*)

about **Fight against smallpox**
1796   Edward Jenner dis-
       covers a method of
       vaccination against
       smallpox.

1803   **Atomic theory devel-
       oped**
       John Dalton an-
       nounces the atomic
       theory.

1803   **New papermaking
       method**
       Henry and Sealy
       Fourdrinier invent a
       machine for making
       cheap paper quickly.

1826- **Photography invented**
1839   Joseph Niepce and
       Louis Daguerre invent
       a method of photogra-
       phy.

1831   **Electricity induced**
       Michael Faraday in-
       duces an electric cur-
       rent with a moving
       magnet. This leads to
       the development of
       the electric motor as
       an important source of
       energy.

1839   **Cell theory proposed**
       Matthias Schleiden
       and Theodor Schwann
       theorize that all living
       things are composed
       of cells.

1856   **Bessemer process**
       Henry Bessemer per-
       fects a method for
       producing steel from
       pig iron.

1860   **Electromagnetic theory**
       James Clerk Maxwell
       develops the electro-
       magnetic theory.

1860   **New power source**
       Jean Joseph Étienne
       Lenoir builds one of
       the first practical in-
       ternal-combustion en-
       gines.

1866   **Mendel's laws**
       Gregor Mendel pub-
       lishes his explanation
       of the laws of hered-
       ity.

1867   **Dynamite invented**
       Alfred Bernhard No-
       bel of Sweden invents
       dynamite.

1868   **Typewriter perfected**
       Three Americans de-
       velop the first practi-
       cal typewriter.

1869   **The Periodic Table**
       Dmitri Mendeleev de-
       velops the periodic ta-
       ble of elements, clas-
       sifying them by their
       atomic weights and
       properties.

1869   **Railroads span U.S.**
       The Union Pacific and
       Central Pacific Rail-
       ways jointly complete
       the first transcontinen-
       tal railroad across the
       United States.

1876   **Pasteur's discoveries**
       Louis Pasteur finds
       that microorganisms
       cause fermentation
       and disease.

1879   **Psychology grows**
       Wilhelm Wundt
       founds the first labora-
       tory of experimental
       psychology.

1882   **Great medical advance**
       Robert Koch discov-
       ers that bacteria cause
       tuberculosis.

1884   **Linotype invented**
       Ottmar Mergenthaler
       patents the Linotype
       machine. The machine
       speeds up the typeset-
       ting process and
       makes printing less
       costly.

1884   **Rayon invented**
       An artificial silk,
       called rayon, is in-
       vented by Hilaire
       Chardonnet in
       France.

1885   **Railroad spans
       Canada**
       The Canadian Pacific
       Railway is built
       across Canada.

1889   **Photography improved**
       George Eastman de-
       velops a practical
       photographic film.

1895   **X-rays discovered**
       Wilhelm K. Roentgen
       discovers X-rays.

1895   **Wireless invented**
       Guglielmo Marconi in-
       vents the wireless tel-
       egraph.

1898   **Radium isolated**
       Marie and Pierre
       Curie isolate the ele-
       ment radium.

Since 1900

Political Events

1900   Boxer Rebellion
The Chinese rebel unsuccessfully against foreign domination of China.

1904-   Russo-Japanese War
1905   Japan enters world politics as a great power by defeating Russia.

1911-   Chinese revolution
1912   Sun Yat-sen helps to overthrow the Manchus and establish the Republic of China.

1914-   World War I
1918   Germany, Austria-Hungary, the Ottoman Empire, and their allies battle Britain, France, Russia, the United States, and their allies.

1917   U.S. in the war
The entrance of the United States on the side of Britain and France tips the balance against Germany.

1917   Russian revolution
Led by Nikolai Lenin, the Bolsheviks (Communists) overthrow a provisional government that had gained power on the abdication of the czar.

1919   The war ends
Monarchies in Germany, Austria, and Turkey are overthrown. New nations, such as Poland, Czechoslovakia, and Yugoslavia, are created. Germany is blamed and punished for the war as a result of the Versailles conference.

1920   Nations unite
The League of Nations is founded.

1922   Rise of Fascism
The Fascist Party, led by Benito Mussolini, seizes control of Italy.

The Treaty of Versailles is signed on June 28, 1919.

1922   U.S.S.R. founded
Led by Nikolai Lenin,
the Communist Party
reorganizes Russia as
the Union of Soviet
Socialist Republics.

1923   Turkish reform
The Young Turk
Movement, led by
Kemal Atatürk, forms
the Republic of Tur-
key.

1929   The Great Depression
Caused by economic
reverses in the United
States, a major
depression sweeps the
world.

1931   Canada independent
The Statute of West-
minster grants Canada
independence within
the British Common-
wealth.

1933   Nazis rise
Nazi leader Adolf Hit-
ler becomes dictator
of Germany.

1935-   Ethiopia invaded
1936   Italian troops conquer
Ethiopia.

1937   Japan expands
Japan and China, bat-
tling on and off since
1928, open general
hostilities.

1938   German expansion
Germany annexes
Austria.

1938   Munich Pact
To avoid a general
war, British and
French leaders agree
to Hitler's seizure of
part of Czechoslova-
kia.

1939   Spanish Civil War
Spanish Fascists, led
by Francisco Franco,
complete the over-
throw of the Spanish
Republic.

1939   World War II begins
Germany invades Po-
land. Britain and
France declare war on
Germany.

**1941   Hitler invades
the Soviet Union**
With Britain the only
major European na-
tion still standing
against him, Adolf
Hitler leads Germany
and her allies in a
massive invasion of
the U.S.S.R.

1941   U.S. in the war
The Japanese bomb
American naval facili-
ties at Pearl Harbor.
The United States en-
ters the war.

1945   UN founded
Representatives of 50
nations meet in San
Francisco to organize
the United Nations.

1945   German collapse
After Hitler commits
suicide, German
forces surrender on
May 7.

1945   The atomic bomb
The first atomic
bombs used in warfare

are dropped by the
United States on the
Japanese cities of Hi-
roshima and Naga-
saki.

1945   Japan falls
Japanese forces sur-
render on September 2.

**1946   Philippine independ-
ence**
The United States
grants independence
to the Philippines.

1946   Cold War begins
The capitalist nations
and the communist
nations, allies in the
battle against fascism,
turn hostile toward
each other.

1947   Truman Doctrine
President Harry S.
Truman declares
American support for
any nation that resists
communism.

1947   India independent
The British withdraw
from their former col-
ony of India. Two na-
tions are formed, In-
dia and Pakistan.

1948   The Marshall Plan
The Marshall Plan,
sponsored by the
United States, pro-
vides aid to the war-
torn nations of Eu-
rope.

**1949   Communists rule
China**
The Chinese Commu-
nist party ends a long
civil war by driving

the Chinese Nationalist government to the Island of Taiwan and establishing the People's Republic of China.

1950 **War in Korea**
Communist troops from North Korea invade the Republic of South Korea. Led by the United States, UN troops intervene.

1956 **The Suez crisis**
UN-sponsored forces halt a British-French-Israeli invasion of Egypt caused by conflict over control of the Suez Canal.

1957 **Vietnam War widens**
Conflict in Vietnam, going on since 1946, expands as the United States enters the civil war on the side of South Vietnam.

1957 **Common Market**
The Common Market, an economic alliance of European nations, is formed.

1959 **Communist Cuba**
Fidel Castro establishes a communist dictatorship in Cuba.

1967 **Arab-Israeli War**
An Arab alliance is smashed by Israeli forces.

1970 **Unrest in Canada**
French Canadian separatists begin a terrorist campaign against the government of Canada.

1975 **New African age**
Although some small colonies remain, Portugal grants independence to the last large European colony in Africa.

1975 **Vietnam War ends**
The communist government of North Vietnam defeats the government of South Vietnam.

1979 **Revolution in Iran**
The Shah's government falls; under the leadership of the Ayatollah Ruhollah Khomeini, Iran is declared an Islamic republic.

1979 **Peace in Middle East**
Egypt and Israel sign a treaty in Washington, D.C., ending 30 years of war.

1980 **War in Afghanistan**
Soviet troops fight in Afghanistan to support the leftist Afghan government against rebel tribes.

1980 **Unrest in Poland**
Thousands of Polish workers strike, demanding independent labor unions and economic and political reform.

1982 **Falklands war**
Britain defeats Argentina in air, land, and sea battles to retain control of the Falkland Islands in the South Atlantic Ocean.

1982 **Lebanese massacre**
Lebanese Christian militia kill hundreds of Lebanese and Palestinian civilians living in refugee camps in Beirut.

1983 **Korean airliner tragedy**
A Soviet fighter plane shoots down a Korean civilian airliner flying in Soviet airspace, killing all 269 persons on board. The incident sparks worldwide concern and protest.

1983 **Bomb kills U.S. troops**
A terrorist bomb explodes in marine headquarters in Lebanon, killing more than 200 U.S. troops.

1983 **Grenada invaded**
Pan American troops, including 1,900 U.S. military personnel, invade Grenada to overthrow the Marxist government in power there.

1983 **Civil war in Nicaragua**
Several thousand anti-Sandinistas invade northeastern Nicaragua.

1984 **Apartheid in South Africa**
Desmond Tutu leads a nonviolent campaign against racial segregation in South Africa.

1985 **Iran-Iraq war**
The territorial war between Iran and Iraq enters its fifth year.

Since 1900
Political Events (*Continued*)

1986 War against terrorism
President Reagan orders U.S. air strikes against military and suspected terrorist centers in Libya.

1987 New president for Philippines
Corazon Aquino becomes the first woman president of the Philippines after former president Ferdinand E. Marcos fled the country.

1987 Nuclear Forces Treaty
Reagan and Gorbachev sign the Intermediate-Range Nuclear Forces Treaty.

1988 New prime minister for Pakistan
Benazir Bhutto becomes the first woman ever to head an elected government in an Islamic nation.

1988 Soviet troops withdraw from Afghanistan
Soviet troops begin withdrawal; however, hostilities continue between the rebels and Afghanistan's government forces.

1989 Massacre in China
University students hold demonstrations in Beijing's Tiananmen Square, calling for more democracy in China. The military crush the demonstrations and kill hundreds of protesters.

1989 Freedom in Eastern Europe
Peaceful demonstrations topple the Communist regimes in Hungary, Romania, Czechoslovakia, and Poland. The people of these nations win the right to vote in free elections.

1989 Berlin Wall crumbles
Huge public protests in East Germany bring down the country's governing Socialist Unity Party. The borders between East and West Germany open, and the wall no longer separates East and West Berlin.

1990 Nelson Mandela is freed
After 28 years of imprisonment in a South African jail for his protests against apartheid, Mandela is released. The South African government begins to relax its apartheid policies.

1990 Germany votes to reunify
The people of East and West Germany vote to unite politically and economically.

1990 Lithuania demands freedom from the Soviet Union
The people of Lithuania, one of the Soviet Union's 15 republics, demonstrate for freedom and are granted some autonomy.

Social Events

1906- Women gain vote
1919   Finland grants suffrage to women in 1906, Norway in 1913, and Denmark in 1915. Britain and the U.S. follow suit in 1918 and 1919.

1911 Chinese upheaval
China's social structure, which had remained unchanged since acceptance of the thought of Confucius, is completely overturned with the fall of the Manchu dynasty.

1920- Gandhi prominent
1948   Mohandas Gandhi uses nonviolent resistance to gain independence from British control for India.

1922 World Court organized
The League of Nations forms an International Court of Justice.

1946 UNESCO established
The United Nations Education, Scientific and Cultural Organization is established.

1948 WHO founded
The World Health Organization is established.

1955 Concern over the atom
The first international conference on peaceful uses of atomic energy is held in Geneva, Switzerland.

1955 **Caste attacked**
India passes legisla-
tion attacking the
caste system which
has governed society
in India since the Ar-
yan invasions.

1960- **Women's rights**
Pres- The modern feminist
ent movement influences
social and cultural
changes around the
world.

1970- **Environmental move-**
Pres- **ment**
ent Groups in many na-
tions hold demonstra-
tions and take political
action to fight air and
water pollution. Oth-
ers express concern
about the potential
hazards of nuclear
power plants.

1970- **Energy concerns**
Pres- The costs of oil and
ent other energy sources
contribute to world-
wide inflation. Many
nations around the
world promote energy
conservation and the
development of alter-
nate energy sources.

1981 **Antinuclear protests**
Huge antinuclear dem-
onstrations in West
Germany, Britain, and
elsewhere in Europe
mark the start of a
new upsurge in public
concern over the pos-
sibility of nuclear war.

1981 **Prince marries**
Prince Charles, heir
apparent to the British
throne, marries Lady
Diana Spencer, a Brit-
ish aristocrat.

1984 **Aid to Ethiopia**
Band Aid, a group of
British rock music
stars, produces a re-
cording to raise funds
for famine victims.
The record earns
more than $11 million.

1988- **Glasnost**
Pres- Under Mikhail Gor-
ent bachev, the Soviet
Union pursues a pol-
icy of domestic and
international openness
known as *glasnost*.

Religion

1942- **The Holocaust**
1945 In the most extensive
persecution of all
time, the Nazis
slaughter six million
Jews during World
War II.

1947 **Dead Sea scrolls**
The oldest known
manuscripts of books
of the Bible are dis-
covered in caves near
the Dead Sea.

1948 **Israel founded**
The United Nations
establishes the state of
Israel, in Palestine.
This is the first sover-
eign Jewish state since
Roman times.

1962- **Vatican Council II**
1965 Vatican Council II
permits the use of lo-
cal language in place
of Latin in the Roman
Catholic liturgy and
liberalizes the
church's position on
relations with non-
Catholics.

1977 **Women in religion**
For the first time,
women are ordained
as priests in the Angli-
can Church. Their or-
dination causes a split
in the Church's hierar-
chy.

1979 **Islam and government**
Iran and Pakistan
form governments
ruled by the law of Is-
lam. Movements in
Saudi Arabia, Bangla-
desh, Egypt, Kuwait,
and Turkey also work
for a return to Islamic
rule.

1982 **Pope in Britain**
Nearly 450 years after
England broke away
from the Roman Cath-
olic Church, Pope
John Paul II travels to
Great Britain. He
joins the archbishop
of Canterbury in a his-
toric religious service
symbolizing the goal
of Christian unity.

Philosophy

1918- **Pessimism grows**
1922 Oswald Spengler pub-
lishes his influential
*The Decline of the
West,* predicting the
collapse of Western
civilization because of
its materialism.

1920- **Logical positivism**
pres- Positivist thinkers
ent claim that a statement
or experience is
meaningful only if it is
verifiable by appeal to
experience.

1921 **Wittgenstein**
Ludwig Wittgenstein,
an Austrian philoso-

Since 1900
Philosophy (*Continued*)

pher living in England, greatly influences the philosophical movement called "positivism."

1927   Analyzing our existence
The writings of Martin Heidegger analyze reality in terms of human existence, the form of being we know best. He is considered an "existentialist."

1929   Whitehead writes
English philosopher Alfred North Whitehead writes *Process and Reality*. His writings attempt to narrow the gap between philosophy and science, between realism and idealism.

1932   Jaspers publishes
Karl Jaspers, a leading German existentialist philosopher, writes *Philosophy,* publicizing the existentialist position in Germany.

1934-   *A Study of History*
1961   Arnold Toynbee revives the idealist philosophy of history through publication of his monumental 12-volume work.

1935-   Camus gains fame
1960   Albert Camus, winner of the 1957 Nobel prize, writes novels and plays which explore the existentialist problem.

1943   Sartre's existentialism
French philosopher Jean-Paul Sartre becomes the leading exponent of the philosophy of existentialism.

1950   Nobel prize for Russell
British philosopher Bertrand Russell receives the Nobel prize for literature "as a defender of humanity and freedom of thought."

1960-   Philosophy on hold
pres-   The influence of se-
ent   manticism and existentialism grows. Eastern philosophies derived from Hinduism and Buddhism begin to penetrate Western thought. Commentaries on earlier thinkers rather than original works become the norm.

1979   Postmodernism
Jean Lyotard publishes an influential pamphlet on postmodernism, a movement that is in reaction against the theory and practice of modern art or literature.

1980   Sartre dies
French existentialist Jean-Paul Sartre, who influenced two generations of thinkers, dies in April.

1985   Postmodernism criticized
Jurgen Habermas, a major opponent of Lyotard's theory, publishes a collection of lectures disputing the validity of postmodernism.

Literature

1902   Gide publishes
André Gide publishes the new romanticist novel *The Immoralist*.

1904   Chekhov famous
Anton Chekhov publishes his most famous work, *The Cherry Orchard*.

1908   D'Annunzio's influence
The writings and political activities of poet Gabriele D'Annunzio strengthen the nationalist movement in Italy.

1910   Mystical revival
Such writers as Paul Claudel, Jacques Maritain, and Stefan George exhibit a new mysticism.

1912   Claudel publishes
French playwright Paul Claudel writes *Tidings Brought to Mary*.

1912   A Shaw masterpiece
George Bernard Shaw, who becomes the leading English language dramatist, writes *Pygmalion*.

1918   Proust prominent
Marcel Proust publishes the second volume of *Remembrance of Things Past*.

1921   Drama by Pirandello
Luigi Pirandello writes *Six Characters in Search of an Author*, one of many philosophical plays.

1921 Social themes grow
In his play, *R.U.R.*, a study of social dehumanization. Czech writer Karel Čapek introduces the word "robot."

1922 War novels
The writings of German war hero Ernst Jünger emphasize war and suggest the rebirth of Germany, influencing radical conservative thinking in that country.

1922 Eliot famous
T. S. Eliot publishes a long poem, *The Waste Land*. It is an outcry against the spiritual bankruptcy of Western culture.

1922 Joyce publishes
James Joyce's novel *Ulysses* is published, setting new forms for the 20th century novel.

1923 Nobel for Yeats
William Butler Yeats, leader of the Irish Literary Revival, wins the Nobel prize for literature.

1924 Europe's despair
Thomas Mann captures the gradual collapse of European culture in his symbolic novel *The Magic Mountain*, which becomes popular in the 1920's.

1925 Hesse prominent
The German pessimist novelist Hermann Hesse gains great prominence among Europe's youth.

1926 Kafka's alienation
Franz Kafka, the apostle of modern man's alienation from himself, writes his cryptic novel *The Trial*.

1927 Akutagawa dies
Ryunosuke Akutagawa, Japan's best known modern novelist, dies.

1928 Lawrence shocks Europe
English novelist D. H. Lawrence writes *Lady Chatterley's Lover*, shocking Europe with its realistic portrayal of modern morality.

1929 Anti-war classic
Erich Maria Remarque, German novelist, publishes the classic, *All Quiet on the Western Front*.

1934 Thomas begins
The Welsh poet Dylan Thomas publishes his first work, *Eighteen Poems*.

1936 Trilogy completed
The American author John Dos Passos gains a worldwide reputation with his three-novel study of the disintegration of American culture titled *U.S.A.*

1940 Canadian epic written
Canadian poet E. J. Pratt writes *Brébeuf and His Brethren*, the epic poem of early French-Canadian history.

1945 Nobel for Mistral
Poet Gabriela Mistral of Chile is the first Latin-American writer to win the Nobel prize for literature.

1946 Guatemalan masterpiece
Miguel Angel Asturias of Guatemala publishes what many believe to be his finest novel, *Mr. President*.

1947 The Frank diary
The Diary of Anne Frank, written by Anne Frank, a German-Jewish child who was eventually killed by the Nazis, is published.

1951 Classic Anouilh
Jean Anouilh, prominent French playwright, publishes his most famous drama, *The Waltz of the Toreadors*.

1961 Hemingway dies
Ernest Hemingway, noted American author, dies. His work is world famous as having broken new ground for the novel form.

1963 Sartre's autobiography
Noted French author and philosopher Jean-Paul Sartre publishes *Words*, the first volume of his long-awaited autobiography.

Literature (*Continued*)

1963   Auden's essays
The Dyer's Hand, a collection of critical essays by the distinguished British author W. H. Auden, is published.

1964   Behan dies
Brendan Behan dies. This most famous of 20th century Irish authors wrote such works as *Borstal Boy* and *The Hostage.*

1966   Nabokov's memoirs
Noted Russian author Vladimir Nabokov publishes *Speak, Memory,* a remembrance of his life as an internationally known author.

1973   Greene publishes
The noted English author Graham Greene publishes *The Honorary Consul,* the best of his later novels.

1973   Neruda dies
Pablo Neruda, Chilean poet who has achieved worldwide fame, dies. Neruda was the recipient of the 1971 Nobel prize for literature.

1973-1976   Russian classic
Russian author Alexander Solzhenitsyn publishes his three-volume study of repression in the Soviet Union, *The Gulag Archipelago.*

1976   Bellow established
Saul Bellow, an American author, solidifies his worldwide influence by winning the Nobel prize for literature.

1978   More from Grass
West German novelist Günter Grass publishes *The Flounder,* perhaps his finest work.

1982   Nobel to García Márquez
Colombian novelist Gabriel José García Márquez wins the Nobel prize for literature.

1986   Borges dies
Jorge Luis Borges, an Argentine man of letters, dies. Borges is best known for his distinctive *fictions,* short stories with many features of the essay.

1989   Death sentence
Ayatollah Khomeini of Iran claims that Salman Rushdie's book, *The Satanic Verses,* is offensive to the Islamic people. Khomeini orders his followers to hunt down the British-born author and execute him.

1990   Beckett dies
Samuel Beckett, an Irish author best known for such avant-garde plays as *Waiting for Godot* and *Endgame,* dies. Beckett received the Nobel prize for literature in 1969.

The Arts

1900   Cubism begins
Paul Cézanne leads the way to a new art form—cubism and the abstract. He paints *The Clockmaker.*

1905   Fauvism popular
Henri Matisse leads the fauvist movement and creates *Landscape at Collioure.* He uses bright colors and flat patterns.

1905   Debussy prominent
Claude Debussy writes *La Mer,* an orchestral composition that represents a revival of romanticism in music.

1906   Early Wright
Frank Lloyd Wright designs Unity Temple in Oak Park, Ill.

1907   Artists' group
Robert Henri forms a group of eight artists. They specialize in presenting realistic scenes from everyday life, and are called the "Ashcan School."

1910   *Der Rosenkavalier*
Richard Strauss writes the music, Hugo von Hofmannsthal the libretto, for the opera *Der Rosenkavalier.*

1913   New musical forms
Igor Stravinsky's ballet, *The Rite of Spring,* is performed for the first time.

1913   Expressionism grows
Wassily Kandinsky

paints *Little Pleasures, No. 174,* a landmark of expressionist art.

1919 Bauhaus founded
The designer Walter Gropius founds the Bauhaus, school of design, in Weimar, Germany. The "Bauhaus Style" of modern design developed at this school still influences architects and designers.

1919 Spanish ballet
The Spanish composer Manuel de Falla produces his famous ballet *The Three-Cornered Hat.*

1920 Dadaism
The Dadaists attempt to purge art of its pretensions. They describe their works as "anti-art."

1922 German revival
Paul Klee of Germany completes the *Red Balloon.* His work typifies the post-World War I revival of the arts in Germany.

1925 Mondrian a leader
Lozenge Composition in a Square, a painting by Piet Mondrian, is presented. His style influences architecture and commercial design as well as painting.

1929 Surrealism grows
Accommodations of Desire, a surrealist painting by Salvador Dali, is completed.

1931 Mexican artist
Diego Rivera, noted Mexican muralist, paints *Agrarian Leader Zapata.* It is part of a large mural featuring the history of Mexico.

1942 Hopper prominent
Edward Hopper of New York captures loneliness in his painting *Nighthawks.*

1943 Bartók composes
Hungarian composer Béla Bartók writes the *Concerto for Orchestra.*

1952 New abstractionism
Willem de Kooning, an abstract painter, completes *Woman, I.*

1954 Andrew Wyeth
Teel's Island, a painting by Andrew Wyeth, is completed. His rural scenes are reminders of American life during an earlier age.

1958 Electronic music
Edgard Varèse, called the father of electronic music, composes *Poème Electronique.*

1960 African art revival
Ondongo of Africa paints a watercolor of *Musicians with Three Drums.*

**1960- Music history made
1970** The Beatles, an English rock group, changes the form of popular music through its compositions, arrangements, and methods of presentation.

1962 War Requiem
Benjamin Britten's composition, *A War Requiem,* is performed for the first time. It is called by many one of Britten's finest works.

1964 Chagall triumphs
Marc Chagall completes his monumental painting for the ceiling of the Paris Opera House.

1965 Artistic landmark
English sculptor Henry Moore's *Reclining Figure* goes on display at Lincoln Center in New York City.

1968 American contemporary
Artist Robert Bechtle completes a photographic-like oil painting, *60 T-Bird.* The painting symbolizes a new return to realism in the arts.

1971 Social art
Black American artist William Walker uses art as social comment in his mural *Wall of Love.*

1973 Architectural landmark
The Sears Tower, the world's tallest skyscraper, is completed in Chicago, Ill.

1973 Picasso dies
Pablo Picasso, the giant of art in the 20th century, dies.

1976   Michelangelo revisited
Several large wall decorations thought to be by Michelangelo are discovered in a basement room in Florence, Italy.

1983   Balanchine dies
George Balanchine, one of the most influential choreographers in ballet history, dies.

1983   Miro dies
Joan Miro, a Spanish painter who won fame for his highly abstract forms, dies.

1985   Chagall dies
Marc Chagall, a forerunner of the surrealism movement, dies.

1989   Dali dies
Salvador Dali, whose surrealist paintings made him one of the most publicized figures in modern art, dies.

1989   Horowitz dies
Vladimir Horowitz, a Russian-born pianist and one of the world's greatest musicians, dies.

Science and Technology

1900   The quantum theory
Max Planck advances the quantum theory to explain certain properties of heat energy.

1900   Psychoanalysis founded
Sigmund Freud develops psychoanalysis to treat hysteria.

1903   Powered flight
Wilbur and Orville Wright fly the world's first power-driven, heavier-than-air machine at Kitty Hawk, N.C.

1904   Vacuum tube perfected
Sir John A. Fleming perfects the diode, a vacuum tube that can detect radio signals.

1905   Einstein's theory
Albert Einstein presents his Special Theory of Relativity.

1909   Bakelite invented
Leo H. Baekeland, an American chemist, invents the first synthetic resin, Bakelite.

1910   Chemotherapy used
Paul Ehrlich originates chemotherapy, the treatment of disease with chemicals.

1911   The atomic structure
Ernest Rutherford explains his theory of atomic structure.

1913   Assembly lines used
Henry Ford pioneers the use of the assembly line method to produce Model T cars.

1920   First radio programs
Station KDKA in Pittsburgh, Pa., schedules the first regular radio broadcasts.

1923   Television tried
Pictures are televised between New York City and Philadelphia.

1928   Penicillin discovered
Alexander Fleming discovers penicillin, the first antibiotic.

1930   First analog computer
Vannevar Bush invents the analog computer.

1938   Atomic age begins
Otto Hahn and Fritz Strassmann find lightweight atoms after bombarding uranium with neutrons.

1941   First TV shows
Commercial television is started in the United States.

1942   First chain reaction
Enrico Fermi and his associates achieve the first successful nuclear chain reaction.

1946   Electronic computer
John W. Mauchly and John P. Eckert, Jr., develop the first electronic computer, called "ENIAC."

1947   Transistors developed
American scientists invent the transistor, which replaces the vacuum tube.

1953   Polio conquered
Jonas Salk produces the first effective vaccine against polio.

**1954-   St. Lawrence Seaway
1959**   Canada and the United States build

the St. Lawrence Seaway. It opens the Great Lakes to seagoing vessels.

1955 **Solar battery used**
A solar battery is used to send telephone messages.

1957 **First satellite**
Russia launches the first artificial satellite.

1957 **DNA produced**
Arthur Kornberg produces artificial DNA, the basic chemical of the gene, in a test tube.

1960 **First laser**
Scientists in the United States construct and operate the first ruby laser.

1961 **First people in space**
Yuri Gagarin of Russia and Alan B. Shepard, Jr., of the United States become the first people to fly in space.

1962 **New energy source**
The first Canadian nuclear-powered electric generating station begins operating at Rolphton, Ontario.

1962 **Laser breakthrough**
The first semiconductor laser is built and demonstrated.

1965 **Tunnel completed**
The world's longest automobile tunnel, the 38,280-foot (11,688-meter) Mont Blanc Tunnel is completed in the Alps.

1966 **Mystery solved**
Scientists discover the secret of the structure of the genetic code, thus adding greatly to our understanding of heredity.

1969 **People on the moon**
Two Americans land on the moon and bring moon rocks and dust back to earth for study.

1978 **"Test-tube" babies**
Two babies, the first to be conceived in a laboratory and implanted in the mother's body, are born in England and India.

1979 **Elementary glue**
An international team of physicists conduct experiments in West Germany that may prove the existence of gluon, a fundamental particle of matter.

1980 **Medical breakthrough**
Scientists in Switzerland and the U.S. use gene-splicing techniques to create bacteria capable of producing human interferon in the laboratory.

1981 **Space shuttle**
The United States launches the space shuttle *Columbia,* the first reusable spaceship.

1983 **Second solar system**
The Infrared Astronomical Satellite (IRAS), a joint British-Dutch-U.S. project, provides scientists with the strongest evidence ever found for the existence of a second solar system, located around the star Vega.

1984 **AIDS virus discovered**
American researchers isolate a virus as the cause of AIDS, calling it the human T-lymphotropic virus type III.

1986 **Space shuttle tragedy**
The U.S. shuttle *Challenger* exploded into a ball of fire shortly after its launch.

1986 **Chernobyl accident**
An explosion and fire at the Chernobyl nuclear power plant in the U.S.S.R. kills 26 people.

1986 ***Voyager* sets record**
American pilots Dick Rutan and Jeana Yeager shatter previous records for long-distance flight without refueling when they fly nonstop around the world in nine days in the experimental aircraft *Voyager.*

1989 **Probe departs**
The U.S. *Voyager 2* unmanned space probe heads out of the solar system after sending spectacular data and images from Neptune. Surveying Neptune and its moons was the last major task in the probe's 12-year journey of 4.4 billion miles.

2

American
History

The following section outlines some important dates in U.S. history. The section is divided into seven categories: (1) political events, (2) social events, (3) religion, (4) philosophy, (5) literature, (6) the arts, including music, and (7) science and technology. Chronologically, history is divided into these broad headings: America Before Colonial Times (1492-1606); The Colonial Heritage (1607-1753); The Movement for Independence (1754-1783); Forming a New Nation (1784-1819); Expansion (1820-1849); The Irrepressible Conflict (1850-1869); Industrialization and Reform (1870-1916); A New Place in the World (1917-1929); Depression and a World in Conflict (1930-1959); and The Contemporary Period (since 1960).

You can use this unit to help you review significant dates in U.S. history and to gain an overall sense of the development of the United States. Viewed as a whole, the chronology illustrates the highlights of American life.

America Before Colonial Times

Political Events

1492 Columbus sees New World
Christopher Columbus sails from Spain and discovers the Western Hemisphere.

1513 Florida explored
Ponce de León of Spain searches for the Fountain of Youth in the West Indies; he finds instead a place that he names Florida.

1521 Cortés defeats the Aztecs
The Spanish conquistador Hernando Cortés defeats the Aztec Indians in Mexico.

1534 Cartier reaches Canada
Jacques Cartier of France is the first European to arrive in Canada.

**1540- American Southwest
1542 explored**
Francisco Coronado of Spain explores the American Southwest.

1565 Oldest U.S. city founded
Spaniards found St. Augustine, Fla., the oldest city in what is now the U.S.

1585 Raleigh settlement fails
Sir Walter Raleigh fails in his attempt to establish a permanent, British settlement in what is now the state of North Carolina.

The Arts

1600's Folk arts flourish
Folk arts and household arts flourish in the Colonies. Craftworkers produce furniture, pottery, glassware, silverware, quilts, embroidery, signs, and weather vanes—to name just a few things.

1600's Colonial architecture
Many buildings, like the Paul Revere House in Boston, Mass., are built in the Colonies. The various European styles of architecture are blended, and the resulting new style is called colonial architecture.

1600- Limners ply trade
1700   Folk artists called *limners* travel through the Colonies, painting simple portraits of local residents.

1600- Gravestone carvings
1700's Stonecutters make ornamental carvings, in various decorative motifs, on gravestones.

The Colonial Heritage

Political Events

1607 Jamestown founded
The first permanent British settlement is founded in Jamestown.

1619 First blacks arrive
The first blacks in the English colonies are brought to Jamestown by a Dutch vessel.

1619 First legislature founded
Virginia establishes the House of Burgesses.

1620 Mayflower Compact signed
English Pilgrims sign the Mayflower Compact, the first agreement for self-government in America.

1735 Freedom of press affirmed
New York newspaper publisher Peter Zenger is acquitted of a libel charge that grew out of his criticism of the British government.

Social Events

1636 First college founded
Harvard College, the first college in the Colonies, is founded on October 28.

1647 Public schools started
The first public school system supported by taxes is set up in Massachusetts.

1731 Franklin founds library
Benjamin Franklin founds the first subscription library in the U.S., the Library Company of Philadelphia. Members pay dues, which are pooled to buy books.

Religion

1607 Colonists worship
The Anglican Church begins holding regular services in Jamestown.

1639 Baptist church set
The religious leader Roger Williams founds a Baptist church in Providence, in the Rhode Island Colony.

1649 Religious freedom set
Maryland passes the first religious tolerance act in North America.

1654 Jews arrive
A group of 24 Jews land in New Amsterdam (now New York City) in the New World. The governor does not want them to perform military service but he is overruled by the Dutch West India Company.

1658 Jews to Rhode Island
Jews found a second community in the Colonies, this one in Newport, Rhode Island.

The Colonial Heritage
Religion (*Continued*)

1682   Pennsylvania founded
Quaker William Penn
founds the colony of
Pennsylvania as a ha-
ven for English Quak-
ers suffering from per-
secution.

1689   Mather on witchcraft
Cotton Mather pub-
lishes his *Memorable
Providences Relating
to Witchcraft and
Possessions.* This
work is credited with
stirring up hatred of
"witches" in Salem,
Mass.

1690's   Salem witch trials held
Twenty persons are
executed as a result of
the Salem witch trials.

1701   Mather fired
Increase Mather is re-
moved from his post
as president of Har-
vard College. He and
his son Cotton, both
conservative Congre-
gationalists, have been
outspoken in attacking
their liberal col-
leagues.

1706   Presbyterians meet
Presbyterians in the
colonies of Maryland,
Delaware, and Penn-
sylvania form an in-
formal presbytery, or
church body.

Philosophy

1733-   Franklin's almanac
1758   In this period, Benjamin Franklin pub-
lishes his *Poor Rich-
ard's Almanac.* The
Almanac contains a

great number of brief
proverbs, many of
them witty. Taken as
a whole, Franklin's
proverbs had a strong
influence on the politi-
cal and social philoso-
phy of the Colonies.

Literature

1608   Smith on the Colonies
John Smith's book *A
True Relation of such
occurrences and acci-
dents . . . as hath
hapned in Virginia* is
published in England;
it is probably the first
personal account of
life in the Colonies.

1640   First book published
The Bay Psalm Book,
a collection of psalms
in verse, is published.
It is the first book
published in the Colo-
nies.

1650   First poetry book
Anne Dudley Brad-
street publishes the
first volume of original
poetry written in the
Colonies.

**1702   Cotton Mather's fa-
mous book**
Cotton Mather, a min-
ister, publishes what
may be his greatest
work, *Magnalia
Christi Americana
(Ecclesiastical History
of New England).*

Science and
Technology

1621   Blast furnace operates
The first blast furnace
in the Colonies is
placed in operation at
Falling Creek, Va.

1646   Ironworks built
The first successful
American ironworks is
built north of Boston,
Mass.

1672   Major cities linked
The completion of the
Boston Post Road
links Boston and New
York City.

1724   Irrigation employed
South Carolina rice
growers use irrigation
systems to increase
the size of their rice
crops.

1728   First botanical garden
John Bartram, a fa-
mous botanist, plants
the first botanical gar-
den in America.

1739   First glass factory
The first successful
American glass fac-
tory is started in
Salem County, N.J.

1743   Science group formed
Benjamin Franklin
founds the American
Philosophical Society,
which becomes the
chief center of colo-
nial science.

1751   Hospital started
One of the first public
hospitals in America
is chartered in Phila-
delphia, Pa.

1752   Franklin's famous kite
Benjamin Franklin
flies a kite during a
storm in a basic ex-
periment. He proves
that lightning is a form
of electricity.

The Movement for Independence

Political Events

1763 **Treaty of Paris signed**
France loses most
possessions in North
America after defeat
by British and Ameri-
cans.

1765 **Stamp Act unites
Americans**
Colonists protest taxa-
tion without represen-
tation after Parliament
passes the Stamp Act.

1770 **Boston Massacre
occurs**
On March 5, British
troops fire on and kill
American civilians.

1773 **Colonists dump tea**
Rebelling against Brit-
ish laws, colonists dis-
guised as Indians
dump British tea in
the harbor at Boston
on December 16.

1774 **Intolerable Acts passed**
Parliament passes the
Intolerable Acts as a
punishment for colo-
nial rebellion.

1774 **The Colonies organize**
Meeting in Philadel-
phia, delegates from
12 colonies hold the
First Continental Con-
gress.

1775 **Revolutionary War
begins**
The Revolutionary
War begins on April
19, as British soldiers
attack the patriots at
Lexington and Con-
cord.

1775 **Battle of Bunker Hill**
On June 17, the Brit-
ish Army defeats the
patriots.

1776 **Independence declared**
On July 4, the Decla-
ration of Independ-
ence is adopted.

The original Declaration of Independence is displayed
in the National Archives Building in Washington, D.C.

Political Events (*Continued*)

1777   Burgoyne defeated
Britain's General John
Burgoyne surrenders
at Saratoga on Octo-
ber 17.

1777   Winter at Valley Forge
General George Wash-
ington leads his army
to its winter quarters
at Valley Forge, Pa.,
on December 19.

**1778   France allies with
patriots**
The United States and
France sign an alli-
ance on February 6.

1779   Patriots win at sea
Captain John Paul
Jones captures a ma-
jor British ship, the
Serapis, on September
23.

1781   British fleet defeated
The French drive a
British naval force
from Chesapeake Bay
on September 15.

**1781   British Army surren-
ders**
A British Army sur-
renders at Yorktown,
Va., on October 19,
officially ending the
war.

1781   Articles signed
The first central gov-
ernment is established
by the Articles of
Confederation.

1783   Treaty of Paris signed
The Americans and
the British sign the
Treaty of Paris on

September 3; the Rev-
olutionary War is offi-
cially over.

Religion

1725-   Revivalism grows
1775   The sermons of Jonathan Edwards, a Puri-
tan minister, inspire a
religious revival
movement in New
England called "The
Great Awakening."

1763   Synagogue dedicated
The Jewish synagogue
at Newport, R.I., is
dedicated. It is the
oldest synagogue in
the U.S. still standing
in contemporary
times.

1769   Missions in California
Junipero Serra, a
Franciscan missionary
from Spain, estab-
lishes the first Catho-
lic mission in Califor-
nia—near what is
today San Diego.

Philosophy

1754   Edwards publishes
Jonathan Edwards, a
Puritan minister, pub-
lishes his major philo-
sophical work, *Free-
dom of Will.*

1774   Jefferson on rights
Thomas Jefferson's
pamphlet *A Summary
View of the Rights of
British America* is
printed. In this pam-
phlet, Jefferson sets
forth a political philos-
ophy that will lead to
revolution—namely,
that England has no
right to govern the
Colonies from afar.

**1776   Paine's rallying state-
ment**
Tom Paine's pamphlet
Common Sense is
published. The pam-
phlet contains a stir-
ring demand for inde-
pendence and lists
reasons why inde-
pendence is abso-
lutely necessary.

Literature

1770   Wheatley's first poem
Black poet Phillis
Wheatley publishes
her first poem, "An
Elegiac Poem on the
Death of that cele-
brated Divine . . .
George Whitefield."

1771-   Franklin on his life
1790   Benjamin Franklin begins writing his auto-
biography in 1771 and
works on it, without
finishing it, for the
rest of his life. The
book is still consid-
ered a classic today.

**1782   Crèvecoeur on
America**
Jean de Crèvecoeur
publishes his *Letters
from an American
Farmer.* The book
presents a vivid de-
scription of life in the
new, young nation.

The Arts

**1766   Copley shows in
London**
John Singleton Cop-
ley, perhaps the great-
est portrait painter in
the Colonies, exhibits
his work in London.

Science and Technology

1756 **Stagecoach line opens**
A stagecoach line links New York City and Philadelphia.

1757 **City lights up**
The first street lights in the Colonies are installed in Philadelphia.

1760 **First wagons built**
The first Conestoga wagons are built in Pennsylvania. The pioneers use these sturdy covered wagons in their move westward.

1765 **First medical school**
The first medical school in the Colonies is established in Philadelphia.

1775 **Iron production grows**
Colonial ironworks are producing one-seventh of the world's iron.

1776 **Smith on economics**
Adam Smith publishes the first systematic classification of classical economics.

Forming a New Nation

Political Events

1787 **Constitution adopted**
The Constitution of the United States is signed on September 17 in Philadelphia; it replaces the Articles of Confederation.

1789 **Washington elected President**
In February, George Washington is elected the first President of the United States.

1790 **Political parties formed**
Disputes over government policies lead to the formation of political parties.

1791 **Bill of Rights adopted**
By December 15, 10 amendments to the Constitution are approved, guaranteeing freedom of speech, religion, press, and peaceful assembly.

1792 **Washington reelected**
George Washington is reelected President.

1800 **Capital moved**
The federal government is moved from Philadelphia to Washington, D.C.

1803 **Judicial review set**
In deciding the case *Marbury v. Madison,* the Supreme Court of the U.S. establishes the principle of judicial review.

1803 **Louisiana Purchase made**
The size of the U.S. doubles when President Jefferson buys the Louisiana Territory from France.

1804- **West is explored**
1806   The Lewis and Clark expedition explores the lands west of the Mississippi River.

1812- **War of 1812 waged**
1814   The U.S. goes to war with Great Britain to protect freedom of the seas and the American shipping trade.

Social Events

1787 **Prison reformers meet**
A group of Philadelphia Quakers organizes a prison reform group; it is later called the Pennsylvania Prison Society.

1792 **First local union set**
Philadelphia, Pa., shoemakers organize the first local union in the U.S.

1800 **Library of Congress set**
The Library of Congress is established by the U.S. Congress; the Library is to serve as the national library and to provide research assistance to Congress.

Forming a New Nation

Religion

1789   **Catholic bishop elected**
Roman Catholic priests in the U.S. elect John Carroll as the first bishop in the U.S.

Philosophy

1785   **Madison on liberty**
James Madison writes his *Memorial and Remonstrance on the Religious Rights of Man.* This was a statement advocating religious freedom and defining civil rights as separate from religion.

1787-   **The Federalist papers**
1788   Alexander Hamilton, James Madison, and John Jay write most of the essays that are later published as *The Federalist.* In the Federalist papers, the authors lay out their political philosophy—especially, the need for a strong central government.

Literature

1817   **"Thanatopsis" published**
William Cullen Bryant writes "Thanatopsis,"

a brilliant poem about death.

The Arts

1795   **Peale's master work**
Painter Charles Willson Peale completes his picture *The Staircase Group,* a portrait of his family.

1795-   **Stuart and Washington**
1796   President George Washington sits for three different portraits by artist Gilbert Stuart.

1814   **National anthem composed**
During the War of 1812, Francis Scott Key writes "The Star-Spangled Banner."

Science and Technology

1787   **First steamboat**
John Fitch demonstrates the first workable steamboat in the U.S.

1790   **Cotton-spinning machine**
Samuel Slater builds the country's first successful water-powered machine for spinning cotton.

1791   **Banneker and the Capital**
Benjamin Banneker, a free black and a math-

ematician, helps survey the city of Washington, D.C. He later publishes an annual almanac of weather predictions and tide calculations.

1793   **Cotton gin invented**
Eli Whitney builds the first cotton gin. This machine cleans cotton faster than 50 persons working by hand.

1798   **Mass production**
Eli Whitney makes muskets, or guns, using the first mass-production methods.

1807   **Steamboat perfected**
Robert Fulton demonstrates the first commercially successful steamboat. It revolutionizes the shipping industry of the new nation.

1811   **National Road begun**
Work begins on the National Road, which will eventually link the East and the Midwest.

1819   **Plow improved**
Jethro Wood produced an improved cast-iron plow, which features replaceable pieces at points of greatest wear.

Expansion

Political Events

1820   **Missouri Compromise set**
The Missouri Compromise is approved by

Congress in March; Missouri is admitted as a slave state, Maine is admitted as a free state at the same

time, and slavery is forbidden in all other areas of the U.S. north of the 36°30′ latitude.

1823   **Monroe Doctrine issued**
On December 2, President James Monroe announces the Monroe Doctrine, which warns European nations not to interfere with free nations in the Western Hemisphere.

1838-   **"Trail of Tears" forged**
1839   Troops drive thousands of Cherokee and Choctaw Indians from their homes, west across the Mississippi River on a "Trail of Tears."

1845   **"Manifest destiny" rises**
Many Americans come to believe that it is their "destiny" to control all of North America.

1846-   **Mexican War fought**
1848   In a dispute over territory, the U.S. goes to war with Mexico. The new land that is gained becomes the southwestern U.S.

1848   **Gold Rush begins**
The discovery of gold at Sutter's Mill in California on January 24 triggers a frantic gold rush.

Social Events

1836   **First child labor law**
Massachusetts passes the first law limiting child labor in the United States.

1840's **Immigration stepped up**
"Great waves" of immigration to the United States begin; Germany, Ireland, Italy, Sweden, Norway, and the Austro-Hungarian empire are some of the countries from which the migrants come.

1841   **Mental patients aided**
Dorothea Dix begins her drive to provide better care for the mentally ill.

1842   **Unions ruled legal**
A Massachusetts court legalizes labor unions.

1846   **Smithsonian founded**
The Smithsonian Institution is founded in Washington, D.C.; the Smithsonian is a national institution devoted to research and learning.

1848   **Feminists organize**
Meeting in Seneca Falls, N.Y., delegates to the first Women's Rights Convention publicly declare that "all men and women are created equal."

Religion

1824   **Sunday School movement**
The American Sunday School Union is formed, as the Sunday School movement grows.

1825   **Unitarian Church founded**
Clergyman William Ellery Channing organizes the American Unitarian Association.

1830   **Mormon Church founded**
Joseph Smith and his associates start the Church of Jesus Christ of Latter-day Saints, or Mormon Church, on April 6.

1834   **Convent burned**
Amid an atmosphere of fear and prejudice, the townspeople in Charlestown, Mass., burn down a Roman Catholic convent of the Ursuline order.

1838   **Mormons to Nauvoo**
Ordered out of Missouri, about 15,000 Mormons migrate to Illinois and found the city of Nauvoo.

1838   **Missionary to Indians**
Jesuit Pierre De Smet begins his long career of converting Indians to Christianity. Other Catholic orders and other denominations also send missionaries to work among the Indians.

1840-   **Immigrants arrive**
1900   Great waves of immigration increase the population of the U.S. and alter the religious composition of the country. The Roman Catholic Church increases in size, as many Catholics arrive from central and eastern Europe. The Lutheran Church also

Expansion
Religion (*Continued*)

grows, as many Lutherans arrive from the Scandinavian countries.

1844   **Joseph Smith killed**
A newspaper in Nauvoo that has opposed Mormon leader Joseph Smith is burned down. Smith and his brother are jailed at Carthage for the crime; a mob breaks into the jail and kills Smith and his brother.

1845   **Southern Baptists meet**
The Southern Baptist Convention is organized in Augusta, Ga. Baptists in the South have been arguing with Baptists in the North over the slavery issue.

1847   **Mormons settle in Utah**
Brigham Young, the new Mormon leader, starts a Mormon settlement in the Great Salt Lake Valley, in what is now the state of Utah.

1848   **Oneida group formed**
John Humphrey Noyes founds a cooperative religious settlement called the Oneida Community in Putney, Vt. The community is based on personal communication with God and harmonious living with peers.

1849   **Apply for statehood**
The Mormons, who have set up a civil government in the Great Salt Lake Valley, apply for admission to the Union as the *State of Deseret.* Instead of granting statehood, Congress sets up the Territory of Utah the next year.

Philosophy

1830   **Alcott publishes**
Bronson Alcott publishes his *Observations on the Principles and Methods of Infant Instruction.*

1834-   **Alcott runs school**
1839   Philosopher Bronson Alcott operates the experimental Temple School in Boston, Mass.

1839-   **Fuller lectures**
1844   Margaret Fuller, a transcendentalist philosopher, conducts a series of "conversations" for women in Boston, Mass. The lectures—which cover philosophy, literature, and education—are a successful experiment in adult education.

1840   **Fuller edits magazine**
Margaret Fuller becomes the editor of the *Dial,* a magazine of transcendentalist philosophy.

1841   **Emerson's first essays**
Ralph Waldo Emerson publishes his brilliant *Essays, First Series.* The famed essay "Self-Reliance" is included in this series.

1841   **Parker gives major talk**
Theodore Parker, a Unitarian clergyman and transcendentalist philosopher, delivers a sermon called "Discourse on the Transient and Permanent in Christianity." Parker's ideas were to prove influential in the areas of religion, philosophy, and social reform.

1841-   **Brook Farm set up**
1847   A group of transcendentalists, led by philosopher George Ripley, operate Brook Farm, an experimental community. Brook Farm is located in West Roxbury, Mass.

1844   **Emerson's second essays**
Essays, Second Series, by Ralph Waldo Emerson, is published.

1845-   **Emerson lectures**
1846   Philosopher Ralph Waldo Emerson delivers a lecture series called *Representative Men.*

Literature

1820   **Short story set**
Washington Irving completes "Rip Van Winkle." With this piece, he creates a new literary form, the short story.

1823-   **Cooper on the frontier**
1841   James Fenimore Cooper writes a series of five novels about the frontier called *The*

Leatherstocking Tales. The five include *The Deerslayer* and *The Last of the Mohicans.*

1845 **"The Raven" by Poe**
Edgar Allan Poe writes "The Raven," a sad poem about a man who feels haunted after the death of his love.

1846 **Poems by Emerson**
The transcendentalist philosopher Ralph Waldo Emerson publishes *Poems,* a volume of his verse.

1847 **Longfellow's poetry**
Henry Wadsworth Longfellow publishes one of his best poems, *Evangeline.*

1849 **Parkman on Indians**
Historian Francis Parkman publishes *The Oregon Trail,* an account of life among the Indians of the Northwest.

The Arts

1820 **Actor's debut**
One of the first great American actors, Edwin Forrest, makes his initial stage appearance.

1825 **Recognition for Cole**
Painter Thomas Cole first receives recognition for his landscapes of the Hudson River Valley in New York state.

1832 **Catlin on Indians**
George Catlin completes his portrait of the Mandan chief

Four Bears. Catlin paints many Indian chiefs and tribesmen during his career.

1840 **Trinity Church**
Building begins on the Trinity Church in New York City, which was designed by architect Richard Upjohn. The architect has adapted traditional Gothic design to the New World.

1840 **A Greenough sculpture**
Horatio Greenough completes his massive sculpture of George Washington.

1840's **Minstrels entertain**
Minstrel shows become a popular form of musical entertainment. Troupes such as Christy's Minstrels dance and sing, usually in blackface makeup.

1846 **Song hit by Foster**
Composer Stephen Foster writes the song "Oh! Susanna," perhaps the most popular of his 200-plus songs.

Science and Technology

1825 **Erie Canal completed**
The Erie Canal is opened, providing a water passage between New York and the Great Lakes.

1830 **Passenger train travel**
Peter Cooper builds the "Tom Thumb," the first American-made steam locomotive. It pulls one of the first passenger trains.

1834 **Reaper helps farming**
Cyrus McCormick patents a reaping machine that makes it possible to harvest larger wheat crops.

1834 **Threshing machine**
John and Hiram Pitts patent the first threshing machine, advancing the development of large-scale farming.

1835 **Colt perfects revolver**
Samuel Colt develops the first successful repeating pistol.

1837 **Steel plow developed**
John Deere builds the first steel plow. This plow is especially suitable for the heavy prairie sod.

1837 **First telegraph message**
Samuel F. B. Morse demonstrates the first successful telegraph, which proves to be the fastest communication available to date.

1839 **Rubber industry advanced**
Charles Goodyear makes rubber stronger through a process called vulcanization.

1842 **Ether kills pain**
Crawford Long uses ether as an anesthetic in surgery.

1846 **Sewing machine improved**
Elias Howe patents a practical sewing machine.

The Irrepressible Conflict

Political Events

1850 **The Compromise of 1850**
A series of laws are passed to deal with the issue of slavery in the new territory acquired from Mexico. The chief terms are the banning of slavery from California and the enactment of the Fugitive Slave Law to tighten the slavery system.

1854 **Kansas-Nebraska Act**
Congress passes the Kansas-Nebraska Act, which sets up the two territories of Kansas and Nebraska and allows the citizens of those territories to vote on whether they wish to have slavery or not.

1857 **Dred Scott ruling made**
In the Dred Scott decision, the U.S. Supreme Court rules that blacks are not citizens.

1859 **John Brown raids arsenal**
John Brown, a radical abolitionist, captures the arsenal at Harpers Ferry, Virginia, hoping to start a slave revolt.

1860 **Lincoln elected President**
Abraham Lincoln, a Republican from Illinois, is elected 16th President of the United States; he is dedicated to preserving the Union.

1860 **South Carolina secedes**
In December, the state of South Carolina becomes the first to secede from the Union.

1861 **Confederacy is formed**
On February 4, South Carolina and five other states that have seceded from the Union meet in Montgomery, Ala., and declare the formation of a new nation, the Confederate States of America; a total of 11 states eventually join the Confederacy.

1861 **Civil War begins**
On April 12, Southern troops fire on Fort Sumter in Charleston Harbor. The Civil War begins.

1861 **First Battle of Bull Run**
One of the first major battles of the war occurs at Manassas, Va.; the army of the North is defeated at Bull Run.

1862 *Monitor* **and** *Merrimack*
On March 8 the Confederate ironclad ship *Merrimack* sinks two Northern ships, but on March 9 the Union ironclad *Monitor* appears and fights the *Merrimack* to a draw.

1862 **Union wins at Shiloh**
General Ulysses S. Grant wins the Battle of Shiloh at Pittsburg Landing, Tenn., for the Union on April 6 and 7.

1862 **Lands in the West open**
The Homestead Act is passed, offering free land to settlers in the West.

1862 **Bull Run revisited**
The Second Battle of Bull Run takes place August 29 and 30; the South wins again.

1863 **North wins in the West**
General Grant leads the Union Army to victory in the Siege of Vicksburg, Miss., from May 19 to July 4.

1863 **North wins at Gettysburg**
Confederate General Robert E. Lee leads his army in an attack on Gettysburg, Pa., July 1-3; the Northern victory here is a turning point in the war.

1863 **Slaves are freed**
President Lincoln is-
sues the Emancipation
Proclamation on Janu-
ary 1; slaves in the
Confederate States are
declared free.

1864 **Truth visits
White House**
Sojourner Truth, a
former slave who has
traveled widely to
speak out against
slavery, visits Presi-
dent Lincoln in the
White House.

1864 **Grant forges on**
The North under Gen-
eral Grant and the
South under General
Lee fight an inconclu-
sive battle, the Battle
of the Wilderness, in a
heavily wooded area
of northern Virginia
on May 5 and 6;
Grant and his army
continue moving
south.

1864 **Sherman marches**
Union General Wil-
liam Tecumseh Sher-
man begins his
"March through Geor-
gia" by leaving At-
lanta in flames on No-
vember 15 and moving
southeast throughout
the state.

1865 **Civil War ends**
On April 9, General
Lee surrenders to
General Grant at the
Appomattox Court
House in Virginia.

865 **Lincoln assassinated**
On April 14, John
Wilkes Booth shoots
President Abraham
Lincoln at Ford's
Theatre in Washing-
ton, D.C.

1865- **Reconstruction pro-**
1877 **ceeds**
The South is gradually
returned to the Union
in the Reconstruction
era; amendments to
the U.S. Constitution
abolish slavery, make
blacks citizens, and
grant them voting
rights.

1867 **Alaska purchased**
The United States
buys Alaska from
Russia for $7.2 mil-
lion.

1868 **Andrew Johnson
on trial**
The House of Repre-
sentatives votes im-
peachment charges
against President An-
drew Johnson, but the
Senate votes not to
remove him from of-
fice.

1869 **Women seek the vote**
Susan B. Anthony and
Elizabeth Cady Stan-
ton found the National
Woman Suffrage As-
sociation, to help win
the vote.

Social Events

1862 **Land-Grant
colleges set**
The Morrill, or Land-
Grant, Act of 1862
provides land to each

state; the land is to be
sold to finance a col-
lege for agriculture
and the mechanical
arts in each state.

1867 **Farmers organize**
The National Grange
is founded to assist
farmers in obtaining
fairer prices for their
products.

Religion

1866 **Black Baptists meet**
A state convention of
black Baptists is
formed in North Caro-
lina.

Philosophy

1854 **Major work by
Thoreau**
Henry David Thoreau
publishes a book of
essays; called *Walden,*
the book discusses na-
ture and the human
spirit.

1859 **Darwin on evolution**
Charles R. Darwin
publishes his theory of
evolution in *On the
Origin of Species by
Means of Natural Se-
lection, or the Preser-
vation of Favoured
Races in the Struggle
for Life.* Though Dar-
win is a British natu-
ralist, *The Origin of
Species*—as it comes
to be known—has a
profound impact on
U.S. philosophy and
psychology.

The Irrepressible Conflict
Philosophy (*Continued*)

1860   **Lectures published**
Ralph Waldo Emerson's lectures on *The Conduct of Life* are published. The lectures were first given in 1851.

Literature

1850   **Hawthorne on sin**
Nathaniel Hawthorne's *The Scarlet Letter* is published. It is a novel about the tragic consequences of sin.

1851   **Melville's masterpiece**
Moby Dick, by Herman Melville, is published. *Moby* is a novel about whaling and about the nature of life.

1851-   **Stowe on slavery**
1852   Harriet Beecher Stowe writes *Uncle Tom's Cabin,* a famous antislavery novel.

1855   **Poetry by Walt Whitman**
Walt Whitman publishes a volume of poetry called *Leaves of Grass.* This great volume contains the moving poem "Song of Myself."

1861   **Dickinson begins writing**
Emily Dickinson begins writing poetry seriously and in volume. Only a few of her poems are published during her lifetime, however.

1866   **Whittier's "Snow-Bound"**
Poet John Greenleaf Whittier publishes what may be his best work, "Snow-Bound," a long poem about winter in a Quaker community.

The Arts

1862   **Popular Civil War song**
Walter Kittredge writes the rousing Civil War song "Tenting on the Old Camp Ground."

1867   **Currier and Ives**
Home for Thanksgiving, a Currier and Ives print, is first published.

Science and Technology

1852   **Otis improves the elevator**
Elisha Otis builds an elevator that uses safety devices to protect against falling.

1859   **Petroleum industry**
The first commercially successful oil well is drilled near Titusville, Pa.

1861   **Telegraph across nation**
The transcontinental telegraph line, connecting the eastern U.S. with California, is completed.

1865   **Railway sleeping cars**
George Pullman introduces a new sleeping car for overnight train travel.

1866   **Cable across Atlantic**
After four unsuccessful attempts, a telegraph cable is laid across the Atlantic Ocean by Cyrus Field.

1867   **Typewriter developed**
Christopher Sholes plays a major role in developing the typewriter; it is patented in 1868.

1868   **Air brakes perfected**
Trains are made faster and safer with the addition of new air brakes, perfected by George Westinghouse.

1869   **Transcontinental railway**
In Promontory, Utah, the last spike is driven into the first transcontinental railway line.

Industrialization and Reform

Political Events

1876 Sitting Bull defeats Custer
A band of Sioux and Cheyenne defeats General George Armstrong Custer at the Little Bighorn River in Montana in June.

1877 Federal troops leave South
The Reconstruction period ends officially as federal troops are withdrawn.

1884 Statue of Liberty erected
The people of France give a 150-foot statue to the U.S. as a symbol of friendship.

1896 Segregation upheld
The Supreme Court of the U.S. rules in *Plessy v. Ferguson* that a state may provide "separate but equal" facilities for whites and blacks.

1898 Hawaii annexed
The Hawaiian Islands are annexed by the U.S.

1898 U.S. battleship sinks
In February, the battleship *Maine* explodes in the harbor at Havana, Cuba; "yellow journalists" in the U.S. use this event to agitate for war with Spain.

1898 War with Spain
On April 25, war with Spain is declared by the U.S.

1898 War ends
On December 10, the Paris Peace Treaty is signed, ending the Spanish-American War; the U.S. gains possession of Guam, Puerto Rico, and the Philippines as part of the settlement.

1901 McKinley assassinated
President William McKinley is assassinated in September.

1904 Canal land leased
The United States purchases the rights to the land in Central America on which the Panama Canal is scheduled to be built.

1914 Canal opened
On August 15, the U.S. opens the Panama Canal.

Social Events

1870-1916 Population doubles
More than 25 million immigrants enter the U.S.; the population more than doubles.

1876 ALA founded
The American Library Association (ALA) is founded to help organize and encourage U.S. libraries; in the same year, Melvil Dewey publishes his Dewey Decimal Classification system.

1879 Willard seeks temperance
Frances E. Willard, an educator and social reformer, becomes president of the Woman's Christian Temperance Union; she organizes a drive toward national prohibition.

1881 Red Cross started
Clara Barton, a nurse known as "the angel of the battlefield" in the Civil War, helps establish the American branch of the Red Cross.

1881 Tuskegee Institute set
Booker T. Washington, an influential black leader and educator, starts the Tuskegee Institute in Alabama, a vocational school for blacks.

1883 Civil service reformed
Congress passes the Civil Service Reform Act, also called the Pendleton Act; it eventually improves the morale and efficiency of the federal civil service.

1886 Labor group formed
The American Federation of Labor (AFL) is founded by Samuel Gompers in Columbus, Ohio.

1889   Hull House founded
Jane Addams and Ellen Starr found a Chicago settlement house called Hull House; they use Hull House as a base from which to work with slum dwellers.

1892   Lynching at peak
Some 230 persons, mostly blacks, are lynched, or hanged by mobs without trial. This is the peak of lynching, which began about 1882 and which continued to 1968.

1892   Labor deaths at Homestead
Ten persons die when guards attack strikers at the steel mills in Homestead, Pa.

1894   Pullman clash violent
Federal troops battle strikers at the Pullman plant in Chicago, with heavy loss of life and considerable property damage.

1896   "A cross of gold"
Populist leader William Jennings Bryan makes an impassioned speech before the Democratic National Convention in Chicago, asking the delegates not to "crucify mankind upon a cross of gold"; Bryan supports free coinage of silver to benefit "the producing masses."

1903   University founded
The University of Puerto Rico is founded in San Juan; a branch campus is later opened in Mayaguez.

1909   NAACP founded
The National Association for the Advancement of Colored People (NAACP) is founded to work for the rights of blacks.

1911   Urban League founded
The National Urban League is founded to assist blacks in getting jobs and housing.

1914   Family planning aided
Margaret Sanger founds the American Birth Control League, to provide birth control information and devices. The group later changes its name to Planned Parenthood-World Population (PPWP).

1916   Child labor law passed
Congress passes the first federal law regulating child labor.

Religion

1875   Eddy publishes
Mary Baker Eddy publishes her major work, *Science and Health with Key to the Scriptures*.

1879   Christian Science set
Mary Baker Eddy and her husband found the Church of Christ, Scientist—also known as the Christian Science Church.

1880   Baptists organize
The National Baptist Convention of America is formed, to bring unity to the Baptists in the U.S.

1880   Salvation Army arrives
The Salvation Army, founded two years earlier in England, is introduced into the U.S. The Army provides shelter, food, and other types of aid to the poor within a religious framework.

1886   Bible school founded
Dwight L. Moody founds the Moody Bible Institute in Chicago; the Institute is a school for training workers in various fields of Christian service.

1887   Catholic University founded
The Catholic University of America is established in Washington, D.C.; it is designated the official Roman Catholic university in the U.S.

1890   Abandon polygamy
The Mormons outlaw the practice of polygamy, or having more than one wife at the same time. Congress has blocked statehood for Utah because of strong feelings in the U.S. against polygamy.

1901   Pentecostal landmark
A worshiper at an evangelical meeting of

the Holiness move-
ment in Topeka,
Kan., begins "speak-
ing in tongues"— or
speaking unintelligible
words in a spirit of re-
ligious ecstasy. This
incident is the start of
the spread of the Pen-
tecostal movement.

1915 **Baptists split**
The Baptist church is
split by factions, in a
dispute over church
property and church
publications. The Na-
tional Baptist Conven-
tion, U.S.A., Inc., is
formed. It proves to
be a larger group than
the parent group, the
National Baptist Con-
vention of America.

Philosophy

1870 **Philosophy club
formed**
A group of philoso-
phers, including
Charles Sanders
Peirce, William
James, Chauncey
Wright, and Oliver
Wendell Holmes Jr.,
meet in Cambridge to
discuss philosophy;
they call their group
"the Metaphysical
Club."

1870's **Birth of pragmatism**
The term "pragma-
tism" is added to the
language of philoso-
phy. American philos-
opher Charles Sanders
Peirce coins the term
to refer to a particular
method of logic.

1877 **Wright publishes**
A collection of the
writings of Chauncey
Wright is published;
the book is called
*Philosophical Discus-
sions.*

1879- **Philosophy school**
1888 The Concord Summer
School of Philosophy
and Literature is oper-
ated in this period.
The school begins in
the home of Bronson
Alcott, a leading tran-
scendentalist philoso-
pher. Later the school
is moved to a center
dedicated to transcen-
dentalism.

1892 **Idealism movement
begins**
Josiah Royce, leader
of the movement
called idealism, pub-
lishes *The Spirit of
Modern Philosophy,*
the first of five famous
books.

1896 **Essay on pragmatism**
Philosopher William
James publishes the
essay "The Will to Be-
lieve." The essay is a
major work on prag-
matism.

1899 **Dewey on education**
In his book *School
and Society,* John
Dewey sets forth the
principles of progres-
sive education.

1901- **James lectures**
1902 William James deliv-
ers a series of lectures
in Scotland called *The
Varieties of Religious
Experience.*

1905- **Santayana publishes**
1906 Philosopher George
Santayana completes
a five-volume work,
The Life of Reason.

1909 **Pragmatism debated**
William James pub-
lishes *The Meaning of
Truth,* a collection of
writings debating var-
ious aspects of prag-
matism.

1912 **Empiricism explored**
A series of essays by
William James is pub-
lished posthumously
under the title *Essays
in Radical Empiri-
cism.*

Literature

1876 **Twain on the river**
Mark Twain's novel
*The Adventures of
Tom Sawyer* is pub-
lished. The book por-
trays a boy's adven-
tures on the
Mississippi River.

1881 **James in flower**
*The Portrait of a
Lady,* a novel by
Henry James, is pub-
lished.

1881 **Another Twain classic**
*The Prince and the
Pauper,* a novel by
Mark Twain, is pub-
lished.

1884 **Twain's masterpiece**
Mark Twain's novel
*The Adventures of
Huckleberry Finn* is
published. Like *Tom
Sawyer, Huck Finn* is
set on the Mississippi
River.

Industrialization and Reform
Literature *(Continued)*

1885   Howells on success
William Dean Howells' novel *The Rise of Silas Lapham* is published. The novel deals with the life of a self-made success.

1889   Twain on King Arthur
Mark Twain publishes his take-off on the Arthurian legends, *A Connecticut Yankee in King Arthur's Court.*

1901   Realism from Norris
Frank Norris' novel *The Octopus* is published. The book is a realistic account of the struggles surrounding railroad expansion.

1903   A classic by London
Jack London's novel *The Call of the Wild* is published.

1903   Mature James
Henry James's novel *The Ambassadors* is published.

1913   Major poem by Lindsay
Vachel Lindsay's poem "General William Booth Enters into Heaven" is published. Lindsay's poetry features strong rhythms and vivid images.

1914   Amy Lowell's poetry
Sword Blades and Poppy Seeds, a volume of imagist poetry, is published by Amy Lowell.

The Arts

1872   Whistler's famous work
James McNeill Whistler paints the portrait known as *Whistler's Mother.*

1876   Winslow Homer
Painter Winslow Homer completes one of his most famous paintings of the sea, *Breezing Up.*

1880   Sousa leads band
John Philip Sousa, the "march king," is appointed leader of the U.S. Marine Band.

1880's   Barnum joins Bailey
Two "greats" in the circus world, P. T. Barnum and James A. Bailey, become partners. Their joint circus is called Barnum & Bailey's "Greatest Show on Earth."

1883   Met founded
The Metropolitan Opera House opens in New York City, with *Faust* as its first offering.

1884-   Early skyscraper
1885   The Home Insurance Building, designed by William LeBaron Jenney, is erected in Chicago. This building is usually considered the first skyscraper.

1885-   Richardson master-
1887   work
The Marshall Field Wholesale Store in Chicago, designed by architect H. H. Richardson, is completed.

1886-   Adler and Sullivan
1889   The Auditorium Building, designed by Dankmar Adler and Louis H. Sullivan, is erected in Chicago.

1887   Residential architecture
The firm of McKim, Mead, & White designs the W. G. Low house in Bristol, R.I.

1892   Work by Cassatt
Mary Cassatt completes her famed painting *The Bath.*

1893   Famed Stieglitz photo
Winter on Fifth Avenue, New York, a photograph by Alfred Stieglitz, first appears.

1893   Columbian Exposition
The World's Columbian Exposition opens in Chicago. Featured is the Great White City of vast buildings designed by famous architects. Also featured are large statues by prominent sculptors like Augustus Saint-Gaudens and Daniel Chester French.

1898   Work by Eakins
Realistic painter Thomas Eakins completes *The Clinic of Dr. Agnew.*

1899   Isadora Duncan
The modern dancer Isadora Duncan performs in Chicago.

1903 **Remington painting**
Painter Frederic Remington completes his *Fight for the Waterhole*. Remington paints mostly scenes of the American frontier.

1910 **Black orchestra**
James Reese Europe, leader of a black dance band, starts a black symphony orchestra.

1911 **Ives's third symphony**
Charles Edward Ives completes his *Third Symphony*. It is not until 1947, however, that he receives the Pulitzer prize for music for this work.

1911- **Woolworth Building**
1913 The Woolworth Building is erected in New York City. The building is a Gothic skyscraper designed by Cass Gilbert.

1914 **"St. Louis Blues"**
Black composer W. C. Handy writes "The St. Louis Blues." Handy's work has a major effect on ragtime and jazz music.

1916 **Wright hotel**
The Imperial Hotel in Tokyo, Japan, is begun; the quakeproof hotel was designed by the American architect Frank Lloyd Wright.

Science and Technology

1876 **Telephone is invented**
Alexander Graham Bell invents the telephone.

1877 **Phonograph invented**
Thomas Edison, the "Wizard of Menlo Park," creates the phonograph, which he calls his favorite invention.

1879 **Electric light invented**
Thomas Edison adds the electric light to his long list of inventions.

1884 **Linotype patented**
Ottmar Mergenthaler patents the linotype, which speeds the printing process. Two years later, the New York City *Tribune* uses the new machine to set type.

1884 **First skyscraper begun**
Work on the world's first skyscraper, the Home Insurance Building, is begun in Chicago.

1896 **Ford builds first car**
Henry Ford completes his first automobile, paving the way for later mass production.

1897 **First U.S. subway built**
The first U.S. subway is built in Boston.

1903 **First airplane**
Wilbur and Orville Wright fly the first power-driven airplane at Kitty Hawk, N.C.

1909 **Peary reaches North Pole**
On April 6, Commander Robert E. Peary of the U.S. Navy is the first person to reach the North Pole.

1916 **Carver receives acclaim**
George Washington Carver is honored by the Royal Society of Arts in London for his agricultural research with peanuts and other products.

A New Place in the World

Political Events

1917 **U.S. enters World War**
Following a period of unlimited submarine warfare by Germany, the U.S. enters World War I on the Allied side.

1918 **Fourteen Points listed**
President Woodrow Wilson announces his Fourteen Points necessary to conclude a peace settlement to World War I.

1918 **Armistice signed**
The armistice ending World War I is signed on November 11 in France.

1919 **Prohibition begins**
The 18th Amendment

A New Place in the World
Political Events (*Continued*)

to the U.S. Constitution is enacted, prohibiting the manufacture and sale of alcoholic beverages.

1919   **Women get vote**
The 19th Amendment to the U.S. Constitution is enacted, granting women the vote.

1920   **Versailles Treaty spurned**
The U.S. Senate votes not to ratify the Treaty of Versailles, drawn up after Germany surrendered in World War I.

1924   **Teapot Dome scandal**
A Senate investigation in February and March uncovers a major scandal, called the Teapot Dome scandal, in the Administration of President Warren G. Harding.

1924   **Indians made citizens**
By Act of Congress, Indians born in the U.S. are declared citizens.

1927   **Sacco and Vanzetti die**
Nicola Sacco and Bartolomeo Vanzetti are executed in August for killing a paymaster and his guard during a robbery in South Braintree, Mass.;

many believe they have been condemned for their political ideas.

1929   **Stock market crashes**
On October 24, the stock market crashes, ruining many if not most investors; the crash heralds the beginning of the Great Depression.

Social Events

1919   **First public strike**
Police in Boston, Mass., go on strike; this is the first strike by public workers in the U.S.

The right to vote is assured for American women when the 19th Amendment to the Constitution is ratified.

Religion

1922 McPherson builds temple
Evangelist Aimee Semple McPherson builds the Angelus Temple in Los Angeles. She is the founder of the International Church of the Foursquare Gospel and is well-known for her revival meetings.

Philosophy

1919 Adams wins Pulitzer
Philosopher and historian Henry Brooks Adams wins a Pulitzer prize for his best-known work, *The Education of Henry Adams*.

1924 Whitehead to Harvard
English philosopher Alfred North Whitehead joins the faculty of Harvard University in Cambridge, Mass.

1926 Durant publishes
Will Durant publishes the major work *The Story of Philosophy*.

1928 Summary work
V.L. Parrington's important work *Main Currents in American Thought* is acclaimed. The book surveys the important trends in American philosophy.

1929 Whitehead's major work
While on the faculty of Harvard University, English philosopher Alfred North Whitehead publishes the book *Process and Reality*.

Literature

1917 O. Henry collected
The complete works of O. Henry, mainly short stories, are published.

1918 Sandburg on war
Carl Sandburg's poem "Grass" is published. The poem deals with the horrors of war.

1918 Cather on the prairie
Willa Cather's novel *My Ántonia* is published; it deals with the struggles of an immigrant girl on the prairie.

1919 Anderson's short stories
Sherwood Anderson published his first collection of short stories, entitled *Winesburg, Ohio*.

1919 Pulitzer for Tarkington
Booth Tarkington wins the Pulitzer prize for literature for his novel *The Magnificent Ambersons*.

1920 Romantic poet
A Few Figs from Thistles, a volume of poetry by Edna St. Vincent Millay, is published.

1923 Cummings innovates
Tulips and Chimneys, a book of poems by e e cummings, is published. The literary world is startled by cummings' revolutionary approach to titles, punctuation, and line breaks.

1925 Jay Gatsby appears
F. Scott Fitzgerald publishes the novel *The Great Gatsby*.

1925 Dreiser's naturalism
Theodore Dreiser, a leading writer in the naturalism movement, publishes the novel *An American Tragedy*.

1926 Hemingway emerges
Publication of *The Sun Also Rises* signals the emergence of Ernest Hemingway as a major novelist.

1926 Lewis refuses prize
Sinclair Lewis is awarded the Pulitzer prize for literature for the novel *Arrowsmith*. He turns down the prize, apparently feeling that he should have received it sooner—for *Main Street* or *Babbitt*.

1929 Hammett begins
Dashiell Hammett publishes two detective novels, *Red Harvest* and *The Dain Curse*.

A New Place in the World
Literature *(Continued)*

1929 Wolfe on youth
Thomas Wolfe's first novel, *Look Homeward, Angel,* is published.

1929 Thurber and White unite
Is Sex Necessary?, a humorous book by James Thurber and E. B. White, is published.

1929 A classic by Faulkner
The novel *The Sound and the Fury,* by William Faulkner, is published. The novel uses the stream-of-consciousness technique in a striking manner.

The Arts
1917 Ryder dies
Romantic painter Albert Pinkham Ryder dies. His works are colorful, strange, and imaginative.

1920's Jazz in flower
Jazz composers and artists win a wide audience. Popular jazz personalities include Louis Armstrong, Sidney Bechet, Bix Beiderbecke, Edward (Duke) Ellington, Earl (Fatha) Hines, and Joseph (King) Oliver.

1920- The blues flourish
1940 Singer Bessie Smith reigns as "empress of the blues." Other prominent blues performers include Billie Holliday, Blind Lemon Jefferson, and Huddie (Leadbelly) Ledbetter.

1921 Famed Steichen photo
Photographer Edward Steichen takes his photograph *Three Pears and an Apple.*

1924 Gershwin's major work
Composer George Gershwin completes his *Rhapsody in Blue,* on a commission from jazz bandleader Paul Whiteman.

1924 Varèse experiments
Edgard Varèse composes *Octandre,* an instrumental piece that utilizes disordered sounds.

1927 Kern's major hit
Show Boat, perhaps the greatest musical by composer Jerome Kern, is first produced.

1928 Mickey Mouse
Cartoonist Walt Disney produces the film *Steamboat Willie,* in which he introduces the character of Mickey Mouse—who proves to be a beloved figure in U.S. popular culture.

Science and Technology
1920 Panama Canal opens
The Panama Canal opens on July 12; work had begun in 1904. Official opening had been in 1914.

1921 Einstein honored
Albert Einstein wins the Nobel prize in physics for his study of quanta.

1926 Rocket launched
Space pioneer Robert H. Goddard launches the first liquid-fuel rocket.

1927 Lindbergh's flight
Charles A. Lindbergh makes the first non-stop solo flight across the Atlantic Ocean.

1927 Compton honored
American scientist Arthur Holly Compton is co-winner of the Nobel prize in physics. He is honored for discovering "the Compton effect," or variations in the wavelengths of X rays.

1929- Plastics industry grows
1937 Chemists learn to make cellulose acetate, acrylics, and polystyrene.

1932 Earhart's flight
Amelia Earhart becomes the first woman to fly solo across the Atlantic Ocean.

Depression and a World in Conflict

Political Events

1933 New Deal begins
President Franklin D. Roosevelt begins the "New Deal" in an effort to end the depression.

1939-1940 Neutrality weighed
The U.S. remains officially neutral as Germany invades Poland and World War II begins.

1941 Lend-Lease begins
The U.S. decides to expand its aid to the Allies. The Lend-Lease Act gives the President the power to transfer arms and food to the Allies.

1941 Pearl Harbor attacked
On December 7, Japan launches a surprise attack on the U.S. military installations at Pearl Harbor on the island of Oahu in Hawaii.

1941 Europeans declare war
On December 11, Germany and Italy declare war on the U.S., and the U.S. declares war on Germany and Italy.

1942 Japan takes Philippines
From January to May, Japan's troops successfully battle U.S. troops for control of the Philippine Islands.

1942 Allies land in Africa
On November 8, American and British troops land in North Africa, in the largest amphibious invasion to date in World War II.

1942 Solomon Islands won
United States forces claim victory on November 12 after a three-day naval battle for control of the Solomon Islands.

1943 Allies land on Sicily
On July 10, American, British, and Canadian troops land on Sicily, in the second largest amphibious invasion of the war.

1944 Normandy invaded
On June 6, D-Day, Allied troops invade the Normandy coast of France.

1944 Philippines recaptured
United States troops led by Gen. Douglas MacArthur land on Leyte on October 20, in the first stage of the battle to recapture the Philippine Islands.

1944 Allies hold the line
American and British troops hold back the German Army at the Battle of the Bulge in December.

1945 Iwo Jima captured
In February and March, U.S. troops battle to capture from the Japanese the island of Iwo Jima in the Pacific.

1945 Okinawa invaded
The U.S. invades the island of Okinawa near Japan; the battle lasts for 3 months.

1945 Victory in Europe
Following the death of Germany's dictator, Adolf Hitler, on April 30, Germany's military leaders sign surrender terms on May 7 in Reims, France.

1945 United Nations founded
The United Nations (UN) Charter is adopted on June 26 by the 50 nations meeting in San Francisco, Calif.

1945 Atomic bombs dropped
Atomic bombs are dropped on Hiroshima, Japan, on August 6 and on Nagasaki, Japan, on August 9.

1945 Japan surrenders
Japan offers to surrender on August 10. The official terms of surrender are signed on September 2.

Political Events (*Continued*)

1947   **Cold war heats up**
President Harry S.
Truman announces
his "Truman Doc-
trine": the U.S. will
give aid to any nation
striving to resist Com-
munism; the U.S. and
Soviet Union are en-
gaged in the cold war.

1948   **Marshall Plan set**
The European Recov-
ery Program, or Mar-
shall Plan, begins sup-
plying massive
amounts of financial
aid to Western Euro-
pean nations.

1948- **Berlin blockade**
1949   **broken**
The Russians block-
ade West Berlin on
June 24, 1948, hoping
to drive out the West-
ern allies; the allies
use an airlift of gigan-
tic proportions to
break the blockade.

1949   **NATO organized**
The U.S. and 11 Eu-
ropean nations form
the North Atlantic
Treaty Organization
(NATO).

1950   **"McCarthyism" in**
flower
Senator Joseph R.
McCarthy, Republi-
can from Wisconsin,
accuses the U.S. De-
partment of State of
harboring Commu-
nists.

1950   **Troops to Korea**
On June 30, President
Truman sends troops
to South Korea,
which was invaded by
North Korea on June
25.

1950   **Troops land at**
Inchon
United States troops
land at Inchon, Ko-
rea, behind enemy
lines in September
and move north to the
Yalu River.

1950   **Allies retreat**
China enters the war
on the side of North
Korea on October 25;
the Chinese attack the
Allies, who begin re-
treating on November
26.

1951   **MacArthur fired**
President Truman re-
moves Gen. Douglas
MacArthur as com-
mander in chief of
U.S. forces in Korea.

1953   **Korean truce set**
A truce ending the
Korean War is signed
on July 27.

1954   **Army-McCarthy hear-**
ings
Senator Joseph R.
McCarthy begins na-
tionally televised
hearings in April on
possible Communist
influences in the U.S.
Army; he accuses the
Army of "coddling
Communists."

1954   **Court says**
desegregate
On May 17, the Su-
preme Court rules in
Brown v. Board of
Education of Topeka
that segregated public
schools are a denial of
blacks' civil rights.

1954   **Censure McCarthy**
In December, the
U.S. Senate votes to
censure Senator Jo-
seph R. McCarthy for
"contemptuous" con-
duct.

1955   **King begins rights cru-**
sade
Dr. Martin Luther
King, Jr., begins orga-
nizing a movement to
protest discrimination
against blacks.

1959   **Two new states added**
Alaska and Hawaii
are admitted to the
Union; they are the
49th and 50th states.

Social Events

1932   **Injunctions limited**
The Norris-La Guar-
dia Act limits the use
of federal court in-
junctions in strikes
and labor disputes.

1935   **NLRB created**
Congress passes the
National Labor Rela-
tions Act, or Wagner
Act, to protect the
rights of labor; the
National Labor Rela-

tions Board (NLRB) is created to settle disputes.

1942 Japanese interned
The U.S. government moves all Japanese on the West Coast, including aliens and native born, to relocation camps in Arkansas, Colorado, Utah, and other states.

1946 New suburb started
Construction begins on the town of Levittown, N.Y., a new type of suburb; a "planned community," Levittown features mass-produced houses that look alike and a master plan for streets and highways.

1947 Taft-Hartley Act set
The Labor-Management Relations Act, or Taft-Hartley Act, is passed by Congress and passed again over the veto of President Harry S. Truman; the Act limits union activities in a variety of ways.

1953 HEW founded
A new department is added to the U.S. Cabinet, the Department of Health, Education, and Welfare (HEW), which is designed to coordinate federal policies in those three broad areas.

1955 AFL-CIO created
The Congress of Industrial Organizations (CIO), a collection of industrial unions, merges with the American Federation of Labor (AFL), a collection of craft unions, to form one "umbrella" organization, the AFL-CIO.

1957 Crisis at Little Rock
Arkansas Governor Orval E. Faubus sends national guardsmen to block black students from entering Central High School in Little Rock, Ark.; the students are admitted after President Dwight D. Eisenhower sends federal troops to the school.

Religion

1930 Black Muslims founded
Elijah Muhammad and W.D. Farad found the Nation of Islam, or the Black Muslim movement.

1933 Day founds paper
Dorothy Day founds the *Catholic Worker,* a monthly publication. Day is a leader in the Catholic Worker movement in the U.S., and she works to further social change in New York City.

1937 Catholic Unionists meet
The Association of Catholic Trade Union-

ists is formed, to extend the church's influence and ideology to labor matters.

1948 Brandeis opens
Brandeis University is founded; located in Waltham, Mass., Brandeis is sponsored by the American Jewish community but is a nonsectarian institution.

1949 Graham begins crusades
Billy Graham, an evangelist preacher, begins his large-scale campaigns for converts throughout the world.

1950 Unity sought
The National Council of the Churches of Christ in the U.S.A. is formed. A number of Protestant and Eastern Orthodox denominations form the Council to promote Christian unity.

1950 Graham goes on radio
Evangelist Billy Graham starts a radio program, called "The Hour of Decision."

1950's Bishop Sheen to TV
Roman Catholic Bishop Fulton J. Sheen is the host for a television series called "Life Is Worth Living"; Bishop Sheen becomes a well-known personality in America.

Philosophy

1931   Cohen publishes
Morris R. Cohen, a
noted defender of reason and scientific
thinking, publishes
the book *Reason and
Nature.*

1934-   Mumford published
1951   Lewis Mumford, philosopher and social
critic, completes *The
Renewal of Life,* a
four-volume philosophy of civilization.

1935   Peirce's papers published
The *Collected Papers
of Charles Sanders
Peirce* are published
posthumously. The
Papers are edited by
Charles Hartshorne
and Paul Weiss.

1938   Alcott published
Selected writings of
transcendentalist philosopher Bronson Alcott (1799-1888) are
published posthumously under the title
The Journals of Bronson Alcott.

1939   Dewey on culture
Freedom and Culture,
a book by John
Dewey, is published.

1951   Major article by Quine
The American philosopher Willard Van Orman Quine publishes
his article "Two Dogmas of Empiricism."
This article is one of
Quine's chief contributions to epistemology, or the study of
knowledge.

1953   Book by Quine
Willard Van Orman
Quine, the influential
logician and philosopher, publishes the
book *From a Logical
Point of View.*

1954   Nagel publishes
Sovereign Reason, a
book by science philosopher Ernest Nagel, is published.

1958   Randall on function
In his book *Nature
and Historical Experience,* John Herman
Randall presents a traditional concept of the
function of philosophy.

Literature

1930-   Trilogy on U.S. culture
1936   John Dos Passos
writes the three novels that make up the
trilogy *U.S.A.*

1931   Buck's best
Pearl Buck's novel
The Good Earth is
published. The story
is set in China and is
the first in a series.

1935   Maxwell Anderson
Winterset, a play by
Maxwell Anderson, is
published. The play is
based on the Sacco-
Vanzetti case.

1938   Play by
Thornton Wilder
Our Town, a play by
Thornton Wilder, receives the Pulitzer
prize for drama.

1939   Sandburg on Lincoln
Carl Sandburg's *Abraham Lincoln: The War
Years* is published in
four volumes.

**1940   Landmark in black
fiction**
Richard Wright's first
novel, *Native Son,* is
published.

1940   Pulitzer for Steinbeck
John Steinbeck receives the Pulitzer
prize for literature for
his novel *The Grapes
of Wrath.*

1941   Hellman on Nazism
Lillian Hellman's play
Watch on the Rhine is
published. The play
centers on a man of
integrity pursued by
Nazis.

1943   Saroyan on life
William Saroyan's
novel *The Human
Comedy* is published.

1943   Frost wins Pulitzer
Robert Frost is
awarded the Pulitzer
prize for poetry for
the fourth time. "Stopping by Woods on a
Snowy Evening" is
one of his best-known
poems.

1945   Gwendolyn Brooks
A Street in Bronzeville, the first book of
poems by Gwendolyn
Brooks, is published.
Bronzeville deals with
life in the black ghettos of Chicago.

1945   Williams to the fore
The Glass Menagerie,
a play by Tennessee

Williams, is first performed.

1949   **Willy Loman appears**
Arthur Miller's play
Death of a Salesman
is published. The play
is a tragedy about the
life of salesman Willy
Loman.

1950   **Bradbury and fantasy**
The Martian Chronicles, a book of stories
by Ray Bradbury, is
published.

1951   **Salinger's major work**
J. D. Salinger's novel
*The Catcher in the
Rye* is published.

1952   **Vonnegut's first novel**
Player Piano, the first
novel by Kurt Vonnegut, Jr., appears.

1954   **Bellow emerging**
Saul Bellow wins the
National Book Award
for fiction for his
novel *The Adventures
of Augie March.*

1957   **O'Neill's final work**
*A Long Day's Journey
into Night,* a play by
Eugene O'Neill, is
published—four years
after the playwright's
death.

1957   **Pulitzer for Wilbur**
Richard Wilbur receives the Pulitzer
prize for poetry for
his volume *Things of
This World.*

1959   **Roth to prominence**
Goodbye, Columbus,
a book of stories by
Philip Roth, is published.

1959   **Updike's first novel**
The Poorhouse Fair, a
novel by John Updike, appears.

The Arts

1931   **Still premiere**
*The Afro-American
Symphony,* by black
composer William
Grant Still, is first performed.

1936   **Balanchine on
Broadway**
The ballet *Slaughter
on Tenth Avenue,* by
choreographer George
Balanchine, is produced as part of the
musical *On Your
Toes.*

1943   **Robeson on stage**
Black actor and singer
Paul Robeson stars in
the title role of
Othello, a dramatic
play that becomes a
long-running hit.

1944   **Rodgers and Hammerstein**
Richard Rodgers and
Oscar Hammerstein II
win the Pulitzer prize
for drama for their
musical play *Oklahoma!*

1949-   **Television expands**
1951   The number of television sets in American
homes expands from
1,000,000 to
10,000,000 in just two
years.

1951   **Cage's music**
Composer John Cage
completes *Music of
Changes.* In his work,
Cage breaks away
from many of the old

conventions regarding
sound.

1953   **Pollock's painting**
Jackson Pollock, the
abstract painter, completes his *Ocean
Grayness.*

1954   **Landmark jazz festival**
The first large American jazz festival is
held in Newport, R.I.

Science and Technology

1934   **Urey honored**
Harold C. Urey wins
the Nobel prize in
chemistry for the discovery of deuterium,
or heavy hydrogen.

1937   **Vitamin C**
Albert Szent-Györgyi
wins the Nobel prize
in physiology or medicine for the isolation
of Vitamin C, or ascorbic acid.

1938   **Nobel for Fermi**
Enrico Fermi wins the
Nobel prize in physics
for his discovery of
radioactive elements.

1938-   **Blood plasma research**
1940   Black physician
Charles Drew conducts research on
blood plasma. Dr.
Drew helps set up
blood banks, which
save many lives.

1942   **Manhattan Project**
The Manhattan Project is organized by
the U.S. Army Corps
of Engineers to supervise the development
of an atomic bomb.

Depression and a World in Conflict
Science and Technology (*Continued*)

1944 Mark I developed
The Mark I digital computer is developed, after years of research.

1951 Two share Nobel
Glenn T. Seaborg and Edwin M. McMillan win the Nobel prize in chemistry for the discovery of plutonium and other transuranic elements.

1951 UNIVAC computer
The UNIVAC is first of a variety of electronic computers mass-produced during the fifties.

1953 Color broadcasts begin
The first television broadcasts in color begin.

1954 Solar energy explored
Bell Telephone Laboratories develops the solar battery.

1955 Nuclear submarine built
The U.S. builds the *Nautilus,* the first nuclear-powered submarine.

1955 Polio vaccine developed
Dr. Jonas Salk develops a vaccine to prevent polio.

1957 Nuclear energy
The first full-scale U.S. nuclear power plant opens in Shippingport, Pa.

1958 Statellite orbits earth
The first U.S. satellite orbits the earth.

1958 Heredity studies
Americans George W. Beadle, Edward L. Tatum, and Joshua Lederberg win the Nobel prize in physiology or medicine. The three are honored for their studies of heredity.

1959 Two honored on DNA
Severo Ochoa and Arthur Kornberg win the Nobel prize in physiology or medicine. The two are honored for their synthesis of ribonucleic acid and deoxyribonucleic acid (DNA).

The Contemporary Period

Political Events

1962 Cuban missile crisis
The U.S. learns that the Soviet Union has missile bases in Cuba; President John F. Kennedy orders a naval blockade of Cuba and forces removal of the missiles.

1963 Rights marchers to capital
More than 200,000 persons take part in the civil rights demonstration called the March on Washington on August 28 in Washington, D.C.

1963 President Kennedy slain
President John F. Kennedy is shot and killed in Dallas, Tex., on November 22; Lee Harvey Oswald is arrested for the crime but is then shot and killed himself.

1964 Civil rights laws passed
Congress passes the Civil Rights Act of 1964 and other legislation guaranteeing equal protection of the laws to blacks.

1964 Gulf of Tonkin incident
North Vietnamese PT boats attack U.S. destroyers in the Gulf of Tonkin.

1964 Gulf of Tonkin resolution
Congress passes the Gulf of Tonkin resolution, which authorizes the President to "take all necessary measures to repel any armed attack against the forces of the United States and to prevent further aggression."

1965   Bomb North Vietnam
President Lyndon B. Johnson orders the bombing of military targets in North Vietnam.

1965   LBJ sends troops
President Johnson sends U.S. Marines to Da Nang, South Vietnam, in March; they are the first U.S. ground troops, as opposed to advisers, to be sent to Vietnam.

1965   Rights confrontation
Police use tear gas and whips to turn back voting rights marchers in Montgomery, Ala.

1965   Voting Rights Act
Congress passes the Voting Rights Act of 1965 in August, to equalize standards for voting in the 50 states.

1965   Urban riots touched off
Blacks riot in the Watts section of Los Angeles, Calif., in August, calling national attention to conditions in U.S. inner city areas.

1967   More riots hit cities
In the "long, hot summer," riots occur in about 75 U.S. cities.

1968   Dr. King slain
On April 4, in Memphis, Tenn., civil rights leader Dr. Martin Luther King, Jr., is shot and killed.

1968   Peace talks begin
Preliminary peace talks begin between the U.S. and North Vietnam.

1969   Troops massed
Some 543,000 U.S. troops are in Vietnam by February, the largest number of the war.

1969   Antiwar protests escalate
Peace demonstrators march in major U.S. cities on Moratorium Day, October 15; about 300,000 persons march on Washington, D.C., on November 15 to protest the continuation of the war and the bombing of Cambodia.

1970   Senate acts on war
On June 24, the U.S. Senate repeals the Gulf of Tonkin resolution which gave the President broad powers to wage war.

1972   Watergate burglary foiled
On June 17, a group of people are arrested for breaking into the Democratic Party headquarters in the Watergate complex in Washington, D.C.; the men arrested prove to be employees of President Richard M. Nixon's reelection committee.

1973   War ends officially
The U.S., North Vietnam, South Vietnam, and the Viet Cong sign a cease-fire agreement in January.

1973-   Watergate facts dis-
1974   closed
Investigators reveal that high officials of the Nixon Administration were involved in covering up the Watergate break-in in 1972.

1973   Vice-President resigns
Vice-President Spiro T. Agnew resigns from office on October 10; at the time, he was under investigation on bribery charges in Maryland.

1973   Ford appointed
Gerald R. Ford is appointed Vice-President by President Nixon.

1974   Nixon resigns
On August 8, President Nixon announces that he is resigning from office effective the following day; he denies any wrongdoing but most observers link his resigning to threats of impeachment.

1978   Canal treaties ratified
The Senate ratifies treaties providing for the transfer of the Panama Canal to Panamanian control on December 31, 1999.

1978   Camp David accords
Egypt and Israel agree to a framework for peace at a 12-day summit mediated by President Carter at Camp David, Maryland.

The Contemporary Period
Political Events (*Continued*)

1979   U.S.-China ties
The United States and China establish full diplomatic relations after a break of nearly 30 years.

1981   Hostages released
On January 20, Iranian militants release 53 Americans who had been held hostage in the U.S. Embassy in Teheran since November 4, 1979.

1983   Reagan urges aid
President Ronald Reagan urges increased aid for the government of El Salvador in its fight against leftist rebels, and for antileftist forces elsewhere in Central America.

1983   U.S.-Soviet chill
U.S.-Soviet relations plummet after a Soviet jet fighter shoots down a civilian Korean airliner, killing all 269 persons on board, including 61 Americans.

1983   Fighting in Lebanon
U.S. military forces stationed in Lebanon as part of an international peace-keeping effort become involved in fighting among various factions. A terrorist bomb explodes in marine headquarters in Lebanon, killing more than 200 U.S. troops.

1983   Grenada invaded
Pan American troops, including 1,900 U.S. military personnel, invade Grenada to overthrow the Marxist government in power there.

1983-
1984   Contra aid
The U.S. aids the contras by placing mines in Nicaraguan harbors.

1984   Ferraro nominated
Geraldine Ferraro becomes the first woman named to the top of a major-party ticket when she is nominated as Democratic vice-presidential candidate.

1986   Terrorist centers attacked
President Reagan orders U.S. air strikes against military and suspected terrorist centers in Libya.

1986   Iran-contra affair
The public learns that profits from the sale of weapons to Iran have been diverted to Nicaraguan rebels.

1987   Nuclear Forces Treaty
Reagan and Gorbachev sign the Intermediate-Range Nuclear Forces Treaty.

1988   Iranian plane shot down
The U.S.S. *Vincennes,* a U.S. Army plane, shoots down an Iranian civilian airliner that it mistook for a warplane. All 290 people on board are killed.

1989   Panama invasion
U.S. military forces invade Panama in an effort to oust the country's leader, General Manuel Noriega. Noriega flees but finally surrenders to U.S. authorities.

Social Events

1961   Peace Corps started
President John F. Kennedy gets congressional approval to start the Peace Corps, a government agency that sends American citizens to foreign countries to promote peace, health, and welfare.

1962   Meredith enrolls
James Meredith becomes the first black to enroll in the University of Mississippi at Oxford. Attorney General Robert F. Kennedy sends U.S. marshals to maintain order when whites riot.

1962   Chavez organizes
Cesar Chavez founds the National Farm Workers Union to organize farm laborers in the grape fields.

1962   School prayer banned
The Supreme Court of the U.S. rules that required prayers and devotional Bible readings in public schools are unconstitutional.

1963   Right to counsel
In *Gideon v. Wainwright,* the Supreme Court rules that states

must provide free legal counsel to any person accused of a felony who cannot afford to pay for counsel.

1964 **"Freedom summer" set**
A number of civil rights groups, including the Student Nonviolent Coordinating Committee (SNCC), send students to Mississippi to register black voters; three workers are killed by whites.

1964 **War on poverty set**
President Lyndon B. Johnson initiates the creation of the Office of Economic Opportunity (OEO), a government agency designed to wage the "War on poverty."

1966 **"Black power" urged**
Stokely Carmichael urges that blacks be militant in seeking "black power," politically and economically.

1966 **NOW founded**
The National Organization for Women (NOW) is founded by a group of persons including Betty Friedan, author of *The Feminine Mystique*.

1966 **Miranda expands rights**
Ruling in the case *Miranda v. Arizona*, the Supreme Court of the U.S. states that criminal suspects must be fully informed of their rights when they are

arrested; otherwise, confessions or statements by the suspect may not be used in court.

1969 **Desegregation ordered**
The Supreme Court of the U.S. rules that desegregation of all public school systems must take place "at once."

1972 **Indians protest**
The American Indian Movement (AIM) and other Indian rights groups hold a sit-in at the headquarters of the U.S. Bureau of Indian Affairs in Washington, D.C., to protest the bureau's policies.

1973 **Seize Wounded Knee**
Members of the American Indian Movement (AIM) seize the village of Wounded Knee, S. Dak.; they demand the return of certain lands taken from Indians in violation of treaty agreements.

1973 **Abortion rights ruling**
The Supreme Court of the U.S. rules that states may not prohibit a woman's right, under certain conditions, to have an abortion during the first six months of pregnancy.

1976 **Death penalty approved**
On July 2 the Supreme Court of the U.S. rules that the

death penalty may be used again in the U.S.; the Court says that state laws passed since its 1972 decision against the death penalty are fair and just in their application of capital punishment.

1978 **Taxpayers revolt**
California voters approve Proposition 13, which sharply limits state and local authority to tax. Similar proposals begin in other states, indicating growing resistance to steadily rising taxes.

1978 **Bakke decision**
In the case of *Regents of the University of California v. Allan Bakke*, the Supreme Court rules that rigid quota systems used to achieve racial balance may constitute unfair discrimination against non-minority persons.

1979 **Inflation rate soars**
The inflation rate tops 13 per cent, the highest rate since 1946.

1982 **Unemployment soars**
The U.S. unemployment rate rises to over 10 per cent—the highest level in 40 years.

1982 **ERA defeated**
The Equal Rights Amendment is defeated when only 35 of the necessary 38 states ratify it before the June 30 deadline. The amendment was proposed as the 27th Amendment to the

Constitution to assure equal treatment of men and women under the law.

1986   **PLUS campaign**
ABC and PBS television networks begin a joint effort to inform public about the problem of illiteracy. The PLUS (Project Literacy U.S.) campaign includes documentaries, public service announcements, and incorporation of illiteracy theme into popular shows.

1986   **Books banned**
Fundamentalist parents succeed in banning some textbooks from schools in several southern states.

1989   **Abortion issue**
The Supreme Court rules that states may outlaw abortions in public hospitals and clinics. Supporters of free choice and anti-abortionists stage demonstrations across the country.

Religion

1960   **Pentecostal revival**
Father Dennis Bennett tells his congregation at St. Mark's Episcopal Church in Van Nuys, Calif., that he has experienced the Pentecostal spirit.

1960's   **Catholic Church changes**
In the wake of the Second Vatican Coun-

cil, the Roman Catholic Church in the U.S. undergoes a series of changes. The liturgy of the Mass is changed from mainly Latin to mainly English, special Masses utilize folk music and folk dancing, and dress codes for nuns are relaxed.

1972   **"Jesus movement" grows**
The International Student Congress on Evangelism is held in Dallas, Tex., and more than 75,000 young people attend.

1974   **Women ordained**
On July 29, eleven women are ordained priests of the Episcopal Church by three bishops jointly celebrating a service in Philadelphia, Pa.; the ordinations are considered "irregular" because the denomination has not yet approved ordination for women.

1979   **Pope visits U.S.**
Throngs of Americans welcome Pope John Paul II to six U.S. cities.

1983   **Presbyterians reunite**
Representatives of the United Presbyterian Church in the U.S.A., a northern group, and the Presbyterian Church in the United States, a southern group, vote to create a unified body called the Presbyterian Church (U.S.A.). The two groups had split in 1861.

1987   **Division in the Catholic Church**
Divisions in the Roman Catholic Church punctuate Pope John Paul II's visit to the U.S.

1988   **Jim Bakker charged**
Jim Bakker, leader of the fundamentalist Christian organization Praise the Lord, is charged with fraud and jailed.

Philosophy

1963   **Moral responsibility**
The *Journal of Philosophy,* a publication associated with Columbia University in New York City, publishes a "Symposium on Human Action." The symposium discusses moral freedom, moral responsibility, and the relationship of knowledge to action.

1966   **Quine's papers**
Various papers by Willard Van Orman Quine are published in two volumes, *Selected Logic Papers* and *The Ways of Paradox and Other Essays.*

1971   **Essays published**
The U.S. philosopher Horace M. Kallen publishes a volume of essays, *What I Believe and Why—Maybe.*

1972   **Women as philosophers**
The Society for Women in Philosophy holds its first conference in Chicago, Ill.

1975   Eastern philosophy
Robert M. Pirsig's
book *Zen and the Art
of Motorcycle Mainte-
nance: An Inquiry into
Values* is published.
The novel deals in a
popularized form with
Oriental and classical
Greek philosophy.
The popularity of Pir-
sig's book is but one
indication of a current
interest in Eastern
philosophy.

1983   Hoffer dies
Eric Hoffer, a self-ed-
ucated longshoreman
who became a well-
known political and
social philosopher,
dies in May. His first
book, *The True Be-
liever,* was published
in 1951.

Literature

**1961   Surrealism and
comedy**
Joseph Heller's novel
Catch-22 is published.

1963   Baldwin essays
The Fire Next Time, a
nonfiction work on
race relations by
James Baldwin, is
published.

1965   Vintage O'Connor
*Everything That Rises
Must Converge,* a
book of short stories
by Flannery O'Con-
nor, is published a
year after her death.

1967   Pulitzer for Albee
Playwright Edward
Albee is voted the Pu-
litzer prize for drama
for his play *A Delicate
Balance.*

1971   A new look at history
Dee Brown's *Bury My
Heart at Wounded
Knee* is published and
becomes a best seller.
The book is a nonfic-
tion account of the
U.S. actions against
the American Indians
in the 19th century.

1976   Searching for roots
The biographical
novel *Roots,* by Alex
Haley, is published.
Roots is a fictional ac-
count of Haley's fam-
ily saga, ranging from
Africa to the U.S.

1977   Robert Lowell dies
Poet Robert Lowell
dies in September. He
is generally consid-
ered the leading con-
temporary American
poet.

1980   Eudora Welty honored
Eudora Welty wins
the National Medal
for Literature for the
"excellence of her
past and continuing
contribution to litera-
ture."

1982   Cheever dies
John Cheever, noted
author of novels and
short stories, dies in
June. Cheever won a
Pulitzer prize in 1979
and received the Na-
tional Medal for Liter-
ature shortly before
his death.

1984   Capote dies
Truman Capote, best
known for his account
of the brutal murder
of a Kansas farm fam-
ily *(In Cold Blood),*
dies at the age of 60.

1987   Baldwin dies
James Baldwin, a
black American au-
thor who wrote about
racial conflict and in-
justice in the United
States, dies at the age
of 63.

1989   Barthelme dies
Donald Barthelme, a
postmodern author of
short stories and nov-
els, dies. Barthelme's
novel *The King,* a
parody of the King
Arthur legend, is pub-
lished a year after his
death.

The Arts

**1961   A major work by
Kahn**
The Richards Medical
Research Building at
the University of
Pennsylvania is com-
pleted. The building
was designed by ar-
chitect and planner
Louis I. Kahn.

1967   Geodesic dome
An innovative and
startling structure, the
geodesic dome, is
erected as the Ameri-
can exhibit at Expo 67
in Montreal, Canada.
The dome is designed
by R. Buckminster
Fuller.

1969   Mies dies
Architect Ludwig
Mies van der Rohe
dies. Mies, who
worked by the princi-
ple "less is more," is
often considered the
leading U.S. contem-
porary architect.

The Contemporary Period
The Arts (*Continued*)

1974   **Graham to Far East**
The U.S. Department
of State sponsors a
tour of the Far East
by modern dancer
Martha Graham and
her troupe.

1976   **Calder show**
"Calder's Universe,"
an exhibition of more
than 200 works by the
American sculptor Al-
exander Calder, opens
in New York City.

1980   **Copland honored**
Orchestras and dance
companies across the
U.S. celebrate com-
poser Aaron Cop-
land's 80th birthday
by performing his
works.

1983   **Award to Pei**
Architect I. M. Pei, a
Chinese-born Ameri-
can known for his cre-
ative urban designs,
receives the Pritzker
Architecture Prize.

1983   **Williams dies**
Award-winning play-
wright Tennessee Wil-
liams, whose works
include *The Glass Me-
nagerie* and *A Street-
car Named Desire*,
dies in February.

1984   **Adams dies**
Ansel Adams, famous
landscape photogra-
pher and environmen-
tal activist, dies.
Adams' work, span-
ning more than five
decades, helped pho-
tography gain recogni-
tion as an art form.

1986   **O'Keeffe dies**
Georgia O'Keeffe, an
American artist who
found inspiration in
nature for most of her
paintings, dies at the
age of 99.

1986   **"Helga" paintings discovered**
Painter Andrew
Wyeth reveals a previ-
ously unseen collec-
tion of 246 works, cre-
ated between 1970 and
1985, using Helga Tes-
torf as a model almost
exclusively.

1986   **Kelly applauded**
Dancer Gene Kelly re-
ceives the American
Film Institute's 13th
Life Achievement
Award for his work in
creating a more mas-
culine, athletic style
of dancing in motion
pictures.

1987   **Huston dies**
Film director John
Huston dies at age 81.
Huston had directed
41 films over 46 years
and co-adapted and
acted in more than 20.
Among his many films

In 1969, two American astronauts from Apollo
XI become the first people to walk on the moon.

are *The Maltese Falcon, The Treasure of the Sierra Madre,* and *The African Queen.*

1987   **Warhol dies**
Andy Warhol, a leading figure in the pop art movement of the 1960's, dies.

1989   **Berlin dies**
Irving Berlin, who composed many famous American popular songs, including "White Christmas" and "God Bless America," dies.

Science and Technology

1960   **Communications satellite**
The U.S. launches *Echo I,* the first passive communications satellite.

1962   **Glenn in orbit**
Astronaut John Glenn becomes the first American to orbit the earth in space.

1962   **Watson honored**
American scientist James D. Watson shares the Nobel prize in physiology or medicine with two British colleagues. The three are cited for their research on the molecular structure of DNA.

1964   **Townes and lasers**
American scientist Charles H. Townes shares the Nobel prize in physics with two Soviet scientists. The three are honored for their research on lasers and masers.

1966   **Mulliken and molecules**
Robert S. Mulliken wins the Nobel prize in chemistry for his research on the structure of molecules.

1969   **Man walks on moon**
Astronaut Neil Armstrong becomes the first person to walk on the moon.

1972   **Bardeen wins again**
John Bardeen becomes the first person to win the Nobel prize twice for work in the same field. He wins the physics prize for his work in superconductivity; in 1956 he was honored for inventing the transistor.

1977   **Human-powered flight**
A group of Californians headed by Paul MacCready, Jr., sponsor a successful test flight of the "Gossamer Condor." The "Condor" is a human-powered aircraft.

1979   **Three Mile Island**
A failure in the cooling system of the Three Mile Island nuclear power plant near Harrisburg, Pennsylvania, causes the worst nuclear accident in U.S. history.

1979-   **Planetary discoveries**
1981   Unmanned planetary probes discover new moons and rings around Jupiter and Saturn as *Pioneer 11* and 2 *Voyager* spacecraft relay photographs back to Earth.

1980   **Volcano erupts**
On May 18, a massive eruption of Mount St. Helens blow away more than 1,000 feet (300 meters) of the mountaintop and kills at least 34 persons.

1982   **Artificial heart**
The first permanent artificial heart implant is performed in Salt Lake City, Utah.

1984   **Animal heart transplanted**
The heart of a baboon is transplanted into the body of a human infant known as Baby Fae. The infant dies but survives longer than any other recipient of an animal heart.

1989   **Oil spill**
The U.S. tanker *Exxon Valdez* strikes a reef near the port of Valdez, Alaska, resulting in the largest oil spill ever to occur in North American waters.

1990   **Hubble telescope**
NASA launches the Hubble Space Telescope. This powerful instrument can see about seven times farther into space than all previous telescopes and will allow the discovery of millions of new objects.

abstract expressionism A school of painting that flourished after World War II until the early 1960's. The artists believed that painting should be a natural act of free expression. Their paintings were studies in color and form often created through means other than brush strokes.

humanism *(HYOO muh nihz uhm)* A way of looking at our world that emphasizes the importance of human beings, our nature, and our place in the universe. Although humanism had its roots in the life and thought of ancient Greece and Rome, it actually flourished as a historical movement in Europe from the 1300's to the 1500's. The humanist approach to the study of man formed the intellectual core of the cultural reawakening called the *Renaissance.*

idealism A philosophical theory that sees the universe as being made up of mind, or reason. Some idealists recognize that matter exists but believe that mind is far more important. Others insist that consciousness, or reason, forms the basis for all reality. Philosopher George Berkeley took the position that nothing was real except ideas and impressions. He explained the apparent reality of objects by the theory that all objects were ideas in the mind of God.

pragmatism *(PRAG muh tihz uhm)* A philosophy developed by William James, Charles Peirce, and John Dewey that stated an idea must be judged by how it works, rather than by how it looks or sounds. Pragmatists consider a proposition true so long as it proves effective in linking the past and future. An idea may be true under certain circumstances, but false under others. Pragmatism has been called a peculiarly American philosophy.

realism In the arts, the attempt to portray life as it is. To the realist, the artist's main function is to describe as accurately and honestly as possible what can be observed through the senses. Realism began in the arts in the 1700's and by the mid-1800's was a dominant art form. In part, it was a revolt against classicism and romanticism, styles of art that idealized life.

romanticism *(roh MAN tuh sihz uhm)* A style in the arts and literature that emphasizes passion rather than reason, and imagination and inspiration rather than logic. The style favors full expression of the emotions and free, spontaneous action rather than restraint and order. Romanticism contrasts with another style called *classicism,* which stresses reason and order. The term *romantic movement* usually refers to the period from the late 1700's to the mid 1800's.

social contract A theory published by Rousseau in 1762, that government should rest on the consent of the governed.

surrealism A movement of art and literature, founded in Paris in 1924 by poet André Breton. Surrealism uses art as a weapon against the evils and restrictions that surrealists see in society. Surrealists claim to create forms and images not primarily by reason, but by unthinking impulse and blind feeling—or even by accident. Much of the beauty sought by surrealism is violent and cruel. In this way, surrealists try to shock the viewer or reader and show what they consider the deeper and truer part of human nature to be.

symbolism A literary movement started by a group of French poets between 1885 and 1895, led by Stéphane Mallarmé. The movement gave a spiritual atmosphere to the world by attributing to it a sacred, mystical quality. Visible realities became symbols for the invisible world of the spirit.

transcendentalism (*TRAN sehn DEHN tuh lihz uhm*) A philosophy that became influential during the late 1700's and 1800's. It was based on the belief that knowledge is not limited to, or solely derived from, experience and observation. Transcendentalism also stated that the solution to human problems lies in the free development of individual emotions. According to this philosophy, reality exists only in the world of the spirit. What people observe in the physical world are only appearances, or impermanent reflections of the world through their senses and understanding. But they learn about the world of the spirit through another power, called *reason*.

utilitarianism (*yoo TIHL uh TAIR ee un nihz uhm*) The doctrine that the goal of life is "the greatest happiness of the greatest number." Whatever brings about this happiness has "utility." Utilitarians hold that the most definite mark of happiness is pleasure. Philosopher Jeremy Bentham first developed this idea in England.

4

People Who Made History

When did Charlemagne die? Who was Benito Juarez? Your classwork probably often presents you with the names of unfamiliar people. These people may have been heads of government, soldiers, scientists, artists, any people who left a mark on history.

This unit is a quick reference biographical dictionary of historically significant people. While the unit makes no pretense at being all-embracing, effort has been made to include those persons who are most often referred to in the average student's classwork.

Marie Curie, a Polish-born chemist, earned Nobel prizes for her work in physics and chemistry.

1

Famous People

Abraham (about 1800 B.C.), whose name means "father of nations," was the founder of the ancient kingdom of Israel. A native of Ur, Abraham obeyed God's command to lead the Hebrew people to Palestine, where he established his people as a nation. He is considered a patriarch of the Jewish people.

Adams, Samuel (1722-1803), an American patriot and politician during the Revolutionary War period, was a leader of the independence movement. He opposed British tax laws such as the Stamp Act and the Tea Act and helped organize demonstrations against them. Adams was one of the signers of the Declaration of Independence and after the war served as governor of Massachusetts.

Addams, Jane (1860-1935), was a social worker and humanitarian. She established Hull House, a neighborhood center in Chicago for immigrants and the poor. Addams worked for numerous reforms, was active in women's movements and peace movements, and wrote several books. In 1931, she shared the Nobel peace prize.

Aeschylus (525?-456 B.C.), a tragic dramatist, ranked with Sophocles and Euripides as one of the most important playwrights of ancient Greece. His plays emphasized divine justice and power. Aeschylus wrote about 80 plays in all, of which only 7 survive, including *Seven Against Thebes, Prometheus Bound,* and *Agamemnon.*

Aesop (620?-560? B.C.), a legendary character, probably a Greek slave and reputedly ugly and deformed, was credited as the author of fables—short stories with moral lessons. His tales about animals such as the slow tortoise and the swift hare, and the frugal ant and the wastrel grasshopper, have been enjoyed for centuries and remain popular today.

Albertus Magnus, Saint (1206?-1280), born Count Albert von Bollstadt in Swabia, Germany, joined the Dominican order as a young man. He became a learned scholar in theology, philosophy, and science. He taught for many years in various universities, and his pupils included Thomas Aquinas. Albertus Magnus was canonized by the Roman Catholic Church in 1932.

Alcott, Louisa May (1832-1888), an American writer, is best known for her novel *Little Women,* the largely autobiographical story of the girlhood experiences of four sisters. She was a member of the New England literary group that included Henry David Thoreau, Ralph Waldo Emerson, and her father, Bronson Alcott.

Alexander the Great (356-323 B.C.), a pupil of the Greek philosopher Aristotle, at the age of 20 succeeded his father, Philip II of Macedon, to the throne. He united the Greek city-states and conquered the Persian Empire, Egypt, and northern India. Alexander ruled over the greatest empire of the time and founded the city of Alexandria in Egypt.

Alfred the Great (849-899), a Saxon king in England, defeated the Danes who tried to conquer his kingdom in Wessex. With his kingdom as the center, he paved the way for the unification of England and issued a code of laws for governing the people. A learned man, Alfred promoted education and Christianity and translated books from Latin to Anglo-Saxon.

Al-Mansur (712?-775), whose father was descended from a first cousin of Muhammad, the founder of Islam, was the second caliph in the Abbasid dynasty. He built Baghdad, which he made his capital, into a great city. Interested in learning, Al-Mansur had Greek and Latin writings translated into Arabic.

Ampère, Andrè Marie (1775-1836), was a French physicist and mathematician who formulated the laws of electromagnetism. He discovered that electric currents moving in the same direction attract but that those moving in opposite directions repel. Ampère also discovered that a coil of electrically charged wire acts as a magnet.

Amundsen, Roald (1872-1928), was a Norwegian explorer who determined the exact position of the North Pole and in 1911 became the first person to reach the South Pole. He also navigated the Northwest Passage through North America and crossed the North Pole in a dirigible. Amundsen disappeared on a North Pole rescue attempt.

Anthony, Susan B. (1820-1906), was a leader of reform movements in the United States who worked for women's suffrage, temperance, and the abolition of slavery. She edited the magazine *The Revolution,* was arrested for voting in 1872, and was president of a national women's suffrage group for several years.

Antony, Mark (82?-30 B.C.), a friend and fellow commander of Julius Caesar, became a consul in the Roman government. After Caesar's assassination, he was a member of the triumvirate that ruled Rome and later commanded the eastern empire. Pursuing Cleopatra of Egypt while trying to widen his control over the empire, he was defeated by Octavian and committed suicide.

Aquinas, Saint Thomas (1225?-1274), an Italian theologian who was influenced by the teachings of the Greek philosopher Aristotle, constructed a system of theology that became the basis for many doctrines of the Roman Catholic Church. Among his writings are *Summa contra Gentiles* and *Summa Theologica,* considered the most complete account of his theology.

Archimedes (287?-212 B.C.), although he considered himself to be a mathematician, is best remembered for his inventions. His inventions included a screw to raise irrigation water and a catapult for military use. Living in Syracuse on the island of Sicily, he also developed the laws of displacement and buoyancy in water and a more precise figure for pi.

Aristophanes (445?-385? B.C.), who wrote during the Golden Age of Athens in ancient Greece, is considered one of the greatest writers of comedy of all time. In his plays, he satirized many contemporary figures and events. His known works include *Clouds, Wasps, Birds, Frogs,* and *Lysistrata.*

Aristotle (384-322 B.C.), a student of Plato, was the greatest Greek philosopher after Plato's death. Considered one of the greatest of logicians, he also lectured on government and ethics and laid the foundations for psychology. Aristotle established a school in Athens; earlier, Alexander the Great had become his pupil.

Armstrong, Neil A. (1930-   ), an American astronaut, was the first person to set foot on the moon. A naval pilot between 1949 and 1952, he made his first space flight in 1966. A part of the crew of *Apollo XI,* Armstrong and another astronaut stepped onto the moon on July 20, 1969, and briefly explored the lunar surface. Armstrong later became a professor of engineering.

Arnold, Benedict (1741-1801), although remembered as a traitor, was one of the best Revolutionary War generals. He fought in several important battles. Passed over for promotions and court-martialed by enemies, Arnold arranged for the British to take over West Point.

When the plot was discovered, he joined the British.

Astor, John Jacob (1763-1848), a German by birth, was the founder of a wealthy American family. He became successful in the fur trade and shipped furs to Europe and to China. He extended his control over the fur trade throughout much of North America and established a post at Astoria, Ore. Astor accumulated real estate in New York City and left a fortune of about $20 million.

Atahualpa (1500?-1533) became the emperor of the Inca empire after defeating his brother Huáscar in a civil war. He was the last Inca to rule Peru before Spaniards under the command of Francisco Pizarro invaded the empire and conquered it. Alleging that he might arouse his people against the Spaniards, Pizarro had Atahualpa put to death.

Atatürk, Kemal (1881-1938), was the first president of the Turkish Republic, serving from 1923 until his death. He led armies against the British in World War I, and after the war he worked for the independence and unification of Turkey. Atatürk modernized Turkey, abolishing ancient dress, old penal codes, and the practice of polygamy. He achieved many other social, economic, and religious reforms.

Attila (406?-453), called the "Scourge of God," was a fierce leader of the Huns. He led his soldiers to conquer much of eastern and central Europe. Turned back in France, he invaded Italy but withdrew when the Pope interceded. The Huns returned to the Danube area, where Attila died while celebrating his wedding.

Attucks, Crispus (1723?-1770), often assumed to have been a black man, was a leader of the mob in the Boston Massacre. He was one of three men killed by British soldiers. His background, however, is uncertain. He may have been a mulatto, or he may have been of mixed Negro and Indian blood. Attucks' place of birth and his occupation, like his ancestry, are also unknown.

Audubon, John James (1785-1851), a failure in business, found success as a painter of American birds. His first group of 435 paintings, *Birds of America,* was first published in England between 1826 and 1838. Audubon later published numerous editions of his paintings of birds and other animals.

Augustine, Saint (354-430), as an intelligent and well-educated Italian youth, led a carefree, worldly life before converting to Christianity at about the age of 30. He became one of the important philosophers of early Christianity and served as the bishop of Hippo in North Africa for more than 30 years. Augustine's writings include *City of God* and his autobiographical *Confessions.*

Augustus Caesar (63 B.C.-A.D. 14), known originally as Octavian, became the first Roman emperor in 27 B.C. He expanded the empire to the north and east. During his reign, the Roman Empire reached the peak of its glory in a period of peace and great artistic production, particularly by literary figures such as Virgil, Ovid, and Horace.

Aurangzeb (1618-1707), the last effective Mogul emperor of India, took the throne by imprisoning his father and killing two of his brothers. He was a harsh ruler, and his religious persecutions of both Muslims and Hindus led to widespread revolts. These and other outbreaks brought about the end of the Mogul empire in India.

Austen, Jane (1775-1817), an English author, wrote six novels, including *Pride and Prejudice, Sense and Sensibility,* and *Northanger Abbey.* As she herself had experienced them, she portrayed the attitudes, hopes, fears, and superficialities of the English middle class with sympathy and understanding.

Bach, Johann Sebastian (1685-1750), a giant among composers, was also a great organist who was attached to many important churches and courts in his native Germany. Among his religious works are the *Mass in B Minor* and *The Passion According to St. Matthew.* His instrumental music includes the *Brandenburg Concertos, The Well-Tempered Clavier,* and *The Art of the Fugue.*

Bacon, Francis (1561-1626), an English philosopher, politician, and writer, is best remembered for his practical essays. Particularly interested in learning, he planned but never completed an encyclopedia of all knowledge. In *Novum Organum,* Bacon stressed the inductive scientific method of collecting data and arriving at tentative conclusions.

Bacon, Roger (1214?-1292?), a medieval philosopher probably born in England, emphasized experience as a means of knowing. Interested in science, he stressed the superiority of conclusions based on observation over those based on reason. A Franciscan, he was imprisoned for some of his views. His greatest work was *Opus Maius,* a discourse on scientific subjects.

Balboa, Vasco Núñez de (1475-1519), was one of the early Spanish explorers of America. He became the governor of Darién in Panama and led expeditions seeking gold. In 1513, he led 200 men on an expedition to discover the Pacific Ocean. Under charges of treason, probably false, Balboa was condemned and executed by beheading.

Balzac, Honoré de (1799-1850), a prolific French writer, studied law but turned to literature as a profession. He wrote many novels, including *The Human Comedy,* a group of novels that deal with the lives of more than 2,000 different characters representing all walks of life. Among his best-known books are *Old Goriot* and *Droll Stories.*

Banneker, Benjamin (1731-1806), was a black mathematician who published an almanac containing weather predictions and astronomical calculations. Also a surveyor, Banneker came to the attention of Thomas Jefferson, who helped him win appointment to the group that laid out the boundaries of the District of Columbia.

Barnum, Phineas T. (1810-1891), perhaps the greatest American showman, created the modern circus. Barnum presented the Swedish singer Jenny Lind, as well as the midget General Tom Thumb and the elephant Jumbo, to American audiences. Because of Barnum, expressions like *white elephant* (fake) and *ballyhoo* (strident publicity) became a part of the English language.

Barton, Clara (1821-1912), won acclaim as a battlefield nurse during the Civil War and was appointed superintendent of nurses for one of the Union armies. Serving as a nurse in Europe during the Franco-Prussian War, she became interested in the Red Cross movement. Barton later organized the American National Red Cross and served as its president.

Becket, Saint Thomas à (1118?-1170), an English cleric and archbishop of Canterbury, opposed the plans of King Henry II to weaken the authority of the Roman Catholic Church in England. When Henry II indicated that he wanted to be rid of Becket, four knights took this to mean his death and killed Becket at Canterbury. Two years later, the church made him a saint.

Bede (673?-735), an English Roman Catholic priest, wrote more than 30 works on history, science, hymns, the lives of saints, grammar, and the Bible. His most famous work is the *Ecclesiastical History of the English Nation,* covering events up to the year 731. For his many achievements, he was given the title "the Venerable Bede" and was canonized.

Beebe, William (1877-1962), became famous for designing the bathysphere, in which he made many undersea explorations to observe marine life. Curator of ornithology at the New York Zoological Society, Beebe traveled widely throughout the world, particularly in tropical regions. His popular books include *Beneath Tropic Seas.*

Beethoven, Ludwig van (1770-1827), a German-born composer generally credited with beginning the romantic movement in music, expanded musical form and used daring harmonies. His compositions include nine symphonies, an opera, five piano concertos, a violin concerto, more than 30 sonatas, and numerous string quartets and religious works.

Bell, Alexander Graham (1847-1922), a painter and a teacher of the deaf, invented the telephone. With the aid of his assistant, Thomas A. Watson, Bell carried out many experiments that in 1876 produced one of the first instruments that successfully transmitted voices over a distance.

Ben-Gurion, David (1886-1973), promoted the creation of the state of Israel and became the nation's first prime minister, serving from 1948 to 1953 and again from 1955 to 1963. Born in Poland, he emigrated to Israel and became a Zionist (independence) leader. In 1930 he formed the United Labor, now the Mapai, political party.

Bentham, Jeremy (1748-1832), an English jurist and philosopher, taught that the morality of ideas, actions, and institutions should be judged on the basis of how well they promote the greatest good for the greatest number of people. His philosophy, called utilitarianism, brought about some court and other reforms.

Bessemer, Sir Henry (1813-1898), an English inventor and engineer, developed a means of removing impurities from iron ore. Called the Bessemer process, it greatly increased the quantity and quality of steel production in the 1800's. He established steelworks at Sheffield, England, to produce parts for guns and steel rails.

Bethune, Mary McLeod (1875-1955), a black educator, founded a school for black women in 1904 in Daytona Beach, Fla., that later merged with a men's school to become Bethune-Cookman College. She was the school's president for many years and later held several positions in the federal government. Bethune also established mission schools for blacks.

Bismarck, Otto von (1815-1898), became the first chancellor of the German Empire in 1871 after he had unified his country after wars with Austria and France. To solidify and secure Germany's position, he created the Triple Alliance through a series of treaties with Austria-Hungary and Italy that lasted until the outbreak of World War I.

Blackstone, Sir William (1723-1780), an English jurist, wrote the influential *Commentaries on the Laws of England.* This extensive treatise was frequently quoted in the 1700's and became the basis for legal education in England. It was also influential in the American Colonies, where it served as a source book on English law.

Blackwell, Elizabeth (1821-1910), was the first woman physician in the United States. Born in England, she moved to the United States as a child. She graduated from medical school in 1849 and opened a hospital for women and children in 1853. Elizabeth and her sister, Emily, founded the Women's Medical College of the New York Infirmary for Women and Children in 1857.

Blake, William (1757-1827), was an English mystic, poet, engraver, and painter, He illustrated his own books as well as the writings of others. A romantic poet, Blake's works include two volumes, both entitled *Songs of Innocence,* which treat similar subjects from contrasting points of view. His engravings include *Illustrations of the Book of Job.*

Boccaccio, Giovanni (1313?-1375), an Italian author, wrote *The Decameron,* a collection of tales supposedly related by a group of men and women isolated in Florence, Italy, during a plague. The stories are humorous and earthy and were retold by many later writers. Boccaccio also served in several diplomatic posts for the Florentine government.

Bohr, Niels (1885-1962), a Danish physicist, elaborated on Ernest Rutherford's theory that the atom consists of a positively charged nucleus with negatively charged electrons revolving around it. Bohr's research was a major step toward the practical use of nuclear energy. Bohr won the Nobel prize in physics in 1922.

Boleyn, Anne (1507-1536), was the second wife of Henry VIII of England. When Henry divorced his first wife to marry Anne, the act brought about the separation of England from the Roman Catholic Church and the establishment of the Church of England. Anne's daughter became Elizabeth I. Charged with infidelity after Henry tired of her, Anne was beheaded.

Bolívar, Simón (1783-1830), born into the middle class, joined the Latin-American independence movement and fought many successful battles against the Spanish. Colombia, Ecuador, Venezuela, and other countries gained their freedom from Spain because of Bolívar's military leadership. For several years, Bolívar was president of Colombia and unsuccessfully worked for Latin-American unity.

Boone, Daniel (1734-1820), an almost legendary frontiersman, participated in the French and Indian Wars and later led an early group of first pioneers into Ken-tucky. He helped lay out the Wilderness Road and found settlements. In 1799, Boone moved West to become a pioneer in Missouri.

Booth, John Wilkes (1838-1865), an actor and member of a prominent theatrical family, assassinated President Abraham Lincoln in Ford's Theatre in Washington, D.C., on April 14, 1865. A Southerner, he considered Lincoln to be a tyrant and an enemy of the South. Fleeing the theater after the shooting, Booth was hunted down in Virginia, where he was shot to death.

Brahe, Tycho (1546-1601), a Danish astronomer, made important discoveries through systematic observation of the planets, an innovation at the time. He observed a new star and suggested that comets originate in outer space, not in the earth's atmosphere, as had been thought. Brahe's theories and astronomical tables were of great value to succeeding astronomers.

Brahms, Johannes (1833-1897), a German romantic composer, wrote music in all major forms except opera and ballet. His compositions include *Variations on a Theme by Haydn, Academic Festival Overture,* four symphonies, two piano concertos and a violin concerto, Hungarian dances, and many songs. His music is known for its dramatic qualities.

Braille, Louis (1809-1852), a Frenchman blinded by an accident at the age of 3, studied music and became an organist. As a teacher at the National Institute for the Blind in Paris, he developed a system of writing using raised points that could be read with the fingertips. His system, called braille, opened a new means of communication for the blind.

Brooks, Gwendolyn (1917-   ), a black American poet and writer, published several collections of poetry, including *A Street in Bronzeville*. A Guggenheim scholar, she won the Pulitzer prize in 1950 for her volume of poetry *Annie Allen*. The first black woman to win the prize, Brooks was named poet laureate of Illinois in 1968.

Brown, John (1800-1859), an American abolitionist, embodied the hostility between the North and the South in the decade before the Civil War. He helped blacks escape from slavery and fought proslavery groups in Kansas. In 1859, Brown and his followers briefly seized the federal arsenal at Harper's Ferry, Va. The arsenal retaken, Brown was convicted of treason and hanged.

Bryan, William Jennings (1860-1925), a politician, served from 1891 to 1895 in the House of Representatives. A spokesman for the free-silver movement, he ran unsuccessfully for the presidency as a Democrat in 1896, 1900, and 1908. Bryan served as secretary of state during the administration of President Woodrow Wilson and later attacked the teaching of evolution in schools.

Buddha (563?-483? B.C.) developed a philosophy of peace based on enlightenment, on which he founded a religion. Born Prince Siddhartha Gautama in Nepal, he taught his followers to forsake desire, seek goodness, escape from sorrow, and follow an eightfold path to righteousness and enlightenment.

Burr, Aaron (1756-1836), an American politician, was Vice-President under Thomas Jefferson from 1801 to 1805. Under the system of that time, Jefferson won the Presidency over Burr on the 36th ballot in the House of Representatives. In a duel in 1804, Burr killed Alexander Hamilton, who was largely responsible for Burr's having lost the Presidency and another office. Later, he was involved in a mysterious plot to establish an independent nation in the Southwest.

Byrd, Richard (1888-1957), an American admiral and explorer, greatly furthered knowledge of the Antarctic region. Beginning in 1928, he led numerous expeditions to Antarctica. During the last expedition in 1955 and 1956, he flew over the South Pole for the third time. Byrd became the foremost authority on Antarctica of his time.

Cabot, John (1450?-1498?), a navigator and explorer born in Italy, made two voyages for King Henry VII of England. Although he was sailing for Asia, both times he reached islands in the North Atlantic. On the first voyage, he landed on Cape Breton Island or Newfoundland. Setting out again, Cabot and his party were lost; however, his voyages helped England establish claims on the islands.

Caesar, Julius (100?-44 B.C.), a Roman general and politician, conquered what is now France and twice invaded England. He later took over the Roman government and fought several wars, one in Egypt. Fearing a dictatorship, Caesar's enemies conspired together and assassinated him.

Calhoun, John C. (1782-1850), a powerful politician, was the foremost spokesman for states' rights before the Civil War. He was a representative and a senator from South Carolina and was Vice-President from 1825 to 1832. Calhoun's last speech in the Senate opposed the Compromise of 1850, a measure that was meant to settle the slavery issue (see "Millard Fillmore" in Unit 5, page 275).

Calvin, John (1509-1564), a Swiss theologian born in France, developed a stern and forbidding Protestant theology based on faith rather than good works. He believed in predestination and free will. Calvinism was a highly individualistic religion, and vestiges of it can be found today in Presbyterian, Congregational, and other faiths.

Carnegie, Andrew (1835-1919), born in Scotland, became an American industrialist and philanthropist. He emigrated to the United States at age 13 and worked his way up to an important position in a railroad company. Carnegie later became a steel manufacturer and eventually accumulated a fortune of some half billion dollars. He gave away much money to philanthropic causes.

Carroll, Lewis (1832-1898), was the pen name of Charles L. Dodgson, an English mathematician and writer. For a girl named Alice, he developed imaginative stories that were later published as *Alice's Adventures in Wonderland*. When the book quickly became a children's favorite, he wrote a sequel, *Through the Looking Glass*. A professor, he also published works on mathematics.

Cartier, Jacques (1491?-1557), a French sailor, became an explorer of Canada for King Francis I. In 1534, he discovered the Gulf of St. Lawrence and the St. Lawrence River. On other voyages, he journeyed far up the St. Lawrence River and located the future sites of Quebec and Montreal. His voyages gave France huge land claims in North America.

Caruso, Enrico (1873-1921), was perhaps the greatest operatic tenor of his time. Born in Italy, he sang in opera houses in Russia, Italy, England, and in South American countries but had his greatest success with the Metropolitan Opera Company of New York City. Caruso had a large repertoire of more than 40 operas.

Carver, George Washington (1864-1943) was a black American scientist who won international fame for his agricultural research. Carver was especially noted for his work with peanuts; he made more than 300 products from them, including printer's ink, soap, and face powder. In addition to his scientific contributions, Carver worked to promote the interests of black people and to improve relations between blacks and whites.

Castro, Fidel (1926-   ), a Cuban revolutionary leader, became prime minister after he overthrew dictator Fulgencio Batista in 1959. He established a Communist state, nationalized businesses, and began land reforms. Castro reportedly aided guerrilla movements in other Latin-American countries, and he sent Cubans to support Communist movements in Africa.

Catherine of Aragon (1485-1536) was the first of the six wives of King Henry VIII of England. The daughter of Ferdinand and Isabella of Spain, she was the mother of Mary I. Henry's insistence on divorcing her led to England's break with the Roman Catholic Church and the establishment of the Church of England. After her divorce, Catherine lived a life of religious devotion in prison (see "Henry VIII" in this unit).

George Washington Carver, shown in his laboratory, devoted his career to improving agricultural methods.

Catherine II (1729-1796) was an empress of Russia who became known as "the Great." When her husband Peter was deposed and murdered, Catherine took the throne. Although interested in European liberalism, she ruled autocratically, and the misery of the serfs increased during her reign. Catherine extended Russian borders to include a part of Poland and the Crimea. She also conquered Siberian tribes.

Cato, Marcus Porcius, the Elder (234-149 B.C.), a Roman consul and senator, helped bring about the destruction of Carthage in northern Africa in the Third Punic War. He viewed Carthage as Rome's mortal enemy and closed all of his speeches in the senate with a plea for its destruction. Known as Cato the Elder, he tried to revive values that Rome had held in its early days.

Cavour, Camillo Benso (1810-1861), an Italian statesman, served as prime minister of Sardinia from 1852 to 1861. Under his leadership, Sardinia joined France to drive Austria from Lombardy. Sardinia then took control of Lombardy and other areas of Italy. Working with Giuseppe Garibaldi and others, Cavour succeeded in making Italy a unified nation.

Cervantes, Miguel de (1547-1616), a Spanish author, wrote *Don Quixote,* sometimes called the world's greatest novel. Begun while Cervantes was in prison, the work tells the adventures of the idealistic Don Quixote and his servant Sancho Panza and is a satire on chivalry. Cervantes held several minor military and diplomatic posts and wrote plays, poems, and other works.

Cézanne, Paul (1839-1906), a French painter, used forms such as the cone, the cube, and the sphere in his works. Trained in the impressionistic school of art, he established his own style in painting that emphasized solid masses of color. Cézanne influenced the cubist school of painters.

Champlain, Samuel de (1567?-1635), was a French explorer of the New World and for several years served as governor of the French colony at Quebec in Canada. He discovered Lake Champlain and explored extensively along the St. Lawrence River, Georgian Bay, and Lake Ontario. Champlain promoted the fur trade and maintained a friendship with the Algonkian Indians.

Charlemagne (742-814) was king of the Franks (Germans) and emperor of the Romans. Defeating the Saxons, the Bavarians, the Avars, the Lombards, and others, he created an empire sprawling over much of central and western Europe. A patron of culture, he did much to promote scholarship and education within his realm.

Chaucer, Geoffrey (1340?-1400), an English public official, diplomat, and poet, wrote *The Canterbury Tales*. In the poem, a group of pilgrims journeying to Canterbury tell stories for their amusement as they proceed. Chaucer also wrote several other poems, including *The Book of the Duchess*.

Chavez, Cesar (1927-   ), was the first labor leader who effectively organized migrant workers. A migrant worker himself, he worked to unionize field laborers in the 1960's in spite of much opposition. Chavez established the National Farm Workers Association and in 1966 signed the first contract with California growers.

Chekhov, Anton (1860-1904), a Russian author, wrote many plays and short stories in which he stressed human loneliness and people's failure to understand one another. Among his stories are "Kashtanka," "The Party," "The Darling," and "Ward No. 6." Chekhov's plays include *The Cherry Orchard, Uncle Vanya,* and *The Three Sisters*.

Chopin, Frédéric (1810?-1849), a pianist and composer born in Poland, was a child prodigy and wrote lyrical works for the piano, many based on popular dance forms. Settling in Paris with George Sand, a woman writer, Chopin composed two piano concertos and many shorter works—mazurkas, polonaises, preludes, études, nocturnes, ballades, and songs.

Churchill, Winston (1874-1965), a British statesman and author, began his career as a soldier and reporter. He later entered Parliament and headed various ministries. In 1940, he became prime minister, leading Great Britain during World War II. He also served as prime minister again from 1951 to 1955. Churchill wrote on English history and also wrote a history of World War II that won him the Nobel prize in literature in 1953.

Cicero (106-43 B.C.), a Roman lawyer, statesman, and writer, served as a consul. Exiled for refusing to support the First Triumvirate, he devoted himself to writing. He later became a leader of the senate and opposed Mark Antony's ambition to rule Rome. Feared because of his ability as an orator, Cicero was condemned to death and was killed while trying to escape.

Cincinnatus, Lucius Quinctius (519?-439? B.C.), a Roman patriot, was appointed dictator and led an army that defeated the Aequians in central Italy. After his victory, he resigned. Given absolute power a second time, he once more resigned after slaying a traitor threatening Rome. To later Romans, Cincinnatus became a symbol of old-fashioned virtues.

Clark, George Rogers (1752-1818), led troops against the British in the Northwest Territory during the Revolutionary War. He financed his own campaigns and was never reimbursed for his expenses. Clark's successes helped secure the Northwest for the United States under the peace treaty of 1783 that ended the war.

Clay, Henry (1777-1852), represented Kentucky for many years in the House of Representatives, where he served several terms as speaker, and in the Senate. He tried unsuccessfully for the presidency three times. Clay's greatest renown came from the Missouri Compromise and the Compromise of 1850—agreements that he worked out to ease the conflict between the North and South over the slavery issue.

Cleopatra (69-30 B.C.), an Egyptian queen who at various times ruled with her two brothers (who were also her husbands), became the mistress of Julius Caesar and bore him a son. She later became the lover of Mark Antony and bore him twins. When Antony was defeated in Egypt by Octavian, Cleopatra committed suicide to avoid the humiliation of being taken to Rome for exhibition as a captive.

Clinton, De Witt (1769-1828), promoted the Erie Canal, completed in 1825 when he was governor of New York. The canal helped New York City develop as the country's most important port. Clinton also served as mayor of New York City, as a state senator, and as lieutenant governor. He was an unsuccessful Federalist candidate for the presidency in 1812.

Cochise (?-1874), a chief of the Chiricahua Apache, was captured by white soldiers under a flag of truce and accused of a crime he had not committed. Escaping, the embittered Cochise led his warriors in 10 years of intermittent warfare against whites. A brilliant leader, he finally was forced to accept life on a reservation.

Columbus, Christopher (1451-1506), an Italian navigator, made four voyages of exploration of the Americas for Spain in the 1490's and early 1500's. He was searching for a route to Asia and reached what he thought were the Indies. Because of his efforts, Spain made vast land claims in the Americas, but Columbus died in poverty and obscurity.

Confucius (551?-479? B.C.), a Chinese philosopher, centered his teachings on human relationships, not gods. He taught moral responsibility, kindness and generosity, filial piety, respect for elders and superiors, and the duty of rulers to govern wisely and well. Confucianism came to be one of the most influential philosophies in Chinese society.

Conrad, Joseph (1857-1924), a Polish-born British author, wrote mostly about sailors and the sea, which he knew from firsthand experience. Among his writings are *Lord Jim* and *Heart of Darkness*. Although he did not learn English until he was 20 years old, Conrad became an elegant stylist in the language.

Constantine (275?-337), called "the Great," was an emperor of the Roman Empire. He favored Christianity during his rule and moved his capital from Rome to Byzantium, renaming the city Constantinople. In 325, Constantine called Christian leaders together at the

Council of Nicaea to settle disputes over doctrine.

Cook, James (1728-1779), a British mariner, made voyages of exploration throughout the world. He mapped portions of the eastern coasts of North America and of New Zealand, Australia, and New Guinea; sailed across the Antarctic Circle; reached New Caledonia; charted much of the western coast of North America; and explored the Bering Strait. Cook was killed in Hawaii.

Copernicus, Nicolaus (1473-1543), a Polish astronomer, is considered the founder of modern astronomy. He developed the theory that the earth is a moving planet, and he attacked Ptolemy's theory—then generally accepted—that the earth was fixed in the universe and never moved. Copernicus' major work was *Concerning the Revolutions of the Celestial Spheres* (1543).

Cortés, Hernando (1485-1547), a Spanish explorer, conquered the Aztec Indians after bitter fighting and won Mexico for Spain. As the first governor of Mexico (then called New Spain), he spread Spanish control and influence and began the first settlement in Lower California.

Crick, Francis H. C. (1916-   ), a British biologist, shared the Nobel prize for physiology or medicine in 1962 for his work with deoxyribonuleic acid (DNA), the substance that transmits genetic information. Crick also helped develop radar during World War II.

Cromwell, Oliver (1599-1658), an English Puritan, led parliamentary forces to defeat, depose, and behead King Charles I in 1649. Beginning in 1653, he ruled England as Lord Protector Cromwell, mostly without the aid of Parliament, until his death. After a short rule by Cromwell's son Richard, Charles II, the son of Charles I, came to the throne.

Curie, Marie (1867-1934), a Polish-born chemist, made important discoveries in radioactivity with her husband Pierre. Together, the Curies discovered radium and polonium and shared the Nobel prize in physics in 1903 with another scientist. A professor at the Sorbonne in Paris, she won the Nobel prize in chemistry in 1911.

Curie, Pierre (1859-1906), a French physicist and chemist, did his first important work on the magnetic properties of metals, and with his wife Marie made important discoveries in radioactivity. The Curies discovered radium and polonium, for which they shared the Nobel prize in physics in 1903. Curie was a professor of physics and chemistry.

Cyrus the Great (reigned 559-529 B.C.) established the ancient Persian Empire. He extended his empire by defeating several rulers—including Astyages, the king of Media; King Croesus of Lydia; and Nabonidus, the king of Babylon. Cyrus freed the Jews from captivity, allowing them to return to Palestine.

Da Gama, Vasco (1469?-1524), a Portuguese navigator, rounded the Cape of Good Hope with an expedition in 1497 and sailed to India. He was the first to establish an all-water route from Europe to the East and was instrumental in opening the spice trade of the Indies to the Portuguese. Da Gama established Portuguese colonies on Mozambique and Sofala.

Dalton, John (1766-1844), an English chemist, developed the first clear statements of the atomic theory of matter. He also established the law of multiple proportions, developed formulas of molecular atomic composition, and although it proved to be inaccurate, produced a table of atomic weights. He also made the first detailed description of color blindness (Daltonism).

Dante Alighieri (1265-1321), an Italian poet, wrote the *Divine Comedy*. Inspired by his love for a woman named Beatrice, the allegorical work describes the narrator's struggle through hell, purgatory, and heaven. Dante also wrote love poems, as well as prose works.

Darius I (558?-486 B.C.), called "the Great," ruled the Persian Empire as its king. In an invasion of Greece, his armies were defeated at the Battle of Marathon. Darius ran his empire efficiently, reorganizing the administration, building roads, and reforming the tax system. He died while preparing for a second invasion of Greece. His son Xerxes succeeded him.

Darwin, Charles (1809-1882), a British naturalist, in 1859 published *The Origin of Species,* a theory of evolution. He first began to develop the theory as the result of observations he made on a five-year voyage around the world. Darwin also wrote *The Descent of Man,* which deals with human evolution from lower animals.

David (?-973? B.C.), the successor to Saul, was the second king of Israel. He won fame as a boy for killing Goliath, the Philistine giant. A harpist, poet, and composer of psalms, David tried to make his kingdom secure with the defeat of several surrounding tribes, but his reign was troubled by rebellions. David was succeeded by Solomon, his son by Bathsheba.

Da Vinci, Leonardo (1452-1519), an Italian genius of the Renaissance, was a scientist, inventor, engineer, sculptor, and painter. Among his many accomplishments, he drew up plans for a flying machine, designed fortifications for Italian rulers, and wrote on astronomy and botany. His paintings include *The Last Supper* and *Mona Lisa.*

Davis, Jefferson (1808-1889), became president of the Confederate States of America in 1861. He had earlier served the United States government as a soldier, as a representative and senator, and as secretary of war. After the Civil War, he spent two years in prison and then retired to Mississippi, where he wrote a defense of the Confederacy and of his presidency.

Davy, Sir Humphry (1778-1829), an English chemist, was the first scientist to isolate a number of elements, including potassium, sodium, strontium, calcium, and magnesium. He invented the Davy lamp, used in coal mining, and also experimented with "laughing gas" (nitrous oxide) as an anesthetic. Davy's interests were wide ranging, and he wrote several books on various subjects in chemistry.

Debs, Eugene V. (1855-1926), an American labor leader, formed the American Railway Union in the 1890's and as the result of a strike went to prison for contempt of court. Debs became a Socialist and ran for the presidency five times between 1900 and 1920. He conducted his last campaign while in prison for opposing United States participation in World War I.

Degas, Edgar (1834-1917), a French impressionistic painter, developed a style using pastel colors for spectacular effects. Although he painted some still lifes, his favorite subjects were the people of everyday life. He often painted ordinary people, such as women ironing or bathing.

De Gaulle, Charles (1890-1970), a French military leader and statesman, was the leader and symbol of the French resistance movement during World War II. As prime minister and later president of the Fifth Republic in the 1960's, he improved France's economy and ended the war with Algeria by granting independence to that colony. Although he was criticized for his dictatorial rule, De Gaulle brought stability to postwar France.

Demosthenes (384?-322 B.C.), an Athenian statesman who was regarded as the greatest of the Greek orators, was a lifelong defender of Greek independence. He spoke out frequently against Philip of Macedon's designs on Greece and formed an army to resist Macedonian invasion. When the Greeks met defeat, Demosthenes committed suicide rather than allow himself to be captured.

Descartes, René (1596-1650), a French mathematician and philosopher, devoted himself to settling questions about existence and reality. As a starting point, he argued that thought is proof of one's existence. From the existence of the self, he developed proofs of the existence of other realities and of the existence of God. Descartes' writings turned modern

philosophy away from the concerns of the Middle Ages.

De Soto, Hernando (1500?-1542), a Spanish adventurer, accompanied Francisco Pizarro in the conquest of the Incas of Peru. Although he gained much wealth from the conquest, he later searched for more gold by leading a party to explore the lower Mississippi River Valley, the Ozark Mountains, and portions of the American Southeast, including Florida. De Soto died on the banks of the Mississippi and was buried in the river.

Dewey, John (1859-1952), an American philosopher, had a great influence on American educational practices. He taught that experience is fundamental and that the value of an idea lies in its results. In education, he emphasized learning through activity rather than lectures or memorization. Dewey became one of the leaders of the "progressive" movement in education.

Dias, Bartolomeu (1457?-1500), a Portuguese navigator, discovered the Cape of Good Hope in 1488, opening the path by sea from Europe to the East. Ten years later, Vasco da Gama duplicated Dias's feat but continued eastward to India, beginning Portuguese domination of the spice trade with the Indies. Dias also traded with Africa and sailed to Brazil.

Dickens, Charles (1812-1870), an English novelist, portrayed the lives of the lower classes in the 1800's. He often included social comments on the wretched conditions under which the poor lived and was credited with some social improvements that were made. His novels include *Pickwick Papers, David Copperfield, A Tale of Two Cities, Great*

Expectations, Bleak House, and *A Christmas Carol.*

Dickinson, Emily (1830-1886), a poet who was unknown to the public in her lifetime, came to be considered among the greatest writers in American literature. Apparently because of her unfulfilled love for a married man, she withdrew from society to write on death, immortality, and love. By her own wish, her poems were not published during her lifetime. The first volume of Dickinson's poems was published in 1890.

Didérot, Denis (1713-1784), a French writer, edited an encyclopedia, a task that took him 20 years. A monumental work, the encyclopedia stressed scientific objectivity. Several other important French writers aided Didérot in his project, and it contained contributions from such influential French thinkers as Rousseau and Voltaire.

Diocletian (245?-313) was proclaimed Roman emperor at a time of great disunity. Dividing the empire into four separate and self-ruled districts, he tried to bring order after 50 years of civil war. Trying to restore the traditional Roman gods, Diocletian carried on severe persecutions of the Christians during much of his reign.

Disraeli, Benjamin (1804-1881), a British politician and statesman, was the only Jewish person to serve as prime minister of England. A novelist early in his life, he was elected to Parliament in 1837, becoming prime minister in 1868 and serving again from 1874 to 1880. During his terms, Disraeli strengthened British imperialism abroad.

Dostoevsky, Fyodor (1821-1881), a Russian novelist, often wrote about people who sought salvation through suffering as they struggled with good and evil. Accused of political conspiracy, he spent several years in prison in Siberia and was plagued by poverty and misfortune throughout his life. Among his novels are *The Brothers Karamazov, The Idiot,* and *The Possessed.*

Douglas, Stephen A. (1813-1861), a powerful representative and senator from Illinois, helped pass the Compromise of 1850. He promoted the idea of popular sovereignty—that the people of a territory should decide on slavery. His Kansas-Nebraska Bill in 1854, which was based on popular sovereignty, led to civil war in Kansas. His debates with Abraham Lincoln over slavery gained national attention for Lincoln, and Douglas was defeated in his bid for the presidency in 1860.

Douglass, Frederick (1817-1895), escaped slavery to become a writer and a leader in the antislavery movement. He founded a newspaper, during the Civil War raised black Union regiments, and later held several government posts. In the *Narrative of the Life of Frederick Douglass,* he wrote about his upbringing as a slave in Maryland and his life after escaping.

Drake, Sir Francis (1540?-1596), an English navigator and plunderer of Spanish treasure ships, sailed the *Golden Hind* around the world between 1577 and 1580. Returning to England with much Spanish wealth, he was knighted by Queen Elizabeth I. Drake later participated in the successful battles against the Spanish Armada that was sent to invade England.

Du Bois, W. E. B. (1868-1963), a black educator, writer, and leader, argued for black-white equality rather than gradual economic improvement for blacks. Du Bois wrote several books, including *The Souls of Black Folk,* about the lives of blacks in the United States. He helped form the National Association for the Advancement of Colored People in 1909.

Dunbar, Paul Laurence (1872-1906), a black American poet, became famous for poems written in dialect that expressed blacks' feelings. His poems were often humorous and were published in volumes that include *Majors and Minors, Joggin' Erlong, Lyrics of the Hearthside,* and *Lyrics of Lowly Life.* Dunbar became a model of achievement for blacks, and many schools were named after him.

Duns Scotus (1265?-1308), an English theologian, disagreed with his contemporary Thomas Aquinas on several theological and philosophical doctrines and founded a system called Scotism. He studied at Oxford and became a professor of theology there and at Paris and Cologne. Duns Scotus wrote commentaries on the Bible and on the Greek philosopher Aristotle.

Earhart, Amelia (1897-1937?), an American aviator, was the first woman passenger to cross the Atlantic Ocean by air and the first woman pilot to fly solo across the Atlantic. She was the first woman pilot to fly from Hawaii to the mainland of the United States and the first to cross the continent solo in both directions. Earhart disappeared in the Pacific Ocean under mysterious circumstances while on a round-the-world flight.

Edison, Thomas Alva (1847-1931), perhaps the foremost technological genius of his time, invented the electric light bulb and the phonograph. Edison also made improvements on the typewriter, storage battery, ticker tape machine, electric-powered train, and electric generator. Altogether, he produced more than 1,000 inventions.

Edward the Confessor (1002?-1066) codified Anglo-Saxon laws and built a church on the site of Westminster Abbey, where he is buried. Placed on the throne by the powerful Earl Godwin, Edward spent much of his reign quarreling with Godwin over policies involving both the state and religion. The king became interested in religion early in his life and was canonized by the Roman Catholic Church in 1161.

Einstein, Albert (1879-1955), a German-born mathematician and physicist, developed the theory of relativity and contributed to the quantum theory and numerous other discoveries in modern physics. A resident of the United States after 1933, he influenced the government to begin work on an atomic bomb. Einstein was awarded the Nobel prize for physics in 1921.

Eleanor of Aquitaine (1122?-1204) was the wife of Louis VII of France and later of Henry II of England. She was the mother of two English kings—Richard I, the Lion-Hearted, and John, the signer of the Magna Carta. England fought several wars to hold her lands in France, the beginning of centuries of hostility between the two countries. Eleanor herself was a party to intrigues involving her faithless English husband and her sons (see "Henry II" in this unit).

Eliot, T. S. (1888-1965), an American who became a British subject in 1927, was one of the most influential poets and critics of his time. Among his best-known poems are "The Love Song of J. Alfred Prufrock," *The Waste Land,* "Ash Wednesday," "The Hollow Men," and "Gerontion." Many of his poems involve religious themes. Eliot won the Nobel prize for literature in 1948.

Elizabeth I (1533-1603) ruled during a time of great expansion of English power and a time of great literary production. William Shakespeare lived during her reign, and English exploration and discovery overseas increased the country's position among European nations. In 1588, Elizabeth's navy defeated the Spanish Armada to make England the greatest sea power of the age.

Elizabeth II (1926-   ) is Queen of the United Kingdom of Great Britain and Northern Ireland. She is also head of the Commonwealth of Nations. Elizabeth was 25 years old when she succeeded to the throne of her father, George VI, in 1952. Her reign has been marked by frequent state visits to all parts of the Commonwealth. Elizabeth married Philip Mountbatten in 1947.

Emerson, Ralph Waldo (1803-1882), an American poet, philosopher, and essayist, was among the leading writers of his time and an associate of such literary figures as Henry David Thoreau and Walt Whitman. Emerson based his philosophy on individualism and self-reliance. *Concord Hymn* is among his most popular poems.

Engels, Friedrich (1820-1895), a German Socialist, collaborated with Karl Marx on *The Communist Manifesto.* Involved in revolutionary activity in Germany, Engels fled to England where he was a manufacturer and a leader of the Socialist movement. He edited and published many of Marx's writings. Engels' own writings include *The Condition of the Working Class in England.*

Erasmus, Desiderius (1466?-1536), a Dutch scholar, was a Christian humanist of the Renaissance. He favored internal reform of the Roman Catholic Church, rather than a break with the church. He stressed faith and grace over works. Erasmus lived and studied in several important university centers.

Ericson, Leif (about 1000), a Norse sailor and adventurer, has been credited with discovering North America long before Columbus. Sailing west, he came upon a land that he named Vinland because of the grapevines he found there. The land Ericson reached has been identified by different historians as the Labrador Peninsula, Newfoundland Island, or New England.

Euclid (about 300 B.C.), a Greek mathematician, was the founder of geometry. His work *The Elements* remained the foundation of geometry until the early 1900's. The text is a model of mathematical and logical thinking. Euclid lived in Alexandria, Egypt, during the reign of Ptolemy I, and founded a school for mathematicians there.

Faraday, Michael (1791-1867), an English physicist and chemist, made important discoveries in electromagnetism. He discovered that passing a magnet through a coil of copper wire produces a flow of electric current, a principle on which the electric motor and generator are based. As a chemist, Faraday developed the law of valences.

Farragut, David G. (1801-1870), was a Union naval commander in the Civil War. Known as "Old Salamander," he commanded Union forces blockading the South along the lower Mississippi River, and won fame for his victory at Mobile Bay, Ala., in 1864. Farragut also participated in many other military actions, including the Mexican War. He was a native of Virginia.

Faulkner, William (1897-1962), a Mississippi writer, portrayed Southern life in a place called Yoknapatawpha County that he created. He regretted the loss of traditional Southern values. Among his novels are *Sartoris, The Sound and the Fury, Absalom, Absalom!, Intruder in the Dust,* and *As I Lay Dying.* Faulkner won the Nobel prize for literature in 1949.

Fermi, Enrico (1901-1954), was a physicist whose work led to the development of the atomic bomb. He became professor of theoretical physics at the University of Rome in 1926, but he left Italy for the United States in 1938 after winning the Nobel prize for physics. At the University of Chicago in 1942, Fermi led a team that produced the first atomic chain reaction.

Fleming, Sir Alexander (1881-1955), a British bacteriologist, discovered penicillin, probably the most useful of all antibiotics. It proved to be an extremely useful drug during World War II and was credited with saving many lives. For his work in bacteriology, Fleming shared the Nobel prize in medicine in 1945.

Ford, Henry (1863-1947), a pioneer American automaker, made the automobile available to the middle class when he introduced the Model T—a plain but sturdy, reliable, and relatively inexpensive automobile. He developed the use of moving assembly lines and interchangeable parts in the manufacture of automobiles. He and his son established the Ford Foundation, a philanthropic organization.

Francis of Assisi, Saint (1181?-1226), an Italian cleric, abandoned a life of wealth and ease to embrace poverty. He founded the Franciscan order in 1209. Known as a gentle man, Francis was a missionary in Italy, Spain, and Egypt, and he visited Palestine. He was canonized by the Roman Catholic Church two years after his death.

Franklin, Benjamin (1706-1790), was perhaps the best-known person in the American Colonies. A signer of the Declaration of Independence and the Constitution, he was a philosopher, politician, inventor, scientist, diplomat, writer, printer, statesman, and civic leader of Philadelphia. Among his many literary works was *Poor Richard's Almanac.*

Frederick I (1121?-1190), known as Barbarossa or Red Beard, was a king of Germany and the Holy Roman Emperor. Often involved in unsuccessful conflicts with the pope, he set out on the Third Crusade, during which he drowned while crossing a river. His reign was marked by the advancement of learning and the development of towns and cities as well as by internal peace in his kingdom.

Frémont, John C. (1813-1890), was an explorer of the Western United States who won the nickname "the Pathfinder." He explored the area that is now Oregon, Nevada, and California and organized the seizure of California during the Mexican War. In 1856, Frémont became the first Republican candidate for the presidency. He led Union troops during the Civil War. Later, he served as territorial governor of Arizona.

Freud, Sigmund (1856-1939), an Austrian physician, founded psychoanalysis, a method of treating emotional problems through recall of repressed thoughts and feelings. Freud believed that the unconscious is a collection of memories that can govern human behavior. Freud also investigated the importance of infantile experiences, sexuality, and dreams. Among his writings are *The Interpretation of Dreams, Three Essays on the Theory of Sexuality,* and *General Introduction to Psychoanalysis.*

Frobisher, Sir Martin (1535?-1594), an English navigator during the reign of Elizabeth I, searched unsuccessfully for the Northwest Passage through North America. He reached Frobisher Bay, explored Labrador, and entered the Hudson Strait. He later participated in the sea battles against the Spanish Armada.

Fulton, Robert (1765-1815), an American artist, engineer, and inventor, developed the first practical steamboat, the *Clermont,* which in 1807 steamed up the Hudson River from New York City to Albany. He also invented a machine for spinning thread, a machine for weaving rope, a dredge for cutting channels for canals, and a successful submarine.

Gagarin, Yuri (1934-1968), a Soviet air force pilot, was the first human to travel in space. The Soviet cosmonaut circled the earth on April 12, 1961, in the spacecraft *Vostok 1.*

Galen (130?-200?), the foremost physician of the Roman world, made discoveries about human anatomy that became the basis of medicine for centuries. He wrote several books, and, even though his works contained many errors, his authority went unquestioned throughout much of the Middle Ages.

Galileo (1564-1642), an Italian astronomer and physicist, made important astronomical observations that confirmed the Copernican theory that the planets revolve around the sun. The Roman Catholic Church rejected his evidence and forced Galileo to recant his view. He built telescopes, discovered the law of the pendulum, and experimented with gravity.

Gandhi, Mohandas K. (1869-1948), the father of modern India, led the movement that forced Great Britain to grant India its independence in 1947. Trained as a lawyer, he fought discrimination in South Africa but returned to India to work for independence. Gandhi practiced passive resistance and civil disobedience and was frequently jailed for his actions.

Garibaldi, Giuseppe (1807-1882), was a leader of the movement that united Italy and was later a member of the Italian parliament. He led troops that freed Lombardy from Austria and conquered the Kingdom of the Two Sicilies. These areas became part of the Kingdom of Italy and were joined by Rome in 1870 to form the modern nation of Italy.

Gauguin, Paul (1848-1903), a French painter, produced brilliant canvases in bright colors with sweeping brushwork. Beginning his career as an impressionist, he was not well accepted. He left France for Tahiti, where he lived for most of the remainder of his life. In Tahiti, Gauguin produced some of his greatest paintings and won acclaim in Europe.

Gauss, Karl Friedrich (1777-1855), a German mathematician and astronomer, established the mathematical theory of electromagnetism. A child prodigy, he produced his first important original work at the age of 19. Gauss made numerous contributions to astronomy, geometry, algebra, and number theory. He also invented a form of the telescope.

Genghis Khan (1167-1227), a Mongol conqueror, successfully invaded northern China and turned his forces toward the west. He also conquered parts of the Middle East. Though a military genius, he left few permanent influences on the lands he conquered. His grandson, Kublai Khan, founded the Mongol dynasty in China.

Geronimo (1829-1909) was a chief of the southern Apache Indians, who resisted control by whites. Rather than go to a reservation, Geronimo moved his people from Arizona to Mexico. From there he led raids on American settlements. After surrendering in 1886, he and his tribe were sent to Oklahoma, where Geronimo spent the rest of his life.

Giacometti, Alberto (1901-1966), a Swiss sculptor, portrayed exaggeratedly long and slender human figures. At first, his work brought him little attention or praise, but he began to receive recognition after World War II. His use of bronze and terra cotta and his unusual sense of space and proportion earned him a secure place among modern sculptors.

Giotto (1267?-1337), an Italian painter, architect, and sculptor, was among the first to portray human figures realistically in three instead of two dimensions. *The Descent from the Cross* and *The Madonna Enthroned with Saints* are two of his most famous paintings.

Gladstone, William Ewart (1809-1898), a British politician, began his long tenure of more than 60 years in Parliament as a Conservative but switched to the Liberal Party. He worked to expand suffrage, to increase elementary education, and to provide relief for Irish tenant farmers. Between 1868 and 1894, Gladstone served four terms as British prime minister.

Glenn, John (1921-   ), in 1962 became the first American astronaut to orbit the earth. In the spacecraft *Friendship 7,* he made three orbits during a flight of nearly five hours. As a naval pilot in 1957, Glenn made the first transcontinental nonstop flight in a supersonic aircraft. Glenn later became active in Democratic politics and was elected a senator from Ohio.

Goddard, Robert Hutchings (1882-1945), an American physicist, was a pioneer in the development of rockets. His experiments with solid and liquid rocket fuels, his work in the mathematical foundations of rocketry, and his many other discoveries led to the development of satellites, space exploration, and nuclear missiles.

Goethe, Johann Wolfgang von (1749-1832), a German poet and writer, inaugurated the romantic and modern movements in German literature. Among his works are the novel *The Sorrows of Young Werther,* a romantic love story, and the verse play *Egmont.* His play *Faust* is considered one of the most important works in modern Western literature.

Gompers, Samuel (1850-1924), an American labor leader born in England, was, except for one year, president of the American Federation of Labor from 1886 to 1924. He worked to improve the position of trade unionists and to abolish the court injunction as means of stopping strikes. Gompers supported free collective bargaining between employees and employers.

Gorgas, William Crawford (1854-1920), a United States Army physician, led a successful battle against yellow fever in Havana, Cuba. He became the chief sanitary officer of the Panama Canal Commission and eliminated yellow fever as a threat to workers building the canal. In 1914, Gorgas was made surgeon general of the Army.

Goya, Francisco (1746-1828), a Spanish artist, became the court painter, a position that brought him prosperity. His position, however, did not prevent him from painting subjects, including the royal family, as he saw them. Among his works are *The Family of Charles IV* and *The 3rd of May,* which depicts the French invasion of Spain. Goya also painted scenes of torture and of bullfighting.

Greco, El (1541?-1614), a painter, was born Domenikos Theotokopoulos in Crete but became famous in Spain, where he produced most of his work, as "the Greek." He painted many mystical religious scenes and landscapes, including *Christ Carrying the Cross* and *View of Toledo.*

Greeley, Horace (1811-1872), a newspaper editor and publisher, founded the *New York Tribune* in 1841. Greeley was influential in the antislavery movement and in efforts to ban alcoholic beverages. A Republican, he worked for the election of Abraham Lincoln. In 1872, the Liberal Republicans and Democrats formed a coalition to nominate Greeley for the presidency, but he lost the election to Ulysses S. Grant.

Gropius, Walter (1883-1969), a German-born architect, founded the Bauhaus school to coordinate the work of architects, artists, and building craftsmen. He created spare, functional designs that used materials in innovative ways. Beginning in 1937, Gropius taught at Harvard University and designed many buildings in the United States.

Gutenberg, Johannes (1395?-1486?), a German printer, invented type molds for casting individual letters. His invention made movable type practical. Gutenberg could produce any quantity of individual letters, arrange them into words, and place the type in a frame. His most famous production was the *Mazarin* (or *Gutenberg*) *Bible*.

Hadrian (76-138), a Roman emperor, improved the empire's fortifications, patronized the arts, curbed graft, and built many edifices in Rome. He had Salvius Julianus draw up a legal code that later became the basis for the Justinian Code. Hadrian established the Euphrates River as the empire's eastern boundary and visited Britain, where he supervised the building of Hadrian's Wall.

Haile Selassie I (1892-1975), the last emperor of Ethiopia, claimed descent from King Solomon and the Queen of Sheba. He established a constitution in 1931, but lost his throne when Italy conquered Ethiopia in 1936. He returned to power after Italy's defeat in Africa during

World War II and ruled until he was deposed in 1974.

Hamilton, Alexander (1755?-1804), who helped draft the United States Constitution, was the first secretary of the treasury. As an advocate of a strong federal government, he established a tax system, a mint, and a central bank. An able but controversial politician and diplomat, Hamilton was killed in a duel with Vice-President Aaron Burr.

Hammurabi (ruled about 1850-1750 B.C.) ruled the Babylonian empire during its greatest period of growth and prosperity. He enlarged the empire, established price and wage controls, and set up an efficient system of taxation. He established the Code of Hammurabi, a set of laws containing almost 300 definitions of crime and punishment.

Handel, George Frideric (1685-1759), a composer born in Germany who became a British subject, wrote both religious and secular music. He wrote several oratorios, including the *Messiah;* more than 40 operas; and many instrumental works. A favorite of the British royalty and people, he wrote *Water Music* and *Fireworks Music* for royal occasions.

Hannibal (247-183 B.C.) began training for the military early in life and became Carthage's greatest general. He fought the Romans in Spain, and led an army through the Alps on Rome in the Second Punic War. Finally defeated in North Africa by Scipio, Hannibal became the civilian leader of Carthage. Faced with Roman captivity, he committed suicide.

Hardy, Thomas (1840-1928), a British novelist and poet, studied architecture but devoted most of his life to literature, becoming one of the most popular writers of his time. Among his novels are *Tess of the D'Urbervilles, The Return of the Native, Far from the Madding Crowd, Jude the Obscure,* and *The Mayor of Casterbridge.*

Harvey, William (1578-1657), an English physician, demonstrated the route of the circulation of blood in the human body. Many who clung to the theories of the Greek physician Galen attacked Harvey vigorously. However, his conclusions, which were based on sound observations, were eventually accepted. Besides working in anatomy, Harvey also made contributions to embryology.

Hawthorne, Nathaniel (1804-1864), an American writer, used symbolism to explore moral issues and human psychology. His novels include *The Scarlet Letter* and *The House of the Seven Gables.* Hawthorne's best-known short stories include ''Young Goodman Brown'' and ''Ethan Brand.''

Haydn, Joseph (1732-1809), an Austrian composer, mastered the forms of the symphony and string quartet and established standards that influenced later composers. He wrote Masses, several operas, oratorios, including *The Creation,* trios, more than 80 string quartets, and more than 100 symphonies. For many years, Haydn was supported by the Esterhazy family in Vienna.

Hearst, William Randolph (1863-1951), a powerful newspaper publisher, became famous for sensational news stories called ''yellow journalism.'' He was partly responsible for arousing public opinion against Spain, which led to the Spanish-American War in 1898. Hearst's chain of newspapers made him wealthy, and he established a 240,000-acre estate, San Simeon, in California.

Hegel, Georg Wilhelm Friedrich (1770-1831), a German philosopher, was one of the most influential thinkers of the 1800's. He integrated earlier philosophies into a new system that stressed the historical sequence of philosophical ideas. His works include *Logic, Encyclopedia of the Philosophical Sciences,* and *Philosophy of Right.*

Hemingway, Ernest (1899-1961), one of the most popular American writers, was a master of a simple, terse prose style used to describe adventures that were concerned with moral values. He won the Pulitzer prize for fiction in 1953 and the Nobel prize in literature in 1954. Among his novels are *A Farewell to Arms, To Have and Have Not, The Sun Also Rises,* and *For Whom the Bell Tolls.*

Henry, Patrick (1736-1799), an American patriot known for his oratory, supported the Revolutionary cause in Virginia. A member of the Virginia House of Burgesses, he also served in the First Continental Congress and was on the committee that wrote Virginia's first state constitution. Henry was governor of Virginia during the Revolutionary War.

Henry II (1133-1189), through his marriage to Eleanor of Aquitaine, ruled over western France as well as England. When he quarreled with Thomas à Becket, the archbishop of Canterbury, over the power of the Roman Catholic Church, four of his knights murdered Becket. Henry II established the English common law and circuit courts. Late in his reign, his two sons led rebellions against him.

Henry VIII (1491-1547), who had six wives, brought about a church-state crisis with the divorce from his first wife. The divorce led to England's break with the Roman Catholic Church and the establishment of the Church of England. Two of his wives, Anne Boleyn and Catherine Howard, were executed. Henry VIII unified power in England and improved the English navy.

Henson, Matthew (1867-1955), a black man, gained fame as the only American to accompany American explorer Robert E. Peary to the North Pole in 1909. For more than 20 years, he went on expeditions with Peary and was often honored for his part in the explorations. Henson wrote *A Negro Explorer at the North Pole.*

Heraclitus (500's or 400's B.C.), a Greek philosopher, made change the basis of his teachings. He believed that everything constantly changes but that change is guided by logos, or intelligent laws. Heraclitus became known as "the weeping philosopher" because of his gloomy view that there are no lasting things in life.

Herodotus (484?-424? B.C.), called the "Father of History," traveled throughout most of the known world of the time and reported and commented on the customs, religion, and behavior of the people he came in contact with. Born in Asia Minor, he wrote a comprehensive history of the Persian empire, describing its beginnings, rise, and unsuccessful invasions of Greece.

Hertz, Heinrich (1857-1894), a German physicist, discovered electromagnetic waves and described their important characteristics. He demonstrated that the transmission of ultrahigh-frequency waves would produce oscillations in a distant wire loop. The development of radio, radar, and television was made possible by Hertz's discoveries.

Heyerdahl, Thor (1914-   ), a Norwegian ethnologist, in 1947 sailed a balsawood raft from Peru to islands in Polynesia to demonstrate that Polynesia could have been settled by ancient Peruvians. He told of his adventures on the trip in *Kon-Tiki.* Later, Heyerdahl and others built a reed boat, called *Ra-2,* in which they sailed from Africa to the West Indies.

Hidalgo, Miguel (1753-1811), a revolutionary Mexican priest, was one of the early leaders in the Mexican independence movement. Rallying followers in the village of Dolores, he marched south toward Mexico City. Although Hidalgo won some victories, the Spanish finally defeated his forces and captured him. Hidalgo was put to death, but his campaign began the war for Mexican independence.

Hillary, Sir Edmund (1919-   ), a New Zealand mountain climber and author, in 1953 with a companion became the first person to reach the top of Mount Everest in the Himalaya. He later led an expedition to climb Mount Makalu I. His books describing his experiences include *High Adventure* and *High in the Thin Cold Air.*

Hippocrates (460?-377? B.C.), a Greek physician called the "Father of Medicine," was the first to show that diseases have natural causes. He prescribed medicines and diets, practiced surgery, and set broken bones. Hippocrates formulated rules of conduct for doctors that

became the basis for the Hippocratic oath.

Hitler, Adolf (1889-1945), the leader of the Nazi Party, ruled Germany from 1933 to 1945. He rearmed Germany and began World War II with an invasion of Poland in 1939. Hitler planned to conquer Europe and to exterminate all Jews. At first successful, German armies later met defeat by the Allies. Hitler committed suicide in an underground bomb shelter.

Hobbes, Thomas (1588-1679), an English philosopher, developed the theory that government arises as a social contract to protect the rights of individuals. He argued that, because humans are selfish, they need the rule of an all-powerful sovereign. Also a writer on physics and psychology, he believed that only matter exists. His most famous work is *Leviathan,* in which he describes his political theory.

Ho Chi Minh (1890-1969) led Vietnam to independence from France after World War II and became the founder and president of the Democratic Republic of Vietnam (then North Vietnam). A Socialist and later a Communist, he conducted a long war to unify North and South Vietnam, a campaign that eventually succeeded in 1975, after his death.

Holmes, Oliver Wendell (1809-1894), an American physician and medical educator, was better known as an essayist, poet, and novelist. His *The Autocrat of the Breakfast-Table* is a collection of essays, many humorous. Holmes's most popular poems include "Old Ironsides," "The Last Leaf," and "The Wonderful One-Hoss Shay."

Holmes, Oliver Wendell, Jr. (1841-1935), an American jurist, served for nearly 30 years on the Supreme Court of the United States, after having been a law professor at Harvard University and a justice on the Massachusetts Supreme Judicial Court. He believed in judicial restraint and in social experimentation. Holmes won attention for his dissenting opinions on many Supreme Court cases.

Homer (about 800? B.C.) was the reputed author of the Greek epic poems *The Iliad* and *The Odyssey,* which tell the story of the Trojan War and of Odysseus' long journey from Troy back to Greece. There has been a long controversy among scholars over whether the epics were the work of several authors or of only one. Other poems once attributed to Homer are now thought to be the work of other poets.

Homer, Winslow (1836-1910), was a painter who portrayed objects realistically but with drama and vitality. A war correspondent with Union troops during the Civil War, he painted such popular war pictures as *Prisoners from the Front.* Homer painted many seascapes of the Atlantic Coast.

Hooke, Robert (1635-1703), an English scientist, described the law of elasticity and the kinetic theory of gases. He made important astronomical observations and discoveries about the earth's and the moon's gravity. He also developed a reflecting telescope, a marine barometer, and a spring to regulate watches. Hooke is also credited with having discovered plant cells.

Houston, Samuel (1793-1863), born a Virginian, represented Tennessee in Congress and was governor of the state. He moved to Texas and worked for independence from Mexico and for admission of Texas to the Union. Houston became president of the Republic of Texas and, later, governor of the state and a senator from Texas.

Howe, Elias (1819-1867), an American inventor, in 1846 became the first person to patent a workable sewing machine. He found little interest for his invention in the United States and scarcely more in England, where he sold manufacturing rights. When other people in the United States began to manufacture sewing machines, Howe began a long and successful lawsuit to protect his patent.

Hudson, Henry (?-1611), an English navigator and explorer, made discoveries in the New World for Holland and England, giving each country some claims to land. He explored the Hudson River, Hudson Strait, and Hudson Bay. On his fourth voyage, his crew mutinied and cast him and eight others adrift in a small boat that apparently was lost.

Hughes, Langston (1902-1967), was a black American poet and writer. Many of his poems were set to music, and they were translated into several languages. His works include *Not Without Laughter, Shakespeare in Harlem, I Wonder As I Wander, The Weary Blues,* and *The Ways of White Folks.*

Huygens, Christian (1629-1695), was a Danish astronomer, mathematician, and physicist. The first to use a pendulum to regulate a clock, he also developed the wave theory of light, improved methods of grinding lenses, constructed telescopes, and discovered a satellite and a ring of Saturn. Huygens also invented the measuring device known as the micrometer.

Ibn Khaldun (1332-1406), considered the greatest Arab historian, wrote a history of the known world. Born in Tunis in North Africa, he saw history as a series of civilizations, each growing and expanding through cooperation and then declining because of corruption and selfishness. Ibn Khaldun held government posts in Egypt for several years and also wrote an *Autobiography*.

Ibsen, Henrik (1828-1906), a Norwegian playwright, is often called the father of modern drama. His works are realistic—that is, they deal with real-life social problems in a direct manner. Some of Ibsen's best-known plays are *A Doll's House, An Enemy of the People,* and *Hedda Gabler*. Ibsen worked in the theater in Norway, as a stage manager, and later received a grant to travel and write.

Ikhnaton (1300's B.C.), an Egyptian pharaoh also known as Akhenaton, was married to Nefertiti and was the first Egyptian ruler to promote the worship of one deity. He tried to abolish belief in many gods among the Egyptians and to make Aton, the sun god, the only deity. The movement did not survive his death. Ikhnaton was the father-in-law of Tutankhamon.

Innocent III (1160?-1216) exercised perhaps the greatest power of any Roman Catholic Pope. Using his power to excommunicate and to mete out spiritual punishment, he dealt harshly with European monarchs such as Otto IV of Swabia and John of England. He promoted the Fourth Crusade, which resulted in the capture of Constantinople. Innocent

III convened Lateran IV, a council that dealt extensively with Church doctrine.

Ivan IV (1530-1584) was the first czar of Russia. He conquered the area along the Volga River, expanded Russia into Siberia, made Moscow the capital, and reduced the power of the nobility. He acquired the name "the Terrible" because of his cunning and cruelty and because he killed his own son.

Jackson, Thomas J. (1824-1863), a Confederate general of the Civil War, earned the nickname "Stonewall" for his stand against Union forces at the first battle at Bull Run, Va., in 1861. A religious man much loved by his troops, Jackson was considered one of the Confederacy's finest generals. He was accidentally killed by his own men during a battle at Chancellorsville, Va.

James, Henry (1843-1916), an American novelist and short-story writer, often wrote from the point of view of one of his characters and emphasized human relationships and the individual in relation to society. Among his novels are *The American, The Portrait of a Lady, Daisy Miller, Washington Square* and *The Bostonians*. James spent much of his life in Europe.

Jay, John (1745-1829), was the first chief justice of the United States. A diplomat and lawyer, he served in the Continental Congress, conducted foreign affairs, worked for the ratification of the Constitution, and negotiated a treaty with England. Jay served on the Supreme Court from 1790 to 1795. He was elected governor of New York and resigned from the Supreme Court in 1795.

Jenner, Edward (1749-1823), a British physician, discovered vaccination. He developed a smallpox vaccine that used cowpox virus to immunize against the disease. By 1800, Jenner's vaccine was widely accepted. He received many honors, including a grant from Parliament and an honorary degree in medicine from Oxford University.

Jesus Christ (dates uncertain, but about 8 B.C. to A.D. 29) proclaimed the moral and theological teachings that became the foundation of the Christian religion. Accompanied by twelve disciples, He was a critic and teacher who was credited with healing and other miracles. Although many accepted Jesus as the Messiah, Jewish religious leaders condemned Him. He was executed by crucifixion but, according to the Gospels, arose in three days and, after many days teaching His disciples, ascended into heaven.

Joan of Arc, Saint (1412-1431), a French peasant girl, believed that she heard voices directing her to aid her country. She led a French army to victory over the English at Orleans in 1429 and defeated the English in other battles. Later imprisoned by the English, she was tried as a witch and heretic by the French and burned at the stake. The Roman Catholic Church canonized her in 1920.

Jones, John Paul (1747-1792), was an American naval commander during the Revolutionary War. He won several engagements against the British, the greatest as commander of the *Bonhomme Richard,* which defeated the British ship *Serapis.* After the war Jones wrote on naval tactics and, at the invitation of the Empress Catherine, served for a time in the Russian navy.

Joyce, James (1882-1941), an Irish writer, created some of the most complex and difficult masterpieces of modern literature in the English language. His major works include the novels *A Portrait of the Artist as a Young Man* and *Finnegans Wake* and the short-story collection *Dubliners.* Though Joyce lived away from Ireland after 1904, he set all of his work in Ireland and continued to explore the character of the Irish people.

Juárez, Benito (1806-1872), worked to establish constitutional government in Mexico and to end foreign interference in the government. An Indian, he was elected president of Mexico in 1861. When the French invaded Mexico, Juárez led a successful war against them and captured Maximilian, who had been offered the throne by Mexican nobles under French influence. Juárez was elected to two additional terms as president; he is regarded as a great hero of Mexican independence.

Jung, Carl (1875-1961), a Swiss psychologist and psychiatrist, was influenced by Sigmund Freud but also developed his own theories, called analytical psychology. Like Freud, Jung stressed the importance of the unconscious, but he also emphasized the importance of "racial memory" and the will to live. In treating patients, he focused on present problems rather than childhood trauma. Jung originated the distinction between introverts and extroverts.

Justinian I (482-565), called "the Great," was an emperor of the eastern Roman Empire. In wars against Vandals, Huns, and Franks, he won back much of the original empire that had been lost. He was responsible for the Corpus Juris

Helen Keller, shown
here with her teacher,
Anne Sullivan, became
an advocate for the
blind and deaf-blind.

Civilis, known as the Justinian Code, a
body of civil law he had drawn up to
govern his realm. The code became the
basis for most European law.

Kant, Immanuel (1724-1804), a German
philosopher, examined the nature and
limits of human knowledge in the *Critique of Pure Reason*. For Kant, knowledge comes from the mind's involvement
with the objects it experiences, and so
the nature of human knowledge depends
partly on the nature of the mind. He also
wrote *Critique of Practical Reason,* a
work on ethics that argued for absolute
moral standards.

Keats, John (1795-1821), was an English
romantic poet who expressed experiences of the senses, as well as ideas, in
his works. Among Keats's best known
poems are "Endymion," "Hyperion,"
"The Eve of St. Agnes," "On a Grecian

Urn," and "La Belle Dame sans Merci."
Plagued by poor health, he contracted
tuberculosis and died in Italy, a young
man.

Keller, Helen (1880-1968), became a famous American lecturer and writer even
though she had lost her sight and hearing
before she was 2 years old. Taught to
speak and to read and write in braille,
she graduated from high school and college. She devoted her life to working on
behalf of the blind and published several
books about her experiences.

Kelvin, William Thomson, Lord (1824-1907), a British mathematician and physicist, invented the mirror galvanometer
and the siphon recorder and was an electrical engineer in charge of laying the Atlantic cable. He established a thermodynamic scale with -273.15 C as absolute
zero. Lord Kelvin also contributed in-

ventions and discoveries in numerous other fields.

Kenyatta, Jomo (1890?-1978), a leader for African independence, fought for the freedom of Kenya from British rule after World War II. He spent some time in jail for anti-British activities. When Kenya became free in 1963 after years of strife, Kenyatta became president of the new nation and become one of the important spokesmen for Africa in the 1970's.

Kepler, Johannes (1571-1630), a German astronomer and mathematician, discovered three important laws of planetary motion. One of these laws states that planets have elliptical, or oval, orbits— rather than circular orbits. Kepler was the first astronomer to support Copernicus' findings openly. When his friend and colleague Tycho Brahe died, Kepler was appointed imperial mathematician by Rudolph II, the Holy Roman Emperor.

Key, Francis Scott (1779-1843), an American lawyer, wrote the poem that was used as the lyrics of "The Star-Spangled Banner." From an American warship, he witnessed the bombardment of Fort McHenry in the harbor of Baltimore during the War of 1812. The successful American defense of the fort inspired Key to write the poem which Congress made the national anthem in 1931.

Keynes, John Maynard (1883-1946), an English economist who was an adviser to the British government, achieved worldwide attention with his book *The Economic Consequences of the Peace.* He argued that governments should stimulate the economy with spending during times of slowdown to prevent un-

employment and depression. His writings on government and economics became very influential.

King, Martin Luther, Jr. (1929-1968), was the foremost black leader of the civil rights movement in the 1950's and 1960's. A Baptist minister who believed in passive resistance and nonviolent civil disobedience, Dr. King led many demonstrations against racial discrimination in the United States and spent time in jail. One of his most important public rallies was a "March on Washington" that brought thousands to the capital. Dr. King received the Nobel peace prize in 1964. He was assassinated in Memphis, Tenn.

Kipling, Rudyard (1865-1936), an English writer, was born in India and lived there for several years. India was the setting for many of his stories, novels, and poems. Among Kipling's popular works are *The Jungle Book, The Light That Failed, Just So Stories,* and *Barrack-Room Ballads,* which includes the poems "Gunga Din" and "On the Road to Mandalay." He was awarded the Nobel prize in literature in 1907.

Klee, Paul (1879-1940), a Swiss artist, developed an original style used to express the subconscious mind and fantasy. Living much of his life in Germany, he founded a movement called Blue Four in collaboration with German abstract artists. Klee taught for a time at the Bauhaus, a German school of design founded by the architect Walter Gropius.

Knox, John (1515?-1572), a Scottish Protestant theologian, statesman, and writer, successfully worked to develop the Presbyterian denomination in Scotland to establish Presbyterianism as the official religion. Knox preached a stern and righteous doctrine and was a bitter enemy of Mary, Queen of Scots, a Roman Catholic who was queen of Scotland.

Koch, Robert (1843-1910), a German physician and bacteriologist, developed a method of growing and observing bacteria and found a vaccine for preventing anthrax in cattle. He also isolated the germ that causes tuberculosis and conducted research on bubonic plague in India and on other diseases. Koch won the 1905 Nobel prize in physiology or medicine.

Kosciusko, Thaddeus (1746-1817), a Polish patriot, arrived in America in 1776 to take part in the Revolutionary War. He participated in the Battle of Saratoga and built fortifications on the Hudson River. Returning to Poland, Kosciusko fought unsuccessfully to prevent the partition of his country among Prussia, Russia, and Austria.

Kublai Khan (1216-1294), established the Yüan, or Mongol, dynasty of China after expanding the conquests of his grandfather, Genghis Khan. He completed the conquest of China and made Peking his capital. Kublai Khan attempted unsuccessfully to conquer Java and Japan. He treated the people he conquered humanely and was a patron of arts and letters.

La Salle, Robert Cavelier, Sieur de (1643-1687), a French explorer in the New World, explored the Mississippi River Valley and claimed to have first reached the Ohio River. He named Louisiana and claimed the Mississippi Valley for France. Named viceroy of North Amer-

ica by Louis XIV, La Salle attempted unsuccessfully to establish a colony at the mouth of the Mississippi.

Lavoisier, Antoine Laurent (1743-1794), a French chemist wrote the first chemical equation. He also gave the first scientific analysis of fire. Lavoisier was the author of *Elements of Chemistry,* the first modern chemistry textbook. Because he was a member of a financial company associated with the government, Lavoisier was put to death as an aristocrat during the French Revolution.

Lee, Robert E. (1807-1870), a Confederate general, commanded troops in the East in the Civil War. For a time, he successfully fought off Northern invasion of the South. When he tried to carry the war to the North, he met disastrous defeat at Gettysburg. His army was worn down by General Ulysses S. Grant, and in 1865 Lee surrendered at Appomattox Court House in Virginia.

Lewis, Meriwether (1774-1809), an American explorer, led an expedition with William Clark to explore the Louisiana Purchase. The party moved up the Missouri River from a point near St. Louis, crossed the Great Divide, and traveled down the Columbia River to the Pacific Ocean. The expedition returned with much valuable information on the new territory.

Liliuokalani (1838-1917), the last queen of Hawaii, had only a two-year reign. Wealthy American settlers on the islands led a revolt against her and established a republic in 1893. She tried in vain to reclaim her throne. After some hesitation because of the circumstances under which the queen had been deposed, the

United States Congress in 1898 voted to annex Hawaii as a territory.

Lindbergh, Charles A. (1902-1974), became in 1927 the first person to fly solo nonstop across the Atlantic Ocean. Taking off from Long Island, N.Y., he landed in Paris 33½ hours later. A rich and famous man, he promoted commercial and military aviation. The kidnapping and murder of his son was the most sensational crime of the 1930's. Lindbergh's biography, *The Spirit of St. Louis,* won a Pulitzer prize in 1954.

Linnaeus, Carolus (1707-1778), a Swedish botanist and naturalist, developed a system for classifying plants and animals according to genus and species. Also a physician, a teacher, and a writer of several books on plants, Linnaeus is considered the founder of the modern system of botanical names.

Lister, Sir Joseph (1827-1912), an English surgeon, founded antiseptic (germ-free) surgery. Realizing the role played by bacteria in infections, Lister used carbolic acid to kill bacteria in operating rooms and on instruments. Because of his work, mortality rates after surgery, formerly very high, were reduced to a small percentage of those operated on.

Livingstone, David (1813-1873), a Scottish missionary and explorer in Africa, reached Lake Ngami, explored the Zambezi River, and reached Victoria Falls. Disappearing for a time, he was found and rescued by Henry M. Stanley, a newspaperman. Livingstone continued exploration and missionary work in Africa until his death there.

Livy (59 B.C.-A.D. 17), a Roman historian during the reign of Augustus, wrote *History from the Founding of the City,* a history in 142 volumes. Written over a period of 40 years, only 35 of the books have survived. Although Livy included legends and myths in his work, it is considered a principal source on the history of Rome.

Locke, John (1632-1704), an English philosopher, also wrote on education, psychology, and political theory. Locke believed that a government exists to promote the welfare of the people, and that if it does not do so, the people have a right to change it. His ideas were used to justify the American Revolution.

London, Jack (1876-1916), an American writer, became famous for novels and short stories about dogs, such as *The Call of the Wild* and *White Fang,* and his tales of the sea. An adventurer in Alaska and at sea, in his writings London reflected his interest in primitive violence as well as his socialistic political opinions.

Longfellow, Henry Wadsworth (1807-1882), was a poet and a teacher of languages and literature. He was the most popular American literary figure of his time. Longfellow spent 18 years as a professor at Harvard University. Among his best known poems are *The Courtship of Miles Standish,* an account of life among the Pilgrims, and *The Song of Hiawatha,* which he based on an Indian legend.

Louis XIV (1638-1715), the Sun King, became the ruler of France at the age of 4. Presiding over a glittering court, he encouraged the arts, and the writers of his time contributed much to French literature. Louis XIV also led France into four major wars. Although a great monarch in many respects, his wars left France in debt with declining influence in Europe.

Louis XVI (1745-1793) suffered the consequences of misrule by the French monarchy when the French Revolution began. He was forced to call a meeting of the national assembly, which had not met for 175 years. Captured while trying to flee France, Louis XVI and his queen, Marie Antoinette, were executed by guillotine.

Luther, Martin (1483-1546), originally a German priest in the Roman Catholic Church, criticized corruption and broke with the church in 1517 to establish the Protestant Reformation. He believed that faith, rather than works, is the basis of salvation. Luther's teachings became the foundation for the Lutheran and other Protestant denominations that were formed in Europe.

MacArthur, Douglas (1880-1964), commanded United States forces in the Pacific area during World War II. His "island-hopping" strategy pushed Japan toward defeat. He later headed the occupation government in Japan. MacArthur commanded United Nations forces in the Korean War until 1951 when, following disputes with President Harry S. Truman, he was relieved of his command.

Machiavelli, Niccoló (1469-1527), an Italian Renaissance literary figure and statesman, wrote *The Prince,* a book on practical politics. He was a member of the Florentine government from 1498 to 1512. Machiavelli's political writings emphasized that the first consideration of a ruler must be success, not morality.

Magellan, Ferdinand (1480?-1521), a Portuguese navigator, led the first expedition to sail around the world. Leaving Spain in 1519, the fleet rounded Cape Horn on South America and proceeded across the Pacific Ocean. Although Magellan was killed in the Philippine Islands, one ship survived the remainder of the journey and reached Spain in 1522.

Malthus, Thomas Robert (1766-1834), an English clergyman and economist, wrote *Essay on the Principle of Population,* in which he argued that population growth tends to outrun food supplies and that excessive population growth encourages war and disease epidemics. He was pessimistic about the possibility of human survival unless population growth were checked. Malthus was also a history professor.

Manet, Édouard (1832-1883), a French painter, was a forerunner of the impressionists. Influenced by painters such as Goya, Velázquez, and Rembrandt, Manet produced flatly silhouetted forms that became popular. Among his works are *Le Bon Bock, Luncheon on the Grass, The Absinthe Drinker, Argenteuil,* and *Boating.*

Mann, Horace (1796-1859), was a politician and educational reformer who did much to promote free public schools in the United States. He founded the first state normal school in the nation, in Lexington, Mass., and improved public control and financial support for schools in the state. He later served as president of Antioch College in Ohio.

Mann, Thomas (1875-1955), had a long literary career in which he became perhaps the foremost German novelist of the 1900's. He left Germany in 1933 when the Nazis came to power. Among his many complex and difficult works are *Buddenbrooks, Joseph and His Brothers, Doctor Faustus, Mario and the Magician, Death in Venice, Tonio Kröger,* and *The Magic Mountain.*

Mao Zedong (1893-1976), the leader of the Chinese Communist revolution, based his movement on the peasants. In the 1930's, he led his followers to northern China, established a government, and fought Japanese invaders. After the Communist victory over Nationalist Chinese forces in 1949, Mao became both chairman of the party and head of state.

Marconi, Guglielmo (1874-1937), an Italian engineer and inventor, developed wireless telegraphy. He produced the first practical wireless telegraph in 1895 and sent the first transatlantic signal in 1901. His other inventions included a magnetic detector and a directional aerial. In 1909, Marconi shared the Nobel prize in physics.

Marcus Aurelius (121-180), a Roman emperor, was also a learned Stoic philosopher. Although he is considered one of the few "good emperors" of Rome, his reign was marked by barbarian invasions, wars, epidemics, severe economic difficulties, and persecution of Christians.

Maria Theresa (1717-1780), was the Holy Roman empress, the archduchess of Austria, and the queen of Hungary and Bohemia. The War of the Austrian Succession and the Seven Years' War shrank her empire, but she remained an influential monarch during her long reign of nearly 40 years.

Marie Antoinette (1755-1793), the daughter of Maria Theresa, was the wife of King Louis XVI of France. She was blamed for being extravagant, frivolous, and insensitive, particularly to the poor. During the French Revolution, she and the king attempted to flee the country. They were captured, tried, and executed by guillotine.

Marquette, Jacques (1637-1675), a French Jesuit missionary and explorer, made an expedition with the fur trader Louis Jolliet that followed the Mississippi River as far south as the Arkansas River. For a number of years, he did missionary work among American Indians. One of the most important French explorers of America, Marquette kept a journal of his Mississippi voyage, which was published posthumously.

Marshall, John (1755-1835), was one of the most influential justices of the United States. During his 34-year term, he made the Supreme Court of the United States an important branch of the government. By affirming the power to declare laws unconstitutional, many of his decisions strengthened the power of the Court. He also increased the power of the federal government over the states.

Marx, Karl (1818-1883), a German philosopher, collaborated with Friedrich Engels on *The Communist Manifesto.* A Socialist who was forced to leave Germany for England, he wrote *Das Kapital,* an analysis of capitalism that became the basis for the Communist movement. Marx believed that economic conditions govern human behavior.

Mary, Queen of Scots (1542-1587), the daughter of King James V of Scotland and the mother of James I of England, was one of the last Roman Catholic rulers of Scotland. When revolt forced her to flee Scotland in 1568, she found refuge in England with her cousin, Queen Elizabeth I. Found guilty of aiding a plot to overthrow Elizabeth, Mary was beheaded.

Mather, Cotton (1663-1728), was an influential Puritan clergyman. The son of a minister, Increase Mather, Cotton Mather was considered a prime mover behind the witchcraft trials in Massachusetts in the 1690's. He wrote on many subjects, including the history of New England. Deeply interested in science and education, Mather became one of the founders of Yale College.

Mazzini, Giuseppe (1805-1872), an Italian patriot, spent many years in exile for his efforts to unify Italy. An advocate of a republic, he was displeased when Italy, except for Rome, was unified in 1861 under a king. He tried to organize a republican revolt in Sicily but failed. Mazzini died before his dream of a united republican Italy was fulfilled.

Mead, Margaret (1901-1978), an anthropologist, made firsthand studies of island societies in the South Pacific. She was also a commentator on the problems of contemporary American society. She was curator of technology at the American Museum of Natural History in New York City. Among her writings are *Coming of Age in Samoa, Growing Up in New Guinea,* and *Male and Female.*

Medici, Lorenzo (1449-1492), known as "the Magnificent," was a member of the Medici family that ruled Florence, Italy,

during the Renaissance. Although an immoral and tyrannical ruler, he encouraged the building of libraries and other public structures, making Florence one of the world's most beautiful cities. He himself was a learned man and an accomplished writer and poet.

Meir, Golda (1898-1978), born in Russia and a long-time resident of Milwaukee, emigrated to Palestine, became active in the Zionist movement, and served as prime minister of Israel from 1969 to 1974. She was also a minister to the Soviet Union, minister of labor, and minister for foreign affairs. Meir was secretary-general of the Mapai (Labor) Party from 1966 to 1969.

Melville, Herman (1819-1891), an American writer, based several of his books on his experiences as a seaman in the South Pacific. His most famous novel, *Moby-Dick,* recounts the destructive efforts of Captain Ahab to capture a whale. Melville's other works, most of which are about the struggle between good and evil, include *Redburn, Billy Budd,* and *The Confidence-Man.*

Mendel, Gregor Johann (1822-1884), an Austrian monk and botanist, established that certain characteristics of animals and plants are inherited. He also determined that certain characteristics are dominant and others recessive. His conclusions were based on extensive work in breeding garden peas. Mendel laid the foundations for the modern study of heredity and genetics.

Mendeleev, Dmitri (1834-1907), a Russian chemist, developed the periodic table of the elements, which gave a system to the properties of elements. On the basis of the table, he predicted the existence of elements that were then unknown but were later discovered. Mendeleev also made contributions to meteorology as well as to petroleum chemistry.

Metternich, Prince von (1773-1859), an Austrian statesman and minister of foreign affairs, guided the establishment of the Holy Alliance in 1815 following the Napoleonic Wars. He created a European balance of power that lasted until 1914. Antidemocratic in his politics, Metternich helped suppress nationalistic and democratic revolts in Europe in the 1840's.

Michelangelo (1475-1564) was an Italian painter, architect, sculptor, and poet of the Renaissance. He painted the frescoes on the ceiling of the Sistine Chapel in Rome and *The Last Judgment* on one wall. Michelangelo designed a chapel and tombs for the Medici family. Among his sculptures are the *Pietà* and a colossal figure of David.

Mies van der Rohe, Ludwig (1886-1969), a German-born architect, used glass, steel, and brick to create buildings with simple, even austere, lines. His work includes the Seagram Building in New York City; several buildings on the campus of the Illinois Institute of Technology in Chicago, where he taught after 1938; and apartment buildings in Chicago.

Mill, John Stuart (1806-1873), an English economist and philosopher, favored women's rights, higher pay for workers, and cooperative agriculture, among other progressive causes. Among Mill's works are *System of Logic, On Liberty,* and *Principles of Political Economy.* His book *Utilitarianism* explains his philoso-phy that pleasure, in its widest sense, is the basis for human action.

Milton, John (1608-1674), an English poet, wrote his greatest works, *Paradise Lost, Paradise Regained,* and *Samson Agonistes,* after he had become totally blind. A Puritan, he wrote on politics and on religion in such works as *The Tenure of Kings and Magistrates* and *Of Reformation in England.* Milton also wrote *Areopagitica,* a defense of freedom of the press.

Monet, Claude (1840-1926), a French painter, was a leader of impressionism, a name that derived from his painting *Impression: Sunrise.* His technique was to place separate spots of color side by side in such a way that the eye would blend them from a distance. Among his other paintings are *The Haystacks* and *The Thames.*

Montesquieu (1689-1755), was a French philosopher and writer who satirized contemporary French society and wrote a history of Rome. His *The Spirit of the Laws* deals with different forms of government. Montesquieu believed that governmental checks and balances among the executive, judicial, and legislative branches are necessary. His ideas formed the basis for the separation of powers in the United States Constitution.

More, Saint Thomas (1477?-1535), an English statesman, served King Henry VIII as lord chancellor. He opposed Henry's plan to divorce his first wife. After Henry VIII established the Church of England, More continued his opposition and was tried for treason and beheaded. He wrote *Utopia,* a futuristic work describing practices such as communal ownership, universal education, and religious toleration.

Morgan, John Pierpont (1837-1913), was one of the most powerful financiers in American history. His banking house in New York City financed many new industries across the country and marketed government bonds. He helped organize the United States Steel Corporation. Although he gave much money for education and philanthropy, Morgan was criticized for the considerable financial power that he wielded.

Morse, Samuel F. B. (1791-1872), best known for his invention of the telegraph, was also a painter and a sculptor. He spent many years developing a device that would transmit sound by means of electric wires, and with associates carried out a successful test of the telegraph in 1844. His success won Morse fame and wealth.

Moses (1200? B.C.), a great leader of the Israelites, was born in Egypt. To escape Egyptian persecution, Moses led his people across the Red Sea to the Promised Land of Palestine. On the journey, he received the Ten Commandments from God on Mount Sinai. Although he saw Palestine from a distance, Moses did not live to enter the Promised Land.

Mozart, Wolfgang Amadeus (1756-1791), an Austrian composer, wrote operas, chamber music, concertos, symphonies, and church music. He was a child prodigy. Among his most popular works are the operas *Don Giovanni* and *The Magic Flute*. Mozart wrote 41 symphonies, including the *Jupiter* (Number 41).

Muhammad (570?-632), the Prophet, founded the religion of Islam, whose followers are called Muslims. A trader in Mecca in Arabia, at about age 40 he experienced visions that led him to become a prophet and teacher. He became a civic as well as a religious leader in Medina and attracted many converts. Many of his teachings were collected in the Koran.

Muñoz Marín, Luis (1898-1980), formerly a journalist, in 1949 became the first elected governor of Puerto Rico. Under his leadership, Puerto Rico became a commonwealth of the United States. Muñoz Marín worked to attract industry that would provide jobs, in order to raise the people's economic level and to improve living conditions on the island.

Mussolini, Benito (1883-1945), founded the Fascist Party and in the 1920's became the dictator of Italy. Under his rule, Italy conquered Ethiopia and attacked Albania and Greece. Italy fought in support of Germany in World War II but was defeated by Allied armies in 1943. Mussolini was captured and executed by partisans.

Napoleon I (1769-1829), emperor of France, seized control of the government in 1799 and began to conquer Europe. A brilliant military leader, he created a vast empire but met a disastrous defeat in Russia in 1813. Exiled, Napoleon returned to France in 1815 but was defeated by English and Prussian forces at Waterloo. He died in exile.

Nasser, Gamal Abdel (1918-1970), an Egyptian army officer, led a revolt against King Farouk in 1952 and later became president of Egypt. He took control of the Suez Canal in 1956 and adopted a more militant policy toward Israel and the West. Nasser did not succeed in uniting Arab nations under Egyptian leadership, but he did bring about economic reforms in Egypt.

Nebuchadnezzar II (died 562 B.C.), a Babylonian king, built Babylon into one of the most beautiful cities of the ancient world. He may have been responsible for building the Hanging Gardens. He destroyed Jerusalem and placed the Israelites in captivity. According to the Bible, Nebuchadnezzar suffered periodically from debilitating delusions.

Nehru, Jawaharlal (1889-1964), was a leader in the independence movement in India and became the country's first prime minister in 1947. He supported state-controlled economy and favored neutrality in the Cold War between the Communist powers and the United States. Nehru retained control of the Ruling Congress Party and was prime minister until his death.

Nero (37-68), an emperor of Rome, led a dissipated private life that included acts such as the murder of his mother. The creature of his advisers, he ruled well during the first part of his reign when he had competent aides. Under later advisers, his reign was marked by misrule and persecution of Christians. Nero was deposed as emperor, and he committed suicide.

Newton, Sir Isaac (1642-1727), an English scientist and mathematician, made revolutionary contributions in mathematics, astronomy, and physics that became the foundations of modern physical science. He developed the law of gravity, discovered that sunlight is a mixture of colors,

established laws of motion, invented calculus, and constructed a reflecting telescope. His writings include *Mathematical Principles of Natural Philosophy* and *Optiks*.

Nietzsche, Friedrich (1844-1900), a German philosopher and writer, was a critic of Christianity who searched for a morality outside religion. He valued the "superman," a person who uses power creatively. As a psychologist, Nietzsche valued the power more than morality or feelings. *The Antichrist* and *Thus Spake Zarathustra* are among his writings.

Nightingale, Florence (1820-1910), an English nurse, hospital reformer, and philanthropist, introduced sanitary practices into hospitals and thereby reduced the incidence of infectious diseases. Born into wealth, she became a nurse and directed nursing operations in the Crimean War. Known as "The lady with the lamp," she later founded the Nightingale Home for Nurses in London and was an adviser for many countries concerning military hospitals.

Nkrumah, Kwame (1909-1972), led the African nation of Ghana to independence from Great Britain in 1957 and became the nation's president in 1960. He promoted education, health and welfare, and industrialization, but he tended to rule dictatorially. When the country had economic difficulties, the army ousted him in 1966. Nkrumah lived in exile in Guinea.

Nobel, Alfred Bernhard (1833-1896), a Swedish chemist, became a wealthy man through his invention of dynamite. The use of his invention in warfare troubled him, and he set up the Nobel Fund, with an initial sum of more than $9 million, to award annual prizes for those who make contributions to international peace and other fields. The Nobel prize has become the world's most important award.

Nyerere, Julius Kambarage (1922-   ), was a leader in the African independence movement. After Tanganyika became free from British rule in 1961, he became prime minister and then president of the country. As head of the government, Nyerere developed socialistic programs for his country, though he promoted democracy. Tanganyika later joined Zanzibar to become Tanzania.

O'Higgins, Bernardo (1778-1842), was the leader of the movement to free Chile from Spain. With José de San Martín of Argentina, he led an army across the Andes Mountains to defeat the Spanish at Chacabuco and won final victory in 1818. O'Higgins became the ruler of Chile but was deposed in 1823.

O'Keeffe, Georgia (1887-1986), an American artist, created lyrical paintings of flowers and scenes of the Southwest that often included animal skulls. She painted in both abstract and realistic styles. O'Keeffe's paintings include *Lake George, Black Iris, Canada, Farmhouse Window and Door,* and *A Cross by the Sea.*

Paine, Thomas (1737-1809), born in England, became the foremost pamphleteer of the American Colonies. His most famous pamphlet, *Common Sense,* succinctly stated the patriot cause and inspired popular support for it. Later works included *Rights of Man* and *The Age of Reason.*

Pasteur, Louis (1822-1895), a French chemist and bacteriologist, developed pasteurization, a process that destroyed bacteria in wine and milk. He also investigated plant diseases, advanced the knowledge of immunity from disease, and developed a successful vaccine against rabies. The Pasteur Institute in Paris was founded in his honor. He is buried in a magnificent tomb in the building that houses the Institute.

Peary, Robert E. (1856-1920), an American naval officer and explorer, led numerous Arctic expeditions. In 1909, with Matthew Henson and four Eskimos, he reached the North Pole. Controversy over prior discovery arose, however, between him and Frederick A. Cook, who claimed to have reached the pole on an earlier expedition. A congressional investigation awarded the honor to Peary.

Penn, William (1644-1718), an English Quaker, founded the colony of Pennsylvania in 1681, primarily as a refuge for those suffering religious persecution. Although he owned Pennsylvania, he visited America only twice. Penn did not achieve wealth from the colony, but he frequently had to fight off efforts to take it from him.

Pepin the Short (714?-768) was the king of the Franks who founded the Carolingian dynasty. He helped Pope Stephen II expel the Lombards from Ravenna in northern Italy and expanded his own kingdom to include Aquitaine in France. Pepin carried out educational and religious reforms and left his kingdom to his sons Carloman and Charlemagne.

Pericles (490?-429 B.C.), an Athenian statesman, encouraged art, literature, and architecture during his rule, known as the "Age of Pericles." He expanded democracy in the city and Athenian influence throughout the Mediterranean world. Pericles also prepared Athens for war with Sparta; he led Athenians in the Peloponnesian War against Sparta from 431 B.C. to 429 B.C., when he died of the plague.

Peter I (1672-1725), called "the Great," was a czar of Russia who expanded Russian power in wars with Turkey, Persia, and Sweden. He improved his army and built a navy. Peter modernized Russia, introducing Western civilization and making the country an important European power. He founded the city of St. Petersburg (now Leningrad) and made it his capital.

Philip II (1527-1598), king of Spain, was a defender of the Roman Catholic faith who promoted the Inquisition and Counter Reformation. Trying to invade and conquer Protestant England, he launched the Great Armada, a Spanish naval force that the English defeated in 1588. The defeat of the Armada marked the beginning of a decline in Spanish power.

Philip II (382-336 B.C.), king of Macedonia, was a military genius who conquered the Greek city-states. He organized the Greek cities into the League of Corinth, which later helped them mount their attack against Persia. Philip was assassinated and was succeeded by his son Alexander the Great, who carried on his father's conquests.

Picasso, Pablo (1881-1973), a Spanish-born artist, painted in nearly every modern art form, including cubism. He did most of his work in France and produced a prodigious number of paintings and drawings. Among his paintings are *The Three Musicians, Guernica,* and *Les Demoiselles d'Avignon.* Picasso also produced many works of sculpture.

Pablo Picasso, a leading artist of the 1900's, is shown in his studio with some of his works.

Piccard, Jacques (1922-   ), a member of a distinguished family of scientists, became an oceanographer and designer of equipment for undersea exploration. He descended 35,800 feet (10,910 meters) into the Pacific Ocean in a bathyscaph and studied ocean currents while submerged in the Gulf Stream. Piccard became a spokesman against pollution of the oceans and the environment as a whole.

Pitt, William (1708-1778), an English statesman, was an influential member of Parliament, who as secretary of state helped organize the British victory over France in the Seven Years' War. At times out of favor with the king, he later entered the House of Lords as Earl of Chatham and frequently spoke in favor of American colonial rights.

Pitt, William, The Younger (1759-1806), an English statesman, entered Parliament at the age of 21 and became prime minister almost three years later, serving until 1801 and again from 1804 to 1806. He is considered one of the greatest prime ministers of Britain, surpassing even the excellent reputation of his father. Pitt's most important foreign achievements were in dealing with the effects of the French Revolution, the early years of Napoleonic rule, and French expansion.

Plato (427?-347? B.C.), a Greek philosopher who was a pupil of Socrates, opened an academy in Athens and made it the intellectual center of Greece. In his dialogues, Plato taught that ideas are more real than the physical world, and in *The Republic* described an ideal state ruled by philosopher kings. Aristotle, who succeeded Plato as the intellectual leader of Greece, was his pupil.

Pliny the Elder (23-79), a Roman writer, admiral, and lawyer, produced many works on history, science, rhetoric, and military tactics. Only one work survives, his monumental *Natural History,* an encyclopedia of science. Pliny was killed by the eruption of Mount Vesuvius that destroyed the city of Pompeii.

Pliny the Younger (61?-113?), a Roman writer who was a nephew of Pliny the Elder, served for a time as the Roman governor of Bithynia and Pontica in the Near East. His description of the treatment of early Christians was one of the first historical accounts of the new religion. In his *Letters,* Pliny described the scholarly and gentlemanly life he led.

Pocahontas (1595?-1617) was the daughter of the chief of the Powhatan tribe in Virginia. As a young girl, she reportedly saved the life of Captain John Smith. Colonists took her hostage during a conflict with her father and his warriors. She met John Rolfe, whom she married and accompanied to England. About to return to Virginia, Pocahontas died of smallpox.

Poe, Edgar Allan (1809-1849), an American writer, created poems and short stories of mystery and horror that focused on human madness. His tales of mystery include "The Purloined Letter," "The Murders in the Rue Morgue,"and "The Masque of the Red Death." Among his well-known poems are "Ulalume," "The Raven," and "Annabel Lee."

Polo, Marco (1254?-1324?), a member of a Venetian merchant family, made a journey to China with his father and uncle. During the visit, Marco entered the diplomatic service of the Chinese ruler, Kublai Khan. Leaving China, the Polos returned to Venice in 1295 after a 24-year absence. Marco wrote *Description of the World.*

Pompey (106-48 B.C.), a Roman statesman and general known as "the Great," gained prominence in the Roman civil wars and was elected consul. With Caesar and Marcus Crassus he ruled Rome as a part of the First Triumvirate. After disagreements with Caesar, he was defeated in battle, and fled to Egypt, where he was killed by Ptolemy.

Ponce de León, Juan (1474-1521), a Spanish explorer, accompanied Christopher Columbus on his second voyage and later became governor of Puerto Rico. Searching for Bimini, reputed to be the site of the mythical Fountain of Youth, he explored part of Florida. Trying to found a colony in Florida, he was wounded in a battle with Indians and died.

Ptolemy I (367?-283 B.C.), a general under Alexander the Great, became king of Egypt after Alexander's death. Making Alexandria his capital, he expanded his rule to include Cyrene, Crete, and Cyprus. He encouraged education and was responsible for establishing the great library and museum at Alexandria.

Pulaski, Casimir (1748-1779), was a Polish patriot who, after an unsuccessful revolt against Russian rule, came to America to join in the Revolutionary War. After service under George Washington, he was made a brigadier general and was in charge of the cavalry corps. Pulaski died from wounds suffered during the American siege of Savannah, Ga.

Pythagoras (500's B.C.), a Greek mathematician and philosopher, developed the Pythagorean Theorem in geometry. As a philosopher, he taught that numbers are central to all things and believed in the transmigration of souls. Pythagoras apparently was the first philosopher to believe that the earth is a sphere and that the sun, moon, and planets move.

Raleigh, Sir Walter (1552?-1618), an English courtier, navigator, historian, and poet, attempted unsuccessfully to found a colony in America. He was at times a favorite of the English court and at other times was in disfavor. Charged with treason and imprisoned by King James I, he wrote *History of the World.* Released to conduct an expedition for gold in South America, he disobeyed the restrictions that had been placed on him, for which he was beheaded.

Rembrandt (1606-1669), a Dutch artist, used sharp contrasts of light and dark in his paintings. In his many portraits, he often painted himself and members of his family. Rembrandt produced many drawings and etchings. Among his works are *The Night Watch, Aristotle Contemplating the Bust of Homer,* and *The Prodigal Son.*

Renoir, Pierre Auguste (1841-1919), a French painter who was a leader of the impressionists, produced many landscapes, paintings of flowers, and works featuring children and young girls. He frequently used his children and his wife as models. Among his works are *The Luncheon of the Boating Party, The Bathers,* and *Mme. Charpentier and Her Children.*

Revere, Paul (1735-1818), was a colonial silversmith and patriot who participated in the Boston Tea Party. In 1775, he was one of those who rode from Boston with a warning of the British advance on Lexington, Mass. He fought in the Revolutionary War and also cast bronze cannons for the army. After the war Revere returned to his trade in Boston.

Richard I (1157-1199), the English king known as the Lion-Hearted, joined a crusade that captured some territories from the Muslims. On his return he was taken prisoner in Austria and freed only after ransom was paid. Leaving his government in his advisers' hands, Richard embarked on a war against France, during which he was killed.

Richardson, Henry Hobson (1838-1886), an American architect, first attracted attention with his design for Boston's Trinity Church, which he based on the Romanesque style of the Middle Ages. He eventually developed an innovative style in designs for commercial buildings, public buildings, and houses. Richardson strongly influenced architects such as Louis Sullivan. Only a few of his buildings remained standing in the 1980's; these included Glessner House in Chicago.

Richelieu, Cardinal (1585-1642), was a French cleric and statesman who virtually ran the government of King Louis XIII. He rescinded political privileges of the Huguenots, curbed the nobility's power, conducted war against Spain, and furthered French interests during the Thirty Years' War. Richelieu encouraged the arts and the founding of the French Academy.

Ride, Sally Kristen (1951-   ), was a United States astronaut who became the first American woman to travel in space. In June 1983, she and astronauts Robert L. Crippen, John M. Fabian, Frederick

H. Hauck, and Norman E. Thagard made a six-day flight on the space shuttle *Challenger*. Ride made her second shuttle flight in October 1984.

Rivera, Diego (1886-1957), a Mexican artist, painted murals in which labor and revolution were the major themes. He was a Communist, and many of his paintings embodied his view of the oppression of workers. He has been credited with influencing social changes in Mexico that have improved the lives of the lower classes. Rivera helped persuade the Mexican government to allow artists to decorate the interiors of public buildings.

Robespierre (1758-1794) was a leader in the French Revolution. As a radical Jacobin, he successfully urged the execution of King Louis XVI. A member of the ruling group, he was partially responsible for the Reign of Terror, which executed thousands of people. When his fortunes turned, Robespierre himself was executed by guillotine.

Rockefeller, John D. (1839-1937), founded the Standard Oil Company and became wealthy from the oil business. He was strongly criticized for building monopolies and for such business practices as demanding rebates on freight rates from railroad companies. He established the Rockefeller Foundation for philanthropic endeavors.

Rodin, Auguste (1840-1917), was an influential French sculptor. He developed a realistic and perfectionist style in early works like the *Age of Bronze* that many people found startling. Rodin's other statues and busts include *The Gate of Hell, Saint John the Baptist, The*

Bather, Adam and Eve, and *The Thinker.*

Roentgen, Wilhelm (1845-1923), a German physicist, through investigations of the mysterious fogging that appeared on photographic plates placed near glass tubes charged with electricity, discovered X rays. He found that X rays would pass through flesh but not bone, a discovery that revolutionized medicine. Roentgen won the first Nobel prize in physics, in 1901, for his discovery.

Rousseau, Jean Jacques (1712-1778), a French philosopher and writer, believed that human beings are naturally good but are corrupted by social and political institutions. He championed the "natural" man and natural rights. Rousseau emphasized feelings over reason and impulsiveness over restraint, particularly in education. His writings include *Émile* and *The Social Contract.*

Rubens, Peter Paul (1577-1640), a Flemish painter, was also a diplomat and a scholar. A master of several languages, he undertook diplomatic missions to Spain and England. He is remembered chiefly as a painter, however. His landscapes, portraits, and religious and historical paintings include *Elevation of the Cross, The Descent from the Cross,* and *The Battle of the Amazons.*

Russell, Bertrand (1872-1970), an English philosopher and mathematician, wrote *Principles of Mathematics* and, with Alfred North Whitehead, *Principia Mathematica,* works that established the foundations for modern mathematics and logic. He frequently espoused such unpopular causes as pacifism, which sometimes got him dismissed from teaching positions and arrested. A writer on many subjects, Russell won the 1950 Nobel prize in literature.

Salk, Jonas (1914-   ), an American scientist, developed a vaccine against poliomyelitis that was tested on nearly two million children. Found safe, it became the first effective means of reducing frequent epidemics of polio. Salk made other important contributions in the field of immunization.

San Martín, José de (1778-1850), an Argentine soldier and statesman, helped free South America from Spanish rule. He joined Bernardo O'Higgins to defeat Spanish forces in Chile and later fought for the independence of Peru. He became disenchanted with political quarreling in South America and withdrew from politics. San Martín's achievements, however, allowed other statesmen to complete the battle for independence.

Schiller, Johann Christoph Friedrich von (1759-1805), a German playwright and poet, is generally considered to be the greatest dramatist ever to write in the German language. Political freedom is a frequent theme in his plays, which include *Wallenstein, Don Carlos, The Robbers, Maria Stuart,* and *William Tell.*

Schweitzer, Albert (1875-1965), a German clergyman, philosopher, physician, and musician, served for many years as a medical missionary in Africa. He established a hospital in Lambaréné, in what is now Gabon, and treated thousands of patients. When he won the Nobel peace prize in 1952, Schweitzer used the money to establish a leper colony. An organist, he was an authority on Bach.

Scipio, Publius Cornelius (236?-184? B.C.), a Roman general known as Scipio the Elder, defeated the Carthaginians in Spain and invaded Africa from Sicily. He defeated the great Carthaginian general Hannibal in battle at Zama. His victory ended the Second Punic War between Rome and Carthage and earned Scipio the title "Africanus Major."

Shakespeare, William (1564-1616), generally considered the greatest dramatist and poet in any language, prospered as an actor and playwright at the Globe Theatre in Elizabethan London. His comedies include *The Comedy of Errors, A Midsummer Night's Dream,* and *Taming of the Shrew.* Among his tragedies are *Romeo and Juliet, Hamlet,* and *Macbeth.*

Shelley, Percy Bysshe (1792-1822), an English poet, wrote romantic lyric poems. A revolutionary, he lived much of his life outside England. Many of his works reflect his hatred of tyranny and his belief in human perfectibility. Among his poems are "Ode to the West Wind," "To a Skylark," and "Adonais."

Sherman, William Tecumseh (1820-1891), was a Union general in the Civil War. He captured and burned Atlanta in a destructive "march to the sea" through Georgia that ended at Savannah. After the war, he became commanding general of the Army. Sherman wrote an account of his military experience in his *Memoirs.*

Siqueiros, David Alfaro (1898-1974), a Mexican artist, painted frescoes and murals upholding revolutionary ideals. A radical, he joined revolutionary forces when he was 15 years old and was later imprisoned in Mexico and expelled from the United States. His murals can be seen in buildings in Mexico City.

Sitting Bull (1834?-1890), a Sioux leader and medicine man, helped prepare Sioux warriors for battle against the whites led by Lieutenant Colonel George A. Custer at Little Bighorn. Retreating to Canada after the battle, Sitting Bull returned in 1881 and was imprisoned for two years. He was later killed by an Indian policeman, allegedly while resisting arrest.

Smith, Adam (1723-1790), a Scottish economist, wrote *The Wealth of Nations,* arguing that labor is the basic source of wealth. He urged that markets and trade be free from government control. Smith believed that unfettered economic self-interest produces the greatest good for the greatest number of people.

Smith, Joseph (1805-1844), was the founder of the Church of Jesus Christ of Latter-day Saints, or the Mormon Church. His converts met persecution in several Midwestern states, sometimes because of their practice of polygamy. When a mob killed Smith and his brother Hyrum in Illinois, many Mormons migrated to the Great Salt Lake Valley in Utah.

Socrates (469?-399 B.C.), a Greek philosopher, taught mainly by asking questions, a technique called the "Socratic method." He tried to develop principles for good conduct but was accused of corrupting youth by destroying their faith in the gods. Put on trial, he was found guilty and carried out his sentence by drinking poison hemlock. Socrates left no writings but is a character in most of the dialogues of his student Plato.

Solomon (around 973-around 933 B.C.) succeeded his father David as king of Israel. Under Solomon, the kingdom reached its peak in prosperity and influence. His greatest accomplishment was the building of the Temple of Jehovah in Jerusalem. Known for his wisdom, Solomon was the reputed author of books of the Bible, including Proverbs and Ecclesiastes.

Solon (639?-559? B.C.) was a Greek poet and lawgiver. Elected a ruler of Athens, he carried out many economic and political reforms. Solon's greatest achievement was a constitution that provided for rule by a council of 400 and for a system of public courts, a milestone in Athenian democracy.

Sophocles (496?-406? B.C.), a Greek tragedian, wrote 100 plays, of which only 7 have survived. His central characters are people who choose courses of action that can lead only to suffering or death, a fate they face heroically. Among Sophocles' works are *Electra, Antigone,* and *Oedipus Rex.*

Stalin, Joseph (1879-1953), dictator of the Soviet Union from 1929 until his death, eliminated his political enemies and ruled his country through secret police terrorism. He formed agricultural collectives and developed industry. Stalin led the Soviet Union during World War II and later expanded Soviet influence in Eastern Europe.

Stevenson, Robert Louis (1850-1894), a Scottish author, wrote many popular novels, essays, and poems. He traveled widely and lived the last few years of his life in Samoa in the South Pacific Ocean. His works include *Treasure Island, Kidnapped, The Strange Case of Doctor Jekyll and Mr. Hyde,* and *A Child's Garden of Verses.*

Stowe, Harriet Beecher (1811-1896), an American writer and the daughter of a noted Congregational minister, wrote the antislavery novel *Uncle Tom's Cabin.* The novel was very popular, but aroused much antipathy in the South. It was credited with making the question of slavery a moral issue and helping to bring on the Civil War.

Sullivan, Louis (1856-1924), an American architect, changed American design from historical imitation to the development of a distinctly American style. He adapted traditional principles to modern requirements in his designs for skyscrapers. His buildings included the Wainwright Building in St. Louis and the Stock Exchange Building in Chicago. Sullivan wrote *Autobiography of an Idea.*

Sun Yat-sen (1866-1925), a Chinese revolutionary, helped bring about the downfall of the Ch'ing dynasty. When the revolution succeeded in 1911, the Chinese Republic was established. Sun failed to unify China, however, and carried on several years of struggle with rival political leaders. It was only after his death that unity was achieved.

Swift, Jonathan (1667-1745), an English writer and Anglican clergyman who was born and lived much of his life in Ireland, satirized many of the cruelties and excesses of his time. His most famous work, *Gulliver's Travels,* satirized political institutions. He wrote about poverty in Ireland in *A Modest Proposal* and about religious corruption in *A Tale of a Tub.* Swift was a friend of many of the important English writers of the time.

Tacitus (about 55-about 120), a Roman politician, orator, and historian, wrote several works on the history of the Roman Empire. Biased in favor of the republican form of government, he criticized the emperors and the imperial system. Among his works are *Histories, Annals, Germania, Life of Agricola,* and *Dialogue on Orators.*

Tchaikovsky, Peter Ilich (1840-1893), a Russian composer, wrote melodic and emotional romantic music. He composed the opera *Eugène Onégin,* the ballets *Swan Lake* and *Nutcracker,* and the symphonic poem *Romeo and Juliet.* Tchaikovsky's symphonies include *Symphony No. 5* and *Symphony No. 6,* the "Pathétique."

Tereshkova, Valentina (1937-   ), a Soviet cosmonaut, was the first woman in space. Untrained as a pilot, she made parachuting a hobby and later joined the Soviet space program. Her historic space flight occurred in June 1963. During the flight, she spent more than 70 hours in orbit and made 48 orbits around the earth.

Thomson, Sir Joseph John (1856-1940), an English physicist, discovered the electron. Experimenting with cathode tubes, he established that the rays they emitted were not light waves but were composed of particles of matter. Thomson also discovered the first isotopes of elements and in 1906 won the Nobel prize in physics.

Thoreau, Henry David (1817-1862), was an American writer and philosopher. Along with his friend and colleague Ralph Waldo Emerson, Thoreau elaborated the transcendentalist philosophy of individualism and mysticism. His works include *Walden, A Week on the Concord and Merrimack Rivers,* and the essay "Civil Disobedience."

Tocqueville, Alexis de (1805-1859), a French writer and politician, wrote *Democracy in America,* after a visit to the United States in 1831 to study prisons. In the book, he skillfully analyzed the American character and American politics. He also wrote *The Old Regime and the French Revolution.* De Tocqueville held several positions in the French government.

Tolstoy, Leo (1828-1910), a Russian novelist, believed in social reform and nonviolence. Born an aristocrat, he later gave up worldly pleasures, adopted a fundamentalist form of Christianity, and lived a simple, pious life. Tolstoy's novels include *War and Peace, Anna Karenina,* and *Resurrection.*

Toulouse-Lautrec, Henri de (1864-1901), a French artist, often painted dance hall scenes, circus performers, and cabaret scenes. An accident early in life left him deformed, and dissipated living brought about his early death. A designer of posters and an illustrator and lithographer, his works include *The Ringmaster* and *In the Circus Fernando.*

Trotsky, Leon (1897-1940), a Russian revolutionary, led the army against forces opposed to the revolution of 1917. After Lenin's death, he lost the struggle for leadership to Stalin. Banished from the country, Trotsky was murdered in Mexico. He wrote several books, including *My Life.*

Tubman, Harriet (1820?-1913), born a slave, escaped to the North in 1849 and began a campaign against slavery. She worked with the Underground Railroad and helped more than 300 blacks escape from slavery. After the Civil War began, she offered her services to the Union Army and worked as a nurse, cook, and spy.

Turgenev, Ivan Sergeevich (1818-1883), a Russian novelist, usually portrayed liberals as ineffectual, even though he was a liberal. His most famous novel is *Fathers and Sons,* in which he popularized the term *nihilist*. Turgenev also wrote the short story "First Love" and the novels *Rudin, A Nest of Gentlefolk,* and *On the Eve*.

Tutankhamon (reigned about 1347-1335 B.C.), an Egyptian pharaoh, ruled for only a few years. After changes by his predecessor, he restored the traditional religion and moved the capital back to Thebes. When his tomb in the Valley of the Kings near Luxor was discovered in the 1920's, it was largely untouched by grave robbers. Thousands of objects, many of them solid gold, were removed from the tomb and placed in the Cairo Museum in Egypt. King Tut's treasures toured the United States in the 1970's.

Twain, Mark (1835-1910), whose real name was Samuel Langhorne Clemens, was an American writer whose novels and stories appealed to children but also made perceptive comments on American society. His boyhood experiences serve as background for *The Adventures of Tom Sawyer* and *The Adventures of Huckleberry Finn*. He also wrote about

Mark Twain, one of the major authors of American fiction, is seen here with his trademark white suit and cigar.

his experiences in the West. Twain's many other writings include *A Connecticut Yankee in King Arthur's Court* and *The Mysterious Stranger*.

Tweed, William Marcy (1823-1878), whose name became synonymous with graft, was the political boss of New York City for many years. He and his associates in the Tweed Ring cost the city millions of dollars through fraudulent supply and building contracts. Tweed was arrested in 1871, convicted, and jailed.

Van Gogh, Vincent (1853-1890), a Dutch painter, used thick brushstrokes to produce works of brilliant color. Many of his paintings seem to reflect the mental illnesses that he experienced for much of his life. Mental disturbances finally drove him to suicide. Among Van Gogh's works are *Self Portrait, The Starry Night,* and *Le Pont d'Arles*.

Vercingetorix (?-46 B.C.) led the Gauls and Arverni in a revolt against the Romans that slowed Julius Caesar's conquest of Gaul. Using guerrilla tactics, he raided Roman supply lines and fought only under favorable conditions. After defeating Vercingetorix, the Romans took him as a captive in chains to Rome, where he was executed.

Verdi, Giuseppe (1813-1901), an Italian composer, wrote operas with dramatic plots and beautiful melodies. Among his best known operas are *Rigoletto, La Traviata,* and *Aida*. Verdi also wrote the *Requiem Mass*. His operas are considered to be among the finest written and are often performed today.

Verne, Jules (1828-1905), a French author, wrote science fiction that accu-

rately forecast many technological developments some years before they actually appeared. Among his novels are *A Journey to the Center of the Earth, Twenty Thousand Leagues Under the Sea, Around the World in Eighty Days, The Mysterious Island,* and *From the Earth to the Moon*.

Victoria (1819-1901), in 63 years as queen of Great Britain and Empress of India, had the longest reign of any English monarch. During her rule, the British Empire was at the peak of its size and power, and the queen commanded domestic and foreign affairs during the latter half of the 1800's. With Victoria as the symbol, the era became known as the Victorian Age.

Virgil (70-19 B.C.), a Roman poet, modeled his greatest work, the *Aeneid,* partly on Homer's *Iliad* and *Odyssey*. Virgil's epic poem, a tribute to Rome, deals with the founding of the city, the growth of its power, and the civilizing effects of the Roman Empire. Virgil's other works include the *Eclogues* and the *Georgics*.

Voltaire (1694-1778) was the pen name of the French writer François Marie Arouet. Perhaps the most influential thinker of his time, he advocated religious toleration in his poem *La Henriade* and satirized social wrongs in *Candide*. Voltaire also wrote histories, encyclopedia articles, and dramas.

Von Braun, Wernher (1912-1977), a rocket engineer, was in charge of Germany's efforts to build rockets during World War II. He developed the V-2 rocket used against England in the latter days of the war. After the war, he worked for the United States contributing to the development of the powerful rockets used in space flights.

Wagner, Richard (1813-1883), a German composer, wrote operas that he called music dramas. His operas are long and costly to stage but are often performed today. His works *The Rhine Gold, The Valkyrie, Siegfried,* and *The Twilight of the Gods* comprise a group called *The Ring of the Nibelung,* based on heroic themes and myths from the ancient German past. Wagner's other operas include *Tristan and Isolde* and *Parsifal.*

Washington, Booker T. (1856-1915), the best-known black leader of his time, organized Tuskegee Institute, a school for blacks in Alabama, and served as its president. Washington accepted separation of the races and believed that education and skills would eventually elevate blacks economically. He wrote *Up from Slavery.*

Watson, James D. (1928-   ), an American biologist and chemist, worked on the development of a model of deoxyribonucleic acid (DNA), the substance that acts as a code in conveying genetic information from one generation to the next. He shared a Nobel prize in 1962. Watson's writings include *The Double Helix.*

Watt, James (1736-1819), A Scottish engineer and inventor, improved the steam engine. He invented the condensing steam engine and made numerous other improvements on existing engines. The patent on the Watt steam engine made him wealthy. The watt, a unit of electric power, is named for him. Watt also did work in metallurgy and chemistry.

Webster, Daniel (1782-1852), a lawyer and politician, served many years as a United States senator from Massachusetts, beginning in 1827. He was an eloquent spokesman for the Union during the states' rights controversy before the Civil War. Webster was also secretary of state under Presidents William Henry Harrison and John Tyler.

Wellington, Arthur Wellesley, Duke of (1769-1852), a British general and statesman, won decisive victories in the Peninsular War against Napoleon. His later victory at Toulouse in 1814 forced Napoleon to abdicate his throne. When Napoleon returned from exile, Wellington defeated him with the aid of Prussian troops at Waterloo in 1815.

Wesley, John (1703-1791), an English Anglican minister, founded the Methodist Church. The church grew out of societies that Wesley organized and before which he preached. Methodism spread rapidly in England and in America. Between 1735 and 1738, Wesley served as a chaplain and missionary to Indians in Georgia.

Wheatley, Phillis (1753?-1784), considered the first black woman poet in America, was brought to America as a slave in 1761. Purchased by John Wheatley, a Boston tailor, she became his wife's personal servant. A child prodigy, she published her first poem in 1770. She moved to England for a year and was very popular there. She published many religious poems.

Whitman, Walt (1819-1892), an American poet, wrote poems praising America and democracy. He was a newspaperman and editor, was active in the antislavery movement, worked as a nurse during the Civil War, and later held minor government jobs. Whitman is considered to be one of the first poets to write in a distinctively American style. His volume *Leaves of Grass* is considered a literary classic.

Whitney, Eli (1765-1825), an American inventor, developed the cotton gin that separated cotton fibers from the seeds. The invention vastly increased the amount of cotton that could be grown and harvested. Later he used interchangeable parts to mass-produce guns for the government. Whitney's arms factory made him wealthy.

Willard, Emma Hart (1787-1870), made important contributions to education for women in the United States. She founded a girls' boarding school in Vermont and later a girls' seminary in New York that became famous as the Emma Willard School. Her school emphasized teacher training and educated hundreds of young women. She also wrote history textbooks and poetry.

William I (1027?-1087), an English king known as "the Conqueror," led an invasion and conquest of England from Normandy in 1066. To centralize his power, he forced all landholders, including the nobility, to swear allegiance directly to him. During his reign, he took an extensive census and survey of the English land, which was compiled in the Domesday Book.

Wolfe, Thomas (1900-1938), wrote long and lyrical autobiographical novels. Born and raised in North Carolina, Wolfe taught at New York University from 1924 to 1930 before turning to writing full time. Among his works are *Look Homeward, Angel; Of Time and the River; You Can't Go Home Again;* and *The Web and the Rock.*

Wordsworth, William (1770-1850), an English poet, was a romantic writer of poems about nature. In collaboration with Samuel Taylor Coleridge, he wrote *Lyrical Ballads,* poems that denounce artificiality and glorify the senses. Among his poems are "I Wandered Lonely as a Cloud," "She Was a Phantom of Delight," "Lines Composed a Few Miles above Tintern Abbey," "The Prelude," and "Ode: Intimations of Immortality."

Wren, Sir Christopher (1632-1723), an English architect, designed plans for the rebuilding of some 50 churches, including St. Paul's Cathedral, after the London fire of 1666. He also designed a master plan for the city of London, but it was not adopted. Wren's other works include the library of Trinity College at Oxford and additions to Hampton Court Palace.

Wright, Frank Lloyd (1867-1959), an American architect, designed hundreds of houses and other buildings. He developed a horizontal "prairie style" for houses and other buildings, and he established architectural schools in Wisconsin and in Arizona. Wright also designed the Imperial Hotel in Tokyo and the Guggenheim Museum in New York City.

Wright, Wilbur and Orville (1867-1912 and 1871-1948), after experimenting with kites and gliders, constructed and flew the first powered airplane on December 17, 1903. They contracted with the United States government for military planes and established factories in France and in Germany. Throughout their lives, the Wright brothers worked for progress in aviation.

Xerxes I (519?-465 B.C.), a Persian king descended from Cyrus the Great and Darius I, invaded Greece with nearly 200,000 men in 480 B.C. The Persians won at Thermopylae but were later defeated at Salamis and Plataea. Xerxes' invasion was the last Persian attempt to conquer the Greeks. He spent the last years of his life in dissolute living and was murdered by a soldier.

Yamato Clan (about 200-646) was a ruling group of Japan that took its name from the Yamato Plain, near the city of Nara. During the period of the Yamato rule, Chinese and Buddhist influences were great in Japan, and the Shinto religion flourished. The period ended with the Taika Reform and the establishment of a strong central government in Japan.

Young, Brigham (1801-1877), was a convert to the Mormon faith who became a leader in the church. Three years after the Mormon leader, Joseph Smith, was killed in Illinois in 1844, Young led the Mormons west to Great Salt Lake Valley where they established settlements. He was the first governor of the Territory of Utah. Partly because he practiced polygamy, the United States government removed him as governor. He was put on trial but was not convicted.

Zapata, Emiliano (1880?-1919), a Mexican revolutionary, joined the revolt against President Porfirio Díaz in 1910. An Indian who remained independent of other revolutionary movements, he was committed to land redistribution and refused to recognize the new Mexican government. Zapata continued his opposition, frequently with armed resistance, until his assassination.

Zenger, John Peter (1697-1746), born in Germany, emigrated to New York and became a printer. When his newspaper criticized the British governor, Zenger was arrested for seditious libel. Represented by the lawyer Andrew Hamilton, who argued truth as a defense for libel, Zenger was acquitted. The case helped establish the principle of freedom of the press in America.

Zwingli, Huldreich (1484-1531), a Swiss clergyman, was among the first clericals to demand reforms in the Roman Catholic Church and to support the Protestant Reformation. Although they had some religious differences, Zwingli supported Martin Luther. Zwingli was killed in fighting between Zurich and the Catholic provinces of Switzerland.

5

Presidents and Prime Ministers

How much do you really know about the people who have filled the office of President of the United States? While most students are able to name many of the Presidents, few students know very much about the backgrounds and terms in office of these persons. Reading about the important events in each Presidency is a convenient way of reviewing important events in American history.

This unit presents a biography of each of the people who have served as President of the United States. And the unit is completed by a handy reference table of Canada's Prime Ministers.

The faces of four great American Presidents are carved
on Mount Rushmore in the Black Hills of South Dakota.

1

Presidents of the United States

The following table lists the Presidents of the United States by terms in chronological order, the order in which they served. Use of the table will enable you to relate the order of presidential succession to the chronological flow of the history of the United States.

A biography of each President follows the table. Presidential biographies have been arranged in alphabetical order for easy reference.

Table of Presidents of the United States

Name	Served	Name	Served
1. George Washington	1789-1797	22. Grover Cleveland	1885-1889
2. John Adams	1797-1801	23. Benjamin Harrison	1889-1893
3. Thomas Jefferson	1801-1809	24. Grover Cleveland	1893-1897
4. James Madison	1809-1817	25. William McKinley	1897-1901
5. James Monroe	1817-1825	26. Theodore Roosevelt	1901-1909
6. John Quincy Adams	1825-1829	27. William Howard Taft	1909-1913
7. Andrew Jackson	1829-1837	28. Woodrow Wilson	1913-1921
8. Martin Van Buren	1837-1841	29. Warren Gamaliel Harding	1921-1923
9. William Henry Harrison	1841	30. Calvin Coolidge	1923-1929
10. John Tyler	1841-1845	31. Herbert C. Hoover	1929-1933
11. James K. Polk	1845-1849	32. Franklin Delano Roosevelt	1933-1945
12. Zachary Taylor	1849-1850	33. Harry S. Truman	1945-1953
13. Millard Fillmore	1850-1853	34. Dwight David Eisenhower	1953-1961
14. Franklin Pierce	1853-1857	35. John Fitzgerald Kennedy	1961-1963
15. James Buchanan	1857-1861	36. Lyndon Baines Johnson	1963-1969
16. Abraham Lincoln	1861-1865	37. Richard M. Nixon	1969-1974
17. Andrew Johnson	1865-1869	38. Gerald R. Ford	1974-1977
18. Ulysses S. Grant	1869-1877	39. James Earl Carter, Jr.	1977-1981
19. Rutherford B. Hayes	1877-1881	40. Ronald Wilson Reagan	1981-1989
20. James A. Garfield	1881	41. George H. W. Bush	1989-
21. Chester A. Arthur	1881-1885		

John Adams

Born: Oct. 30, 1735
Died: July 4, 1826
Place of Birth: Braintree
  (now Quincy), Mass.

Political Party: Federalist
Term: 1797-1801
Electoral Vote: 71
Vice-President:
  Thomas Jefferson

Adams, John (1735-1826), was the second President of the United States. The son of a farmer, John Adams rose to become a prominent lawyer, a key figure in the movement for independence from Great Britain, and a leader among those who shaped the new republic.

Born in Braintree (now Qunicy), Mass., on Oct. 30, 1735, Adams received a degree from Harvard College in 1755. He then studied law, eventually opening an office in Boston. In 1764, he married Abigail Smith, daughter of a minister.

Early in his career, John Adams became involved in opposing British tax and trade policies for the colonies. He was one of the leaders of the successful attack against the Stamp Act of 1765, which placed a tax on legal papers and other documents.

A delegate to the First Continental Congress, Adams spoke out strongly against the Intolerable Acts. These British laws aimed to punish Massachusetts and Boston for the Boston Tea Party of December, 1773. Serving in the Second Continental Congress, Adams spoke out strongly for an end to ties with Britain.

He helped draft, and was one of the signers of, the Declaration of Independence.

During the Revolutionary War, Adams spent much of his time abroad as a diplomat in France and in Holland. In Holland, he obtained a $1,400,000 loan to help America carry on the war. In 1782, Adams joined Benjamin Franklin and John Jay to negotiate the Treaty of Paris, which ended the Revolutionary War. Three years later, he became the first United States minister to Britain, serving until 1788.

By the time Adams sailed for home, a new Constitution had been written and a new government was about to be established. He was chosen the first Vice-President under George Washington, and he remained in that office during Washington's second term.

Two political parties formed during Washington's presidency. One, the Federalist Party, supported Washington's policies and a strong central government. The other, the Democratic-Republican Party, under the leadership of Thomas Jefferson and James Madison, stressed states' rights. Adams ran against Jefferson for the presidency in 1796. Adams won more electoral votes, and, under the provisions of the Constitution at that time, he became President. Jefferson, as runner-up, became Vice-President.

John Adams' single term as President was a troubled one. There had been war between France and England since the beginning of the French Revolution in 1789. Both England and France had seized American ships. Adams wanted the United States to remain neutral. But other Federalists, led by Alexander Hamilton, who had opposed the French Revolution, wanted war with France. Pursuing his neutralist course, President Adams sent delegates to France to work out an agreement. But the French diplomats offered to negotiate only in return for a bribe and other payments. The situation became known as the XYZ Affair, after the unnamed French officials involved. It produced great controversy in the United States and increased the demands for war. Adams supported the

building of more warships, and he made Washington commander of the Army. But Adams refused to abandon his policy of neutrality, and he finally got a treaty with France in 1800.

To curb criticism of their party and policies by Republicans and by Frenchmen in the United States, the Federalists pushed harsh laws through Congress. Under the Alien and Sedition Acts, the President was authorized to deport aliens by a simple order.

Shortly before the election of 1800, John and Abigail Adams moved into the still unfinished White House, living in just a few rooms. By this time, Adams' political fortunes had declined drastically. He had few friends, and many members of his own party would not support him. Still, in 1800, he received 65 electoral votes to Thomas Jefferson's 73.

Leaving the presidency, Adams retired from all political activity. He died on his country's birthday, July 4, 1826, at age 90.

John Quincy Adams

Born: July 11, 1767
Died: Feb. 23, 1848
Place of Birth: Braintree
(now Quincy), Mass.
Political Party:
Democratic-Republican

Term: 1825-1829
Electoral Vote: 84
Vice-President:
John C. Calhoun

Adams, John Quincy (1767-1848), was the sixth President of the United States. Short, stout, bald, aloof, and one of the great intellectuals of his time, John Quincy Adams enjoyed a brilliant governmental career until he achieved the presidency. Then he suffered troubles similar to those that his father, John, had experienced.

The sixth President of the United States was born in the same house as his father in Braintree (now Quincy), Mass., on July 11, 1767. When he was nearly 11, he accompanied his father on a diplomatic mission to France. At age 14, he became secretary to Francis Dana, the first United States diplomat in Russia. Returning home in the 1780's, he graduated from Harvard College and became a lawyer.

During his father's Administration, Adams served as minister to Prussia. In 1797, he married Louisa Catherine Johnson, the daughter of the United States consul general in London.

Adams, a member of the Federalist Party, won election to the Massachusetts senate in 1802 and to the United States

Senate the following year. England and France were at war, and to ensure American neutrality, President Thomas Jefferson in 1807 imposed an embargo on trade with either country. This hurt New England commercial interests, and when Adams supported Jefferson, he was forced to resign from the Senate. But in 1809, Madison appointed him minister to Russia, where he served for five years. Then, in 1814, Adams served in the American delegation that negotiated the Treaty of Ghent, which ended the War of 1812 with England. Adams was minister to Great Britain from 1815 to 1817.

Following the election of Republican James Monroe to the presidency in 1816, Adams became secretary of state. He favored the country's expansion and was especially influential in the development of the Monroe Doctrine in 1823.

Both James Madison and James Monroe had been secretary of state before assuming the presidency. It was expected that Adams would succeed Monroe as President. The presidential campaign of 1824, however, was a four-man race. Adams, Andrew Jackson, Henry Clay, and William Crawford all received electoral votes. Jackson received the highest number of votes, 99, but not a majority. Clay had the least number of votes, putting him out of the race. The House of Representatives decided the winner, and with Speaker of the House Clay supporting him, Adams became President. When Adams made Clay secretary of state, Jackson's followers declared that Adams and Clay had struck a corrupt bargain. They bitterly opposed Adams throughout his Administration.

John Quincy Adams spent four unhappy years in the White House. He refused to pass out political jobs to those who had supported him. This won him no friends. He favored federal spending on roads and canals. This made him unpopular with supporters of states' rights. His attempts to curb speculation in public lands annoyed Westerners. He re-

fused to force Cherokee Indians to move out of Georgia, arousing Southern anger. When Andrew Jackson won the presidency in 1828, Adams left office with relief.

Unlike his father, Adams did not retire from politics after serving as President. He was elected to the House of Representatives in 1830, an accomplishment which pleased him more than gaining the presidency. He remained in the House until 1848, serving with great distinction, as independent and grumpy as ever, but earning the title "Old Man Eloquent" for his speeches. Adams' effort to lead the fight against "gag rules" in the House was his most memorable act as a congressman.

Adams suffered a stroke in 1846 but recovered partially. Then he suffered a second stroke in February 1848. He died two days later.

Chester A. Arthur

Born: Oct. 5, 1829
Died: Nov. 18, 1886
Place of Birth:
    Fairfield, Vt.

Political Party: Republican
Term: 1881-1885
Electoral Vote: None
Vice-President: None

Arthur, Chester A. (1829-1886), was the 21st President of the United States. He

succeeded to the presidency following the assassination of James A. Garfield in

1881. Arthur is remembered as a machine politician who believed firmly in the patronage system of rewarding supporters with government jobs. Yet, during his Administration, the first national civil service reform legislation was enacted.

A New Englander, Chester A. Arthur was born in Fairfield, Vt., on Oct. 5, 1829. His father was a Baptist minister. After graduating in 1848 from Union College in Schenectady, N.Y., Arthur taught school and studied law. He joined a New York City law firm in 1854. As a lawyer, he became known for his defense of civil rights for free blacks. His courtroom successes included winning a case that led to the desegregation of city streetcars in New York City. In 1859, Arthur married Ellen Lewis Herndon, a naval officer's daughter. He also became active in politics as a member of the Republican Party, which had been founded in 1854.

Arthur served as a delegate to the New York Republican state convention in 1860. As a result of his work on behalf of Governor Edwin D. Morgan, who won reelection, Arthur was eventually appointed quartermaster general of New York. In this position, he was responsible for awarding contracts to provide supplies for Union troops in the Civil War.

After the war, Arthur became a member of the faction of the Republican Party known as "Stalwarts," led by Senator Roscoe Conkling of New York. During the Grant Administration (1869-1877), Arthur served as collector of the Port of New York.

The Stalwarts and their rivals, the "Half-Breeds," led by Maine Senator James G. Blaine, clashed at the 1880 Republican presidential convention. The Stalwarts supported former President

Ulysses S. Grant for the nomination, and the Half-Breeds backed Ohio Senator James A. Garfield. Garfield became the candidate, and, in an attempt to gain Stalwart support, the convention named Arthur as his running mate. Garfield and Arthur won.

But Garfield's Administration was short-lived. Only a few months after his inauguration, Garfield was assassinated by Charles J. Guiteau, a disappointed office seeker who claimed to be a Stalwart (see Garfield, James A.). Arthur became President in September 1881.

The assassination led to a public outcry against the "spoils system" of distributing government jobs on the basis of political preference (see Jackson, Andrew). Arthur resisted the calls for reform as long as he could, but yielded after many Republican members of Congress were defeated in the elections of 1882. The result was the Pendleton Civil Service Act of 1883. This legislation established a Civil Service Commission, classified government jobs, and set up a system for advancement. At first, relatively few jobs were placed on the civil service list and freed from political influence. The Pendleton Act, however, was an important piece of legislation that set the stage for later civil service reform.

In 1882, President Arthur signed the first law prohibiting Chinese immigration. He also supported the Anti-Polygamy Act of 1882, which was aimed at Mormons and which made it illegal for a man to have more than one wife.

New York Republicans lost the 1882 governor's race to the reform candidate, Grover Cleveland, a Democrat who later became President. Because they did not think Arthur had given the party sufficient support, Republican leaders blamed him for the defeat. Partly as a result of the 1882 loss, the Republicans in 1884 refused to nominate Arthur for the presidency. Instead, they selected James G. Blaine, leader of the so-called Half-Breed faction.

Soon after his retirement from the presidency, heart trouble and Bright's disease forced Arthur to quit his law practice. He died in 1886.

James Buchanan

Born: April 23, 1791
Died: June 1, 1868
Place of Birth:
    Stony Batter, Pa.
Political Party: Democrat

Term: 1857-1861
Electoral Vote: 174
Vice-President:
    John C. Breckinridge

Buchanan, James (1791-1868), was the 15th President of the United States. With a solid diplomatic and congressional career behind him, Buchanan became President at a time when tension over slavery was building rapidly in the United States. During his Administration, the first of the Southern States withdrew from the Union.

The son of a country store owner, James Buchanan was born near Mercersburg, Pa., on April 23, 1791. He was the second of 11 children. As a boy, he worked in his father's store and later graduated from Dickinson College in Carlisle, Pa. He then studied law and began practice in Lancaster, Pa., in 1812.

Buchanan entered politics in 1814,

winning election to the Pennsylvania legislature. He served two terms. He then resumed his law practice for a brief period, returning to politics following the death of his fiancée in 1819. Buchanan never married.

Beginning in 1821, James Buchanan served 10 years in the United States House of Representatives. A Democrat, he strongly supported President Andrew Jackson. In 1831, Jackson made Buchanan minister to Russia. Buchanan was a senator from Pennsylvania from 1834 to 1845, and secretary of state under President James K. Polk from 1845 until 1849. During Buchanan's time as secretary of state, the United States settled the Oregon boundary dispute with

Britain and won a war with Mexico. The United States gained a large amount of territory in the Southwest as a result of the war.

The Democrats lost the 1848 election, and Buchanan retired from politics. When his party regained power under President Franklin Pierce in 1853, Buchanan became minister to Great Britain.

Running against the first Republican presidential candidate, John C. Frémont, Buchanan was elected President in 1856. He presided over a nation sharply divided over the slavery issue and threatening to disintegrate. Buchanan considered slavery to be immoral, but constitutional. He believed the federal government should not become involved in the issue.

Buchanan avoided taking a strong stand on slavery. He preferred middle-of-the-road positions and compromise. At a time when extremists on both sides demanded action, Buchanan's moderation contributed to his unpopularity.

The slavery issue was most bitterly contested in Kansas, which was about to become a state. Pro- and antislavery factions fought for control of the Kansas government. A state constitution permitting slavery came up for a vote in Kansas in 1857. The antislavery group boycotted the election, and slavery was approved. President Buchanan favored congressional acceptance of the constitution, since both sides had had a chance to express their views. This angered Senator Stephen A. Douglas of Illinois, who wanted Kansas to be a free state. Douglas persuaded Congress to return the constitution to the Kansas voters.

The controversy over "bleeding Kansas" split the Democratic Party into Northern and Southern factions. And in 1860, neither group favored Buchanan as a presidential candidate. The split helped elect Republican Abraham Lincoln to the presidency. Between the time of Lincoln's victory and his inauguration, seven Southern states seceded from the Union.

Early in 1861, Buchanan agreed to send a supply ship to Fort Sumter, in the Charleston, S.C., harbor to relieve the federal garrison there. Firing on the ship, Southerners forced it to withdraw. Because no blood had been shed, Buchanan took no action against the South.

Northerners sharply criticized Buchanan for his lack of action. But his cautious course did postpone the beginning of the Civil War and left open the possibility of a peaceful solution under Lincoln's administration. However, in April 1861, Southerners captured Fort Sumter. Lincoln declared the South in a state of rebellion and called for volunteers to the Army. Buchanan approved this action and urged fellow Democrats to support the new President.

James Buchanan spent the years during and after the war on his estate near Lancaster, Pa. He died there in 1868.

George H. W. Bush

Born: June 12, 1924
Place of Birth:
   Milton, Mass.
Political Party: Republican

Term: 1989-
Electoral Vote: 426
Vice-President: Dan Quayle

Bush, George Herbert Walker (1924-   ), was elected the 41st President of the United States in 1988. A Republican, he defeated the Democratic candidate, Governor Michael S. Dukakis of Massachusetts, in the November 1988 election.

George Bush was born on June 12, 1924, in Milton, Massachusetts, the son of a successful businessman and banker. He attended private schools, and in 1941 joined the Navy to become a fighter pilot on an aircraft carrier.

After the war, Bush graduated from Yale University and then went into the oil business in Texas. With a friend, he later formed an oil-drilling company that made him wealthy.

Bush became interested in politics in the late 1950's, and in 1966 he won election to the first of two terms representing Texas in the U.S. House of Representatives. He made an unsuccessful run for the U.S. Senate in 1970.

During the 1970's, Bush held various positions in government under Presidents Richard M. Nixon and Gerald R. Ford. He was United States ambassador to the United Nations (UN), United States envoy to China, and director of the Central Intelligence Agency (CIA).

In 1980 George Bush sought the Republican nomination for President, but lost to Ronald Reagan. Bush then accepted the nomination for Vice-President. Republican victory in November 1980 swept Reagan and Bush into office.

As Vice-President for eight years, Bush played a more active role in government than most holders of that office. He attended daily security briefings and headed a task force on drug smuggling and illegal immigration. He also took over some of the duties of the President when President Reagan underwent medical treatment.

Bush easily won his party's nomination for President in 1988, and he won election that year by a wide margin of popular and electoral votes. He was the 14th former Vice-President to become President, and the first to be elected President while serving as Vice-President since Martin Van Buren in 1836.

As Bush took over the presidency, U.S. relations with the Soviet Union were better than they had been in some years. The federal government was deeply in debt, however, having spent much more than it took in over several years. There was also a huge trade deficit.

America imported more than it exported—which meant that much money went to foreign countries.

Early in his presidency, Bush had to deal with the worst crisis in the savings and loan industry since the Great Depression of the 1930's. He proposed legislation to rescue and restructure the industry. In other national affairs, Bush took steps to reduce air pollution and reduce the use of illegal drugs in the United States.

The President also took strong stands in international affairs. In May 1989, he called for reductions in U.S. and Soviet troops and weapons in Europe. And in December 1989, he ordered U.S. troops to invade Panama and arrest that country's leader, General Manuel Noriega. When the U.S. military failed to seize Noriega, Bush offered a reward for his capture. Noriega eventually surrendered and was turned over to American authorities. He will stand trial in the United States, where he will face drug trafficking charges.

James Earl Carter, Jr.

Born: Oct. 1, 1924
Place of Birth:
    Plains, Ga.
Political Party: Democrat

Term: 1977-1981
Electoral Vote: 297
Vice-President:
    Walter F. Mondale

Carter, James Earl, Jr. (1924-   ), was elected the 39th President of the United States in 1976. A Georgian, Jimmy Carter became the first person from the Deep South to win the presidency.

James Earl Carter, Jr., was born in Plains, Ga., on Oct. 1, 1924. He graduated from high school there, then attended Georgia Southwestern College at Americus and the Georgia Institute of Technology at Atlanta. He won admission to the United States Naval Academy at Annapolis in 1943, graduating with a commission in 1946. That year, he married Rosalynn Smith, whom he had known since childhood. Carter spent the next seven years in the Navy, serving part of that time in the nuclear submarine program.

The death of his father in 1953 caused Carter to resign from the Navy to take over the family business, which included a peanut warehouse and about 2,500 acres of farmland. He proved a highly successful manager, and, at the same time, became active in local civic affairs and statewide organizations.

From 1962 to 1966, Carter served in the Georgia senate, where he posted a liberal record and spent much of his time on educational matters. In Plains, Carter in 1965 spoke out strongly for the admission of blacks to the Plains Baptist Church, where he was a deacon.

Carter was elected governor of Georgia in 1970. Beginning his governorship in 1971, Carter called for an end to racial discrimination. His most notable achievement as governor was to reduce the number of state agencies from 300 to 22. He also claimed credit for a $166-million surplus in the state treasury upon leaving office.

After leaving the governorship in 1975, Carter began organizing and campaigning for the 1976 Democratic presidential nomination. His efforts paid off. He won a number of 1976 primary elections, presenting himself as a stranger to Washington, not bound by old ways of doing things. At the Democratic National Convention in New York City, he easily won the nomination on the first ballot. Carter chose Walter F. Mondale of Minnesota as his running mate. Carter and Mondale defeated their Republican opponents, President Gerald R. Ford and Kansas Senator Robert J. Dole. Carter won 297 electoral votes, against Ford's 241.

The U.S. economy was Carter's major domestic concern. With Carter's support, Congress passed laws to create jobs, lower the federal income tax, and deregulate much of the nation's transportation system. Carter opposed several costly government projects. His 1980 program to fight inflation called for cut-ting federal spending, restricting credit, and voluntary wage and price restraints. Despite these actions, severe inflation and unemployment continued.

In 1977, Carter created a new Department of Energy. During his term, Congress approved most of his energy program, which was designed to decrease consumption, end dependence on foreign oil, and find new energy sources.

In foreign affairs, Carter came out in favor of human rights around the world. In 1979, the SALT II treaty, limiting the use of nuclear weapons, was negotiated with the Soviet Union. But the Soviet invasion of Afghanistan in late 1979 and 1980 put a strain on U.S.-Soviet relations. In response, Carter called for curtailing trade with the Soviet Union, boycotting the 1980 Olympic games in Moscow, and delaying Senate ratification of SALT II.

Carter achieved several other major foreign policy goals. In 1978, the Senate approved the Panama Canal treaties, gradually returning control of the canal to Panama. Carter was praised for helping to establish full diplomatic relations with China and for helping to bring about the peace treaty between Egypt and Israel.

But he was plagued during the last year of his term with his attempts to gain the release of U.S. hostages being held by militants in Iran. He applied economic and diplomatic pressures and carried on extensive negotiations. A failed military rescue attempt in April 1980 drew sharp criticism. The hostages were not released until the day that Carter left office.

In 1980, Carter was defeated in his bid for a second term by his Republican opponent, former Governor Ronald W. Reagan of California.

Grover Cleveland

Born: March 18, 1837
Died: June 24, 1908
Place of Birth:
 Caldwell, N.J.
Political Party: Democrat

Terms: 1885-1889; 1893-1897
Electoral Vote: 219, 277
Vice-Presidents:
 Thomas A. Hendricks;
 Adlai E. Stevenson

Cleveland, Grover (1837-1908), was the 22nd and 24th President of the United States. He was the only President to serve two nonconsecutive terms in office. As President, Cleveland stood by the principles of conscientiousness, self-control, and government impartiality. However, his beliefs led to some difficulties in his administration during a time of social change.

The son of a poor Presbyterian minister, Grover Cleveland was born on March 18, 1837, in Caldwell, N.J. He went to work at an early age in a general store. At 17, Cleveland left home for Buffalo, N.Y., where he studied law. He worked for the Democratic Party, served as assistant district attorney for Erie County, and then was elected sheriff.

Graft and corruption characterized city governments in the late 1800's. Cleveland won election as mayor of Buffalo in 1881 on a reform ticket. He conducted an honest and impartial administration, believing that government should grant favors to no one group. From 1883 to 1885, he served as governor of New York.

Promoting honest government gave Cleveland a national reputation. There had been corruption in the federal government, and voters were ready for national reform. As a result, Cleveland won the Democratic presidential nomination in 1884 and was elected, though by only 23,000 votes.

President Cleveland opposed veterans' pension bills. He favored lower tariffs. He sought repeal of a law that allowed people to use silver to pay obligations contracted in gold, a practice that was draining the nation's gold reserves. He supported the Interstate Commerce Act of 1887, which permitted the federal government to regulate railroads.

Cleveland became the first President to marry in the White House. He married 21-year-old Frances Folsom, daughter of a former law partner, in 1886.

Cleveland's honesty, impartiality, and willingness to stand on principle made him a popular President. However, his policies on pensions, cheap money, and tariffs gained him enemies among veterans, industrialists, and farmers. In 1888, although Cleveland won the popular vote by 90,000 votes, he lost to Republican candidate Benjamin Harrison in the Electoral College, 233 to 168.

Frances Cleveland predicted that she and her husband would return to the White House in 1893. She was right. President Harrison did many things Cleveland had refused to do. He supported high tariffs, greater coinage of silver, and veterans' pensions. By 1892, American voters were ready for Cleveland again. He easily defeated Harrison.

Cleveland's second term was troublesome. He failed to win a reduction in tariffs. A severe economic depression began in 1893. The drain on gold reserves forced Cleveland to borrow money from New York lenders. Labor unrest was widespread. "Coxey's Army," a group of unemployed workers, marched on Washington, D.C., to demand government relief. In Illinois, workers at the Pullman railroad car plant went on strike. The American Railway Union supported them and refused to handle Pullman cars. Declaring that the strike interfered with mail delivery, Cleveland sent federal troops to bring it to an end.

In 1892, the Populist Party, a splinter group of farmers and some labor representatives, had opposed the two major parties. The Populist candidate for President received a million votes. By 1896, the Populists, who supported the free coinage of silver, had gained control of the Democratic Party. Democrats that year turned to William Jennings Bryan, a free silver advocate, as their presidential candidate.

Cleveland spent the remaining years of his life in Princeton, N.J., serving as a university lecturer and trustee and writing magazine articles. He died there in 1908.

Calvin Coolidge

Born: July 4, 1872
Died: Jan. 5, 1933
Place of Birth:
    Plymouth Notch, Vt.
Political Party: Republican

Terms: 1923-1929
Electoral Vote: 382
Vice-President:
    Charles G. Dawes

Coolidge, Calvin (1872-1933), was the 30th President of the United States. A shy, closemouthed New Englander known as "Silent Cal," Coolidge held public office throughout most of his adult life.

Coolidge was born in the village of Plymouth Notch, Vt., on July 4, 1872. His father was a farmer and storekeeper. After completing secondary school, Coolidge entered Amherst College in Massachusetts in 1891, graduating with honors four years later. In 1897, he became a lawyer in Northampton, Mass.

Politics attracted Coolidge soon after his graduation from college and in 1899, he won election to the Northampton city council. Later, he served two terms as city solicitor. He married Grace Anna Goodhue, a school teacher, in 1905.

In 1906, Coolidge was elected a Republican member of the Massachusetts house of representatives. Then, in 1909, he became mayor of Northampton. Continuing his political climb, he served in the state senate from 1911 to 1915, and became lieutenant governor in 1916. He became governor of Massachusetts three years later.

His action during a strike by Boston policemen in 1919 earned Coolidge a nationwide reputation. Although it was contrary to police department rules, a group of policemen had organized a labor union. As a result, the Boston police commissioner suspended 19 of them. This led to a strike by policemen and a great deal of turmoil in the city. Governor Coolidge acted. Declaring that "there is no right to stike against the public safety by anybody, anywhere, any time," he called out the National Guard. The strike was ended.

In 1920, Calvin Coolidge became the Republican nominee for the vice-presidency, joining presidential candidate Warren G. Harding. The slender, retiring Coolidge stood in sharp contrast to the friendly, outgoing Harding. But they were the team Americans wanted, and they won a resounding victory.

President Harding died early in August, 1923, just as news of wrongdoing among Cabinet and other officials became public (see Harding, Warren G.). Coolidge then became President.

Republicans believed that the government should help business by supporting low taxes and high tariffs. Aside from that, they felt the government should interfere as little as possible in the economy or in people's lives. Coolidge thoroughly agreed. "The business of America is business," he said. Under his administration, high tariff rates continued, taxes—especially on high incomes and inheritances—were reduced, and there was no government aid for farmers suffering from low prices for their products.

In foreign affairs, Coolidge opposed United States participation in the League of Nations. His administration worked out a plan by which Germany could pay the huge damage payments the victorious Allies demanded after World War I. Following the Mexican Revolution in 1917, relations between Mexico and the United States became strained over the question of foreign-owned oil properties. Various disputes with Mexico were settled, and relations improved during Coolidge's presidency.

Referring to the fact that Coolidge's face rarely wrinkled with a smile or a laugh, an observer concluded that he had been "weaned on a pickel." Coolidge treasured silence, saying that "the things I don't say never get me into trouble."

But Americans generally were satisfied with Coolidge and his policies. They overwhelmingly elected him President in 1924.

The Coolidge era was a time of prosperity for millions of people. Industrial wages and farm incomes, however, remained relatively low. Speculation on the stock market went unchecked. Some observers warned that the economy was on a dangerous course, and that disaster would result. But neither Coolidge nor anyone else took action to change things. The stock market crash came in the fall of 1929, the year Coolidge left office.

Calvin Coolidge spent the remaining years of his life on his estate near Northampton. He died in 1933.

Dwight David Eisenhower

Born: Oct. 14, 1890
Died: March 28, 1969
Place of Birth:
   Denison, Tex.
Political Party: Republican

Terms: 1953-1961
Electoral Vote: 442; 457
Vice President:
   Richard M. Nixon

Eisenhower, Dwight David (1890-1969), was the 34th President of the United States. He won acclaim as commander of the Allied forces in Europe during World War II. Like military heroes George Washington and Ulysses S. Grant before him, Eisenhower was twice elected President.

Eisenhower was born in Denison, Tex., on Oct. 14, 1890. The Eisenhower family moved to Abilene, Kans., when he was 2 years old. After high school graduation in 1909, Eisenhower went to work. But the following year, he won appointment to the U.S. Military Academy at West Point. He graduated as a second lieutenant in 1915, and in the summer of 1916, he married Mamie Geneva Doud, a wealthy meat packer's daughter.

During World War I, Eisenhower served as a tank-training officer. After the war, like other military officers in peacetime, his progress through the ranks was slow. He became a colonel in 1941. His record, however, attracted the attention of General George C. Marshall, Army chief of staff. After the United States entered World War II in Decem-

ber, 1941, Marshall appointed Eisenhower to the War Plans Division. Soon thereafter, Marshall had Eisenhower promoted to major general and placed him in command of U.S. forces that were to invade North Africa, Sicily, and Italy. His performance earned him further promotion and appointment as commander of Allied forces preparing for the invasion of France. The invasion on June 6, 1944, was successful, and in less than a year, the war in Europe ended. In November, 1945, Eisenhower succeeded Marshall as Army chief of staff.

With Eisenhower's support, all of the U.S. armed forces were unified under a single secretary of defense in 1947. In 1948, Eisenhower resigned to become president of Columbia University. Two years later, he was appointed commander of the North Atlantic Treaty Organization troops.

In 1948, both Republicans and Democrats sought Eisenhower as their presidential candidate, but he refused to enter politics. Four years later, however, he agreed to stand for the Republican nomination, and he won it easily. With California Senator Richard M. Nixon as his

running mate, Eisenhower defeated
Democrat Adlai Stevenson by more than
6 million popular votes. He was elected
to a second term in 1956, again defeating
Adlai Stevenson.

Americans looked upon Eisenhower
as a father figure, whom they referred to
by his nickname, "Ike." His warm and
ready smile generated confidence. As
President, Eisenhower tended to stress
the power and responsibilities of the
states, rather than the federal government. Even so, he resisted conservative
efforts to diminish or dismantle such federal social programs as Social Security
and welfare aid. He also approved the
establishment of the Department of
Health, Education, and Welfare. He supported a multimillion dollar federal interstate highway program. In 1954, the Supreme Court handed down a decision
declaring that school segregation on the
basis of race was unconstitutional.
Eisenhower did not wholeheartedly approve of the decision, but when the state
of Arkansas defied it in 1957, he sent
U.S. troops to Little Rock to enforce it.

In foreign affairs, Eisenhower brought
the Korean War to a close in 1953 (see
Truman, Harry S.). He insisted on reducing the size of the armed forces and
on keeping the U.S. stockpile of nuclear
weapons at a fixed level. The Cold War,
however, continued (see Truman, Harry
S.). The Eisenhower Administration extended aid to France, which was fighting
a rebellion by Nationalist and Communist forces in Indochina, its colony in
Southeast Asia. Eisenhower also sent
U.S. military advisers into Indochina.
The President in 1957 announced the Eisenhower Doctrine, which committed
U.S. forces to the Middle East if they
were necessary to halt what might be
perceived as Communist aggression. Under the doctrine, he ordered troops into
Lebanon to help defend that nation's
government against left-wing forces. In
1960, the Soviets shot down a U.S. spy
plane over Russia. Eisenhower took responsibility for the spying. He refused,
however, to apologize for it. As a result,
the Russians canceled a summit meeting
scheduled for that year.

The 22nd Amendment, adopted in
1951, prevented Eisenhower from running for a third term, which he might
have won. Leaving the presidency in
1961, he retired to his farm near Gettysburg, Pa., where he wrote his memoirs.
Eisenhower died in March 1969.

Millard Fillmore

Born: Jan. 7, 1800
Died: March 8, 1874
Place of Birth:
  Locke Township,
  N.Y.

Political Party: Whig
Term: 1850-1853
Electoral Vote: None
Vice-President: None

Fillmore, Millard (1800-1874), was the 13th President of the United States. He became the second Vice-President to succeed to the presidency, but that was not his only claim to recognition. During the bitter sectional controversy over slavery in the early 1850's, Fillmore kept the nation on a compromise course.

Fillmore was born into a farm family in Locke Township, N.Y., on Jan. 7, 1800. He received little formal schooling, and at age 15 became apprenticed to a clothmaker. After buying his freedom from his master, Fillmore taught school and studied law. He began practicing law in 1823 in East Aurora, N.Y. Three years later, he married Abigail Powers, a Baptist minister's daughter.

A seat in the New York assembly, to which he was elected in 1828, marked Fillmore's first political experience. In 1832, he won election to the U.S. House of Representatives, where he served two terms.

Fillmore joined the Whig Party when it was formed in the 1830's. In Congress, he generally supported Whig policies of high tariffs and federal aid for domestic improvements. After serving in Con-

gress, he ran for the governorship of New York in 1844, but lost.

Fillmore remained prominent enough to gain the Whig nomination for the vice-presidency in 1848. War hero General Zachary Taylor was the presidential nominee. Democrats split that year, many of them voting for the Free Soil Party, a group that opposed the extension of slavery. Taylor and Fillmore won the election.

Taylor died 16 months after his inauguration, and Millard Fillmore became President. The United States had won a war with Mexico in 1848, and had acquired vast new territories in the West, including California (see Polk, James K.). A gold rush in California rapidly increased the population there, and by 1849, the territory was ready for admission to the Union. The issue of California statehood brought the slavery issue to the surface again. With the admission to statehood of Iowa and Wisconsin, the number of slave and free states stood at 15 each. California's admission would upset the balance, giving antislavery forces more representation in Congress. President Taylor had opposed compromise on the California question. But in Congress, such men as Daniel Webster, Henry Clay, and Stephen A. Douglas proceeded with compromise measures anyway.

President Fillmore proved as willing to bend on the issues as Taylor had been opposed. Fillmore signed the bills that made up the Compromise of 1850. One of the bills admitted California as a free state. Another organized New Mexico and Utah as territories, allowing the people there to settle the slavery question when the territories were admitted as states. Another bill forbade the slave trade in the District of Columbia. Finally, to appease the South, a fourth bill provided for a stronger fugitive slave act.

Millard Fillmore wholeheartedly supported compromise, and he urged the nation to accept it. But historians disagree on whether the Compromise of 1850 was really a compromise, or only a truce between the North and the South. The Fugitive Slave Law, which increased the use of federal power to return runaway slaves to their masters, up-

set those who wanted slavery abolished. Agitation against the law in Wisconsin eventually caused the supreme court there to declare the Fugitive Slave Law null and void within the state. Similar action occurred in Pennsylvania. Fillmore, however, insisted on rigid enforcement of the Fugitive Slave Law, and this cost him support in the North. In 1852, the Whigs passed him over to nominate an antislavery candidate, General Winfield Scott, for President.

A month after he left office in 1853, Fillmore's wife died. He remarried in 1858. He resumed his law practice in New York, but he was not finished with politics. The Know-Nothings, an anti-Catholic, anti-immigrant group, nominated him for the presidency in 1856. The Whigs that year also turned to Fillmore as their nominee. He ran third, however, behind the candidate of the newly formed Republican Party and the Democratic winner, James Buchanan. Although he opposed many of Abraham Lincoln's policies, Fillmore was relatively inactive during the Civil War. He died in 1874.

Gerald R. Ford

Born: July 14, 1913
Place of Birth:
    Omaha, Nebr.
Political Party: Republican

Term: 1974-1977
Electoral Vote: None
Vice-President:
    Nelson A. Rockefeller

Ford, Gerald R. (1913-   ), was the 38th President of the United States. In 1973, Gerald R. Ford became the first appointed Vice-President. A year later, he became the first person to take office as President following a chief executive's resignation.

Ford was born in Omaha, Nebr., on July 14, 1913. Following his parents' divorce in 1915, he lived with his mother in Grand Rapids, Mich. Educated there, Ford went on to the University of Michigan, graduating in 1935. He later attended Yale Law School, earning his degree in 1941.

After serving as a naval officer during World War II, Ford returned to Grand Rapids to practice law. He was elected to the U.S. House of Representatives as a Republican in 1948. That same year he married Elizabeth (Betty) Bloomer, a dancer and fashion model.

In Congress, Ford established a record as a conservative, hard-working, and loyal party member. He served for a time as chairman of the Republican Conference and was a member of the Warren Commission, which investigated the assassination of President John F. Kennedy. He also served as House minority leader, beginning in 1965.

In 1973, Vice-President Spiro Agnew was charged with taking bribes and evading income tax payments. He resigned his office. President Richart M. Nixon then appointed Ford Vice-President, with congressional approval. During the Watergate investigation, Ford made numerous speeches defending the President and proclaiming his belief in Nixon's innocence. Under threat of impeachment, Nixon resigned the presidency on Aug. 9, 1974, and Ford became President (see Nixon, Richard M.). Ford then appointed Nelson Rockefeller Vice-President. For the first time in U.S. history, the two highest offices in the land were filled by persons who had not been elected to them.

Because of the Watergate scandal, public confidence in government was low when Ford took office. Ford's popularity suffered when he granted Nixon a pardon for any crimes he might have committed while President. Ford was also criticized by liberals for his program of limited amnesty to Vietnam draft evaders. The program required up to two years of public service work to avoid prosecution.

Inflation and recession were two of Ford's most difficult domestic problems. The annual rate of inflation topped 10 per cent, and the rate of unemployment went beyond 9 per cent. Ford established the Council on Wage and Price Stability, and approved legislation to lower taxes and to create some federal service jobs. Inflation slowed somewhat, and unemployment dropped only very slowly as the nation moved toward economic recovery in 1975 and 1976.

In foreign affairs, Ford continued Nixon's policy of improving relations with China and the Soviet Union. Ford met with Soviet leaders in Vladivostok and journeyed to China to confer with leaders there. United States aid to South Vietnam continued until early in 1975, when Congress refused the additional funds Ford requested. In April of that year, the Vietnam War ended in a victory for North Vietnam.

Ford's bid for the 1976 Republican presidential nomination was hotly contested by Ronald Reagan, former governor of California. Both men entered numerous primaries and arrived at the Republican convention with an almost equal number of committed votes. Ford won the nomination, however, on the first ballot. He selected Kansas Senator Robert J. Dole as his running mate. Ford and Dole lost the election to Democrats Jimmy Carter and Walter F. Mondale. After leaving the presidency, Ford served on the board of directors of several companies. He also spent much time lecturing at colleges and universities and speaking to organizations.

James A. Garfield

Born: Nov. 19, 1831
Died: Sept. 19, 1881
Place of Birth:
    Orange, Ohio
Political Party: Republican

Term: 1881
Electoral Vote: 214
Vice-President:
    Chester A. Arthur

Garfield, James A. (1831-1881), was the 20th President of the United States. He was the fourth chief executive to die in office and the second to be assassinated. His death stimulated the enactment of important governmental reform.

Born in Orange, Ohio, on Nov. 19,

1831, Garfield received his early education in the local schools. At age 20, he entered what is now Hiram College in Ohio, and after three years there, continued at Williams College, in Massachusetts. After graduating from Williams in 1856, Garfield became a professor of literature and ancient languages at Hiram. At age 26, he was named president of the college. In 1858, he married Lucretia Rudolph, an Ohio farmer's daughter. Garfield served in the Union Army during the Civil War. He rose from lieutenant colonel to major general.

James Garfield's political career had begun in 1856, when he campaigned for Republican presidential candidate John C. Frémont. In 1859, Garfield was elected to the Ohio senate. While still in the army, he won election to the U.S. House of Representatives. After the war, he was reelected to eight additional terms.

The Ohio legislature elected Garfield to the U.S. Senate in 1880, and he became a member of the delegation to the Republican presidential convention. The delegates were deadlocked between former President Ulysses S. Grant and Senator James G. Blaine of Maine. On the 36th ballot, Garfield was chosen as the compromise candidate. Chester A. Arthur was named his running mate. In the election, Garfield and Arthur defeated the Democratic candidates by only about 40,000 votes, but they won in the electoral college, 214 to 155.

The Republican infighting displayed at the convention continued into Garfield's Administration. In his appointments, Garfield favored the faction known as the "Half-Breeds," headed by Blaine. Their rivals were the "Stalwarts," led by Senator Roscoe Conkling of New York. Blaine had been instrumental in swinging the nomination to Garfield, and the President rewarded Blaine by making him secretary of state. Garfield infuriated Conkling and his faction by appointing a Half-Breed as collector of the Port of New York City.

Since the Grant Administration in the late 1860's and 1870's, politics had been characterized by widespread corruption. Garfield himself had been accused of accepting bribes while in the House, though the charges were never proved. He admitted taking $5,000 from a construction company in return for his aid in obtaining a paving contract in Washington, D.C., but he claimed the act was not improper. Political machines controlled state and city governments. At each election, machine workers rounded up the vote, herding recently arrived immigrants to the polls in large cities. Ballots and political favors were bought and sold. Many persons were encouraged to vote "early and often," for a fee, moving from one polling place to another. The "spoils system" of filling jobs continued to be practiced (see Jackson, Andrew).

Garfield's assassination in 1881 stimulated an effort to change the system and reduce the corruption in American politics. In the summer of that year, President Garfield planned to attend a class reunion at Williams College. As he stood at the crowded Washington railroad station on July 2, waiting to board his train, a man stepped from the throng. Firing two pistol shots at the President, the man shouted: "I am a Stalwart, and Arthur is President now!" Garfield fell to the floor, alive, but badly wounded. Police immediately arrested the attacker, Charles J. Guiteau, who turned out to be a disappointed office-seeker.

One bullet had wounded Garfield's arm slightly. The other had lodged in his back, and doctors were unable to locate it. For 80 days, Garfield clung to life, while an uncontrollable infection set in. Gradually, his strength gave way. On Sept. 19, 1881, in a house in New Jersey where he had been moved, the President died.

Ulysses S. Grant

Born: April 27, 1822
Died: July 23, 1885
Place of Birth:
    Point Pleasant, Ohio
Political Party: Republican

Terms: 1869-1877
Electoral Vote: 214; 286
Vice-Presidents:
    Schuyler Colfax;
    Henry Wilson

Grant, Ulysses S. (1822-1885), was the 18th President of the United States. As commander of the Union forces during the Civil War, Ulysses S. Grant became a national hero, and his war record gained him the presidency. But Grant proved incapable as President. Most historians consider his administration one of the poorest on record, because of scandals that involved some of his chief appointees.

Grant was born on April 27, 1822, in Point Pleasant, Ohio. His father was a tanner and farmer. After completing elementary and one year of secondary school, Grant won appointment to the United States Military Academy at West Point. He graduated as a second lieutenant in 1843. He fought at Monterrey and Veracruz during the Mexican War. In 1848, he married Julia Dent, a West Point classmate's sister.

Tired of the loneliness of army life, Grant resigned his commission in 1854. During the next few years, he unsuccessfully tried farming, dealing in real estate, and storekeeping. The outbreak of the Civil War in 1861 brought him an opportunity for success.

Grant began his Civil War service as a colonel in a regiment of Illinois volunteers. He soon rose to the rank of brigadier general. Early in 1862, he led troops against Fort Henry on the Tennessee River. The Union forces captured the fort easily. Later, he fought a Confederate army to a standstill at Shiloh. Grant then captured Vicksburg, Miss., giving Union forces control of the Mississippi River. His next victory came at Chattanooga, Tenn.

Grant's success in the west attracted President Abraham Lincoln's attention. In 1864, Lincoln brought Grant east, and placed him in command of all Union forces. Grant's major strategy was to attack repeatedly. Although his army suffered heavy losses, Grant gradually wore down the Confederate forces under General Robert E. Lee. On April 9, 1865, Lee surrendered to Grant at Appomattox Court House, Va.

Ulysses S. Grant's wartime popularity brought him the Republican nomination for President in 1868. He won election by a huge majority. Grant won a second term in 1872 by easily defeating New York newspaper publisher Horace Greeley, the candidate of both the Democrats and of a splinter Republican group. Although Grant himself was not involved, his administration is best remembered for political corruption.

The first transcontinental railway system from the Midwest to California was completed in 1869. Railroad promoters had formed a separate construction company, Credit Mobilier, to build one of the roads. The company profited handsomely by charging as much as $50,000 a mile for track that actually cost about half that much to lay. To conceal their scheme, company officials bribed some government officials, and several members of Congress. In St. Louis, members of the "Whiskey Ring" sealed their bottles of liquor with counterfeit revenue stamps. As a result, the Treasury lost millions of dollars in taxes, and members of the St. Louis group gained about $2.5 million. Evidence indicated that government officials sold trading post rights on Indian reservations for their own profit. There were other scandals, too.

The Grant administration did succeed in reducing the national debt. It also reached a settlement with Great Britain over the issue of payments for Civil War damages caused by ships built in Britain for the Confederacy. But Grant ran into trouble when he tried to purchase the Dominican Republic for the United States. His action angered those who supported black independence and political rights. And during Grant's second term, his administration had to weather an economic depression that began in 1873.

Grant left the White House in 1877 with about $100,000 in savings. He invested it in a banking firm, and lost it all. To pay his debts, Grant wrote his memoirs, which earned his family half a million dollars. Author Mark Twain was his publisher. He died of cancer in 1885, shortly after completing the work.

Warren Gamaliel Harding

Born: Nov. 2, 1865
Died: Aug. 2, 1923
Place of Birth:
   near Blooming Grove,
   Ohio

Political Party: Republican
Term: 1921-1923
Electoral Vote: 404
Vice-President:
   Calvin Coolidge

Harding, Warren Gamaliel (1865-1923), was the 29th President of the United States. Harding was an able politician. But he is most commonly remembered for the scandals that occurred during his administration.

The son of a farmer, Harding was born on Nov. 2, 1865, near what is now Blooming Grove, Ohio. Following his graduation from secondary school, he taught school, studied law, and sold insurance. In 1884, Harding and two partners bought the *Marion Star,* a failing Ohio newspaper. The paper prospered under Harding's guidance. In 1891, Harding married Florence Kling DeWolfe.

Harding entered politics in 1898, when he won election to the Ohio senate as a Republican. In 1903, he became lieutenant governor of Ohio. He lost the race for the governorship in 1910, but four years later, he won election to the United States Senate. As a senator, he usually supported the Republican leadership.

Urged on by his wife and by Ohio political friend Harry M. Daugherty, Harding made himself available as a compromise candidate at the Republican presidential convention in 1920. He had numerous assets. He was conservative, and the public was ready for conservatism. He was a fine orator. And, people said, the tall, white-haired Harding "looked like a President." He won nomination on the tenth ballot. In November 1920, he was elected by about 60 per cent of the popular vote over Democrat James M. Cox. The election was the first in which women throughout the nation voted.

Harding offered no program. He would, he had said, return the country to "normalcy," a word he made popular, and which meant different things to different people. To Americans weary of war and the affairs of a troubled world, normalcy, whatever its meaning, seemed ideal.

Harding did not believe in a strong presidency. He felt the country's leadership should come mainly from Congress. Congress kept the United States out of the League of Nations. It raised tariff rates to new heights. It imposed immigration quotas for the first time. And it reduced taxes, especially on high incomes.

President Harding made both wise and poor choices in selecting his advisors. Secretary of Commerce Herbert Hoover and Secretary of State Charles Evans Hughes were widely respected. But Harding appointed incompetent friends to several important positions, including Albert B. Fall as secretary of the interior, Daugherty as attorney general, and Charles R. Forbes as head of the Veterans' Bureau. These men, and others, became involved in scandal.

In exchange for bribes, Fall arranged for oil companies to lease government-owned petroleum reserves in California and Wyoming. This affair became known as the Teapot Dome scandal, because one of the oil reserve areas was located in Teapot Dome, Wyo. Forbes took bribes for awarding building contracts for veterans' hospitals to certain construction firms. Daugherty was accused of mismanagement and bribery. Fall went to prison for one year, Forbes was jailed for two years, and Daugherty was eventually freed of charges. Harding was not personally involved in any of the wrongdoing. He was, however, responsible for the men he had placed in office.

The United States suffered a brief economic depression in 1921, and farm prices did not recover rapidly afterward. Partly because of this, Republicans lost a number of congressional seats in 1922. The following summer, to bolster his administration's image, Harding set off on a cross-country speaking tour that took him into Canada and to Alaska. While on the trip, Harding received the first news of the Teapot Dome scandal. Arriving at Seattle on the return journey, the President became ill. He insisted on continuing, but became ill again in San Francisco. He died there on August 2. The precise cause of his death was never made clear. Some evidence of food poisoning seemed to exist, but other evidence indicated a heart attack.

Benjamin Harrison

Born: Aug. 20, 1833
Died: March 13, 1901
Place of Birth:
   North Bend, Ohio
Political Party: Republican

Term: 1889-1893
Electoral Vote: 233
Vice-President:
   Levi P. Morton

Harrison, Benjamin (1833-1901), was the 23rd President of the United States. He was the only grandson of a President also to become President. His grandfather was William Henry Harrison.

Benjamin Harrison was born on his grandfather's estate in North Bend, Ohio, on Aug. 20, 1833. He was named after his great-grandfather, a signer of the Declaration of Independence. After spending his early years on the farm, Harrison attended a small college near Cincinnati. In 1852, he graduated from Miami University of Ohio. The following year, he married Caroline Lavinia Scott, daughter of a woman's college president.

Harrison became a lawyer in 1854 and moved to Indianapolis. He won election there as city attorney in 1857. Beginning in 1860, he served three terms as reporter for the Indiana Supreme Court.

In 1862, Harrison recruited the 70th Regiment of Indiana Volunteers. Although only 5 feet 6 inches tall, he proved an able and fearless commander, leading his unit in numerous battles. He ended the war as a brigadier general.

Following the war, Harrison resumed his law practice. He failed in his attempt to win the Indiana governorship in 1876. But in 1881, he gained a seat in the Senate, as a Republican. Seven years later, Harrison became the Republican nominee for the presidency. His war record and his popularity with Civil War veterans were great assets. And his relationship to William Henry Harrison, the hero of the Battle of Tippecanoe in 1811, helped, too. Harrison did not, however, win the popular vote. He lost by 90,000 votes to Democratic President Grover Cleveland. But Harrison won the electoral vote, 233 to 168, and thus became President of the United States.

Harrison's Administration is best remembered for four pieces of legislation: the Dependent Pension Act, which benefited veterans; the McKinley Tariff Act; the Sherman Silver Purchase Act; and the Sherman Antitrust Act.

As a senator, Harrison had supported a veterans' pension bill, which President Cleveland vetoed. The measure, passed under Harrison's Administration in 1890, raised the federal pension outlay to $159 million from $88 million.

Tariffs were an important issue during the late 1800's. Industrialists wanted high tariffs, or taxes, on imported manufactured goods. Farmers and working people supported low tariffs. The McKinley Tariff Act set rates at the highest they had ever been, increasing the cost of living for everyone.

Low prices for farm products caused farmers to demand an inflationary increase in the money supply. In particular, they wanted an increase in the amount of silver coins in circulation. Owners of silver mines supported the idea. The Sherman Silver Purchase Act allowed the government to buy silver with notes that could be redeemed in silver or gold. Most note holders preferred gold. As a result, the nation's gold supply dwindled. This helped to create a financial crisis in 1893 and eventually a depression.

After the Civil War, some large businesses and industries formed trusts, which gave control of production and markets to a few firms and destroyed competition. Such practices tended to increase prices, to the disadvantage of farmers and other working people and also threatened the well-being of small-business men. The Sherman Antitrust Act of 1890 outlawed trusts that could be shown to hinder trade.

By the 1890's, the industrial growth of the United States had made it one of the world's great powers. In keeping with the spirit of the time, President Harrison approved a program to create a two-ocean navy. His administration also negotiated trade treaties with Latin American countries, and hosted the first Pan-American Conference in Washington in 1889. In far-off Hawaii, American sugar and pineapple planters led a successful revolt against the queen, Liliuokalani, in 1893. The new Hawaiian government wanted Hawaii to be annexed to the United States, and requested territorial status. In the meantime, Harrison had lost the 1892 election to Grover Cleveland. Despite his election loss, Harrison presented the Hawaii annexation bill to the Senate. Before the Senate could act, however, the Cleveland Administration took power and rejected Hawaii's request for annexation.

After leaving the presidency, Harrison returned to his law practice. He died in Indianapolis in 1901.

William Henry Harrison

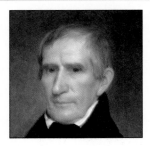

Born: Feb. 9, 1773
Died: April 4, 1841
Place of Birth:
   Charles City
   County, Va.

Political Party: Whig
Term: 1841
Electoral Vote: 234
Vice-President:
   John Tyler

Harrison, William Henry (1773-1841), was the ninth President of the United States. As President, he is remembered for three things. He served the shortest term: about 30 days. He was the first President to die in office. And, most important, after Harrison, presidential campaigns were never the same again.

The youngest son of seven children, Harrison was born in Virginia in 1773. His father, Benjamin, was a signer of the Declaration of Independence.

For most of his adult life, Harrison was either in the army or in government. He joined the army after attending Hampden-Sydney College in Virginia and became an officer. While in the army, Harrison married Anna Symmes, daughter of a wealthy landowner.

In 1798, President John Adams appointed Harrison secretary of the Northwest Territory, an area later divided into the states of Ohio, Indiana, Illinois, Michigan, Minnesota, and Wisconsin. Between 1801 and 1812, Harrison served as appointed governor of the Indiana Territory.

In 1811, Indians of the Northwest became resentful over attempts to settle on

Indian land. Led by Tecumseh, the Indians tried to drive out the settlers. Governor Harrison led U.S. forces to victory over the Indians at Tippecanoe Creek, near present-day Lafayette, Ind. During the War of 1812, Harrison commanded U.S. troops against Indian and British forces at the battle of the Thames, in Canada.

Harrison's military record helped him politically. Following the war, between 1816 and 1828 he served the state of Ohio as a state senator and a U.S. congressman and senator. In 1828, he became minister to Colombia, a position that he held for one year.

Returning from Colombia, Harrison became a member of the new Whig Party, led by such giants in Congress as Daniel Webster and Henry Clay. Because the party was young and made up of opposing interests, Whig leaders in 1836 sought a candidate for President who had taken no strong stand on such issues as high tariffs and internal improvements. In the end, in order to satisfy all interests, the Whigs nominated four regional candidates. Harrison was one of the four, and he was presented as a military hero. Although Harrison made a good showing, he and the other Whigs lost to the sole Democratic candidate, Martin Van Buren, who had been Andrew Jackson's Vice-President.

The Whigs turned to Harrison again four years later, this time as their one candidate. They chose John Tyler of Virginia as their vice-presidential candidate. The Democrats stayed with Van Buren. And the 1840 campaign proved an exciting one, much different from any past presidential campaign.

For the first time, a presidential candidate "stumped" the country, taking his campaign to the people. Harrison gave more than 20 speeches, appearing before as many as 100,000 persons at a time. Besides "stump" speeches, politicians organized barbecues, torchlight parades, and campfire rallies. Campaign slogans and songs found their place in American politics. "Tippecanoe and Tyler Too" became the principal Whig slogan. Others were "To Guide the Ship, We'll Try Old Tip," and "Farewell, Dear Van, You're Not Our Man." One song ran, in part:

Tippecanoe and Tyler too,
Oh, with them we'll best little Van, Van,
Van is a used-up man.

The energetic campaign paid off. In 1836, slightly more than 1,500,000 votes had been cast. In 1840, the total was 2,402,405. Harrison received 53 per cent of the popular vote, defeating Martin Van Buren.

On Inauguration Day, President Harrison caught a cold. He died of pneumonia a month later.

Rutherford B. Hayes

Born: Oct. 4, 1822
Died: Jan. 17, 1893
Place of Birth:
    Delaware, Ohio
Political Party: Republican

Term: 1877-1881
Electoral Vote: 185
Vice-President:
    William A. Wheeler

Hayes, Rutherford B. (1822-1893), was the 19th President of the United States. He won the first disputed presidential election in the history of the United States, the election of 1876.

The son of a store owner, Hayes was born in Delaware, Ohio, on Oct. 4, 1822. His father died before Rutherford was born. Hayes graduated from Kenyon College in Ohio in 1842, then attended

Harvard Law School, and was admitted to the bar in 1845.

After a slow start, Hayes established a successful law practice in Cincinnati, Ohio. In 1852, he married Lucy Ware Webb, a physician's daughter. Appointed city attorney in 1858, he remained in that position until the outbreak of the Civil War. Hayes served as a major of a regiment of Ohio volunteers during the war, and he proved to be an able commander. He rose to the rank of major general.

Hayes was elected to Congress while still in the army. He took his seat in the House as a Republican in December 1865. He served until 1867, when he won the first of three terms as governor of Ohio.

Fraud and corruption in government had marred the Republican Administration of war hero Ulysses S. Grant (see Grant, Ulysses S.). Democrats saw a chance for victory in 1876 as the Republicans split over the corruption issue and could not agree on a candidate. The Republicans eventually chose Hayes as a compromise candidate, but he lost to the Democratic nominee, Samuel J. Tilden, by about 200,000 votes. Returns from four states—Louisiana, South Carolina, Florida, and Oregon—were disputed, and both sides claimed victory. Congress created an electoral commission to decide which electoral votes should go to whom. The issue was not decided until 1877, a few days before the inauguration.

To solve the problem, Southern Democrats agreed not to oppose the Hayes election. In return, the Republicans agreed to the removal of federal troops that had been stationed in the South since the Civil War. The final electoral vote was 185 to 184 in Hayes's favor. He pulled the troops out a month later.

The removal of the troops allowed Southern Democrats to regain political control of the South gradually. Northern Democrats felt that the bargain between the Southerners and the Republicans was corrupt, and many historians agree. But others have concluded that the wounds of war needed healing, and the troops would have soon been withdrawn in any case.

Hayes had won a reputation as an able and honest administrator as governor of Ohio, and he believed that government appointments should be based on merit rather than political connections. He announced that he would not seek a second presidential term so that he could push for a federal merit system, an effort that would gain him enemies. He advocated reform, but Congress refused to accept his proposals. Although he failed, Hayes opened the way to later civil service reform.

True to his word, Rutherford B. Hayes did not seek a second term as President. In 1881, following the inauguration of James A. Garfield, he retired to his home in Fremont, Ohio, and withdrew from politics. Hayes devoted the years following his presidency to religion, prison reform, and philanthropy. He died at his home in 1893.

Herbert Clark Hoover

Born: Aug. 10, 1874
Died: Oct. 20, 1964
Place of Birth:
    West Branch, Iowa
Political Party: Republican

Term: 1929-1933
Electoral Vote: 444
Vice-President:
    Charles Curtis

Hoover, Herbert Clark (1874-1964), was the 31st President of the United States. He enjoyed a reputation as a brilliant engineer, public servant, and government official. Then, blamed for the severe economic depression that began during his presidency, Hoover found his reputation badly tarnished.

West Branch, Iowa, was Hoover's birthplace. He was born on Aug. 10, 1874, and orphaned at age 9. He then lived with relatives in Iowa and later in Oregon. Hoover completed secondary school in Oregon and went on to Stanford University to study mining engineering. At age 23, he got a job managing gold mines in Australia. Returning to the United States, he married Lou Henry, a banker's daughter, in 1899. He and his bride then left for China, where he continued his mining career. Later, Hoover became a partner in an engineering firm in London. In 1908, he opened his own firm, which, by 1914, made him a millionaire.

Hoover won international fame for his direction of relief work in Belgium during World War I. He then became head of the United States Food Administra-

tion, which directed food distribution in the United States during the war. After the war, Hoover administered the distribution of food to millions of people in Europe. His achievements made Hoover a popular figure. He refused to be nominated as the Republican presidential candidate in 1920, but he accepted the position of secretary of commerce under President Warren G. Harding. Hoover remained in that office until he was nominated for the presidency in 1928.

For many people the 1920's were prosperous years. And in 1928, the Republicans had no trouble persuading voters that the Republican Party was responsible for prosperity. The Republicans promised that good times would continue under Hoover. Hoover won an overwhelming victory over Democrat Al Smith, the first Catholic ever nominated for the presidency by a major party.

A shy, retiring man, with a round face and ruddy complexion, Hoover displayed little warmth in public. But he was an excellent administrator.

During his Administration, the London Naval Treaty, limiting the size of navies, was signed. Some friendly over-tures were made toward Latin American nations. Hoover brought home U.S. troops that had been stationed in Nicaragua since 1912 and agreed to withdraw U.S. forces from Haiti, where they had been since 1915. With Hoover's approval, Congress established the Federal Farm Board, which purchased surplus crops and encouraged the formation of cooperatives to raise farm income.

On the other hand, he signed the Hawley-Smoot Tariff Bill, which raised import duties enormously. Because the new tariffs increased the price of manufactured goods and discouraged trade, they contributed to the depression that began in 1929.

Seven months after Hoover's inauguration, the stock market collapsed, causing losses estimated at $40 billion. The market did not recover, and the United States slid into a terrible depression. By 1932, about 12 million persons were out of work.

Hoover favored government aid to business. When the depression continued longer than he had expected it to, he supported the establishment of the Reconstruction Finance Corporation, which offered loans to depression-hit businesses. He opposed direct federal aid to the unemployed. But, when the relief load became unbearable for state and local governments, he approved federal loans to states to help them out. Hoover also supported such federal projects as dam construction to put people to work.

The unemployed and homeless lived in colonies of tar-paper shacks called "Hoovervilles" and slept on park benches under old newspapers called "Hoover blankets." After being persuaded that prosperity would last forever, Americans now blamed Hoover for the depression hardships.

Hoover left office in 1933 an unpopular man, overwhelmed by the Democratic victor, Franklin D. Roosevelt. Hoover spent the rest of his life in public service. He served on numerous commissions, and also wrote his memoirs. He died in 1964, at age 90.

Andrew Jackson

Born: March 15, 1767
Died: June 8, 1845
Place of Birth:
    Waxhaw settlement,
    S.C.?
Political Party: Democrat

Terms: 1829-1837
Electoral Vote: 178; 219
Vice-Presidents:
    John C. Calhoun;
    Martin Van Buren

Jackson, Andrew (1767-1845), was the seventh President of the United States. Unlike earlier Presidents, Andrew Jackson came from a poor frontier family. But he gained a military reputation that greatly aided him in politics. He became the first Westerner and the first "man of the people" to be elected President.

Jackson was born in a log cabin on the border between North and South Carolina on March 15, 1767. His father died a few days before Andrew's birth, and his mother died of cholera when he was 14.

At age 17, Jackson began to study law in Salisbury, N.C. and was eventually admitted to the bar. But he became better known for his brawling and dueling than for his legal talent. Moving west in the late 1780's, Jackson settled in Nashville, Tenn. There he met Rachel Donelson Robards, a divorcée and daughter of a widowed boarding-house keeper. He married her in 1791. At the time of their marriage, however, Jackson and his wife did not realize that her divorce from her first husband had not yet become final. When they learned this, they went

through another marriage ceremony after the divorce was completed. In addition to practicing law, Jackson made money by buying and selling land. By the late 1790's, he owned two plantations. One, the Hermitage, near Nashville, became his lifelong home.

Jackson's political career began when he helped write the Tennessee constitution. After that state's admission to the Union in 1796, he won election to the U.S. House of Representatives. Jackson later served a brief term in the Senate, and served as a Tennessee supreme court justice for six years.

In 1814, as a major general in the Tennessee militia, Jackson led a band of volunteers against the Creek Indians. The Creek had destroyed a fort and massacred more than 200 people in Alabama. Jackson defeated the Creek and forced them to give up millions of acres of land in Alabama and Georgia. Later that year, President James Madison ordered Jackson to New Orleans. There, Jackson organized the city's defenses in preparation for what would be the final battle of the War of 1812 against the

British. The attack came in January 1815, and resulted in a stunning American victory over the British forces. Although a peace treaty had been signed in Europe the month before, Jackson gained a national reputation as the "hero of New Orleans." Following the war, he led an expedition against the Seminole Indians in Florida and then retired to the Hermitage.

Jackson did not remain in retirement long, however. Tennessee politicians were soon talking of him as a presidential nominee. And in 1824, as one of four candidates, Jackson received the highest number of electoral votes, 99. But this fell short of a majority, and the House of Representatives had to choose the winner. Henry Clay, Speaker of the House, had received the lowest number of votes in the election and thus was out of the running. He threw his support behind John Quincy Adams, whom the House then selected as President. After taking office, Adams appointed Clay as secretary of state. This infuriated Jackson and his followers. They charged that Adams had made a corrupt bargain with Clay for the presidency. Jackson's followers spent the next four years preparing for the election of 1828.

During the early 1800's, the West was a land of opportunity. And as more Western states joined the Union, that region grew in political influence. In more and more states, property qualifications for voting were set aside. The frontier, where a person had to depend on his own ability to make a living in the wilderness, was an equalizer. Accomplishment, rather than wealth and social position, was the measure of a person's worth. A broadly based political democracy was developing and a period of history described as the "age of the common man" was about to begin. It was under these circumstances that Andrew Jackson, a "self-made man," helped found and became the leader of the new Democratic Party.

The controversy over Adams' election four years earlier was only one of many issues raised in the 1828 campaign, which became the bitterest of any in American history. Because the Jacksons had been married before her divorce was final, Mrs. Jackson was called an adulteress. Jackson never shook his belief that the vicious accusations against him and his wife contributed to her death from a heart attack in December 1828. With strong support from farmers and working men, Jackson won the election with 56 per cent of the popular vote, and a 95-vote margin in the electoral college.

As a "people's President," Jackson opened the White House to huge crowds on Inauguration Day. They caused considerable damage, arousing criticism of the President among some more dignified observers.

Andrew Jackson believed that loyalty, not just competence, qualified a person for a government job. He also believed that "to the victor belong the spoils" of political office. Jackson is credited with introducing the "spoils system" to presidential politics, though the practice of giving jobs to party loyalists had been followed by previous Presidents.

Numerous other controversies marked the Jackson presidency. In 1828, Congress passed a bill setting high tariff rates on imported manufactured goods. This displeased the South, where many such goods were marketed. In 1832, Congress lowered the rates, but only a little. John C. Calhoun of South Carolina, Jackson's Vice-President, argued that under the Constitution, a state had the right to nullify—declare null and void—any federal law that harmed its interest. South Carolina then voted to nullify both tariff laws. Nullification threatened the Union, and Jackson and Congress responded with legislation that authorized the President to use armed force, if necessary, to collect tariffs. South Carolina withdrew its nullification of the tariff laws, but then nullified the armed force bill. In the meantime, a compromise tariff was worked out.

The Bank of the United States, established during George Washington's presidency, possessed great power over the nation's money system and loan policies. Jackson opposed the bank as a monopoly. He also favored gold and silver over paper currency. In 1832, Nicholas Biddle, the bank president, applied for renewal of the institution's charter. Congress consented, but Jackson vetoed the bill. He later withdrew federal deposits from the bank. In spite of severe criticism from business interests, the President had destroyed the bank. That same year, 1832, he easily won election to a second term.

Jackson's Indian policy also met with criticism. Whites in Georgia wanted the Cherokee Indians removed from the state. Jackson supported the Georgians. The Supreme Court of the United States, however, decided that, by treaty, the Cherokee were an independent nation, outside the limits of state control. Jackson refused to enforce the decision, and the Cherokee finally were forced to move.

During Jackson's second term, land speculation and the issuance of paper money by state banks threatened to cause wild inflation. Jackson, therefore, issued the *Specie Circular* in 1836. It required government officials to accept only gold and silver in the sale of public lands. Jackson succeeded in stopping speculation, but he lost support among Westerners. Overexpansion in business and public works projects continued, however, and led to a panic that caused a depression soon after Jackson left office in 1837.

In foreign affairs, Jackson won a British agreement to open all ports in the West Indies to American shipping. The ports had been closed to the United States since the end of the Revolutionary War. In exchange, all U.S. ports were opened to the British.

During Jackson's Administration, various reform groups intensified their demands that slavery be abolished. Slavery became an issue when Texas, which had won independence from Mexico in 1836, applied for admission to the Union as a slave state. Abolitionists opposed admission. Southerners favored it. Although Jackson himself was a slaveholder, he refused to act on the statehood question. He seemed to understand that the Texas issue, and the related problem of slavery, endangered the Union.

Jackson's second Vice-President, Martin Van Buren, succeeded him as President in 1837. Jackson returned to the Hermitage, where he died in 1845.

Thomas Jefferson

Born: April 13, 1743
Died: July 4, 1826
Place of Birth:
    Goochland (now
    Albemarle) County,
    Va.
Political Party:
    Democratic-Republican

Terms: 1801-1809
Electoral Vote: 73; 162
Vice-Presidents: Aaron Burr;
    George Clinton

Jefferson, Thomas (1743-1826), was the third President of the United States. One of the most talented men ever to occupy the White House, Jefferson was a political philosopher, a writer, an inventor, an educational reformer, an architect, a scientist, and a statesman. He himself wished to be remembered chiefly as the author of the Declaration of Independence and the founder of the University of Virginia.

Jefferson was born on the family plantation in Goochland (now Albemarle) County, Virginia, on April 13, 1743. Jefferson inherited the estate of more than 2,000 acres and more than a dozen slaves at age 14, when his father died. Beginning at age 16, he spent two years at the College of William and Mary, and in 1767, became a lawyer. Five years later, Jefferson married Martha Wayles Skelton, a widow and a lawyer's daughter.

Jefferson's first political experience came in 1769, when he was elected to the Virginia House of Burgesses. His

colleagues in the House of Burgesses included such figures as Patrick Henry and Richard Henry Lee. The Virginia legislators opposed British tax and trade policies for the colonies. And in 1775, as relations with England moved toward the breaking point, Jefferson became a member of the Second Continental Congress. Previously, Jefferson had declared that the British Parliament had no authority over the colonies, but that the colonists owed allegiance only to the king. In Congress, he drafted a "Declaration of the Causes and Necessity of Taking up Arms," but the other delegates considered its language of resistance too strong. In the summer of 1776, however, Jefferson was named to a committee to draft a declaration of independence. The other committee members chose Jefferson to prepare the document. The Declaration of Independence, which the Congress adopted that July, is Jefferson's best-known work.

At the outbreak of the Revolution, Jefferson, who did not wish to serve in the military, returned to the Virginia legislature. Jefferson was interested in curbing aristocratic power, and he successfully worked for the abolition of *primogeniture* and *entail*. Primogeniture required a property owner to will all his land to his eldest son. Under entail, a person could not dispose of land as he wished, but had to will it to a particular individual. The end of primogeniture and entail meant that numerous large estates in Virginia were broken up. At the time, a person needed to own property to vote. Because more land was available for purchase, more people could now vote. Jefferson's efforts also led to the removal of state support from the Anglican Church in Virginia. As an institution established by law, the church had been supported by public tax money. Jefferson served as governor of Virginia for two one-year terms, in 1779, and again in 1780.

Jefferson's wife died in 1782. He accepted election to Congress the following year in the hope that political activity would divert him from his grief. As a congressman, Jefferson became best known for drafting a law that formed the basis for the political organization of western lands. Later, he served as United States minister to France. There, he sympathized with the French Revolution, which began in 1789, viewing it as a democratic movement similar to the one he had supported in the United States.

The Constitution went into effect while Jefferson was abroad. George Washington was elected President. After Jefferson's return from France, Washington appointed him secretary of state.

Jefferson left the Cabinet in 1795, and planned to retire to his estate, Monticello. But he accepted the Democratic-Republican nomination for the presidency in 1796. His opponent was Federalist John Adams. Adams won the Electoral College vote and became President. Under the provisions of the Constitution at the time, Jefferson, as runner-up, became Vice-President.

Although he was a member of the Adams Federalist Administration, Jefferson continued as leader of the opposition. He particularly opposed the Alien and Sedition Acts of 1798, which were aimed at curbing Democratic-Republican criticism of the Adams government (see Adams, John).

In 1800, Jefferson defeated Adams and won the presidency. Jefferson put his political philosophies into practice by reducing taxes and government expenditures and the size of the Army and the Navy. His presidency, however, is best remembered for three things: the Supreme Court case *Marbury v. Madison*, the expansion of the United States, and growing troubles with Great Britain.

Before leaving the presidency, John Adams had appointed about 200 Federalist judges under the Judiciary Act of 1801. Jefferson's secretary of state, James Madison, refused to issue commissions to the appointees. One of the judges, William Marbury, asked the Supreme Court to order Madison to grant his commission. The Judiciary Act had given the Supreme Court the power to issue such orders. But the Court refused to do so. According to Chief Justice John Marshall, the power given to the Supreme Court under the Judiciary Act was unconstitutional. By his decision in the case of *Marbury v. Madison*, Marshall thus established the principle under which the Court could review laws and determine their constitutionality. Part of this decision pleased Jefferson, but he was skeptical about judicial review. He feared that this gave the Court supreme power over the other two branches of government. To curb judicial power, Jefferson tried to remove several judges from office, including Supreme Court Justice Samuel Chase, an ardent Federalist. He succeeded in removing only one district judge in New Hampshire.

One of President Jefferson's greatest accomplishments was the Louisiana Purchase. At the time, Louisiana was a vast expanse of land beyond the Mississippi River. It had belonged to Spain, which had given it up to France in 1800. The Spaniards had allowed Americans to use the port of New Orleans, which gave western farmers a gateway through which they could move crops downriver to the sea and world market. Napoleon Bonaparte, who controlled the territory, closed the port. Jefferson in 1803 instructed James Monroe to help Robert R. Livingston, the minister to France, negotiate with Napoleon for the purchase of New Orleans. To the Americans' surprise, Napoleon offered to sell the entire Louisiana Territory to the United States. Jefferson set aside personal doubts about the constitutionality of federal land acquisition and agreed to the purchase. As a result, at a total cost of about $15 million, or a few pennies an acre, Jefferson doubled the size of the United States.

Jefferson easily won reelection in 1804. He defeated the Federalist candidate, Charles C. Pinckney, by an electoral vote of 162 to 14.

Foreign affairs caused problems during much of Jefferson's second term. Great Britain and France were at war in 1803. Both countries tried to destroy each other's ocean commerce. This ben-

efited U.S. commercial interests, because it opened much of the West Indies-Europe trade to United States shipping. Increased trade, however, made it difficult for President Jefferson to maintain American neutrality in the war and at the same time uphold freedom of the seas. Both Britain and France interfered with U.S. vessels. British sailors began deserting to join American merchantmen. British warships stopped American ships to remove the deserters, but they frequently took American sailors, also. The United States was not prepared for war, and Jefferson thought he could end the British and French conflict by denying both nations goods made in America or transported in American ships. The result was the Embargo Act of 1807. It forbade any American trade with the warring countries.

The embargo did not help the situation. Britain and France survived without American trade. Merchants in New England and elsewhere lost money. Shipbuilders were out of work. Warehouses overflowed with goods. Some shippers evaded the law by smuggling. In 1809, just as Jefferson left the presidency, Congress repealed the Embargo Act.

Jefferson was 65 when he retired to Monticello. He devoted much of the remainder of his life to writing, studying, and corresponding with political leaders. His major achievement in retirement was the creation of the University of Virginia, which opened in 1825. At the end of a long life, Jefferson died on July 4, 1826, 50 years after the adoption of the Declaration of Independence.

Andrew Johnson

Born: Dec. 29, 1808
Died: July 31, 1875
Place of Birth: Raleigh, N.C.
Political Party: Democrat
(National Union)

Term: 1865-1869
Electoral Vote: None
Vice-President: None

Johnson, Andrew (1808-1875), was the 17th President of the United States. A Tennessee Democrat, Johnson became Abraham Lincoln's Vice-President in 1865 and succeeded to the presidency following Lincoln's assassination. Johnson was the only President ever to be tried on impeachment charges.

Andrew Johnson was born on Dec. 29, 1808 in Raleigh, N.C. He was apprenticed to a tailor at age 14, and two years later he ran away to South Carolina. There, Johnson set up a tailor shop. Later, he then moved to Tennessee. In 1827, at age 18, he married 16-year-old Eliza McCardle, a shoemaker's daughter.

Johnson became a Democratic follower of Andrew Jackson, who was first elected President in 1828. Johnson's own political career began that same year, when he was elected an alderman in Greenville, Tenn. He later served as the city's mayor. In 1835, he was elected to the Tennessee House of Representatives, and he later held a seat in the state senate. Johnson became a U.S. congressman in 1843. He was known chiefly as a supporter of cheaper western land for settlers.

Johnson lost his seat in the House in 1853, but won election as governor of Tennessee. Four years later, he returned to Washington as a member of the Senate. A slaveholder himself, Johnson generally upheld slavery interests. He was, however, a staunch Union man. When the Civil War began, he supported the war measures of Republican President Abraham Lincoln. When Tennessee voted to secede, Johnson refused to go along.

Johnson's loyalty earned him the post of military governor of Tennessee after federal armies gained control of the western part of the state in 1862. He prepared Tennessee for reentry into the Union (which was accomplished in 1866). In 1864, the Democratic Party split. One group supported the Democratic peace candidate, General George McClellan for the presidency. Democrats who supported the war then joined with other Republicans to nominate Lincoln for a second term. Since he was considered an outstanding War Democrat, Andrew Johnson received the vice-presidential nomination.

Abraham Lincoln was assassinated six weeks after his second inauguration. Johnson became President. And he soon became embroiled in bitter conflicts with Congress.

The end of the war brought numerous problems for the Johnson Administration. Foremost among these problems were the rebuilding of the South, the reentry of the seceded states to the Union, and provisions for blacks freed from slavery. Lincoln's plan for Reconstruction had been to mend the Union as quickly as possible, and in general, Johnson followed Lincoln's lead. Congress was not in session when Johnson became President. He offered amnesty and a pardon to all Southerners, except leaders of the Confederacy, who were willing to swear loyalty to the Constitution of the United States. He also appointed governors for the former Confederate states, and those states soon sent representatives to Congress.

Southern whites ignored blacks' newly won civil rights. Johnson's plan was too mild for so-called Radical Republicans, who wanted to punish the South and to protect freed blacks. Over Johnson's consistent opposition, the Radicals refused to seat Southern members of Congress. Congress then passed the 14th Amendment, which gave civil rights to blacks. Congress also divided the South into five military districts. Most southern whites were not allowed to vote, and numerous blacks were elected to public office in the South.

Relations between Johnson and Congress grew steadily worse, and to curb his power, Congress in 1867 passed the Tenure of Office Act. It forbade the President to remove any official whom he had appointed with the consent of the Senate without also obtaining senatorial approval for the removal. Johnson ignored the act and fired Secretary of War Edwin M. Stanton, an enemy. As a result, the House of Representatives began impeachment proceedings against Johnson, and he was tried in the Senate. The effort to remove Johnson from office failed by only one vote.

Johnson was not nominated for the presidency in 1868, and he returned to Tennessee. He then ran unsuccessfully for Congress and, in 1874, finally won a seat in the Senate. Back in Tennessee, he suffered a stroke and died in the summer of 1875.

Lyndon Baines Johnson

Born: Aug. 27, 1908
Died: Jan. 22, 1973
Place of Birth: near
  Stonewall, Tex.
Political Party: Democrat

Terms: 1963-1969
Electoral Vote: 486
Vice-President:
  Hubert H. Humphrey

Johnson, Lyndon Baines (1908-1973), was the 36th President of the United States. Johnson took office after the assassination of President John F. Kennedy in 1963. He oversaw the enactment of much social legislation and presided over a nation increasingly divided on the issue of the Vietnam War.

Johnson was born on Aug. 27, 1908, near Stonewall, Tex. He entered Southwest Texas State Teachers College in 1927, but later dropped out because of a lack of funds. After working for a time, he returned and was graduated in 1930. Following a brief career as a teacher, Johnson went to Washington as secretary to Texas Representative Richard M. Kleberg. In 1934, he married Claudia Alta (Lady Bird) Taylor, the daughter of a wealthy family.

During the mid-1930's, Johnson served in the National Youth Administration, which employed young people and enabled them to finish high school or college. Johnson won a seat in the House of Representatives in a special election in 1937. During World War II, while still in Congress, he became a naval lieutenant commander. In 1942, he

was reelected to the House. He moved on to the Senate in 1948.

Johnson became Senate minority leader in 1953 and majority leader in 1955. He thoroughly mastered the mechanics of the legislative process and the art of compromise, and he could be counted on to deliver votes. In 1960, Johnson became a candidate for the Democratic presidential nomination. He lost the nomination to John F. Kennedy, who then chose Johnson as his running mate. Kennedy was assassinated in November, 1963, and Johnson took the oath of office as President.

The following year, Johnson was elected President in his own right by a huge majority. During his administration, he pushed for legislation to launch what he called the "Great Society." Congress passed 226 out of the 252 bills that the President submitted. Various pieces of civil rights legislation curbed discrimination against blacks. Congress established the Office of Economic Opportunity to pour money into job training and other programs to aid the poor. Lyndon Johnson rode a crest of popularity higher than most Presidents before him. Then, the continuing war in Southeast Asia led to his downfall.

Vietnam had been a French colony since the late 1800's, as part of French Indochina. The Japanese took it during World War II. After the war, the Vietnamese resisted French efforts to return as colonial masters. Many of the Vietnamese rebels were Communists. The United States aided France in its fight against the Vietnamese, but by the mid-1950's, the rebels had won. Vietnam then was split into two nations. The North was Communist-controlled. The government in the South was called a republic, and it received United States support. Communists and other rebels in the South tried to overthrow the South Vietnamese government, and eventually they were aided by Communist North Vietnam. The Eisenhower administration sent military advisers to the South. Along with military supplies, the Kennedy Administration began sending troops to South Vietnam in the early 1960's. Troop commitments continued under Johnson, until the total number of U.S. forces exceeded half a million.

Even with massive United States aid, the South Vietnamese government seemed unable to win the war. The government became increasingly corrupt and dictatorial. More and more Americans opposed continued involvement in what appeared to be an unwinnable war, and continued support for an oppressive regime. The conflict was costing thousands of American lives. Johnson resisted the criticism and continued to step up the war effort, declaring that, "I'm not going down in history as the first American President to lose a war." Opposition to the war mounted as thousands of Americans took to the streets to protest. The nation was becoming more and more divided.

Despite his growing unpopularity, nearly everyone expected Johnson to be the Democratic nominee for President in 1968. But in March of that year, he made a surprise announcement. At the conclusion of a televised speech, he declared that he would not be a candidate for reelection. Early in 1969, after nearly 40 years in the nation's capital, Lyndon B. Johnson left Washington, D.C., for the final time. He retired to his Texas ranch and died there in 1973.

John Fitzgerald Kennedy

Born: May 29, 1917
Died: Nov. 22, 1963
Place of Birth:
  Brookline, Mass.
Political Party: Democrat

Term: 1961-1963
Electoral Vote: 303
Vice-President:
  Lyndon B. Johnson

Kennedy, John Fitzgerald (1917-1963), was the 35th President of the United States. Young, witty, and sophisticated, John F. Kennedy promised to lead the nation from the conservative 1950's to a "New Frontier" of bold experimentation and social change. Kennedy was the first Catholic to be elected to the presidency, and he was the fourth President to be assassinated.

Kennedy was born into a wealthy family in Brookline, Mass., on May 29, 1917. He attended elementary schools there and in Riverdale. After a prep school secondary education, he entered Harvard University, graduating in 1940. During World War II, Kennedy saw action as a naval lieutenant in the Pacific. His political career began in 1946, when he was elected to the House of Representatives as a Democrat. He was re-elected twice, then won a Senate seat in 1952. The following year, Kennedy married Jacqueline Lee Bouvier, the daughter of a Wall Street broker.

In 1956, Kennedy unsuccessfully sought the Democratic vice-presidential nomination. He won reelection to the Senate in 1958, and soon began to pre-

pare for the presidential nomination two years later. In 1960, after a hard-driving, tireless campaign that brought him numerous primary victories, Kennedy gained the nomination on the first ballot. His campaign for the presidency was equally energetic and carefully planned. But he defeated Republican candidate Richard M. Nixon by only a narrow popular majority. In the Electoral College, Kennedy won by a vote of 303 to 219.

President Kennedy unleashed a flood of legislative proposals on such matters as unemployment, health care, civil rights, aid to Appalachia and other depressed areas, trade expansion, and an increased minimum wage. Congress, though Democratic, proved to be more conservative than Kennedy. It raised the minimum wage to $1.25 an hour, granted aid to depressed areas, and passed tariff-cutting legislation. But it did not establish a Department of Urban Affairs, as Kennedy requested, nor did it provide health care for the aged. Civil rights legislation made little progress under Kennedy. However, he did use federal troops to integrate the Universities of

Alabama and Mississippi when blacks were denied admission to those institutions. In 1961, Kennedy issued an executive order that established the Peace Corps, which some consider his greatest achievement. Under the Peace Corps, thousands of Americans went to underdeveloped countries to teach and to provide other services.

The Kennedy Administration waged the Cold War vigorously (see Truman, Harry S. and Eisenhower, Dwight David). The U.S. stockpile of nuclear weapons grew. Kennedy continued Eisenhower's policy of sending aid to South Vietnam to combat a rebellion that involved Communists and that was supported by Communist North Vietnam. Closer to home, Kennedy approved a plan to use American-trained Cuban exiles as an invasion force to bring down Cuba's Communist government. The invasion in 1961 at the Bay of Pigs failed miserably, and Kennedy was sharply criticized for the incident. In 1962, the Soviet Union constructed nuclear missile sites in Cuba. Kennedy publicly forced the Soviets to back down

and dismantle the sites. In 1963, the Soviet Union and the United States agreed to limit nuclear testing.

On Nov. 22, 1963, as he rode in a motorcade in Dallas, Tex., Kennedy was assassinated by Lee Harvey Oswald. While in police custody, Oswald himself was shot and killed by nightclub owner Jack Ruby. Some persons questioned whether Kennedy's assassination resulted from a conspiracy, or was simply the act of a single individual. The Warren Commission investigated the assassination and concluded that Oswald had acted alone. However, critics disputed the findings. During the 1970's, a special committee of the United States House of Representatives reexamined the evidence. The committee accepted the testimony of acoustical (sound) experts who claimed that shots were fired from two locations along the motorcade at almost the same time. In 1978, the committee concluded that Kennedy "was probably assassinated as a result of a conspiracy." Other authorities have strongly disputed the committee's conclusion.

Abraham Lincoln

Born: Feb. 12, 1809
Died: April 15, 1865
Place of Birth: Hardin
(now LaRue) County,
Ky.
Political Party: Republican

Terms: 1861-1865
Electoral Vote: 180; 212
Vice-President:
Hannibal Hamlin;
Andrew Johnson

Lincoln, Abraham (1809-1865), was the 16th President of the United States. He governed a nation torn apart by the Civil War, and his major task was to end the conflict and restore the Union. He did not have the opportunity, however, to "bind up the nation's wounds." Shortly after the war ended in 1865, Lincoln was assassinated.

Abraham Lincoln was descended from pioneers who had moved farther and farther west with each generation. He was born in Hardin (now LaRue) County, Ky., on Feb. 12, 1809. When he was 7, his family crossed the Ohio River and settled in Indiana. In 1830, when Lincoln was 21, the family moved again, this time to Illinois.

Settling on his own in New Salem, Lincoln failed in a business venture, served briefly in the Black Hawk War of 1832, and became village postmaster. In 1834, as a member of the Whig Party, he was elected to the Illinois legislature. He served four terms and at the same time studied law. He became a lawyer in 1837 and moved to the state capital, Springfield.

Lincoln remained a Whig, but his ambition for national political office was unfulfilled until 1847, when he won election to the U.S. House of Representatives. In Congress, he became best known for his opposition to the Mexican War (see Polk, James K.). This stand cost him reelection. He returned to his law practice in Illinois. There, in 1842, he married Mary Todd, a Kentuckian.

The extension of slavery into new territories and states was an issue that stirred the nation in the 1850's. Lincoln believed that the Constitution did not prohibit slavery, but he opposed its extension. He expressed his position in his campaign for the Senate in 1854, during which he debated Senator Stephen A. Douglas of Illinois. Douglas refused to take a stand against slavery. Lincoln lost the election. He unsuccessfully ran for Douglas' own seat in 1858, and once more debated the senator on the slavery issue. Newspaper coverage of the 1858 debates brought Lincoln nationwide attention.

By 1860, Lincoln had become a member of the new Republican Party, which was dedicated, among other things, to opposing the extension of slavery. That year, Lincoln became a candidate for the presidential nomination. Because he had spent relatively little time in public life, Lincoln had few enemies. This, plus his moderate views on slavery, appealed to many delegates at the 1860 Republican convention in Chicago. Lincoln won the nomination on the third ballot.

The Democrats split over the slavery issue. Southern party members split among themselves to form two parties, both with presidential candidates. Northern Democrats chose Stephen A. Douglas as their candidate. Lincoln won in the Electoral College, though he failed to gain a majority of the popular vote.

Southerners feared the Republican victory doomed slavery. In December 1860, South Carolina seceded from the Union. In January, Mississippi, Florida, Alabama, Louisiana, and Georgia followed. Later, Virginia, Texas, Arkansas, Tennessee, and North Carolina left the Union to join the Confederate States of America.

As President, Lincoln's immediate task was to hold such border states as Kentucky and Maryland in the Union. He held the border states, but he had to decide what to do about Fort Sumter, a federal fort in the Charleston, S.C. harbor. To withdraw troops from Sumter would arouse Northern criticism. To send supplies and additional troops there would generate Southern hostility. Lincoln chose to send supplies only. But before a ship could arrive, Confederate troops fired on Fort Sumter and forced it to surrender. Lincoln declared the South to be in a state of rebellion and called for volunteers to the Union Army. The Civil War had begun.

Lincoln's major problems lay in the East, where he had difficulty finding a suitable commander for the Army of the Potomac. General George B. McClellan lost the Peninsular Campaign, which was aimed at Richmond, Va., to Confederate General Robert E. Lee in 1862. As a result, Lincoln removed McClellan. The next appointee, John Pope, met defeat at the second Battle of Bull Run in August of that year. Lincoln turned once again to McClellan, who held back Lee at Antietam, but failed to pursue the Confederates. Lincoln then appointed General Ambrose E. Burnside commander. Burnside failed to win at Fredericksburg, and his successor, General Joseph Hooker, lost at Chancellorsville early in May 1863. Lee then invaded the North, moving into southern Pennsylvania. There, at Gettysburg in July, 1863 General George Meade defeated the Confederate forces, and Lee retreated into Virginia.

The Union enjoyed more success in the West. In 1862, General Ulysses S. Grant took the Confederate Fort Henry on the Tennessee River. Next, he fought Southern armies to a standstill at Shiloh, in Tennessee. Then he captured Vicksburg, which put the Mississippi River in Union hands, and later went on to victory at Chattanooga, Tenn. Lincoln made Grant a lieutenant general and brought him east to command all Union forces.

In addition to conducting the war, Lincoln had to keep the loyal states united. This proved difficult. Union failures on the battlefield aroused much discontent. Republicans criticized Lincoln for not pursuing the war more vigorously. "Copperhead" Democrats, who were sympathetic toward the South, wanted to make peace. In addition, various groups demanded the abolition of slavery. Lincoln hesitated to move on the slavery issue, for fear of offending the border states of Kentucky, Missouri,

Maryland, and Delaware, where slavery was permitted. After the Battle of Antietam in 1862, which could be called a Union victory, Lincoln issued the Emancipation Proclamation. The document, which was issued in final form on Jan. 1, 1863, freed slaves in all the states then in rebellion. It could be enforced, however, only where Union troops were in control. Still, the Proclamation cheered abolitionists. It also made the abolition of slavery a war aim, in addition to the preservation of the Union.

As the war dragged on, however, Lincoln lost popularity. He faced strong opposition in his bid for reelection in 1864. Democrats nominated General McClellan as their candidate. The Republicans chose John C. Frémont, a radical Republican who was a general and a famed explorer. Frémont later withdrew, and Lincoln defeated McClellan by 212 to 21 electoral votes. By the time of Lincoln's second inauguration in March 1865, the end of the war was near.

In 1864, General William T. Sherman besieged and captured Atlanta, Ga. He then moved to cut a 60-mile-wide path of destruction from Atlanta to the sea at Savannah, Ga. Much of the South lay in ruins.

In Virginia, troops under Ulysses S. Grant suffered heavy losses as they fought to a series of standoffs with Lee's Army of Northern Virginia. Lee held off Grant in the two-day Battle of the Wilderness in May 1864, but Grant pushed forward to clash again with Lee at the Spotsylvania Court House that same month. Grant proceeded toward Richmond, the capital of the Confederacy, and once more met fierce resistance, at Cold Harbor, in June. Finally, he lay siege to the Southern army at Petersburg. In the meantime, the Northern cavalry under General Philip Sheridan defeated Confederate forces in the Shenandoah Valley of Virginia. The Union destruction of the valley eliminated it as a source of Confederate food. Hemmed in at Petersburg and Richmond, Lee finally asked for terms. He surrendered to Grant at Appomattox Court House in Virginia, on April 9, 1865. The Civil War was over.

In his second inaugural address, Lincoln had called for "malice toward none" and "charity for all," and for an effort "to bind up the nation's wounds" and "achieve and cherish a just and lasting peace." But he himself was not to take part in the nation's reconstruction.

On the night of April 14, 1865, less than a week after the war had ended, Lincoln and his wife attended Ford's Theatre in Washington, D.C. There, in the presidential box, at about 10 o'clock, John Wilkes Booth shot Lincoln in the head. Booth was a well-known actor, a Marylander, and a Confederate sympathizer. Carried to a nearby house, Lincoln died at about 7:30 the following morning.

James Madison

Born: March 16, 1751
Died: June 28, 1836
Place of Birth:
    Port Conway, Va.
Political Party: Democratic-
    Republican

Terms: 1809-1817
Electoral Vote: 122; 128
Vice-Presidents:
    George Clinton;
    Elbridge Gerry

Madison, James (1751-1836), was the fourth President of the United States. Madison was responsible for the system of checks and balances that is built into the American government, and he is known principally as the "Father of the Constitution."

Born on March 16, 1751, in Port Conway, Va., Madison was the son of the owner of a plantation called Montpelier. He received most of his early education at home. At age 18, he entered what is now Princeton University in New Jersey.

In 1774, Madison was elected to the Committee of Safety in Orange County, Virginia. Two years later, after he helped draft a constitution for the state, he was elected to the Virginia legislature. In 1779, he won election to the Continental Congress. He returned to the Virginia assembly in 1783.

Madison served as one of Virginia's representatives at the Constitutional Convention in 1787. His suggestions made him a leader in the process of writing the document. His ideas for a two-house legislature and a sharing of power among the legislative, judicial, and executive branches won acceptance. After the convention, he worked to win ratification of the Constitution by the states.

In 1789, Virginians sent Madison to the U.S. House of Representatives. In Virginia, in 1794, he married Dolley Payne Todd, a young widow. Madison became a leading opponent of the Federalist Party, which favored business and commercial interests and a strong central government. He and Thomas Jefferson formed the Democratic-Republican Party, which favored states' rights. Jefferson was elected to the presidency in 1800, and he made Madison secretary of state. During his term as secretary, the United States purchased Louisiana from France. There were also problems because of a war between Great Britain and France. Both nations interfered with American shipping. In 1807, Congress passed the Embargo Act, which halted trade with both nations. This did more harm than good, however. It hurt American commercial interests, and the Congress repealed the act in 1809.

Madison was elected President in

1808. Problems with France and Britain continued, and Congress passed the Macon Act. The law provided that if either France or Britain would stop interfering with American shipping, the United States would stop trade with the other nation. France declared, falsely, that it would cease harassment. Trade with Britain was halted. When France's trickery was discovered, there were angry outcries in the United States against the French.

Feelings against Britain were aroused when the British in Canada encouraged Indians to attack American frontier settlements. The British also continued to harass American shipping. Americans began to talk of war. Westerners favored war with Britain to stop the Indian attacks. They also hoped to annex Canada. Other factions approved of fighting Britain to restore freedom of the seas. Finally, in 1812, Congress declared war on Great Britain.

Madison was easily reelected President a few months after the war began. But the conflict went badly for Madison and his Administration. The British blockaded the Atlantic Coast. United States shipping declined. In 1814, the British landed troops in Maryland.

Shortly thereafter they occupied Washington, D.C., and burned the Capitol and some other public buildings. James and Dolley Madison fled. Only fierce American resistance at Fort McHenry in the Baltimore harbor prevented the British from taking the capital of the United States.

American forces fought the British to a draw in battles in southern Ontario, and U.S. naval forces won a battle on Lake Erie. In 1815, Andrew Jackson defeated the British in the Battle of New Orleans, shortly before a peace treaty was ratified.

Following the war, the United States entered a period of prosperity and expansion. Road and canal building helped the Westward movement and brought the country's various regions together. Protective tariffs helped the birth and growth of American industries. The downfall of the Federalists gave the Democratic-Republicans dominance over the government.

James Madison retired from the presidency to Montpelier in 1817. He continued his life-long study of government and history and later became president of the University of Virginia. He died in 1836.

William McKinley

Born: Jan. 29, 1843
Died: Sept. 14, 1901
Place of Birth: Niles, Ohio
Political Party: Republican

Terms: 1897-1901
Electoral Vote: 271; 292
Vice-Presidents:
   Garret A. Hobart;
   Theodore Roosevelt

McKinley, William (1843-1901), was the 25th President of the United States. William McKinley was chief executive at a time of great industrial and territorial expansion. In 1901, six months into his second term, McKinley was assassinated.

Born in Niles, Ohio, on Jan. 29, 1843, McKinley received his early education in public and private schools. After serving in the Union army during the Civil War, he studied law. In 1867, he opened an office in Canton, Ohio. Two years later, as a Republican, he was elected prosecuting attorney of Stark County. In 1871, he married Ida Saxton, granddaughter of a Canton newspaper publisher.

In 1876, McKinley was elected to the U.S. House of Representatives. In Congress, he supported protective tariffs, and the tariff law bearing his name set rates at new high levels. He also favored the unlimited coinage of silver, an inflationary measure. After being defeated for reelection to the House in 1890, he was elected to two terms as governor of Ohio.

McKinley became a close friend of

Mark Hanna, a wealthy industrialist who used his influence and financial resources to promote McKinley for the presidency. McKinley easily won nomination at the Republican convention in 1896, and went on to defeat Democratic candidate William Jennings Bryan by more than 600,000 votes.

Industrialization had proceeded rapidly since the end of the Civil War, and by the turn of the century, there was no doubt that the United States was a world power. During the 1890's, the government began a construction program to achieve a two-ocean navy. In 1898, the United States expanded its territory by annexing Hawaii.

The Caribbean colony of Cuba revolted against Spain in 1895. Many American newspapers, particularly those that practiced sensational "yellow journalism," agitated for U.S. involvement. These newspapers printed many stories that emphasized Spanish harshness and oppression. A clamor arose in the United States for intervention in Cuba, but McKinley resisted the demand.

The President did dispatch the battleship *Maine* to Havana harbor, for the stated purpose of protecting American lives and property on the island. On Feb. 15, 1898, the *Maine* blew up. Although the cause of the explosion has never been determined, Spain was blamed. War fever reached a high pitch, and "Remember the Maine" became a common slogan. McKinley finally bowed to the demand for war with Spain.

Less than four months later, the conflict ended. United States naval forces defeated Spanish fleets off the Philippines and in the Caribbean. The United States invaded Cuba and was victorious over Spanish forces there. When the war with Spain ended, the United States gained possession of Cuba, Puerto Rico, the Philippines, and the island of Guam in the Pacific.

The United States gave Cuba self-governing powers in 1901 but reserved the right to intervene there whenever necessary. It kept Puerto Rico as a colony. The status of the Philippines became a controversial issue. Traditionally, the United States had opposed colonialism.

Further, Filipinos wished to be independent. Business groups in the United States tended to favor annexation. So did those who believed it was the United States' mission to educate Filipinos and to convert them to Christianity, though many Filipinos had already become Catholics under Spanish rule. President McKinley finally decided on annexation. His decision touched off a revolt by Filipino Nationalists that cost the United States numerous casualties before peace was restored.

During McKinley's first administration, the nation had enjoyed prosperity. Running for reelection in 1900, he promised four more prosperous years. He won easily. In September 1901, McKinley attended the Pan-American Exposition in Buffalo, N.Y. At a reception in Buffalo on September 6, an anarchist named Leon F. Czolgosz shot the President. Czolgosz said he wanted "to kill a great ruler." McKinley died a week later, and Theodore Roosevelt became President.

James Monroe

Born: April 28, 1758
Died: July 4, 1831
Place of Birth:
    Westmoreland County, Va.
Political Party:
    Democratic-Republican

Terms: 1817-1825
Electoral Vote: 183; 231
Vice-President:
    Daniel D. Tompkins

Monroe, James (1758-1831), was the fifth President of the United States. He was the last of the "Virginia dynasty" of Presidents, which included George Washington, Thomas Jefferson, and James Madison. Monroe is best remembered for the Monroe Doctrine, which he proclaimed in 1823. The doctrine warned European nations against interfering in the affairs of independent countries in the Western Hemisphere.

James Monroe was born on April 28, 1758, in Westmoreland County, Virginia. He entered the College of William and Mary at age 16, but did not finish. He left school to fight in the Revolutionary War.

Monroe's political service began in 1782, when he was elected to the Virginia Assembly. The next year, he was elected to the national Congress, where he spent three years. After marrying Elizabeth Kortright, a New York merchant's daughter, he returned to the Virginia legislature. In 1788, he was a member of the state convention that ratified the U.S. Constitution. He was elected to the United States Senate in 1790, and

helped organize the Democratic-Republican Party (see Jefferson, Thomas).

From 1794 to 1796, Monroe served as minister to France. Then in 1799, he won the governorship of Virginia. In 1803, he was a member of the delegation that negotiated the Louisiana Purchase from France. Afterward, Monroe served as minister to Great Britain. In 1810, he once again was elected to the Virginia legislature. Then, after a brief period as governor, he became President James Madison's secretary of state. In 1816, Monroe won the presidency.

The Federalist Party, concentrated in New England, had opposed the War of 1812, mainly because the conflict damaged that region's trade. As a result, Federalists were accused of a lack of patriotism, and the party dissolved after 1816. The Democratic-Republican Party was the only one in existence in the United States during Monroe's Administration. The absence of interparty battling caused the period to be known as the "era of good feeling."

It was also an era of growing nationalism, prosperity, and expansion. To promote nationalism, Speaker of the House Henry Clay advanced his American System. One part of this plan called for federally supported road and canal construction. It also included a high tariff to protect young American industries from foreign competition. High tariff laws were enacted in 1816, in 1818, and again in 1824. Monroe added territory to the nation in 1819 by buying Florida from Spain.

Slavery and sectionalism became issues in 1820. Missouri had applied for statehood as a slave state in 1819. Its admission would upset the balance between slave and free states that then existed. Southerners favored Missouri's admission to the Union; Northerners opposed it. After months of debate, Henry Clay worked out a compromise. Missouri would come in as a slave state, Maine as a free state, and slavery would be prohibited in the rest of the Louisiana Territory north of Missouri's southern border. Monroe approved the Missouri Compromise, and in that same year, 1820, he was reelected President.

By the early 1820's, most Latin American colonies had won independence from Spain and Portugal. There was some evidence, however, that certain European nations might band together to return the new nations to colonial status. Britain wanted to issue a joint declaration with the United States opposing such a move. But Monroe's secretary of state, John Quincy Adams, advised him that the United States should issue a declaration on its own. Adams assumed that the United States could depend on British seapower to enforce any declaration. The result was the Monroe Doctrine, proclaimed in 1823. It protected the Western Hemisphere from any further European colonization.

The era of good feeling ended in 1825. Four candidates vied for the presidency in 1824 (see Adams, John Quincy, and Jackson, Andrew). None won a majority of the electoral votes, and the House of Representatives decided the election in favor of John Quincy Adams. The result was political bitterness that lasted throughout the 1820's.

After Monroe left the presidency, he retired to his estate, Oak Hill, in northern Virginia. Mounting debts forced him to sell his plantation and move to New York to live with one of his daughters in 1830. He died there the following year.

Richard M. Nixon

Born: Jan. 9, 1913
Place of Birth:
    Yorba Linda, Calif.
Political Party: Republican

Terms: 1969-1974
Electoral Vote: 301; 520
Vice-Presidents:
    Spiro T. Agnew;
    Gerald R. Ford

Nixon, Richard M. (1913-   ), was the 37th President of the United States. From the start to the finish of his political career, Richard M. Nixon remained a controversial figure. In 1974, he became the first person to resign the presidency.

Nixon was born in Yorba Linda, Calif., on Jan. 9, 1913. He attended elementary and high schools in Yorba Linda, Whittier, and Fullerton. He graduated from Whittier College in 1934 and then attended Duke University School of Law, where he received his degree in 1937. He married Thelma Catharine Ryan, known by the nickname Pat, in 1940. Nixon practiced law until 1942, when he went to Washington, D.C., to work for the Office of Price Administration, an agency in charge of price controls and rationing during World War II. Later in 1942, he became a naval lieutenant j. g. and served in the Pacific.

Following the war, Nixon in 1946 ran as a Republican for the seat in the House of Representatives held by Californian Jerry Voorhis, who had served five terms. At the time, there was a rising fear of Communist influence in the United States (see Truman, Harry S.).

Nixon was criticized for taking advantage of this fear by implying that Voorhis, a liberal, was a Communist sympathizer. Nixon won the election.

As a member of the House Un-American Activities Committee, Nixon made a name for himself by conducting a lengthy investigation into the background of former State Department official Alger Hiss, who was accused of having spied for Russia during the 1930's. Hiss was later convicted of perjury. In 1950, Nixon ran for the Senate from California against Representative Helen Gahagan Douglas. He won the election but again was criticized for using campaign tactics similar to those he had employed against Voorhis.

By 1952, Nixon was a well-known public figure, and he was chosen by the Republicans to run for the vice-presidency that year. He and presidential candidate Dwight D. Eisenhower were elected, and re-elected four years later.

As Vice-President, Nixon was more active than most of his predecessors in the office had been. He attended Cabinet and various commission and council meetings, made a tour of Latin America, and journeyed to the Soviet Union.

Nixon was nominated in 1960 by the Republicans to succeed Eisenhower, but he lost the election to Democrat John F. Kennedy in a close race. Two years later, he failed in an attempt to win election as California's governor. He then moved to New York to join a law firm.

In 1968, Nixon returned to politics and again secured the Republican nomination for the presidency. This time he won, defeating Democrat Hubert H. Humphrey by 301 to 191 electoral votes.

Foreign affairs, especially the war in Vietnam, attracted much attention during the Nixon years. Nixon's policy called for the gradual withdrawal of American ground forces and the strengthening of South Vietnam's ability to carry on the war against North Vietnam alone. Troop withdrawal pleased most Americans, but it did not proceed rapidly enough to suit longtime opponents of the war. Then, in April, 1970, Nixon ordered an invasion of Cambodia for the stated purpose of wiping out Communist supply bases. To many people, it appeared that Nixon was widening the war instead of ending it. There were demonstrations against the Cambodian invasion. At Kent State College in Ohio, national guardsmen killed four demonstrating students. Police in Jackson, Miss., killed two students there. United States involvement in Vietnam finally ended in January 1973.

Nixon had been known for his strong stand against Communism and such Communist nations as China and Russia. Yet, in 1972, he took an important step toward improving U.S.-Chinese relations by journeying to China to confer with that nation's leaders. That same year, he flew to Moscow to meet with Soviet officials.

In November 1972, Nixon easily won reelection over Democrat George McGovern. The electoral vote was 520 to 17.

Inflation and recession were problems during Nixon's second term. Both became especially troublesome after the fall of 1973, when oil-producing nations increased petroleum prices.

President Nixon also had problems within his Administration. Vice-President Spiro Agnew was accused of having accepted bribes while serving as a government official in Maryland. Agnew was also charged with income tax evasion. Agnew steadfastly denied his guilt, but in October 1973, he finally pleaded no contest to the income tax charge. He was fined and resigned from the vice-presidency. Nixon appointed Michigan Congressman Gerald R. Ford to the office.

The President's gravest domestic problem, however, stemmed from a burglary. On June 17, 1972, Washington police arrested five men who had broken into the Democratic national headquarters in the Watergate office and apartment building. The men were carrying electronic surveillance equipment. One of the men, James W. McCord, Jr., was a former Central Intelligence Agency (CIA) employee who was connected with the Republican Committee to Re-elect the President. Two additional men were arrested later. They were E. Howard Hunt, a former CIA agent who also worked for the election committee, and G. Gordon Liddy, a former FBI agent. Liddy and McCord pleaded not guilty to burglary and conspiracy charges. All seven were tried and found guilty of burglary.

In 1973, the grand jury that investigated the Watergate break-in uncovered evidence of political spying through electronic means, other politically inspired break-ins and burglaries, illegal Republican campaign contributions, and other improper activities. A Senate committee began its own investigation. It appeared that numerous presidential aides had been involved in the Watergate scandal and related matters. Nixon denied any such involvement by his aides.

Testifying before the Senate committee, however, former White House counsel John W. Dean III insisted that numerous men around the President had been involved, and that Nixon himself, as early as September 1972, had tried to keep his officials from being indicted for participation in the Watergate affair. Dean also revealed an "enemies list" of about 250 persons who the Administration intended to harass by such means as tax audits. He further said that the CIA had been used to block an FBI investigation of Watergate. Nixon continued to deny any cover-up of the Watergate affair by anyone then in the government. He did have the Justice Department appoint a special prosecutor to investigate Watergate.

The Senate committee also learned that Nixon had regularly tape-recorded his conversations in his White House office. A long controversy then began over whether Nixon would give up certain tapes the committee requested for its investigation. But when the prosecutor, Archibald Cox, insisted on obtaining crucial tapes, Nixon had him fired.

Under a new special prosecutor, Leon Jaworski, the Watergate investigation continued into 1974. Nixon at last offered to provide edited versions of certain tapes. These showed that he and his aides had discussed such things as "hush money," clemency for the Watergate burglars, and how to restrain the Watergate investigation. Public confidence in Nixon's integrity eroded.

Many persons began to talk of impeaching Nixon on charges of obstruction of justice. In the meantime, at Jaworski's request, the Supreme Court ordered Nixon to turn over all the tapes the investigators wanted. Nixon complied. These tapes revealed new evidence concerning a cover-up. One tape in particular indicated that, contrary to his repeated denials of involvement, Nixon had known of the cover-up plan less than a week after the Watergate break-in. The House Judiciary Committee now voted to recommend articles of impeachment against Nixon. Nixon resigned from office on Aug. 9, 1974, and left immediately for California. Vice-President Ford was sworn in as President. One of Ford's first acts was to pardon Nixon for any crimes that he might have committed while in office.

The number of people indicted in connection with Watergate for obstruction of justice, burglary, conspiracy, perjury, and other crimes finally totaled more than 50. The leading figures among those sent to prison were such presidential aides as H. R. Haldeman and John D. Ehrlichman, and former Attorney General John Mitchell.

Franklin Pierce

Born: Nov. 23, 1804
Died: Oct. 8, 1869
Place of Birth: Hillsboro,
  N.H.
Political Party: Democrat

Term: 1853-1857
Electoral Vote: 254
Vice-President:
  William R. King

Pierce, Franklin (1804-1869), was the 14th President of the United States. A Democrat, Pierce presided over a nation that was being torn apart by the slavery issue, as the possibility of compromise became more and more remote.

Franklin Pierce was born on Nov. 23, 1804, in Hillsboro, N.H. His father had fought in the Revolutionary War and later became governor of New Hampshire. Pierce was educated in private academies and Bowdoin College, where he graduated in 1824. He then studied law and opened a practice in Concord, N.H. in 1827.

A follower of Andrew Jackson, Pierce was elected to the New Hampshire House of Representatives in 1828. He served a total of three terms. In 1833, he moved on to a seat in the House of Representatives in Washington, D.C., then to the Senate. In 1834, he married Jane Means Appleton, a college president's daughter. Pierce served as an army officer during the Mexican War, and participated in the capture of Mexico City in 1847.

In 1852, the Democratic convention deadlocked over the selection of a presidential candidate. Pierce had supported the Compromise of 1850 and strict enforcement of the Fugitive Slave Law (see Fillmore, Millard). This won him support among Southern Democrats. He gained the nomination on the 49th ballot and was elected President with 254 electoral votes.

President Pierce favored United States expansion. Under his Administration, the country made the Gadsden Purchase, which gave it additional land from Mexico. A railroad was proposed to run over the newly acquired land to California. He also supported the idea that the United States had the right to seize Cuba from Spain. But public opposition to the annexation of Cuba, where slavery existed, forced him to back down.

The extension of slavery was the most important domestic issue during the Pierce years. The Compromise of 1850 had quieted concern over the problem only slightly. Senator Stephen A. Douglas of Illinois wished to organize the Kansas and Nebraska territories, for he had an interest in a company that planned to build a transcontinental railroad through the area. The bill he proposed upheld "popular sovereignty"—the right of the people of a territory to decide for themselves whether to permit slavery. This violated the Missouri Compromise of 1820, however, which prohibited slavery in the Louisiana Territory, north of Missouri's southern boundary. Kansas and Nebraska were to be formed from part of that region. Even though passage of the Kansas-Nebraska bill would destroy the compromise between the North and South, and inflame public opinion, Pierce supported it. After many disagreements, the bill became law. Northerners and Southerners flocked to Kansas, the first of the two territories to be organized, in an effort to load the population for or against slavery. Violence followed as pro- and anti-slavery forces struggled for control of the Kan-

sas government (see Buchanan, James).

Douglas' bill, and the "bleeding Kansas" aftermath, led to turmoil among the nation's political parties. In 1854, a new organization, the Republican Party, was formed. Among other things, the Republican Party came out strongly against the extension of slavery. Democrats, especially those in the South, defended the institution. The Whig Party completely disappeared, as many of its Northern members joined the Republicans.

Pierce found little support for renomination in 1856. His support of the Kansas-Nebraska bill led people to believe he was a Northerner with Southern principles. The Democratic nomination in 1856 went to James Buchanan. Pierce died in 1869.

James K. Polk

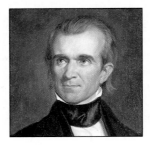

Born: Nov. 2, 1795
Died: June 15, 1849
Place of Birth: near
    Pineville, N.C.
Political Party: Democrat

Term: 1845-1849
Electoral Vote: 170
Vice-President:
    George M. Dallas

Polk, James K. (1795-1849), was the 11th President of the United States. Polk was a supporter of expansion, and he presided over a nation that was growing rapidly.

James Polk was born on Nov. 2, 1795, into a farming family near Pineville,

N.C. When he was 11, his family moved to central Tennessee. Polk graduated from the University of North Carolina in 1818, studied law, and was admitted to the Tennessee bar in 1820.

Polk was first elected to public office in 1823, when he won a seat in the Tennessee House of Representatives. A year later, he married Sarah Childress, a country merchant's daughter.

In 1825, Polk won election to the United States House of Representatives, where he served seven terms. He was Speaker of the House from 1835 to 1838. Jackson supported Polk for governor of Tennessee in 1839, and Polk won. But he lost two tries for reelection.

Polk became a candidate for the presidency in 1844. The principal issues of the time concerned Texas and Oregon. Texas had won independence from Mexico in 1836 and wished to become a state. The boundary of Oregon was the subject of a dispute with Great Britain. Polk claimed that the territories had always belonged to the United States, and so he came out for the "reannexation" of Texas and the "reoccupation" of Oregon.

This position pleased those who believed that the United States was destined to dominate the continent. And when the Democrats at the 1844 convention could not agree on another candidate, Polk received the nomination. During the campaign, he returned to the expansionist theme, and "54-40 or Fight" became the principal Democratic slogan. It referred to the proposed northern boundary of Oregon at 54°40′ latitude. Polk gained the presidency by about 40,000 popular votes over the Whig candidate, Henry Clay.

During the 1840's, thousands of Americans made the long trek to Oregon. Many of them settled north of the Columbia River on territory that Great Britain claimed. Since 1818, the United States and Britain had occupied the area jointly. But Polk and his supporters were determined to gain sole U.S. possession of the territory as far north as the latitude of 54°40′. Polk eventually settled

for a compromise with the British, however, and agreed that the 49th parallel should mark the boundary between Oregon and Canada.

Although Texas had been independent since 1836, its entry into the Union had been blocked by the slavery issue. Northerners opposed the addition of another slave state. Southerners supported it. But with expansionist sentiment in the air, outgoing President John Tyler had persuaded Congress to annex Texas by simple resolution in 1845.

Mexico had not recognized Texas' independence. In addition, the government claimed that the Nueces River, not the Rio Grande, was the true boundary between Mexico and Texas. In January 1846, President Polk ordered General Zachary Taylor to lead troops into the disputed area. Mexican forces responded to what they considered an invasion of their country, and fired on Taylor's men. The Mexican War had begun.

General Taylor quickly defeated the Mexicans in two battles in northern Mexico. Then he took the city of Monterrey. Next he won a smashing victory at the Battle of Buena Vista. General Winfield Scott led another invasion of Mexico, aimed at the capital city, which he took in September 1847.

The following year, Mexico and the United States signed the Treaty of Guadalupe Hidalgo. Under its terms, Mexico gave up claims to Texas, and ceded land forming all or part of Arizona, New Mexico, California, Colorado, Nevada, Utah, and Wyoming. The United States gave Mexico $15 million. President Polk had gained his second foreign policy objective, and much more besides.

Polk had promised not to seek reelection, and he did not. He retired to Nashville, Tenn., where he died of cholera after a short illness in 1849.

Ronald Wilson Reagan

Born: Feb. 6, 1911
Place of Birth: Tampico, Ill.
Political Party: Republican
Term: 1981-1989

Electoral Vote: 489; 525
Vice-President:
  George Herbert Walker Bush

Reagan, Ronald Wilson (1911-   ), was elected the 40th President of the United States in 1980. A Republican, he defeated President Jimmy Carter, the Democrat, and Representative John B. Anderson of Illinois, who ran as an independent.

Reagan was born on Feb. 6, 1911, in Tampico, Ill. In 1928, he attended Eureka College in Illinois. While majoring in economics and sociology, he played football, joined the track team, and served as captain of the swimming team. He had leading roles in many college plays and became president of the student body.

After graduation in 1932, Reagan made a screen test and signed a contract to act in films. He made more than 50 feature films between 1937 and 1964.

Reagan entered the U.S. Army Air Force in 1942 during World War II. He spent most of the war helping to make training films. He had married actress Jane Wyman in 1940. The couple had a daughter and adopted a son. They were divorced in 1948. In 1952, Reagan married actress Nancy Davis. They have two children.

During his movie career, Reagan served five terms as the president of the Screen Actors Guild (1947-52). During the period of strong anti-Communist feeling in the United States, he worked to remove suspected Communists from the movie industry. In 1960, he served a sixth term as president and led the successful strike for payments to actors for sales of their films to television.

Reagan's first public office was the governorship of California from 1967 to 1975. In 1980 Reagan gained the Republican nomination for President. He won the presidency by a large plurality.

Reagan's first major domestic programs were economic. In February 1981, Reagan proposed a plan that included tax cuts with wide reductions in welfare and other social programs, plus a large increase in defense spending. He also worked to curb federal agencies' roles in regulating business and industry. His policies became known as Reaganomics. The economy began to improve in 1983, as economic production rose and unemployment declined.

In foreign affairs, military build-ups and worsening relations with the Soviet Union deepened public concern about nuclear war. In 1983, U.S.-Soviet relations reached a new low after a Soviet jet fighter shot down a Korean civilian airliner flying in Soviet airspace. Conflicts in Central America, Lebanon, and the Caribbean added to international tensions. Reagan urged increased aid for the government of El Salvador in its fight against leftist rebels. In Lebanon, the administration helped arrange a cease-fire in 1982. But new fighting broke out in 1983, and U.S. Marines serving as a peace-keeping force became involved. More than 200 U.S. troops were killed when a terrorist bomb exploded in their headquarters. In the Caribbean, Pan American forces, including U.S. Marines, invaded the island nation of Grenada in an attempt to overthrow the Marxist regime in power there.

Early in his second term, Reagan achieved some major goals. He expanded the Strategic Defense Initiative (known as "Star Wars"), a controversial research program designed to develop a space-based missile defense system. In 1986, Congress approved Reagan's request to create a new, simplified tax system.

In foreign affairs, Reagan acted boldly to combat increasing world terrorism. In October 1985, he ordered U.S. Navy jets to intercept an Egyptian airliner carrying a small group of Palestinian terrorists. In April 1986, Reagan ordered U.S. air strikes against military and suspected terrorist centers in Libya. Tensions between the U.S. and the Soviet Union were eased in December 1987 when Reagan and Soviet leader Mikhail Gorbachev signed the Intermediate-Range Nuclear Forces (INF) Treaty. The treaty calls for the destruction of Soviet SS-20 missiles and U.S. Pershing 2's and cruise missiles.

During Reagan's second term there was increasing conflict in the Persian Gulf. In 1987, Iran laid mines there to disrupt shipping. It fired on U.S. vessels and helicopters in the gulf. Reagan ordered military responses to these actions and ended U.S.-Iranian trade. In May 1987, two missiles from an Iraqi warplane hit the U.S.S. *Stark*, a warship that was patrolling the gulf. Thirty-seven American crewmembers were killed. Iraq said the attack was a mistake. In July 1988, the U.S.S. *Vincennes* shot down an Iranian civilian airliner that it mistook for a warplane. All 290 people on board were killed.

The Reagan Administration suffered a sharp loss of prestige in November 1986 when the public learned about the secret sale of U.S. weapons to Iran. The profits were used to help the Nicaraguan rebels, known as the Contras. Reagan claimed that he knew nothing about the fund diversion, which had been carried out by the National Security Council (NSC). In 1987, televised congressional hearings into what became known as the Iran-Contra Affair revealed deep conflict among members of the Reagan Administration. The congressional hearings also exposed attempts by the NSC to deceive Congress about the arms sale and Contra aid. Later in 1987, Reagan was strongly criticized in a joint report of the congressional committees investigating the affair.

In 1988, Reagan campaigned for Vice-President George Bush, the Republican nominee for President. Bush defeated the Democratic candidate, Massachusetts Governor Michael S. Dukakis.

Franklin Delano Roosevelt

Born: Jan. 30, 1882
Died: April 12, 1945
Place of Birth:
    Hyde Park, N.Y.
Political Party: Democrat
Terms: 1933-1945

Electoral Votes: 472; 523;
    449; 432
Vice-Presidents:
    John Nance Garner;
    Henry A. Wallace;
    Harry S. Truman

Roosevelt, Franklin Delano (1882-1945), was the 32nd President of the United States. Breaking the precedent that had been set by George Washington, Franklin D. Roosevelt ran for and won a third term in office in 1940, and then gained a fourth term in 1944. He presided over a nation struggling to overcome the deepest economic depression in its history, and went on to lead the United States during World War II.

The son of a wealthy New York family, Roosevelt was born on Jan. 30, 1882, on his family's estate in Hyde Park. He was a distant cousin to Theodore Roosevelt, the country's 26th President. Educated by tutors until he was 14, Roosevelt attended Groton preparatory school in Massachusetts, from which he graduated in 1900. He then went on to graduate from Harvard University in 1903, and he later studied law at Columbia University. He married a distant cousin, Eleanor Roosevelt, in 1905.

Politics interested Roosevelt much more than the law. In 1910, as a Democrat, he was elected to the New York senate. Then, as a result of working for Woodrow Wilson in the 1912 presidential campaign, he was appointed Assistant Secretary of the Navy. Roosevelt held this position during World War I.

By 1920, Roosevelt was well known in Democratic circles, and he received the vice-presidential nomination that year. Although the Democrats lost to Republican Warren G. Harding, Roosevelt's participation in the campaign made him known nationally.

About a year after the election, disease threatened to end Franklin D. Roosevelt's political career. He was stricken by polio at the family summer home on Campobello, an island off New Brunswick, in August 1921, and was left partially paralyzed. Roosevelt followed a strict schedule of exercise to overcome the paralysis of his hands and back. But for the remainder of his life, he wore braces on his legs and had to use canes or other assistance in order to walk.

Roosevelt appeared at the Democratic National Convention in 1924 to nominate New York's Governor Al Smith for the presidency. Smith did not receive the nomination that year, but he won it four years later, and Roosevelt once again supported him. Although Smith lost in 1928, that year, Roosevelt was elected to the New York governorship. He was re-elected by a huge majority two years later. His success as governor placed Roosevelt in line as a possible presidential nominee in 1932.

The year 1932 appeared to be as good a year for Democrats as 1920 had been for Republicans. Following a decade of prosperity, the stock market had crashed late in 1929 (see Hoover, Herbert C.). The following year, the deepest economic depression in the country's history set in. Republicans, especially President Herbert Hoover, were blamed for the disaster. By the summer of 1932, more than 12 million people were unemployed.

At their convention in Chicago in 1932, Democrats nominated Roosevelt on the fourth ballot. Roosevelt then flew to Chicago and became the first presidential nominee to make an acceptance speech at a national convention. In his speech, he avoided specifics, but he promised a "new deal" to lift the country out of the depression. Roosevelt won election with a large majority of the popular vote and with 472 electoral votes to Hoover's 59.

After the election, the depression grew worse. There was widespread suffering. Shortly before Roosevelt's inauguration in March 1933, depositors began to take their money out of banks in an effort to protect their savings. As a result of the mass withdrawals, many banks collapsed. Once in office, Roosevelt immediately declared a "bank holiday." All banks were closed until each could be evaluated. The soundest banks then reopened.

Roosevelt next called Congress into a special session that became known as the "Hundred Days." The heavily Democratic Congress, which was actually in session for 99 days, enacted legislation designed to counteract the depression. Among other things, Congress appropriated a half billion dollars for state and city relief programs. It established the Works Progress Administration (WPA), to put people to work on such public projects as road building and school construction. It set up the Civilian Conservation Corps (CCC), which was designed to employ young men on conservation projects. As a further conservation measure, Congress authorized the construction of dams under the Tennessee Valley Authority (TVA). And, in an effort to raise farm incomes, it passed the Agricultural Adjustment Act (AAA).

The New Deal marked an increasing government role in the economy that continued even after Roosevelt's presidency ended. Many New Deal items aroused conservative opposition on the grounds that they were socialistic. The New Deal did not pull the country completely out of the depression, but that fact did not diminish Roosevelt's popularity. He easily won reelection in 1936.

After 1936, Roosevelt's concern shifted more and more to foreign affairs. He initiated the Good Neighbor Policy toward Latin America. But events farther from home attracted more attention. The number of right-wing dictatorships in the world had increased. In Italy, Fascist dictator Benito Mussolini held power. Adolf Hitler and his Nazi Party controlled Germany. In Japan, an aggressive militaristic group governed. Japan occupied Manchuria in 1931, and six years later invaded China. Italy conquered Ethiopia in 1936. In 1938, Germany annexed Austria, and the following year, Czechoslovakia. These actions alarmed Roosevelt. He wished to use United States influence and aid as a counterweight against aggression. He feared that Germany might eventually dominate all of Europe and pose a severe threat to the United States. But the nation favored neutrality, and neutrality laws passed during the 1930's prevented Roosevelt from acting.

In September 1939, World War II erupted in Europe as Hitler conquered Poland, and England and France declared war on Germany. By the spring of 1940, Germany had conquered Belgium, The Netherlands, Denmark, Norway, and finally France. American attitudes toward neutrality began to change. U.S. aid flowed to Britain in ever-increasing amounts as the British stood alone against Germany. Congress enacted a draft law. America began to rearm. Declaring that the nation needed continuous leadership in such times, Roosevelt ran for and won a third term in 1940.

The Roosevelt Administration had opposed Japanese expansion. The opposition grew stronger after the fall of The Netherlands and France, when Japan moved to occupy French and Dutch colonies in Asia. To remove the threat of American power in the Pacific, the Japanese attacked the United States naval base at Pearl Harbor, Hawaii, on Dec. 7, 1941. The American Pacific fleet was badly crippled, but not destroyed, and the United States was now in World War II. Earlier in 1941, Germany had invaded the Soviet Union. Now Germany and its ally Italy declared war on the United States.

Under Roosevelt's command, United States military leaders conducted a global strategy. In the Pacific, U.S. forces took island after island, and gradually pushed the Japanese back. American troops participated in the invasions of North Africa, Sicily, and Italy in 1942-1943. On June 6, 1944, Allied armies crossed the English Channel and invaded France. The German armies fought fiercely, but finally retreated, while the Soviets moved toward Germany from the east.

The strain on Roosevelt of three terms in office was obvious as 1944 began. But the voters elected him to a fourth term in November of that year. Then, on April 12, 1945, Roosevelt suffered a cerebral hemorrhage and died. Vice-President Harry S. Truman became President.

Theodore Roosevelt

Born: Oct. 27, 1858
Died: Jan. 6, 1919
Place of Birth:
    New York, N.Y.
Poltical Party: Republican

Terms: 1901-1909
Electoral Vote: 336
Vice-President:
    Charles W. Fairbanks

Roosevelt, Theodore (1858-1919), was the 26th President of the United States. A flamboyant, decisive man of boundless energy, Roosevelt was a strong and immensely popular President.

Theodore Roosevelt was born into a well-to-do family in New York City on Oct. 27, 1858. Early in his life, Roosevelt displayed great curiosity and determination. He suffered from asthma, but by following a vigorous schedule of exercise, he overcame his affliction and gained great physical strength. Roosevelt was educated by tutors, then entered Harvard University at age 18. He graduated from there in 1880. Shortly thereafter, he married Alice Hathaway Lee, a Bostonian and daughter of a wealthy investment banker. She died in childbirth in 1884.

After briefly attending Columbia University Law School, Roosevelt decided to enter politics. In 1881, at age 23, he was elected to the New York assembly as a Republican. He won reelection twice. Beginning in 1884, he spent two years working on cattle ranches he owned in the West. He also wrote several books. He returned to politics in

1886, when he lost a bid to become mayor of New York. Near the end of that year, he married Edith Kermit Carow.

In 1895, Roosevelt became president of the Board of Police Commissioners for the City of New York. While serving on the police commission, he fought dishonesty in the department. As a result, Roosevelt earned a reputation as a reformer. He took part in the successful presidential campaign of Republican William McKinley in 1896. After McKinley took office, Roosevelt was rewarded with the post of Assistant Secretary of the Navy.

At the time, the United States was becoming more and more prominent as a world power. Roosevelt forcefully supported the expansion of U.S. economic, political, and military influence. In 1895, Cubans began a revolt against their Spanish colonial government. Roosevelt urged that the United States intervene to free Cuba from Spanish rule. The United States finally did declare war on Spain in 1898, and Roosevelt left the government to head a volunteer force known as the Rough Riders, which fought in Cuba.

Roosevelt's military record helped him win election as governor of New York shortly after he returned from Cuba in 1898. As governor, he pursued a course independent from regular party leaders and established a record of reform. In 1900, the Republicans chose him as their vice-presidential nominee to run with President McKinley, who sought a second term. McKinley and Roosevelt won. Roosevelt did not think the vice-presidency would further his career. But then, in 1901, McKinley was assassinated, and Roosevelt became President.

No one was sure of Roosevelt's positions. He was known as a reformer. But progressive Republicans, who favored close government regulation of business and industry, pro-labor legislation, and conservation programs, did not entirely trust him. Conservatives also tended to distrust him.

In practice, Roosevelt managed to steer a middle course. He successfully moved against such business monopolies, called *trusts,* as Standard Oil, American Tobacco, and the Northern Securities Company. As a result, Roosevelt became known as a "trust buster."

In 1904, Roosevelt won election to the presidency by a margin of more than 2½ million popular votes, the largest majority to that time. He continued to uphold reform legislation, including the Hepburn Railroad Rate Act, the Food and Drugs Act, and the Meat Inspection Act.

A French company had tried and failed to dig a canal through Panama. When American officials wanted to take the project over, Roosevelt approved. Panama was then a part of Colombia. Colombia refused the sum offered by the Americans for rights to build the canal.

With the aid of some Americans, and with Roosevelt's tacit approval, Panamanians then staged a rebellion against Colombia. Roosevelt sent a United States warship to prevent Colombian forces from reaching Panama. Panama became independent, and its representatives signed a treaty that gave the United States the authority to build a canal and to control land alongside it. The Panama Canal opened in 1914. In 1905, Roosevelt negotiated a treaty ending the Russo-Japanese War. Two years later, to "show the flag," he sent a fleet of U.S. warships on a goodwill tour around the world.

William Howard Taft succeeded Roosevelt in the presidency in 1909. Roosevelt went off to Africa to hunt big game. After his return to the United States, he became increasingly critical of Taft's performance (see Taft, William Howard). In 1912, Roosevelt decided to try to regain the presidency. Progressive Republicans nominated him as their candidate on the "Bull Moose" ticket, and conservative Republicans remained with Taft. The Republican split helped Democratic candidate Woodrow Wilson win the election.

Roosevelt strongly supported United States preparedness when World War I broke out in Europe in 1914. He constantly criticized President Wilson's efforts to keep the United States neutral.

After the war, Roosevelt opposed United States membership in the League of Nations (see Wilson, Woodrow). He feared such membership would hinder America's freedom in foreign affairs. There was talk of a Roosevelt nomination for the 1920 presidential campaign, but early in 1919, he died suddenly of a blood clot in the heart.

William Howard Taft

Born: Sept. 15, 1857
Died: March 8, 1930
Place of Birth:
   Cincinnati, Ohio
Political Party: Republican

Term: 1909-1913
Electoral Vote: 321
Vice-President:
   James S. Sherman

Taft, William Howard (1857-1930), was the 27th President of the United States. Taft's first love was the law, and he was reluctant to run for the presidency in 1908. In 1921, eight years after leaving office, he achieved his highest goal, appointment as Chief Justice of the United States.

A lawyer's son, William Howard Taft was born in Cincinnati, Ohio, on Sept. 15, 1857. He was a large child, and as President, he stood 6 feet tall and weighed 300 pounds. Taft attended Yale University. He was graduated from Yale in 1878 and from Cincinnati Law College two years later.

Taft's first political job was as an assistant county attorney in Ohio. In 1882, President Chester A. Arthur appointed Taft a district collector of internal revenue. Four years later, he married Helen Herron, the daughter of one of President Rutherford B. Hayes' law partners. In 1901, Taft was made civil governor of the Philippines, which had become a U.S. possession as a result of the United States victory in the Spanish-American War. Taft performed ably in that position, and he became so devoted to his

work in the Philippines that he turned down an appointment to the Supreme Court in 1902. In 1904, however, Taft accepted when President Theodore Roosevelt offered him appointment as secretary of war.

As an administrator, Taft won popular acclaim, and he became Roosevelt's choice for the Republican presidential nomination in 1908. Taft won an easy victory in the election that year.

Taft was uncomfortable in the presidency. He found it difficult to follow the flamboyant Roosevelt, who had been a public favorite. Moreover, Taft presided over a Republican Party that was divided into conservative and liberal factions. The conservatives unabashedly favored big business. The liberals wanted to curb the huge business monopolies, called trusts. They also wanted to increase government regulation of the economy in general, and secure gains for labor. Taft was a conservative but tried to steer a middle course. He eventually lost control of his party.

Taft supported several policies that pleased the liberals. He took more action under the 1890 Sherman Antitrust

Act than had Roosevelt. He also set up the Tariff Board to make detailed studies of tariff rates. During his administration, Congress established the Children's Bureau, set up the postal savings and parcel post systems, passed a law that required the public disclosure of political campaign expenses, and placed the regulation of telegraph, telephone, and cable systems under the Interstate Commerce Commission.

On the other hand, Taft offended the liberals on numerous occasions. He refused to support their efforts to reduce the vast political power wielded by Speaker of the House Joseph Cannon of Illinois. Cannon personally decided which legislation would pass and which would fail. The liberals won the fight against Cannon in spite of Taft's position.

In foreign affairs, Taft followed the policies of his immediate predecessors and extended American economic and political influence. He supported the granting of loans by U.S. banks and businesses to other countries, especially in Latin America. This led to an extension of American economic and political control in the indebted nations. Taft's policy became known as "dollar diplomacy."

As Taft's Administration continued, former President Theodore Roosevelt became more and more critical of Taft. Roosevelt denied any renewed interest in the presidency, but in 1912, he reversed himself and accepted nomination by the liberal wing of the Republican Party. Conservatives chose to stay with Taft. With the Republicans split, Democrat Woodrow Wilson won the presidency.

In 1913, Taft became a professor of constitutional law at Yale. President Warren G. Harding appointed him Chief Justice of the United States in 1921. On the Supreme Court he established a conservative record. Taft died in Washington, D.C., in 1930.

Zachary Taylor

Born: Nov. 24, 1784
Died: July 9, 1850
Place of Birth: near
  Barboursville, Va.
Political Party: Whig

Term: 1849-1850
Electoral Vote: 163
Vice-President:
  Millard Fillmore

Taylor, Zachary (1784-1850), was the 12th President of the United States. Zachary Taylor's popularity as a war hero after 40 years of military service propelled him into the White House. But his term was one of the shortest in presidential history, for he died after only 16 months in office.

A Southerner, Taylor was born on Nov. 24, 1784, near Barboursville, Va. Taylor's father was rewarded with 6,000 acres of land in Kentucky for his Revolutionary War service, and he settled the family there in 1785. Taylor gained his interest in the military from hearing about his father's army experience and from the Indian wars that were being fought in Kentucky during his boyhood. In 1808, he became a lieutenant in the United States Army. Two years later, he married Margaret Mackall Smith, the daughter of a Maryland planter.

Taylor fought against Indians in Indiana during the War of 1812. He later served in Wisconsin during the Blackhawk War in 1832. In 1837, he led a successful expedition against the Seminole Indians of Florida.

Texas won its independence from

Mexico in 1836 and wished to become a state. The dispute over the extension of slavery delayed its admission, however, for Texas would be a slave state, and Northerners opposed its entry into the Union. But in 1845, public opinion favored territorial expansion, and the United States annexed Texas. Mexico, which had never recognized Texan independence, threatened war. In addition, Mexico insisted that the southern boundary of Texas lay along the Nueces River, not the more southerly Rio Grande. Early in 1846, President James K. Polk ordered Zachary Taylor to lead U.S. troops into the disputed area. Mexican forces fired on the Americans and war began.

Taylor, known as "Old Rough and Ready," defeated Mexican troops in two battles. He then took the city of Monterrey. Because of his success, Taylor seemed the logical choice to command the U.S. drive toward Mexico City. But President Polk, a Democrat, thought otherwise. Polk feared that Taylor, who leaned towards the Whigs, might become a political hero. So Polk chose General Winfield Scott to lead the invasion. Taylor, in the meantime, went on to achieve his greatest fame in the Battle of Buena Vista in 1847; he won a two-day battle in which his forces were outnumbered four to one.

The Whigs now had a military hero in their midst, and they capitalized on their opportunity. In 1848, they nominated Taylor for the presidency and selected Millard Fillmore of New York for the vice-presidency. Neither Whigs nor Democrats raised the slavery issue during the campaign. But a third party, the Free Soil Party, entered the contest with a pledge to halt the extension of slavery. Former President Martin Van Buren was the Free Soil candidate. Van Buren drew enough votes away from Democrat Lewis Cass to ensure Taylor's election.

Gold had been discovered in California in 1848, and Americans flocked west. California's population grew rapidly, and the territory was soon ready for state-

hood. But at the time, the number of free and slave states was equal. California's admission would tip the balance in favor of the free states. Compromise or conflict seemed inevitable.

Taylor supported California's admission, and he opposed a compromise on the issue. Since he himself was a slaveholder, this position seemed to go against his interests and his Southern heritage, and it dismayed Southerners. Taylor, however, was first and foremost a nationalist. Further, the time he had spent in the Northwest as a soldier had made him as much a Westerner as a Southerner. Basically, he believed in retaining slavery where it already existed, but he was opposed to its extension.

As Congress debated a compromise, Taylor died in the summer of 1850. Millard Fillmore became President and a compromise was enacted.

Harry S. Truman

Born: May 8, 1884
Died: Dec. 26, 1972
Place of Birth: Lamar, Mo.
Political Party: Democrat

Terms: 1945-1953
Electoral Vote: 303
Vice-President:
  Alben W. Barkley

Truman, Harry S. (1884-1972), was the 33rd President of the United States. The peppery and outspoken Truman was elevated to the presidency upon the death of Franklin D. Roosevelt in 1945.

Lamar, Mo., was the place of Truman's birth on May 8, 1884. He attended elementary and high school in Independence, Mo. After graduation, he worked for a railroad, in a newspaper mailing room, and as a bank clerk. Then he turned to farming. During World War I, Truman served as a captain of artillery.

After the war, Truman opened a men's clothing store in Kansas City. The business failed. He then entered politics. With the support of the Pendergast political machine in Kansas City, he was elected a county judge in 1922. In 1934, again with machine help, Truman won election to the United States Senate. He became known in the Senate for his work as head of a committee investigating fraud in war contracts during World War II. And in 1944, Truman became the Democratic compromise candidate for the vice-presidency, as Roosevelt sought a fourth term. Roosevelt's death in April 1945 made Truman President.

The war in Europe ended in May 1945. Truman's most momentous decision as President concerned the war in the Pacific. He ordered an atomic bomb dropped on Hiroshima and Nagasaki, Japan.

After the Japanese surrender in August 1945, Truman faced many difficult domestic problems. Among them were labor unrest and the question of price controls. There were many strikes during 1945 and 1946, as organized labor sought pay increases to compensate for growing inflation. In some cases, Truman took harsh action. When railroad unions threatened to walk out, tying up the nation's transportation system, the President asked Congress for authority to draft strikers into the Army. The railroad unions backed down. When union leader John L. Lewis refused to send his striking coal miners back to work, Truman had a court injunction served on him. The court levied heavy fines against Lewis and the mineworkers' union. The coal strike ended. Truman lost labor support as a result of these actions, but they made him popular among millions of other Americans.

Foreign affairs attracted much attention during Truman's Administration.

The Soviet Union and the United States had been allies against Germany in World War II. But soon after the war ended, differences began to divide them. The Soviet Union refused to support free elections in Poland, which it had liberated from German control. With Soviet aid, Poland became a Communist nation. The Truman government perceived the Soviet Union as an aggressor. President Truman concluded that the Soviet Union had plans to control Western Europe and probably intended to dominate the world. Truman established the policy of "containment," which endorsed resistance to the advance of Communism anywhere in the world. The period known as the Cold War began.

The foreign policy position against Communism had domestic effects. The discovery of a Soviet spy ring in Canada in 1946 aroused fears that Communist agents might be operating in the United States as well. Truman tended to downplay the fear of domestic Communists, though he set up a loyalty review board to check on government employees. Some employees resigned, and some others were dismissed, but no Communists or evidence of spying were discovered.

Despite this action, Truman was labeled "soft on Communism," and he was criticized by many people for his handling of the strikes and price controls. By 1948, he was an unpopular President. It appeared that for the first time since 1933, Republicans would control the White House. They nominated New York Governor Thomas E. Dewey as their presidential candidate. Democrats had no choice but to go along with Truman. Then, following the party's adoption of a strong civil rights plank, Southern delegates walked out of the 1948 Democratic convention. They formed their own party, known as the Dixiecrats. Many liberal Democrats threw their support behind yet another candidate, Henry Wallace, who headed the Progressive Party. With the Democrats badly split, Republican chances looked better than ever.

But Truman conducted a strong, scrappy, and tireless campaign. He blamed the Republican-controlled Congress for the nation's troubles. And to the surprise of almost everyone, he won the election.

The Allied victory in World War II had freed Korea from Japanese control. The Soviet Union occupied North Korea, and the United States occupied the South. Both nations withdrew their troops later. The Soviet Union left a totalitarian government in the North. South Korea, supported by the United States, formed a republic. In June 1950, North Korea invaded the South. President Truman immediately dispatched U.S. troops to aid South Korea and persuaded the United Nations to send troops also. The invasion was eventually repelled, and the Korean War ended in 1953 with the country divided as before.

Meanwhile, fear of Communists continued in the United States. A group accused of giving atomic secrets to the Soviet Union was uncovered. The members of the group were convicted. Some were imprisoned. Two others, Julius and Ethel Rosenberg, were executed. Alger Hiss, a former state department official, was accused of having spied for the Soviet Union in the 1930's. Convicted of perjury, Hiss was sentenced to five years in prison.

These cases, plus the Communist victory in China and the Korean War, offered some politicians a chance to play upon American fears. Foremost among these politicians was Senator Joseph R. McCarthy of Wisconsin. Beginning in 1950, he kept the country in an uproar for four years with charges that Communists had infiltrated the U.S. government. McCarthy employed highly unethical methods in his investigations, and he proved no cases. Yet for a time, millions of people supported him. Government leaders feared to act against him.

In 1950, Congress passed the McCarran Internal Security Act. One portion of the act required members of the Communist Party in the United States to register with the government. Truman vetoed the bill, calling it unconstitutional. But Congress overrode his veto.

Truman retired from the presidency in 1953 and returned to Independence, Mo. There he oversaw the construction of the Truman Library and wrote his memoirs. He died in Independence in 1972.

John Tyler

Born: March 29, 1790
Died: Jan. 18, 1862
Place of Birth:
    Charles City Co., Va.

Political Party: Whig
Term: 1841-1845
Electoral Vote: None
Vice-President: None

Tyler, John (1790-1862), was the 10th President of the United States. He became the first Vice-President to succeed to the presidency upon the death of a President. He took office after the death of President William Henry Harrison in 1841. Tyler spent his presidential years in conflict with Congress.

John Tyler was born in Charles City Co., Va., on March 29, 1790. He graduated from William and Mary College in Williamsburg, Va., at age 17. He then studied law and became a lawyer in 1809.

Turning to politics, Tyler won election to Virginia's House of Delegates at age 21. He took time out from the legislature to serve briefly in the War of 1812, and in March 1813, he married Letitia Chris-tian, the daughter of a well-to-do Virginia planter. Three years later, Tyler ran for and won a seat in the United States House of Representatives. He remained there until he ran for the Senate and lost in 1821. After serving briefly as chancellor of William and Mary College and two years as governor of Virginia, Tyler finally was elected to the Senate in 1827.

Tyler opposed the second Bank of the United States, which had been chartered in 1816, and federal support for internal improvements. He based his opposition on the belief that such measures led only to a bigger and more powerful federal government. In 1828, Congress passed a tariff law that placed high taxes on imported manufactured goods. Southerners opposed the measure. Andrew Jackson's first Vice-President, John C. Calhoun of South Carolina, later argued that a state had the constitutional right to nullify— declare null and void—any federal law it opposed. South Carolina nullified the high tariff laws of 1828 and 1832. Congress, with Jackson's support, then passed a bill authorizing the President to use force if necessary to collect tariffs. South Carolina backed down. As a senator, Tyler opposed both nullification and Jackson's handling of the matter. Told by the Virginia legislature to support the President, Tyler resigned from the Senate instead. He also withdrew from the Democratic Party.

In 1840, the Whig Party named Tyler as running mate to presidential candidate William Henry Harrison. Whigs had formed their party in the 1830's out of a loose coalition of interests, some of which actually opposed one another. Farmers, manufacturers, and Southerners, for example, could not agree on the tariff question even though all three groups supported the Whig Party. Tyler won the Whig nomination because he had been an anti-Jackson man, and he was a Southerner. Because Harrison was an Ohioan, Tyler gave geographical balance to the ticket. But Harrison died unexpectedly a month after his inauguration, and Tyler became President. His troubles began soon afterward.

Whigs in Congress pushed through bills for internal improvements, high tariffs, and a new Bank of the United States. A Jackson veto in 1832 had abolished the second Bank. Tyler stuck to his principles and responded with vetoes. An armed mob then attacked the White House, shouting insults and pelting windows with rocks. But Tyler stood firm. Congress passed another bank bill, and Tyler again vetoed it. This resulted in another mob scene, and the mob burned Tyler in effigy. The President had kept the Cabinet chosen by Harrison, and now all but Secretary of State Daniel Webster resigned. Tyler next vetoed a Whig measure that gave income from federal land sales to the states. This caused the sponsor of the bill, Henry Clay, to resign from the Senate.

Whigs began to disown Tyler and referred to him as "His Accidency." In January 1843, Whigs in Congress moved to impeach Tyler, but they failed. The fact was that Tyler had never been a Whig in the first place, and he was an accidental President.

Texas won independence from Mexico in 1836. It wished to join the Union. Northerners opposed this, because Texas would be an additional slave state. Southerners, Tyler included, supported annexation. In 1844, Democrat James K. Polk, who favored admitting Texas, was elected President. Before leaving office in 1845, Tyler approved a joint congressional resolution making Texas a state.

Tyler supported Virginia's secession from the Union in 1861, and he served in the Confederate congress. He died in Richmond, Va., in 1862.

Martin Van Buren

Born: Dec. 5, 1782
Died: July 24, 1862
Place of Birth:
    Kinderhook, N.Y.
Political Party: Democrat

Term: 1837-1841
Electoral Vote: 170
Vice-President:
    Richard M. Johnson

Van Buren, Martin (1782-1862), was the eighth President of the United States. He was recognized as a highly skilled political organizer. But he became President shortly before the nation slid into its first severe economic depression. His steadfast refusal to provide government relief proved him to be a man of principle, but it cost him his political popularity.

Martin Van Buren was born in Kinderhook, N.Y., on Dec. 5, 1782, into a Dutch family of long standing in the community. At age 14, he began to study law, and he made his first courtroom appearance as a lawyer when only 15. Van Buren opened a law practice in Kinderhook in 1803, and four years later he married Hannah Hoes, a distant cousin. He entered politics as a member of the Democratic-Republican Party and a follower of Thomas Jefferson, who became President in 1800. Van Buren was elected to the New York senate in 1812, and four years later became that state's attorney general. In 1821, the New York legislature sent him to the United States Senate.

After winning reelection to the Senate

in 1827, Van Buren resigned the following year, when he was elected governor of New York. Then, as a reward for his aid in managing the 1828 presidential campaign, President Andrew Jackson made Van Buren his secretary of state.

In 1831, Jackson nominated Van Buren as minister to Great Britain, but the Senate refused confirmation. Jackson then made Van Buren his vice-presidential running mate in 1832, placing him firmly in line for the presidency. Jackson and Van Buren won the 1832 election. And in 1836, Van Buren was the Democratic presidential candidate. He defeated the leading Whig candidate, William Henry Harrison, by 97 electoral votes.

Martin Van Buren became President at an unfortunate time. During the Jackson presidency, land speculation had run wild. States made unsound investments in canal and road building. Joining in the speculative frenzy, banks extended many insecure loans for land purchases and business expansion. President Andrew Jackson attempted to cool the situation with the *Specie Circular,* issued in 1836. It required that land be purchased only with gold or silver. This halted land speculation, but it did not save the country from a severe depression that began soon after Van Buren took office in 1837. Many banks failed, and the financial crash became known as the Panic of 1837.

The depression threw thousands of people out of work, but President Van Buren turned down all ideas for government action to alleviate the hardship. He clung to the belief that government intervention would do the economy more harm than good. Van Buren concerned himself chiefly with federal government finances. Jackson had destroyed the Bank of the United States, and had placed federal deposits in private and state banks (see Jackson, Andrew). Van Buren feared that those banks might fail, and he wanted to set up an independent treasury to hold federal government funds. Congress finally approved an independent treasury bill in 1840, but it abolished the treasury a year later, after Van Buren had left office.

Van Buren's failure to act against the depression earned him criticism. In addition, abolitionists criticized him for spending federal money to subdue and remove the Seminole Indians in Florida. They believed Florida would become another slave state. Proslavery groups attacked him for refusing to agree to demands that Texas be annexed. Texas had won independence from Mexico in 1836 and would have entered the Union as a slave state. And Van Buren received little credit for peacefully settling a boundary dispute between Maine and New Brunswick, a Canadian province.

Although Van Buren's Administration had been an unhappy one, he was willing to try for another term, and the Democrats renominated him in 1840. The Whigs again turned to war hero William Henry Harrison. Van Buren lost by an electoral vote of 234 to 60. But he managed to gain more than a million of the 2,400,000 popular votes cast. The election had brought out the greatest turnout of voters up to that point in American history.

Martin Van Buren remained a staunch Democrat and active in politics for the remainder of his life. He died in 1862.

George Washington

Born: Feb. 22, 1732
Died: Dec. 14, 1799
Place of Birth:
  Westmoreland County,
  Va.

Political Party: None
Terms: 1789-1797
Electoral Vote: 69; 132
Vice-President: John Adams

Washington, George (1732-1799), was the first President of the United States. Unlike any other American President, Washington has been honored with an unblemished reputation and consistent national acclaim. His unique role in the history of the United States has made him revered as the "Father of His Country."

Washington was born in Westmoreland County, Va., on Feb. 22, 1732. Although he had some formal schooling, most of his education came through his daily experiences living and working on the family plantation.

While in his teens, George Washington became a surveyor, and his work took him on numerous trips to the back country of Virginia. At age 20, he became a major in the Virginia militia. In the fall of 1753, he led a small party into western Pennsylvania to deliver a message from Virginia's Governor Robert Dinwiddie to the French commander of Fort Le Boeuf, near present-day Erie, Pa. Dinwiddie warned the French to evacuate the region but the commander refused. Later, Dinwiddie sent Washington to secure a fort that Virginians had

built at the juncture of the Allegheny and Monongahela rivers in Pennsylvania. The French captured the fort, however, before Washington and his force arrived, and named it Fort Duquesne. Washington's men built another fort, named Fort Necessity, south of Fort Duquesne. Washington not only failed to attack Fort Duquesne, but he was unable—even with British help—to hold Fort Necessity.

The British and Virginians were not finished with Fort Duquesne. In the spring of 1755, Washington and a group of militiamen accompanied a force under British General Edward Braddock on a march against the stronghold. The French and their Indian allies attacked the column and defeated it. Braddock was mortally wounded in the action.

Washington saw little additional action during the French and Indian War. His exploits, though, had made him known throughout the American Colonies. For the next 15 years, Washington devoted himself to managing his plantation, Mount Vernon, on the Potomac River in northern Virginia. In 1759, he married Martha Custis, a wealthy widow. During the years before the Revolutionary War, Washington also served in the Virginia legislature, the House of Burgesses.

George Washington became one of the first persons to express opposition to the British tax and trade policies that led to the Revolution. He was a member of both the First and Second Continental Congresses. After the early battles, in the spring of 1775, the Congress chose Washington as commander in chief of the Continental Army.

Standing 6 feet, 2 inches tall, with an erect posture, Washington was an impressive military figure. But he presided over more defeats than most successful commanders. Desertion and the almost constant lack of adequate supplies caused Washington to be frequently discouraged. His major contribution to the war effort, through determination and sheer force of personality, was to keep an army in the field and to inspire it to continue fighting. With the aid of a French army and navy, Washington won the most important battle of the Revolutionary War, at Yorktown, Va., in 1781. The fighting ended soon afterwards.

Washington returned to his beloved Mount Vernon after the Revolution, and stayed there for five years. He was then called upon to participate in the construction of a new government.

In 1781, Congress had adopted the Articles of Confederation, which provided for a national government and listed the powers to be held by it and by the states. Most of the power rested with the states. The national government could not, for example, levy taxes or regulate trade. A number of prominent Americans, including Washington, concluded that the Articles had to be amended to strengthen the central government. And for that purpose, 55 men

gathered in Philadelphia in the summer of 1787. Washington was chosen president of the convention. The delegates proceeded to throw away the Articles of Confederation and write a new Constitution. After the Constitution had been ratified by the states, Washington became, as everyone expected, the first President of the new nation. He was the only person to be elected to the office unanimously, not only once, but twice.

Washington was inaugurated on April 30, 1789. Because he was the first President, heading a new government, everything he did would set a precedent. How should the President be addressed? As "Mr. President." What about relations with Congress? At first, distant. What should be the President's role in legislation? Advise little, but exercise the veto when necessary. Washington first used his veto power in 1792, when he acted against a bill that would have increased the number of U.S. representatives from 67 to 120. What about advisers? With the cooperation of Congress, Washington established the first Cabinet. It consisted of Alexander Hamilton as secretary of the treasury, Thomas Jefferson as head of the state department, Henry Knox as secretary of war, and Edmund Randolph as attorney general.

During Washington's Administration, the federal government assumed the Revolutionary War debts of the states. It established the First Bank of the United States. It sent an army to put down a threatened rebellion among western Pennsylvanians who refused to pay a tax on whiskey. Following the French Revolution in 1789, Europe was at war. Washington steered a narrow path of neutrality, even though he was beset with demands that the United States side with Britain on the one hand, or France on the other.

As a war measure, both England and France sought to cut off one another's trade with neutral nations. Britain halted U.S. ships on the high seas. The British frequently removed sailors they claimed were deserters from British vessels, some of whom actually were Americans. The British seizure of American sailors added fuel to the demands for war with Britain. Washington, however, stood firm for neutrality, and he dispatched John Jay, chief justice of the United States, to England to work out a treaty. The British consented to trade agreements, and they agreed to give up forts they still held in the northwestern part of the United States. But the Jay Treaty contained no mention of the issue of British harassment of American ships. George Washington realized that he had a highly emotional issue on his hands, and for a time, he did not make the treaty public. There was a public uproar when the news got out, and the Senate split sharply on the issue, though it finally ratified the treaty. After considerable further thought, Washington signed it.

Washington hated factionalism, but he nonetheless presided over the development of political parties in the United States. Originally, those who favored the ratification of the Constitution were known as Federalists. Those opposed were called Anti-Federalists. In the government, those who favored strong central power, business and commercial interests, and Washington's policies in general, were called Federalists. Alexander Hamilton, secretary of the treasury,

was the chief Federalist leader. Those who stressed states' rights and the interests of farmers and small-businessmen became known as Democratic-Republicans. They were led by Thomas Jefferson and James Madison. Jefferson and Hamilton disagreed on such issues as the Bank of the United States, the government's assumption of states' war debts, and on whether the United States should favor Britain or France in the European war. Criticism of the Jay Treaty came chiefly from Democratic-Republican newspapers. This and other criticism disturbed Washington, who believed in discussion of public issues, but not in what he considered unjustified complaint.

Weary of argument, factionalism, and of public service in general, Washington refused nomination for a third term. He thus set a precedent that went unbroken until 1940, when Franklin D. Roosevelt campaigned for and won a third term. In 1797, Washington handed over the reigns of government to John Adams, who had served during both terms as his Vice-President. Washington then retired to Mount Vernon. While he managed his plantation, he kept in touch with government leaders, and from time to time he visited the capital, then located in Philadelphia.

Early in December 1799, while riding in a cold rain, Washington caught a chill. Laryngitis developed. Following the standard medical procedure of the time, Washington's physician drained blood from his veins. This only weakened him. And on December 14, Washington died.

Woodrow Wilson

Born: Dec. 29, 1856
Died: Feb. 3, 1924
Place of Birth: Staunton, Va.
Political Party: Democrat

Terms: 1913-1921
Electoral Vote: 435; 277
Vice-President:
  Thomas R. Marshall

Wilson, Woodrow (1856-1924), was the 28th President of the United States. Woodrow Wilson achieved national acclaim as a university president and as New Jersey's governor before going on to the presidency. As President, he encouraged the enactment of much reform legislation and guided United States participation in World War I.

Wilson was born in the small town of Staunton, Va., on Dec. 29, 1856. He was the son of a Presbyterian minister. He graduated from Princeton University in 1879. Wilson practiced law for a year and then entered Johns Hopkins University for graduate work in government and history, completing a Ph.D. in 1886. A year earlier, he had married Ellen Louise Axson, whose father was also a Presbyterian minister. She died in August, 1914, and about a year later, Wilson married Edith Bolling Galt, a widow.

Wilson taught at Bryn Mawr College, Wesleyan University, and Princeton University. He became president of Princeton in 1902. In 1910, with the New Jersey Democratic Party suffering from the effects of widespread corruption, party leaders needed an outsider with in-

tegrity. They approached Wilson, who accepted their nomination for the governorship and won by a large majority.

As governor, Wilson separated himself from regular party leaders and pushed for reform. He obtained such reforms as a corrupt practices law, a primary election law, and employers' liability legislation. His record as governor brought him national attention, and in 1912, he won the Democratic nomination for the presidency.

Republicans that year were split. One faction followed President William Howard Taft, the other favored former President Theodore Roosevelt. Wilson easily won election with about 6,300,000 popular and 435 electoral votes.

In the presidency, Wilson continued as a reformer. He achieved lower tariff rates, the establishment of the Federal Reserve Board to regulate banks and the nation's currency, and the inauguration of the Federal Trade Commission to oversee trade practices within the country. Beginning in 1914, however, foreign affairs occupied much of his attention.

Relations between the United States and Mexico were frequently troubled during Wilson's first term. Various factions in Mexico struggled for control of the government. Wilson opposed the ruling dictator, Victoriano Huerta, and tried through peaceful means and then by force to remove him from power. Argentina, Brazil, and Chile finally mediated the dispute, and Huerta fled from Mexico in 1914. U.S. soldiers later tangled with soldiers who had rebelled against the new acting president of Mexico. Only a series of dramatic events in the spring of 1916 averted open war. Finally, in 1917 Wilson officially recognized the Mexican government that had been established by a new constitution.

World War I began in Europe in August 1914. With the majority of Americans supporting him, Wilson declared the United States neutral in the conflict and attempted to hold to that policy. But he also insisted on American freedom of the seas. That put United States ships and Americans traveling to Europe in danger of attack by German submarines, which were trying to cut Great Britain and France off from outside contact. Wilson finally obtained German agreement to curb unrestricted submarine warfare.

In 1916, the Democrats used the slogan, "He kept us out of war," and Wilson won election to a second term. But after Germany renewed unrestricted submarine activity early in 1917, neutrality once again became difficult to maintain. War came increasingly near as German submarines sank a number of American ships. Finally, early in April 1917, Wilson asked for and obtained a declaration of war by Congress.

United States troops arriving in France helped turn back a German offensive in 1918 and achieve Allied victory. Wilson hoped to restrain European nationalism, which had been responsible for many wars, and to establish a firm basis for lasting peace. With those goals in mind, he offered Fourteen Points as a basis for settlement, and he promoted them at the peace conference held at Versailles, France, in 1919. Among the points were a ban on secret treaties, freedom of the seas, and an association to settle international disputes and keep the peace. The association became known as the League of Nations.

Wilson won some of his points and lost others. The victorious European allies redrew the map of Europe in their own interests and burdened Germany with a huge bill of compensation for war damages. They agreed on what Wilson considered the most important point, however, the League of Nations.

Returning home temporarily, Wilson found a Republican-controlled Senate unwilling to accept United States membership in the League without amendments providing the U.S. with greater freedom of action as a League member. Wilson returned to the peace conference and won agreement to some changes, but not enough to satisfy the critics in the Senate. Back in the United States once more, Wilson decided to take his plea for American membership in the League to the people. He embarked in the fall of 1919 on a wide-ranging speaking tour. But on September 25, while traveling between Pueblo, Colo., and Wichita, Kans., Wilson fell ill. Early in October, he suffered a stroke. For the remainder of his term, Wilson remained an invalid. His wife helped him carry out necessary presidential duties. The Senate voted twice to refuse to accept the Treaty of Versailles without reservations concerning U.S. participation in the League of Nations.

Crippled, Wilson retired from the presidency in 1921 to a life of relative inactivity. He died in 1924.

2

Prime Ministers
of Canada

Canada's Prime Ministers

Name	Dates served	Party	Birthplace	Birth and death dates
Sir John A. Macdonald	1867-1873	Conservative	Glasgow, Scotland	1815-1891
Alexander Mackenzie	1873-1878	Liberal	Logierait, Scotland	1822-1892
Sir John A. Macdonald	1878-1891	Conservative	Glasgow, Scotland	1815-1891
Sir John J. C. Abbott	1891-1892	Conservative	St. Andrews, Lower Canada (now Quebec)	1821-1893
Sir John S. D. Thompson	1892-1894	Conservative	Halifax, N.S.	1844-1894
Sir Mackenzie Bowell	1894-1896	Conservative	Rickinghall, England	1823-1917
Sir Charles Tupper	1896	Conservative	Amherst, N.S.	1821-1915
Sir Wilfrid Laurier	1896-1911	Liberal	St. Lin (now Laurentides), Quebec	1841-1911
Sir Robert L. Borden	1911-1917	Conservative	Grand Pré, N.S.	1854-1937
Sir Robert L. Borden	1917-1920	Unionist	Grand Pré, N.S.	1854-1937
Arthur Meighen	1920-1921	Unionist	St. Mary's, Ont.	1874-1960
W. L. Mackenzie King	1921-1926	Liberal	Berlin (now Kitchener), Ont.	1874-1950
Arthur Meighen	1926	Conservative	St. Mary's, Ont.	1874-1960
W. L. Mackenzie King	1926-1930	Liberal	Berlin (now Kitchener), Ont.	1874-1950
Richard B. Bennett	1930-1935	Conservative	Hopewell Cape, N.B.	1870-1947
W. L. Mackenzie King	1935-1948	Liberal	Berlin (now Kitchener), Ont.	1874-1950
Louis S. St. Laurent	1948-1957	Liberal	Compton, Que.	1882-1973

Name	Dates served	Party	Birthplace	Birth and death dates
John G. Diefenbaker	1957-1963	Progressive Conservative	Neustadt, Ont.	1895-1979
Lester B. Pearson	1963-1968	Liberal	Toronto, Ont.	1897-1972
Pierre E. Trudeau	1968-1979	Liberal	Montreal, Que.	1919-
Charles Joseph Clark	1979-1980	Progressive Conservative	High River, Alta.	1939-
Pierre E. Trudeau	1980-1984	Liberal	Montreal, Que.	1919-
John N. Turner	1984	Liberal	Richmond, England	1929-
Martin Brian Mulroney	1984-	Progressive Conservative	Baie-Comeau, Que.	1939-

In 1982, Queen Elizabeth II signed the Constitution Act while Prime Minister Pierre E. Trudeau observed.

Index

Respelling Table

The World Book Student Information Finder provides pronunciations for many unusual or unfamiliar words. The pronunciation, when it is used, is placed in parentheses immediately following the word in question. In the pronunciation, the word is divided into syllables and respelled according to the way each syllable actually sounds. For example, here is a word used in the glossary for Unit 3, Important Dates in History:

transcendentalism *(TRAN sehn DEHN tuh lihz uhm)*

The system of respelling used in the *Student Information Finder* is the system used in THE WORLD BOOK ENCYCLOPEDIA. In that system, the syllable that bears the greatest emphasis when the word is spoken appears in capital letters *(DEHN)*. If the word is long enough to have a syllable that receives secondary emphasis, that syllable appears in small capital letters *(TRAN)*. More than one pronunciation may be included for words that have several accepted pronunciations in English, for words that have distinctive pronunciations in other languages, and for names that have distinctive local pronunciations.

See the list on the following page for examples of respelled syllables and respelled words. Note the variety of examples for the syllable "uh."

In addition to the respellings, *The World Book Student Information Finder* uses a number of diacritical marks and special characters to indicate the correct spellings for many words and names in languages other than English. These marks have various meanings, according to the languages in which they are used. For example, an acute accent mark (´) over an *é* in a French word indicates that the *é* is pronounced *ay*. An acute accent mark over an *é* in a Spanish word indicates that the syllable containing the *é* bears the main emphasis in the word. These are probably the two most common accent marks that you will encounter in this volume.

Respelling	Example		Respelling	Example	
a	alphabet	*AL fuh beht*	ow	fountain	*FOWN tuhn*
ay	Asia	*AY zhuh*	s	spice	*spys*
ai	bareback	*BAIR bak*	sh	motion	*MOH shuhn*
ah	armistice	*AHR muh stihs*	u	Fulbright	*FUL bryt*
ch	China	*CHY nuh*		wool	*wul*
eh	essay	*EHS ay*			
ee	leaf	*leef*	oo	Zulu	*ZOO loo*
	marine	*muh REEN*	zh	Asia	*AY zhuh*
ur	pearl	*purl*	uh	study	*STUHD ee*
ih	system	*SIHS tuhm*	uh	blood	*bluhd*
y	Ohio	*oh HY oh*	uh	Burma	*BUR muh*
eye	iris	*EYE rihs*	uh	fiddle	*FIHD uhl*
k	corn	*kawrn*	uh	citizen	*SIHT uh zuhn*
ah	Ottawa	*AHT uh wuh*	uh	lion	*LY uhn*
oh	rainbow	*RAYN boh*	uh	cyprus	*SY pruhs*
	tableau	*TAB loh*	uh	physique	*fuh ZEEK*
aw	orchid	*AWR kihd*	uh	mountain	*MOWN tuhn*
	allspice	*AWL spys*	uh	Georgia	*JAWR juh*
oy	coinage	*KOY nihj*	uh	legion	*LEE juhn*
	poison	*POY zuhn*	uh	anonymous	*uh NAHN uh muhs*

Acknowledgments

The publishers acknowledge the following illustrations. Credits read from top to bottom, left to right, on their respective pages. Charts and diagrams prepared by the *World Book* staff unless otherwise noted.

Cover Illustrations: Yoshi Miyake. Photos: Photri from Marilyn Gartman; NASA: Jointly owned by the National Portrait Gallery, Smithsonian Institution, and the Museum of Fine Arts, Boston (detail); Granger Collection; Sistine Chapel, The Vatican, Rome (SCALA); World Book photo. 1 © Harvey Moshman, Journalism Services. 3 © Alan Carey, The Image Works. 31 © Mark Antman, The Image Works. 45 Granger Collection. 121 Granger Collection. 122 Bettmann Archive. 155 Imperial War Museum, London (detail). 169 World Book photo. 184 Brown Brothers. 198 NASA 203 Bettmann Archive. 213 Brown Brothers. 232 Bettmann Archive. 243 Granger Collection. 251 Mark Twain Memorial, Hartford, Conn. 257 © Kunio Owaki, The Stock Market. 259 Harvard University Portrait Collection, gift of Andrew Carnegie, 1794. 261 Andrew W. Mellon Collection, National Gallery of Art, Washington, D.C. (detail). 262 Corcoran Gallery of Art, gift of William Wilson Corcoran (detail). 264 Corcoran Gallery of Art (detail). 266 David Valdez, The White House. 267 © White House Historical Association, photography by National Geographic Society (detail). 269 National Portrait Gallery, Smithsonian Institution, Washington, D.C. (detail). 271 Union League Club, New York City. 273 © White House Historical Association, photography by National Geographic Society (detail). 275 National Portrait Gallery, Smithsonian Institution, Washington, D.C. (detail). 277 © White House Historical Association, photography by National Geographic Society (detail). 278 Corcoran Gallery of Art (detail). 280 National Portrait Gallery, Smithsonian Institution, Washington, D.C. (detail). 282 National Portrait Gallery, Smithsonian Institution, Washington, D.C. (detail). 284 © White House Historical Association, photography by National Geographic Society (detail). 286 National Portrait Gallery, Smithsonian Institution, Washington, D.C. (detail). 287 © White House Historical Association, photography by National Geographic Society (detail). 289 National Portrait Gallery, Smithsonian Institution, Washington, D.C. (detail). 291 Daughters of the American Revolution, Washington, D.C. 294 © White House Historical Association, photography by National Geographic Society (detail). 297 Tennessee Historical Society. 299 © White House Historical Association, photography by National Geographic Society (detail). 301 © White House Historical Association, photography by National Geographic Society (detail). 303 Huntington Library and Art Gallery, San Marino, Calif. 306 National Gallery of Art, Washington, D.C., Alisa Mellon Bruce Fund (detail). 308 Corcoran Gallery of Art (detail). 310 Pennsylvania Academy of Fine Arts (detail). 312 © White House Historical Association, photography by National Geographic Society (detail). 315 National Portrait Gallery, Smithsonian Institution, Washington, D.C. (detail). 316 Corcoran Gallery of Art (detail). 318 © White House Historical Association, photography by National Geographic Society. 320 © White House Historical Association, photography by National Geographic Society (detail). 323 © White House Historical Association, photography by National Geographic Society (detail). 325 White House Historical Association, photography by National Geographic Society (detail). 327 Corcoran Gallery of Art (detail). 329 © White House Historical Association, photography by National Geographic Society (detail). 331 Corcoran Gallery of Art (detail). 333 Metropolitan Museum of Art, gift of Mrs. Jacob H. Lazarus, 1893 (detail). 335 Jointly owned by the National Portrait Gallery, Smithsonian Institution, and the Museum of Fine Arts, Boston (detail). 338 National Portrait Gallery, Smithsonian Institution, Washington, D.C. (detail). 341 Canapress.